Oxford in India Readings

THEMES IN INDIAN HISTORY

Available in the Series

Ishita Banerjee-Dube (ed.)	*Caste in History* (OIP)
Aloka Parasher-Sen (ed.)	*Subordinate and Marginal Groups in Early India* (Second Edition, OIP)
S. Irfan Habib and Dhruv Raina (eds)	*Social History of Science in Colonial India*
Kaushik Roy (ed.)	*War and Society in Colonial India*
Mushirul Hasan (ed.)	*India's Partition: Process, Strategy, and Mobilization* (OIP)
David Ludden (ed.)	*Agricultural Production and South Asian History* (OIP)
P.J. Marshall (ed.)	*The Eighteenth Century in Indian History: Evolution or Revolution?* (OIP)
Michael H. Fisher (ed.)	*The Politics of the British Annexation of India 1757–1857* (OIP)
Muzaffar Alam and Sanjay Subrahmanyam (eds)	*The Mughal State 1526–1750* (OIP)
Richard M. Eaton (ed.)	*India's Islamic Traditions, 711–1750* (OIP)
Jos J. L. Gommans and Dirk H. A. Kolff (eds)	*Warfare and Weaponry in South Asia 1000–1800* (OIP)
Ian J. Kerr (ed.)	*Railways in Modern India* (OIP)
Ranbir Chakravarti (ed.)	*Trade in Early India* (OIP)

The Middle Class in
Colonial India

The Middle Class in Colonial India

edited by
SANJAY JOSHI

OXFORD
UNIVERSITY PRESS

YMCA Library Building, Jai Singh Road, New Delhi 110001

Oxford University Press is a department of the University of Oxford.
It furthers the University's objective of excellence in research, scholarship, and education by publishing worldwide in

Oxford   New York

Auckland   Cape Town   Dar es Salaam   Hong Kong   Karachi   Kuala Lumpur
Madrid   Melbourne   Mexico City   Nairobi   New Delhi   Shanghai   Taipei   Toronto

With offices in
Argentina   Austria   Brazil   Chile   Czech Republic   France   Greece   Guatemala
Hungary   Italy   Japan   Poland   Portugal   Singapore   South Korea   Switzerland
Thailand   Turkey   Ukraine   Vietnam

Oxford is a registered trademark of Oxford University Press
in the UK and in certain other countries

Published in India
by Oxford University Press, New Delhi

© Oxford University Press 2010

The moral rights of the author have been asserted
Database right Oxford University Press (maker)

First published 2010

All rights reserved. No part of this publication may be reproduced, or transmitted in any form or by any means, electronic or mechanical, including photocopying, recording or by any information storage and retrieval system, without permission in writing from Oxford University Press. Enquiries concerning reproduction outside the scope of the above should be sent to the Rights Department, Oxford University Press, at the address above

You must not circulate this book in any other binding or cover
and you must impose this same condition on any acquirer

ISBN-13: 978-0-19-806382-7
ISBN-10: 0-19-806382-2

Typeset in ITC Legacy Serif STD 10/12.6
by Sai Graphic Design, New Delhi 110 055,
Printed in India at Shri Krishna Printers, Noida
Published by Oxford University Press
YMCA Library Building, Jai Singh Road, New Delhi 110 001

To Sanjam and Aeka....
For pushing me, and giving me the time,
to finally get this done!

Contents

Series Note	ix
Preface	x
Acknowledgements	xiii
Introduction	xv
SANJAY JOSHI	

I. Framing the Middle Class

1. A Microscopic Minority — 3
   THE MARQUIS OF DUFFERIN AND AVA

2. A Cheap Shoddy Import — 10
   AUROBINDO GHOSH

3. The Carriers of Enlightenment, Freedom, Progress, and Prosperity — 14
   THE BENGALEE

4. A Class in Need of Help — 17
   JAWAHARLAL NEHRU

II. Debating the Middle Class

5. The Bourgeoisie Comes of Age — 25
   D.D. KOSAMBI

6. The Middle Class of Colonial India: A Product of British Benevolence — 33
   B.B. MISRA

7. The Myth of a 'Westernized Middle Class' — 47
   MICHELGUGLIELMO TORRI

8. A Pre-History of The Middle Class? — 69
   C.A. BAYLY

9. The Subalternity of a Nationalist Elite 94
   PARTHA CHATTERJEE

10. What about the Merchants? A Mercantile Perspective 118
    on the Middle Class of Colonial India
    CLAUDE MARKOVITS

11. Consumption, Domestic Economy, and the Idea of the 132
    'Middle Class' in Late Colonial Bombay
    PRASHANT KIDAMBI

III. GENDER, CASTE, AND RELIGION IN THE MAKING OF MIDDLE-CLASS MODERNITY

12. Domesticity and Middle-class Nationalism 157
    in Nineteenth-century Bengal
    TANIKA SARKAR

13. Limits of the Bourgeois Model? 178
    DIPESH CHAKRABARTY

14. Re-Publicizing Religiosity: Modernity, Religion, 202
    and the Middle Class
    SANJAY JOSHI

15. Middle Class and Secularization 222
    MARGRIT PERNAU

16. One Step Outside Modernity: 240
    Caste in the Middle-class Imaginary
    M.S.S. PANDIAN

IV. WHITHER MIDDLE CLASS STUDIES? THE MIDDLE CLASS AND THE EVERYDAY WORLD

17. 'In Those Days There Was No Coffee': Consumption, 261
    Popular Culture, and Middle-class Formation in Madras
    A.R. VENKATACHALAPATHY

18. A Case of Indian Exceptionalism: Bengali Middle-class 278
    Patronage of Sport in Colonial Bengal
    BORIA MAJUMDAR

19. Middle-class Cinema 297
    M. MADHAVA PRASAD

Annotated Bibliography 313
Note on Contributors 325

Series Note

The series focuses on important themes in Indian history, on those which have long been the subject of interest and debate, or which have acquired importance more recently.

Each volume in the series consists of, first, a detailed Introduction; second, a careful choice of the essays and book-extracts vital to a proper understanding of the theme; and, finally, an Annotated Bibliography. Using this consistent format, each volume seeks as a whole to critically assess the state of the art on its theme, chart the historiographical shifts that have occurred since the theme emerged, rethink old problems, open up questions which were considered closed, locate the theme within wider historiographical debates, and pose new issues of inquiry by which further work may be made possible.

Preface

Compiling a volume such as this, is simply not possible without the active assistance of a large number of people. It is my pleasure to be able to acknowledge, perhaps too briefly, the generous help of the many who have made this book possible. First, of course, I must thank the scholars who produced the essays comprising this volume. Without their stellar work, this volume would obviously not have been possible. Some, such as Boria Majumdar, wrote new essays for this collection. Sankaran Krishna significantly revised his earlier essay for this collection, and to him I offer also my apologies because factors beyond my control meant his excellent essay had to be eliminated from this volume at the last moment. I also must single out Christopher (now, Sir Christopher) Bayly for his kindness. He went out of his way to intercede with Cambridge University Press (CUP) to facilitate the permission to use his essay in this volume. I am immensely grateful for him for taking the trouble he did, and to CUP for acting on his advice. For the sake of getting to a manuscript of manageable proportions, I have had to edit almost every essay present in this collection. I have changed the titles of many of the essays to better fit this volume. I take this opportunity to apologize to the authors for taking such liberties with their work, and thank them for bearing with a sometimes-heavy editorial hand.

A large number of authors, publishers, and scholars have made it possible to publish this volume, and I am delighted to have the opportunity to acknowledge their assistance. I would like to thank the Sri Aurobindo Ashram Trust, particularly Manoj Das Gupta for the permission to publish the extract from Aurobindo Ghosh's 'New Lamps for Old'. Sonia Gandhi and the Jawaharlal Nehru Memorial Fund were kind enough to give permission to reprint the extract from *Discovery of India*. David Laibman and the editors of *Science & Society* were very prompt and generous with their permission to reprint D.D. Kosambi's essay, and for that my heartfelt thanks. Similarly, my thanks to Katie Gordon, at the Chatham House (The Royal Institute of International Affairs) for permission to republish a section from B.B. Misra's book. Michelguglielmo Torri was generous and prompt with his permission to reprint an older essay, as were a number of parties (John Hill, the editor of the collection, Peter Robb at SOAS which held some rights to the work, and folks at Thomson Publishing Services on behalf of Taylor & Francis Books) from whom I sought permission to republish this esssay. The copyrights to the essays by Madhava Prasad, Partha Chatterjee, and Dipesh Chakrabarty in this collection were held by OUP, which made my own life easier, and Princeton University Press who have the global rights to Partha Chatterjee's book were kind enough to grant their permission to reprint as well. I am particularly grateful to these three authors, who also agreed to let their pieces be included in the volume. Esha Beteille at Social Science Press and Margrit Pernau were equally generous with their responses to my request to reprint Margrit Pernau's essay. The editors at IESHR and Sage Publications gave permission to reprint A.R. Venkatachalapathy's essay, and Venkatachalapathy himself provided a soft copy of his essay to facilitate editing. To all of them my thanks. Tanika Sarkar was one of the first authors to give me her permission to republish her essay, and Rukun Advani came through with the publisher's permission promptly for her essay and that of Claude Markovits, and it gives me pleasure to acknowledge my gratitude to them all. M.S.S. Pandian held the copyright to his own essay, and was very prompt and extremely generous in granting me the permission to republish his essay, which is crucial to this collection. A vote of thanks also to Douglas Haynes who first alerted me to Prashant Kidambi's essay, which is another important part of this volume. Of course, I must thank Prashant himself for not only sending me his [then] forthcoming essay, but also giving me a free hand in editing it to fit the requirements of this volume. Finally, Rutgers University Press gave me permission to reprint an essay I had earlier published in *The Invention of Religion*, for which I am very grateful.

My own procrastination in getting everything together ensured that I worked with two sets of editors at Oxford University Press before I completed this volume! I would like to thank the editorial team for their perseverance and dedication in bringing out the volume.

I cannot end this section without expressing my thanks to Mrinalini Sinha, who responded to an early request for ideas with a list that helped me think through about this collection. Barbara Ramusack's close reading of the Introduction prevented some embarrassing mistakes. To her I am always grateful for her mentoring, friendship and guidance. I had the privilege of discussing this volume in its early stages with Sumit Sarkar, and benefited tremendously from his astute analytical observations and wide bibliographic knowledge. Ever since I joined NAU, Susan Deeds is always the first person I turn to for intellectual advice and for her close proofreading skills. She helped tremendously with this volume as she has with almost all my other writing. It is to Sanjam Ahluwalia, though, as always, I owe my greatest debt of gratitude. Without Sanjam's encouragement, nagging, and, most important, her intellectual inputs, this work would never have been finished. Lastly, I cannot end without acknowledging the joys that our daughter, Aeka's, presence has brought to our lives. To Aeka and her mother, for allowing Baba the time over the last year to finally get this project completed, I dedicate this book.

Sanjay Joshi
Flagstaff

Acknowledgements

The editor and the publisher acknowledge the following for permission to include articles/extracts in this volume.

Cambridge University Press, Cambridge for C.A. Bayly, 'The Indian Ecumene: An Indigenous Public Sphere', *Empire and Information: Intelligence Gathering and Social Communication in India, 1780–1870*, 2000 © Cambridge University Press, pp. 180-211.

Jawaharlal Nehru Memorial Fund, Nehru Memorial Museum and Library, New Delhi for Jawaharlal Nehru, 'The Last Phase (2) Nationalism Versus Imperialism: Helplessness of the Middle Classes Gandhi Comes', *Discovery of India*, 1981, pp. 35-60.

M.S.S Pandian for 'One Step Outside Modernity: Caste in the Middle-class Imaginary', Amsterdam/Dakar: SEPHIS-CODESRIA, 2001.

Permanent Black, New Delhi for Claude Markovits, 'Merchants, Entrepreneurs and the Middle Classes in Twentieth Century India', *Merchants, Traders, Entrepreneurs: Indian Business in the Colonial Era*, 2008, pp. 167-83; and Tanika Sarkar, 'Hindu Wife, Hindu Nation: Domesticity and Nationalism in Nineteenth-century Bengal', *Hindu Wife, Hindu Nation: Community, Religion, and Cultural Nationalism*, 2001, pp. 23-52.

Princeton University Press, Princeton for Partha Chatterjee, 'The Nationalist Elite', *Nation and Its Fragments: Colonial and Postcolonial Histories*, 1999, pp. 35-75.

Royal Institute of International Affairs, Chatham House, London for B. B. Misra, 'Introduction', *The Indian Middle Classes: Their Growth in Modern Times*, 1961, pp. 1-17.

Rutgers University Press, Rutgers for Sanjay Joshi, 'Re-Publicizing Religiosity: Modernity, Religion, and the Middle Class', in Derek Peterson and Darren Walhof (eds), *The Invention of Religion: Rethinking Belief in Politics and History*, © 2002 by Rutgers, The State University. Reprinted by permission of Rutgers University Press.

Sage Publications India Pvt. Ltd, New Delhi for A.R. Venkatachalapathy, '"In Those Days There Was No Coffee": Consumption, Popular Culture, and Middle-class Formation in Madras', *The Indian Economic and Social History Review*, vol. 39, nos 2 and 3, 2002, pp. 301–16.

School of Oriental and African Studies, London and Curzon Press and Taylor & Francis, London, for Michelguglielmo Torri, 'Westernized Middle Class: Intellectuals and Society in Late Colonial India', in John L. Hill (ed.), *The Congress and Indian Nationalism: Historical Perspectives*, 1991, pp. 18–55.

Science and Society, New York for D.D. Kosambi, 'The Bourgeoisie Comes of Age', *Science and Society*, vol. X, 1946, pp. 392–8.

Social Science Press, New Delhi for Margrit Pernau, 'Middle Class and Secularization: The Muslims of Delhi in the Nineteenth Century', in Imtiaz Ahmad and Helmut Reifeld (eds), *Middle Class Values in India and Western Europe*, 2001, pp. 21–41.

Sri Aurobindo Ashram Trust for Aurobindo Ghosh, 'New Lamps for Old—3', *Indu Prakash*, 28 August 1893.

Introduction

SANJAY JOSHI

This volume brings together important writings that illuminate the making and ascendancy of the middle class during the period of British rule in India. Many themes in the essays in this volume have been widely discussed before. Indeed some of the issues they touch upon, such as social reform, caste, gender or religion, have even been the subjects of separate volumes in this series. The intent of this volume is, however, different. By bringing together a variety of writings on and about the middle class in colonial India, I hope we will be able to better understand how being middle class—what we might term 'middle class-ness'—was central to a variety of undertakings in colonial India, including politics related religion, gender, caste, social reform, and, of course, nationalism. Together, they help us better understand the history of the middle class in colonial India, and thus appreciate the strengths and limitations of the very important ideas and practices which have shaped, and continue to shape, modern India.

We cannot write the history of colonial India without centrally engaging with the history of the middle class. Whether in the arena of politics or culture, it is probably not an exaggeration to suggest that the middle class has been central to most conventional histories of modern India. The contribution of the middle class to nationalism, feminism, religious revival, social reform, to the visual arts, to literature, and to a myriad of other fields of endeavor has been well documented in writings on Indian history. With decolonization, a middle-class leadership eventually replaced the British ruling class in India. The ascendancy of the middle class was the product of a relatively long historical process; predicated on the creation of new forms of politics, the restructuring of norms of social conduct, and the construction of new values guiding domestic as well as public life. All of these transformations, whether political, social, or cultural, reflected the concerns, and perhaps the contradictions, constitutive of the middle class. Understanding the making of this middle class and the process through which it acquired its predominance in public affairs, is critical to comprehending much of the cultural and political world around us today.

All historiography is a product of its time. It is appropriate, therefore, to begin by locating this book in its own historical context. This volume has been put together at a time when there is a great deal of interest in the middle class. The very visible and relatively recent affluence of what is called the middle class has no doubt contributed to our interest in this social category. Reading some of the contemporary discussions in newspapers or the electronic media, however, one would think that the Indian middle class became significant only about fifteen years ago, around the 1990s. Evidently, that is far from being the case. Economic liberalization has allowed sections of the Indian middle class to prosper. Linked to global capitalism, sections of this class have sought to match the income and consumption levels of affluent groups in the West. To some extent, they have succeeded. In fact, one could argue that its putative 350 million-strong middle class is what makes India a destination of choice for global capital. Yet, and perhaps especially, in the midst of the contemporary celebrations of the Indian middle class, it is critical to recall its history.

The fact that middle-class cultural entrepreneurs have dominated public sphere discussions in India for over a hundred years is also quite significant for understanding how we discuss the middle class in contemporary India (and beyond its borders). Indian history, society, culture, economics, and politics has for long been viewed through middle-class lenses. Yet, until recently, middle-class journalists, commentators and academics, for the most part preferred to analyse the role and formation of other social groups and other collectivities. For at least three decades from the late 1960s, it was the failure of peasant and other subaltern groups, in Ranajit Guha's words, to 'come into their own,' that dominated discussions of modern Indian history. Before that, nationalist paradigms dominated. Though much of the substance of nationalist historiography was concerned with work done by middle-class activists, the nation and nationalism rather than the middle class-ness of the major actors, was its central analytical focus.

Exploring writings on the middle class in colonial India immediately makes apparent an interesting paradox. We are confronted with a situation that reveals both paucity and plenitude. On the one hand, few scholars have explored what becoming or being middle class in modern India entailed. On the other hand, if we expand our field to include all studies which deal with middle-class activity in modern India, we are faced with such a vast array of scholarship as to make anything approaching a representative sampling virtually impossible. Appropriately perhaps, given its subject, this volume treads a middle path between these two! While preferring essays which directly address the making of this social category, this anthology also takes into account debates and discussions on the subject which indirectly help us better understand the making of a middle class through essays that only deal with some aspect of middle-class activity, such as gender or caste relations. Before discussing the contents of this anthology, however, we must deal with a much thornier question: who or what is 'middle class'?

DEFINING THE MIDDLE CLASS

Despite its wide currency, there is surprisingly little agreement on what defines the social category called the middle class. Most scholars who use this category treat the middle class as an already-understood social group, sometimes dividing it into smaller sub-groups based on economic resources or status (such as the lower middle class, upper middle class, and so on). Scholars and journalists alike treat 'the middle class' as a fully-formed, sociologically bounded, category defined primarily by economic indicators, ignoring the extent to which social classes do not simply 'emerge' but are 'made.'[1] Overemphasizing structure and economic factors, they downplay the significance of 'cultural capital' and human agency as an important basis for middle class, or other class formations.[2] Thus, Indian historiography cannot boast of a large body of scholarship which analyses the *making* of the middle class seriously. Common even amongst those who disagree about its composition, however, is the idea that the category refers to people who belonged to the upper strata of society, without being at the very top. While financially comfortable, they were people who did need to work to earn a living. This was one factor which distinguished them from the richest strata of Indian society, such as the large hereditary landlords or the remnants of an indigenous aristocracy. The other, even more significant factor, was their distance, economic, social, and cultural, from the lower classes. Beyond that, though, objective indicators take us only so far in understanding the middle class.

The middle class in colonial India was not a social group that could be classified as occupying a median position in terms of standard sociological indicators of income, consumption, or status. Though usually not from the traditional landed aristocracy, there is little doubt that the people who came to term themselves middle class were from the upper rungs of Indian society. In fact, measured by any set of objective indicators such as income, consumption, occupation or even education, the social groups described as middle class in colonial India were in the top two deciles of the population. As recent critiques of contemporary usages of the category reveal, in purely economic terms, it would make much more sense to speak of the social group we refer to as an affluent class rather than the middle class.[3] The elitism of the people who claimed this category was even more pronounced during the colonial era. Most of them were male, upper caste Hindus, *ashraf* (high-born) Muslims, or other such high-status groups, and many came from so-called 'service communities,' that is, from families and social groups who had traditionally served in the courts of indigenous rulers and large landlords. Not only did this mean they had sufficient economic resources, but they also possessed sufficient educational training to shape and participate in public debates during the colonial era.[4] Another of the objective indicators distinguishing the middle class in colonial India, therefore, was their exposure to western-style education. But merely the knowledge of English, similarity of family background, or even exposure to western education did not transform these educated people into a middle class. This was achieved through cultural entrepreneurship.

While economic distinctions offer some indication of who the middle classes were, they are insufficient to describe the middle class as a social category. The middle class as a category is better understood if we see it as the product of a group of people sharing a social and economic background who became the producers and products of a new cultural politics in a transformed historical context. It was not simply similarities in education, occupation, or profession, that made a middle class in colonial India. It was the initiation of new cultural politics which allowed them to articulate a new set of beliefs, values, and modes of politics, thus distinguishing them from other social groups both below and above. It was not traditional status alone that upper caste Hindus or ashraf Muslim men deployed to create distinctions between themselves and other social groups in colonial India. Rather, it was by transforming traditional cultural values and the basis of social hierarchy that a distinctive middle class emerged. It was not simply the objective circumstances of their existence that made a group of intellectuals and bureaucrats key political and social figures. Rather, efforts of cultural entrepreneurship made them into a middle class, and a significant player in the social and political life of colonial India.

Important social, economic, and political changes accompanying British rule in India undoubtedly presented new opportunities to educated men and, a little later, to women as well. But ultimately, being middle class in India, as elsewhere, was a project of self-fashioning. In colonial India, as elsewhere around the world probably, a middle class emerged from processes by which intellectuals and activists created a new and distinctive social category through a 'self conscious interposition between people of rank and the common people.'[5] It is, for most part, these self conscious interpositions that essays in this volume examine. To highlight cultural projects as central to middle-class formation is not to deny the significance of either economic structure or indeed the historical context of changes in legal and economic regimes that accompanied the transition to colonialism. At the same time though, it is very important not to overemphasize a false dichotomy between 'objective' factors versus processes stressing the agency of the middle class. The history of the middle class in colonial India is a near-perfect example of how the two actually constitute each other. Objective conditions delimited the number and sort of people who could aspire to be middle class, but the efforts of people also created or transformed these very objective conditions which made the middle class possible. The emergence of a public sphere in India—a critical arena for the creation of the middle class, is an ideal illustration of this point.

A public sphere may have been facilitated by the British in India, but it was ultimately created by the efforts of educated Indians. It was they who invested in presses, worked as journalists, created civic and political associations, and published and debated their ideas either in the press or in the forums of their associations.[6] And it was through these activities as well as control of the public sphere, that educated, respectable, but hardly among the richest, most powerful or influential of men in colonial India, were able to successfully represent themselves as the middle class. Education and literary accomplishments had, of course, been valued for long before the British came to India. Court officials, religious leaders, and men of letters, the north Indian 'ecumene,' did comment on social matters and were occasionally even allowed the license to be critical of the rulers and their administration. Yet their social and political importance was relatively insignificant until the latter half of the nineteenth century. Adept use of the public sphere allowed a group of middling significance in the politics of pre-British courts to emerge as arbiters of native social conduct and aspirants to direct political power under British rule. It was through the public sphere that middle-class norms came to be universalized in colonial India. Using new institutions of the public sphere, these men were able to recast ideas of respectability to distinguish themselves from upper and lower classes in society, and to posit a moral superiority over both. All of these were a crucial element in the constitution of a middle class. An important task of any historical exercise must be to show the processes through which power comes to be created, and to recognize, as Dipesh Chakrabarty puts it, the 'ambivalences, contradictions... the tragedies and ironies that attend' the constitution of power.[7] The aim of this collection is to do exactly that for the history of the middle class in colonial India.

Though my usage of the singular—the middle class—may suggest otherwise, I do not intend to suggest that the middle class in colonial India was a monolithic entity. There were, for one, significant regional differences. Probably due to a different pattern of land tenure in the province, the *rentier* component in the social group which constituted itself as a middle class in Calcutta (described by Tanika Sarkar in this volume) was distinct from those in other towns such as Surat where merchant groups had a much higher profile.[8] There was also diversity of other kinds. The religious diversity of Delhi or Lucknow, for instance, ensured a different sort of public religiosity as compared to Madras.[9] Nor should we assume that even within regions perfect unanimity characterized the middle class. There were significant differences and debates within the middle class, which are noted later in this introduction, and well illustrated in the essays comprising this volume. Very different access to material resources also made the lifestyles and hence cultural preferences of the contributors to the *Kanara Saraswat*, described by Prashant Kidambi in his essay in this volume, quite different from, say, a well-to-do lawyer such as Jawaharlal Nehru. Yet, as the essays will also show, there are significant points where the opinions of the two do coincide. It is precisely such intersections that make it possible to talk about a middle class in colonial India.

It is important to reiterate, perhaps, that there is no particular moment when the middle class is 'finally' made. Rather, much like most other social formations, it is always in the making. Therefore, the essays in this collection highlight different moments in this history. The history of middle-class formations shows both commonalities and differences in the way the class comes to be made at different times. For instance, at most times, the middle class seeks to distinguish itself from the upper, and more vehemently, the lower orders of society. Quite how it does so, depends on the historical moment. In this collection, the author of the editorial in the *Bengalee* does so very differently from Nehru. Middle-class leaders in Prashant Kidambi's essay on early twentieth century Bombay do so quite differently from the directors of films in the 1970s that Madhava Prasad describes. But distancing has to be reinforced at each historical juncture, because it is central to the middle-class project. From this distancing emerge middle-class aspirations to leadership and hopes of establishing social and political hegemony.

We cannot really understand the issues and debates involved in defining the middle class unless we squarely address the issue of comparisons. Comparisons have been central to any discussion of the middle class in colonial India.[10] For most part, these comparisons have been unfavourable. Colonial officials and intellectuals had good reason to disparage the aspirations of the upwardly mobile western-educated men, and did so frequently. But even middle class Indians themselves expressed reservations about their lack of authenticity. Of course there was change over time. There was a huge difference, for instance, between Jawaharlal Nehru's critique of the middle class as 'déclassé intellectuals,' (soon to be redeemed by Gandhi's hyper-authenticity), and the much less confident debates between the advocates of wholesale westernization and neo-conservatives in the nineteenth century. But colonialists and nationalists alike did, implicitly or explicitly, compare the Indian middle class with what they all believed was an authentic model of middle class-ness originating in the West.

Being middle class in colonial India was a project undertaken by a social elite which deployed a category consciously picked up from the history of their rulers, the British. Taking a cue from the enlightened, progressive role attributed to the middle class in British history, western educated elites of colonial India found little trouble in representing themselves in the same way. But this inevitably led to comparisons. The middle class of colonial India thus repeatedly suffered comparisons, and suffered in comparison, to a presumed model of an 'authentic' western middle class. A review of the writing on the Indian middle class from its origins in the late nineteenth century to almost the present day reveals that discussions of the Indian middle class continue to be inhibited by comparisons with an ideal-type of the category derived ultimately from rather simplistic readings of European history. Scholars tend to contrast an idealized notion of class formation and unity with the more messy terrain of historical reality, only, and obviously, to find the latter wanting.

Yet, a more careful examination of the middle class, even in European or North American history reveals some significant ambiguities about the use of this category.[11] Does the industrial bourgeoisie alone constitute the middle class? Surely not, as then we would have to exclude the central role of cultural entrepreneurs—the teachers, the journalists, the novelists, the politicians, and so on—from our understanding of the middle class. What exactly *was* the relationship between these groups and the Industrial Revolution? In fact, recent studies seem to emphasize the extent to which this 'foundational' middle class too was the product of conscious interventions in social and public life of nineteenth century England or the United States.[12] Although the industrial revolution certainly forms an important backdrop to their study of the middle class, Mary Ryan as well as Leonore Davidoff and Catherine Hall focus on the centrality of cultural projects, and particularly the recasting of gender relations within the family, to the construction of a middle class in England or the United States. Dror Wahrman goes further in challenging prevalent ideas about the middle class. Suggesting that arguments about an Industrial Revolution leading to an inevitable 'rise of the middle class' are more a mythical construct than historical reality, Wahrman contends that the idea of a middle class was actually the product of political representations, carried out in the public sphere.[13] Much like colonial India, it seems, the image of Britain as a middle class society came into being through the 'language of writers and speakers as found in those means of public communication geared towards interventions in the political process and towards audiences interested in such interventions.'[14] Instead of a fixed sociological category bounded by income or occupation, Wahrman argues that in Britain 'the precise social referent of the notion of 'middle class' was far from being well defined, and indeed that this vagueness often served the purpose of its users.'[15] But it is precisely this myth which now stands as a model against which non-western historical developments are judged. Increasingly, scholarship in other parts of the world too is examining the middle class not only as a project of self-constitution with only indirect links to economic power, but also emphasizing the importance of social manners, morals, and values as integral to middle-class formation. Such scholarship, for one, questions a causal connection between rapid industrialization and the emergence of a 'middle-class society.' These studies also reveal that public sphere interventions were critical in establishing certain myths about middle-class formation.[16]

With this background then, we can better understand the selections used in this volume. The essays are divided into four parts. The first part, titled 'framing the middle class,' looks at writings from the late nineteenth and first part of the twentieth century that are either by or about the newly emerging middle class. These not only give us a sense of how the 'middle class' enters public discourse in colonial India, but also how many of the later discussions and critiques of the middle class are prefigured in these documents. The second section surveys the major scholarly writings and debates about the middle class in colonial India. Until recently, much of the discussion on this subject took place without any attention to the ways in which gender, caste, and religion have been central to middle-class formation in colonial India. The third section of the book explicitly focuses on the importance of these themes to the historiography of the middle class. In the last section of the book I include essays which explore new fields of study that still need more research. They all engage with concerns of everyday life that have not really been explored in detail by historians of colonial India. Together, the selections included in this anthology seek to explore the dilemmas of being middle class in colonial India and provide a window into how these have been tackled by a variety of scholarly approaches.[17]

FRAMING THE MIDDLE CLASS

One of the purposes of books in this series is to 'chart the historiographical shifts that have occurred since the theme emerged.' The idea of an Indian middle class emerged in the colonial era, and selections used in the first section of this book introduce readers to some of the early discussions about the middle class from the late nineteenth through to the middle of the twentieth century. In no way are these selections meant to be 'representative' of the tremendous regional and linguistic diversity of middle-class writings of the nineteenth and twentieth centuries. Nor does this section even try to represent the canonical figures of middle-class politics and literature—Rabindranath Tagore and Mohandas Gandhi are conspicuous by their absence in this section, for instance, as are any women writers. Rather than try to create an anthology of representative 'primary sources' of middle-class writing (a task which would take more room and much more linguistic competence than I have at my disposal), I have tried to select writing that captures some of the important concerns and anxieties about middle class-ness that were present during the making of the middle class. As we will see, these concerns also permeate later historians' discussions and assumptions about the middle class of colonial India, and in many ways continue to inform contemporary discussions about the middle class.

The middle class was very much a product of British colonialism. I therefore start by looking at how the colonial rulers themselves saw this social group, and use as an example an extract from the farewell speech by the Viceroy to India, the Marquis of Dufferin and Ava, as he prepared to leave the office in November 1888. It is quite apparent that the major purpose of Lord Dufferin's speech was to refute demands being made by the newly-formed Indian National Congress for greater representation of Indians in the colonial administration.[18] Dufferin stressed that given India's tremendous social, economic, cultural, and above all religious diversity, a 'microscopic minority' of educated Indians (he is careful to avoid using the term 'middle class' while describing the social group) could not claim to represent this tremendous diversity.

Despite the overall tone and intent of the Viceroy's address, we can derive a good sense of the historical context that produced the middle class from his speech. Clearly, the middle class was regarded as an important social formation of some significance by the rulers. Else, there would be little reason for Dufferin to have spent a considerable amount of time criticizing the Indian National Congress, then only three years old and with shallow roots in Indian society. That an unsympathetic outgoing Viceroy said he wished to 'enlarge the surface of our contact with the educated and intelligent public opinion of India,' no doubt reinforced the middle class' own sense of self-importance. Equally though, Dufferin's speech also reveals the ways in which the colonial rulers sought to put the middle class in its place. From the rhetoric of English people's love of liberty and egalitarianism he quickly moved to the reminder that the English would never permit any interference in the exercise of their power over India. To reinforce this argument, Dufferin went on to excoriate the unrepresentative character of the western-educated middle class, based on their minuscule numbers in proportion to the Indian population, as well as the parochialism of their agenda. As much as the opportunities offered by colonialism, then, the ways in which colonial officialdom sought to limit, circumscribe, and criticize their influence had a tremendous impact on shaping the middle class of colonial India.

Whatever his personal opinions about the emerging middle class, a public speech by the outgoing Viceroy had to be somewhat guarded in its language. Dufferin chose to display his disappointment over criticism of his administration through sarcasm rather than open hostility. Other supporters of the imperial cause were not limited in the same way. Perhaps the best known of these was the writer Rudyard Kipling. Much more comfortable with an older, authoritarian and paternalist style of administration, Kipling lampooned liberal administrators and commentators as fiercely as he did the emerging westernized middle class of India, through characters such as Hurree Chunder Mookerjee in *Kim* or Grish Chunder De in 'Head of the District.'[19] Kipling was at his vitriolic best when contrasting the superficial veneer of westernization in these characters with others whom he represented as 'real' or authentic Indians, whether they be the Lama or Mahbub Ali in *Kim*, or the rugged Pathan tribesmen of 'Head of the District.' This distinction between authenticity and inauthenticity was to find a significant echo in debates within the emerging middle class of colonial India as well.

Critiques of native social customs such as those articulated by Dufferin, or the charges of cultural inauthenticity exemplified in Kipling's writings, were to have a profound impact on the constitution of the middle class in this time. Some middle-class activists, for instance Mahadev Govind Ranade (and in a different way, Sir Sayyid Ahmad Khan) took colonial critiques seriously enough to devote their energies to social and religious reform.[20] But equally significantly, criticism of the apparently derivative agenda of middle-class reformism arose from *within* the middle class. Bankim Chandra Chatterjee's scathing critiques of the anglicized Bengali Baboo are known to most readers of modern Indian history.[21] Less known perhaps are people such as Sajjad Hussain, a inveterate critic of Sir Sayyid's modernizing efforts, and whom Sajjad never failed to lampoon in his *Oudh Punch*.[22] Debates between the so-called traditionalists and modernizers were, in fact, a staple of the middle-class milieu in the nineteenth and early twentieth centuries. But rather than recapitulate that well-known debate through primary sources, I have chosen to introduce a more unusual primary source next.[23] Aurobindo Ghosh is better known for his advocacy of radical nationalism in his earlier days and for his later incarnation as a spiritual leader and seer. Yet the extract from his famous series of essays in the *Indu Prakash* also reveals the extent to which the colonial critique of cultural inauthenticity remained a very central element of middle-class formation in colonial India.

Aurobindo Ghosh may well have been one of the first to consistently use the label 'middle class' to describe people who had been variously referred to and who had described themselves as the 'educated classes,' or 'the thinking classes' of British India.[24] But his use of this label for this social group (in which he included himself, incidentally), was not particularly complimentary. 'Of all brand new articles we have imported,' Ghosh said, 'inconceivably the most important is that large class of people—journalists, barristers, doctors, officials, graduates, and traders—who have grown up and are increasing with prurient rapidity under the aegis of the British rule: and this class I call the middle class.' The aim of this series of essays was to point out what he considered to be the excessive timidity of the leadership of the Indian National Congress in the face of an oppressive colonial power which did not care a whit for Indian interests. To do so, Aurobindo argued that the party represented not the entire nation, but a small fragment of it— the middle class. What is even more interesting, though, are the terms of Aurobindo's critique of the middle class which go beyond simple critiques of elitism and echo the charges of cultural inauthenticity we noted earlier. Ghosh compared the Indian middle class to low-priced British imports, such as 'cheap Liverpool cloths, [and] shoddy Brummagem wares.' Both were equally responsible, in his opinion, for destroying 'the fine and genuine textures' of traditional Indian society. In fact, his very preference for the term 'middle class' rather than others which were used by the Congress leaders of his time is rooted in this notion. Continuing his comparison of the westernized middle-class leadership to superficially attractive English artefacts, Ghosh concludes that 'when we are so proud of our imported English goods, it would be absurd, when we want labels for them, not to import their English names as well.'

However damning Aurobindo Ghosh's usage may have been, his label was soon to be appropriated in much more positive ways by his contemporaries and successors. An editorial in *The Bengalee* from 1911 clearly reveals a much more confident middle class than was described by Aurobindo. Greater representation in local councils—a demand being made by the middle class for at least twenty five years—was by now asserted with a degree of self assurance that had been lacking earlier. More than simply aspiring to prominence in society, the editorial appears to suggest both a historical inevitability and a moral imperative about the role that the middle class was destined to play in colonial India. This was, in part, based on a (somewhat selective) reading of Euro-Atlantic history. The historical successes of England, France, and the United States are attributed to the presence of the middle class in these countries, whereas the reason for the failures of Russia and Portugal are deemed to be a result of these nations not having a middle class. The very presence of a middle class then, was a necessary condition of success in this modern age, if we are to believe *The Bengalee*, and its absence a recipe for failure and decline. This is so because, the newspaper tells us: 'Wherever you have a middle class, you have enlightenment, freedom, progress and prosperity. Wherever society is sharply divided into upper and lower strata ... you have superstition, reaction, poverty and decay.' It was as champions of enlightenment, freedom, and progress, as well as the crusaders against superstition and reaction that the Indian middle class made their claims to leadership of native society and demanded a greater representation in the running of the country.

Read together, Aurobindo and *The Bengalee* reveal some interesting facets of middle-class formation in colonial India. There is considerable difference in their assessment of the middle class, of course. Whereas for Ghosh the importing of the category signals the extent to which the middle class is alienated from the real textures of Indian society, for *The Bengalee* the presence of the middle class is evidence of India realizing the promises and fruits of modernity. The middle class of *The Bengalee*'s editorial could hardly be accused of the sort of 'mendicancy' that had so infuriated Aurobindo Ghosh. But nor is there any evidence, in *The Bengalee*, of the auto-critique undertaken by Ghosh. Yet, both points of view clearly acknowledge that the middle class is a category whose original home lies in the West. Both base their analysis on a comparison of the Indian middle class with a putatively 'original' Western middle class. For Aurobindo the comparison provides evidence of loss of authentic tradition; for *The Bengalee*, a comparison is the basis of its claim to power.

A facile reading of history might suggest that the gains made by middle-class activists in the decade or so after Aurobindo's critiques gave them the confidence to overcome their earlier reservations. Certainly, the Government of India Act of 1909 strengthened middle-class representation in decision-making bodies. Middle-class publications thrived, and lent greater public visibility to their causes. The partition of Bengal would be revoked later in the year, lending credibility to the claims of political leadership made by the Indian National Congress, described by Aurobindo as a 'middle-class machine.' Yet, reading this as a simple history of growing middle-class confidence would have to ignore the fact that throughout the colonial era (and well beyond, as I will later suggest), middle-class discourse retained a significant degree of anxiety about its purported cultural inauthenticity. This is not to ignore their successes or the greater confidence that success bred. Nor can the historian ignore the considerable amount of anxiety about their own authenticity or lack of it that permeated historical discourse through the colonial era, and beyond.

The last of the readings in this section is from Jawaharlal Nehru's magnificent *Discovery of India*. One would think that more than half a century after Aurobindo's critique, and a new Indian middle-class leadership poised to take power from the British (with the author himself at the helm), there would be fewer anxieties about the authenticity of the Indian middle class. Of course, Nehru's work anticipates decolonization, and that confidence is reflected in the very project he undertakes in the book. Yet, as we shall see, even as late as the 1940s, concerns about cultural authenticity were prominent even in the writing of this quintessential representative of the westernized middle class. Writing about the era following the First World War, Nehru contrasted India's sturdy peasants, tempered by centuries of hardship, with 'déclassé intellectuals' cut off from the land. This contrast itself is revealing. Romanticizing the hardship of the peasants, Nehru believed them to be somehow more authentic than the middle class, whom he chose to represent as belonging neither to the traditional or the modern world. Reflecting some of the ideas first articulated by men like Dufferin or Kipling, Nehru wrote to say that while the middle class were attracted by modernity 'they lacked its inner content.' Nowhere does he tell us what this inner content was, or why educated Indians were incapable of grasping it. Presumably the socialist Nehru perceived some impermeable barrier, undoubtedly related to the very different historical experiences of the western and non-western world, that made Indians lack the 'inner content' of (a presumably irremediably western) modernity. Frustrated by their inability to be real and authentic, Nehru suggests that among the Indian middle classes '[s]ome tried to cling tenaciously to the dead forms of the past....[while] Others made themselves pale and ineffectual copies of the West.' Because neither was effective, men of the Indian middle class became, '...derelicts, frantically seeking some foothold of security for body and mind and mind and finding none, they floated aimlessly in the murky waters of Indian life.'

While we can dwell on the social, political, psychological or cultural reasons for these representations of the Indian middle class, I would like to highlight here the perceptions of the historical. One reason why both the colonialist and nationalist, why traditionalists and modernists in India, could label the Indian middle class inauthentic was because the real history of a real middle class, it was assumed, lay elsewhere, specifically in the West. As we shall see, the concerns about authenticity and inauthenticity, about comparisons, came to shape the debates among later historians too when it came to the study of the middle class in colonial India.

DEBATING THE MIDDLE CLASS

The second section of this book introduces readers to some of the most important scholarly debates about the existence, origins, and working of the middle class in colonial India. It starts with critical review of Jawaharlal Nehru's *Discovery of India* by one of the most remarkable polymaths of his time, Damodar Dharmanand Kosambi. There are many reasons why Kosambi's review kicks off this section of the book, not the least of which is because of the subject of the review. Though Nehru was not a professional historian, his book is an important landmark in the historiography of India. On the middle class, for instance, Nehru makes a compelling argument linking its formation to material conditions initiated by colonialism, and more specifically to certain contradictions inherent in colonial rule over India.[25] Undoubtedly Nehru drew upon the work of Marxist thinkers and activists who had made such connections before him, such as

Manabendra Nath Roy,[26] as well as the work of nationalist historians like Romesh Chunder Dutt.[27] Scholars such as Dhurjati Prasad Mukerji were soon to elaborate on the arguments we encounter in the *Discovery of India*, linking the formation of a 'new middle class' to colonial land-tenure and commercial policies.[28] Yet the sweeping vision, lucid arguments and compelling prose of *Discovery of India* ensured that this work was to play a very important role in shaping the narratives of modern Indian history, including our understanding of the middle class.

Perhaps an even more important reason for starting this section on scholarly debates about the middle class with Kosambi's review is because of its uninhibited use of a Marxist framework (albeit an explicitly unorthodox one) to understand the Indian middle class. Despite its limitations, we really cannot ignore Marxist frameworks while deploying class as a category of social analysis. Yet it is a telling commentary on the changing nature of academic fashion that few of the scholars whose writings follow Kosambi's essay in this volume do so. One reason for this could well be Marx's own emphasis on a bipolar class model, leaving little room for theoretical discussions of intermediate social classes. Yet to overlook Marxist methodology all together would also mean ignoring the importance of Marxism in the shaping of our understanding of modern South Asian history.[29] Even if quoting Marx is no longer fashionable in the era of postcolonial scholarship, the political edge bequeathed by the Marxist tradition—the idea that the point of scholarship is not just to interpret the world but to change it—remains an important one in Indian historiography, even among scholars who find it impossible to overlook the Eurocentricism of Marxist paradigms.[30]

Though appreciative of Nehru's vision, Kosambi takes him to task for virtually ignoring class, class struggle, and capital accumulation as the explanatory framework for understanding the recent history of India. For Kosambi, as the title of his review suggests, the 1940s signal the 'coming of age of the Indian bourgeoisie.' The review reveals quite clearly the many strengths as well as some of the limitations of the Marxist framework Kosambi employs. Evident is a prescient analysis of the strengths and limitations of the middle-class agenda in soon-to-be independent India, including a provocative argument explaining the emerging divergence between the Indian National Congress and the Muslim League. But even Kosambi's unorthodox Marxism cannot overcome the apparent disregard for delving too deeply into the character and composition of an intermediate social group called the middle class. In Kosambi's analysis, intellectuals and political activists are conflated with industrial and financial tycoons, making all elements of the middle class appear to be either tools or representative of financial and industrial capital. However, it must be noted that Kosambi's approach is remarkably free of attempts at explicit or implicit comparisons of the Indian bourgeoisie with an 'original' western model. It is such comparisons, and the inevitable discovery of a lack or lag, which most infuriates critics of Marxist teleologies among contemporary postcolonial critics.[31]

The nation and its toiling millions became the focus of virtually all Indian historiography of the first four decades after independence. It appears that historians were not really interested in the middle class. There were also other factors at work. As Satish Deshpande suggests, 'the middle class may have seemed an 'unworthy' or self-indulgent topic for a generation of social scientists drawn from this class, who believed their mandate was to act on behalf of 'the people' who constituted the nation.'[32] With a focus on the lower orders of society then, there was little attempt at exploring the making of India's middle class.[33] While scholars of the 1950s and 1960s did use the term 'middle class' extensively, for the most part the middle class was assumed to be a self-evident sociological category which did not need further explanation. This is typified in Banke Bihari Misra's seminal work on the Indian middle classes, which follows Kosambi's review in this volume. Misra says that 'since most of us, without the aid of a specialist, understand what we mean when we use the term,' he sees little need or value in trying to reach more precise definitions of the middle class. Instead, Misra presents us with a rich introduction to the history of the commercial, landed, educated, and professional 'middle classes.' To a large extent, this first academic study of the Indian middle class of colonial India concurs with earlier assumptions of colonial administrators and Indian nationalists. Misra, like most of the writers reviewed in the first section of this volume[34] saw the middle class in colonial India simply as the product of English education, the rule of law, and a capitalist economy introduced by the British in India. There was little sense of the middle class' own efforts in their creation. It is a testament to how under-studied the category of the middle class is in Indian history that B. B. Misra's work remains, to date, one of the few comprehensive treatments of the subject by a historian of India.

Though the making of a middle class may not have been the focus of Indian historiography, a large proportion of it during the 1960s, 1970s and even the 1980s, did deal with the activities of middle-class nationalists. It would be inappropriate, even if it were possible, to summarize this vast array of fine historical literature around nationalism. All that is really possible given limitations of space and time is to mention a few exemplary works, by scholars whose study of nationalism was particularly useful for understanding the making of the middle class. Among these would have to be Bipan Chandra's study of economic nationalism, Sumit Sarkar's exploration of the Swadeshi movement in Bengal, and John McLane's excellent study of the early Indian National Congress.[35] While it may be unusual to reference a textbook among specialized monographs, Sumit Sarkar's *Modern India* is far from a usual textbook. For the subject of this volume, I cannot think of a better short introduction to the study of the middle class of colonial India than contained in Sarkar's textbook.[36] In their own very different ways the work of these scholars took our understanding of the middle class well beyond the limited parameters suggested by scholars such as Misra who had easily fallen into describing the middle class much as colonial officials had, by agreeing, for instance, with the argument that 'the Indian middle class which the British aimed at creating was to be a class of imitators, not the originators of new values and methods.'

The body of opinion represented by B. B. Misra, however, remained strong and these assumptions about the middle class came to be shared by scholars in the 1970s and 1980s who denied the existence of a 'real' middle class in India all together. Working on revisionist interpretations of Indian nationalism, historians from Cambridge University in the 1970s saw educated Indians acting as 'clients' of other powerful people, and completely without an independent political agenda.[37] Michelguglielmo Torri built on these ideas to argue that the devastating intervention of the 'Cambridge school' historians exploded a 'master concept' of Indian historiography and signed the 'death warrant' of the middle class as a category of Indian history. Describing them as the urban non-capitalist bourgeoisie, he suggests that it was precisely because of their role as intellectuals, that the so-called middle class suffered the 'delusion' of belonging to an autonomous social group, 'endowed with a political weight of its own.' It is striking to see the extent to which Torri too works with the idea of there being a real middle class against which he can compare the Indian version to find it lacking. This notion of a real middle class located in western history is hardly limited to Torri's work. In fact, one could argue that it has come to acquire the status of historical common sense. For instance, in his otherwise fascinating study of construction of modern Sikhism, Harjot Oberoi rejects the applicability of the term middle class to Indian history because he sees the former as a category which is the product of Europe's historical experience of industrialization. 'In India on the other hand petty bureaucrats and urban professionals could at best only dream of industrialization; thus this non-productive class could not appropriately be named middle class.'[38] Joya Chatterjee repeats the same argument in her work on Bengal's partition.[39]

Given the origins of Torri's inspiration, it is instructive to note the differences between his position and the arguments outlined by Christopher Bayly, earlier identified with the so-called Cambridge school.[40] Refuting the idea that the history of India was so different as to preclude the emergence of public sphere politics comparable to that of Europe (crucial to middle-class formation), Bayly suggests that 'public opinion—the weight of reasoned debate—was not the preserve of modern or western polities.' Tracing a much longer indigenous genealogy for the public sphere activities of the later nineteenth century activists, Bayly suggests that these men, whom he terms the 'north Indian ecumene,' drew upon a tradition of debate, persuasion, and communication 'which owed as much to Indian norms as they did to Comte or Mazzini.' This ecumene, he points out, had long functioned as a critical reasoning public, with the literati or officials using poetry, satire, letter-writing, placarding, festivals, and religious congregations to exercise a degree of critical surveillance on the activities of the state. Though certainly contestable[41], Bayly's point of view provides a unique perspective to the discussion on the Indian middle class. At the very least he allows us to understand the significant continuities that mark the pre-colonial and colonial eras and better understand the nature of the resources—material as well as cultural—that were deployed in middle-class formation during the colonial era.

If Christopher Bayly looked for the pre-colonial traditions of public debate in India, Partha Chatterjee, in contrast, suggests that no real public sphere could ever exist in colonial India. What Chatterjee terms 'the rule of colonial difference,' ensured that any *rights* the middle class may have believed they possessed, that of public criticism of colonial policies, were in fact denied any legitimacy in the colonial milieu. Even as late as the 1880s, the only 'public sphere' that existed in colonial

India, Chatterjee contends, consisted of 'European residents of the country.'[42] The Indian middle class, he suggests in the extract we read from the book, even while contesting 'colonial difference' in the public sphere, came to locate their own project of counter-hegemony in a 'spiritual' or 'inner' domain, over which they claimed sovereignty. It was here that they sought to fashion a middle-class nation that would be both modern and traditional, strong enough to contest colonial rule yet not lose its essential cultural uniqueness. The Calcutta middle class was thus attracted to Ramakrishna's teachings, yet, as Chatterjee demonstrates through his reading of the *Kathamrta*, their attempts also reveal the 'fears and anxieties of a class aspiring to hegemony [and] ... reveals to us the subalternity of an elite.'

Chatterjee's work is an excellent representative of the postcolonial approach to the study of the middle class in colonial India, and displays the significant strengths as well as some of the possible limitations of this approach. It certainly helps to open up ways of thinking about the middle class in colonial India beyond the categories of analysis derived from the European Enlightenment and naturalized through the colonial experience. The advantages of this are many. For one, it eases (though not completely alleviates) the burden of comparisons that has dogged the historiography of the middle class in colonial India which compares the middle class of colonial India and finds it deficient, in many respects, to a presumed liberal and enlightened western middle class. Rather than lamenting a lack of identity with an ideal typical western middle class, Chatterjee's work highlights the contradictions and racism inherent in a colonial milieu that could not but lead to the fashioning of a distinct and different colonial modernity. The Indian middle class Chatterjee describes could not, therefore, be the same as the idealized middle class of the Western tradition. Responding to the colonial milieu, they fashioned their counterhegemonic project in the 'inner domain of cultural identity,' and with a sense of despair at their lack of successes in the public sphere. Their interventions, seeking to create a new middle-class national culture, were consciously created as models that differed from the ideals of western modernity. Second, and equally important, the postcolonial approach that Chatterjee and others employ, allows for a shift in the focus of historiography away from purely political history, so that we finally get some serious attention paid to the 'inner domains' of middle-class politics such as the family and religion.

The limitations of postcolonial approaches have been addressed by a number of scholars. Probably the most articulate of the critics has been Sumit Sarkar, whose own work on the middle class shows how factors such as income, caste, and the new discipline of clock-time, rather than the resistance to a generalized 'colonial discourse,' shaped middle-class identities in colonial Bengal.[43] A critique from a different perspective is made by Claude Markovits in his essay that follows Chatterjee in this collection. Markovits complains that most studies of the middle class in colonial India only look at cultural productions of western educated professionals while ignoring merchant groups—a very justifiable criticism of the existing scholarship. To remedy the situation somewhat, Markovits focuses primarily on entrepreneurial and merchant groups in this essay where, he claims, 'Macaulay and his kind play no role.' Markovits doesn't quite deliver what he promises, as comparisons between merchants and 'Macaulayans' occur through the essay. However, he does succeed in pointing out the distinctness of mercantile middle-class groups, who he argues 'remained largely separate from the world of the English-educated middle classes.' But perhaps the most significant contribution of Markovits' essay is to point out the scant attention historians of the middle class have paid to groups such as the Marwari, Gujarati, or Chettiar merchant and entrepreneurial communities while proffering their analyses of the middle class in colonial India.[44]

The last essay in this section represents one of the most recent interventions on the subject of the middle class in colonial India. Drawing upon some of the newest work on the middle class in India as well as other parts of the world, Prashant Kidambi dispenses with the idea that we can look at the middle class as some sort of given, stable, entity. Focusing on upper-caste white-collar salaried employees in colonial Bombay, Kidambi shows how they invoked a distinctive 'middle-class identity' when demanding better wages and working conditions, and simultaneously distanced themselves from similar demands being made by manual workers in the city. Kidambi is also careful to show how material concerns shaped the making of Bombay's middle class. In doing so his argument contests 'the assumption that there was a clear-cut distinction between the 'material' and 'cultural' domains in the ideological articulation of middle-class identity.'

It is perhaps fitting that an essay calling for attention to material domain of middle-class formation in colonial India closes this section of the book which began with Kosambi's Marxist reading of the role of the Indian bourgeoisie. Kidambi's essay, as important as it is for what it says, is also significant in how it reveals the trajectories taken by the scholarship on the middle class since Kosambi's analysis. Clearly aware of the critiques undertaken by postcolonial interventions, Kidambi never invokes the sort of invidious comparisons with a putatively originary middle class of the kind that informed, for instance, the work of B. B. Misra. Nor is he willing to give up entirely on looking at the middle class as a comparable social formation by emphasizing only the uniqueness of a colonial modernity. But, as Kidambi himself points out, there are certainly limitations in his approach. In its lack of attention to gender, as well as to caste and religion, Kidambi's essay is fairly representative of the mainstream scholarship on the middle class of colonial India. All of these dimensions of middle-class formation certainly need much more attention, and it is to them we turn in the next section of the book.

GENDER, CASTE, AND RELIGION IN THE MAKING OF MIDDLE-CLASS MODERNITY

One of the conceits of a foundational category such as 'class' is to relegate to subordinate status other vectors of social hierarchy, and other forms of social or cultural identity. Engaging with gender, caste and religion, the essays in this section of the book also bring to fore some larger questions. Can a category such as 'class' which clearly has roots in a variety of Eurocentric traditions, be capacious enough to accommodate other social and cultural variables? Even more significantly, does privileging class (in this case, the category 'middle class') help us better understand the ways in which class, caste, and religion played out in the politics of colonial India? The essays in this section of the book suggest that the answer to these questions should be a definite yes.

Despite the fact that being middle class in colonial India (as elsewhere) was a highly gendered project, it took historiography quite a while to recognize and appreciate the fact. In spite of obvious upper-caste dominance, attention to issues of caste in the historiography of Indian middle-class modernity is even more recent. Religion, though, has had a slightly different place in the writings on colonial India. Primarily because the politics of religious identities produced a political division in the subcontinent, and then because of the continued salience of religion in politics, historians of middle-class activities in colonial India have paid attention to religious identities. However, despite a couple of decades of bashing, Orientalist traditions remain well and alive,[45] which explains why a particularly reified notion of religious identities continues to permeate the writing of Indian history.[46]

A large and vibrant body of feminist scholarship has engaged in revealing the extent to which the project of middle-class nationalism was a gendered one. This is a tradition that probably predates the first generation of Indian feminist activism.[47] Despite the limitations under which they operated, early Indian feminists such as Kamaladevi Chattopadhyaya or Uma Nehru made their critique of patriarchal assumptions governing middle-class nationalism quite apparent.[48] It took a much longer time, though, for these critical viewpoints to make their way into mainstream historiography of modern India. It was really only during the 1980s and 1990s, through the efforts of many feminist historians, that the gendering of the middle class of colonial India came to the attention of other historians of the region.[49] Thanks to some of these writings, modern Indian historiography now boasts of stellar scholarship about how colonialism and nationalism recast patriarchy in colonial India to create dutiful daughters, bourgeois *bahu*s (daughters-in-law) or efficient housewives.[50] Increasingly, in fact, feminist historians are turning to examine ways in which middle-class connections cut across lines of metropole and colony to reaffirm patriarchal authority or other elite agenda.[51]

The essay by Tanika Sarkar included in this volume builds on and contributes to the established tradition of feminist scholarship on the gendered nature of the making of the Indian middle class. What stands out in Sarkar's approach is her steadfast refusal to subscribe to either the colonial-nationalist binary, or indeed the divide between materialist and cultural historians. Though paying careful attention to the material circumstances that went into the making of the Bengali middle class, Sarkar's essay reveals that the middle class does not arrive fully-formed as a result of these circumstances, but rather is made through the efforts of people. It is these efforts, as we can clearly see from her essay, that are highly gendered. Despite some significant disagreements, Sarkar does concur with Partha Chatterjee on the extent to which the home represented an autonomous space where the contours of a nationalist middle class were shaped. If, as Sarkar says, 'the home was not merely an escape from this world but its critique and an alternative order' then the relationships within that home, and in particular the conjugal relationship, had to be represented in new terms by the middle class. However, unlike Chatterjee, Sarkar is able to reveal not just the new disciplinary formations that emerge from colonial-nationalist discourse, but also the contested and contradictory nature of this discourse. Characteristic of middle-class politics was not only the struggle for arenas of power against colonial domination, but also, critically, over other social groups, which at this time included women from their own class. This became apparent when women such as Rukmabai, or the Phulmani Devi case, challenged the authority of middle-class men over their own households. Then, the discourse of love and affect quickly transformed itself into another kind of language that reeked of patriarchal authority and misogynistic readings of sacred texts. It only took a challenge to their authority within the home to show the limits of their claim that love, harmony and a general sense of self-fulfillment lay at the heart of middle-class conjugality. Sarkar's essay demonstrates the fractures and contradictions constitutive of middle-class formation in colonial India, containing both the possibilities of egalitarian and highly authoritarian and illiberal political positions.

Dipesh Chakrabarty, although also examining notions of domesticity, gender relations and, in particular, the constructions of an ideal housewife, opens up somewhat different questions about what it means to be 'middle class' in colonial Bengal. While feminist scholars have often read these new ideas as the recasting of patriarchy, Chakrabarty closely examines these constructions to reveal a fundamental disconnect between bourgeois notions of domesticity, and those of the Indian middle class. This Bengali middle-class approach to gender relations in the home, he argues, was constituted by tensions, as it sought to incorporate both the historical and modern as defined by the ideal-type of Western modernity, and the anti-historical modern, 'tied to mythico-religious time' which 'escapes and exceeds bourgeois time.' There was much in the ideals Bengali middle-class men proposed for the housewife which was derivative of the modernity brought by colonialism, he argues, but it was also a modernity which sought to evoke 'formations of pleasure, emotions and ideas of good life that associated themselves with models of non-autonomous, non-bourgeois and non-secular personhood.' His point here, as in large parts of his magisterial *Provincializing Europe*, is to demonstrate the limits of the universality of the model of modernity derived from the EuroAmerican experience. Chakrabarty suggests that these are 'subaltern pasts' which are not really amenable to tenets of modern secular historicization without doing considerable violence to the subjects of these pasts.[52] Chakrabarty's is an important contribution to any attempts at seeking a language for writing about the middle class of colonial India, for it creates space for delving into the specifics of the histories of non-western subjects without necessarily evaluating them by a history they could never replicate, or by a set of standards which would always find them wanting.

Chakrabarty is critical of the existing historiography based on public narratives of private lives as it, 'tells us very little about what went on in the everyday lives of actual, empirical, *bhadralok* families.' Yet, it must be said that for all its historiographical significance, in this respect his essay does not take us as far as some emerging feminist scholarship on the middle-class family.[53] Though perhaps even here, one would have hoped for more attention to the quotidian and greater use of non-official sources for the writing of family history.[54] We are told that Indian history has to be such because India simply lacks the sort of sources that would allow the sort of detailed, local, 'French' style, social history of private life in India.[55] While that may not necessarily be true, there is a problem of master narratives. So much do the themes of colonialism and nationalism frame Indian historiography, that even historiographical traditions which emerge to challenge these master narratives, end up somehow reinforcing their hold. Thus feminist critiques remain grounded in critiques of colonial and nationalist constructions. Though they successfully challenge the prevailing assumptions about colonial and nationalist reforms, through looking at gender relations in the family, they really have not shed light on the more mundane aspects of family politics. Perhaps Chakrabarty is right in concluding that secular historicist narratives are incapable of apprehending non bourgeois personhood—or as he puts it elsewhere, subaltern pasts are not amenable to strategies of radical histories.[56]

M. S. S. Pandian's essay introduces readers to a fracture at the heart of middle-class modernity in colonial and postcolonial India analogous to Tanika Sarkar's argument. Just as Sarkar's essay clearly shows the gendered nature of middle-class formation in colonial India, Pandian turns our attention to the extent to which constructions of middle-class modernity are hugely inflected by caste.[57] Focusing as it does on the processes by which middle-class public sphere activists 'delegitimised the language of caste in the domain of politics,'

Pandian shows that in accounts of modern, middle-class life, 'caste always belongs to someone else; it is somewhere else; it is of another time.' Pandian's essay highlights the denial of the significance of caste by middle-class activists, who were themselves from the upper castes and contrasts their writings with those from people of lower castes, for whom caste is a central fact of their everyday life. His essay makes apparent the discomfort of upper caste intellectuals and scholars (whether the novelist R. K. Narayan or the sociologist M. N. Srinivas) about their own upper caste status, as this highlights for them some of the limits of the 'universal' values and principles they espouse. The championing of an 'unmarked modern' by middle-class activists, he argues, 'is stealthily upper caste in its orientation.' Just as middle-class nationalists sought to deny the inequities of power between men and women, they sought to deny or justify the existence of caste inequalities through explanations and analogies deploying the languages of modernity. Caste was either just another form of division of labour, or else a form of creating boundaries between hygienic and unhygienic practices, according to middle-class nationalists. Yet, as Pandian argues, this reveals middle-class nationalism to be not simply the contestation of colonial domination, but also a strategy to secure 'domination over the subaltern social groups such as lower castes, women, marginal linguistic regions, by the national elite.'

Historiographically, caste and class have had an uneasy relationship in the writings on colonial India. Thanks to a strong Orientalist tradition, some of whose origins have been well explored by Nicholas Dirks, among others,[58] studies of class in India have had, and continue to have, a particularly ambiguous relationship with caste. Louis Dumont, for instance, forcefully argued that hierarchy, exemplified by religion and caste, rather than equality and social mobility characteristic of class society, were emblematic of Indian society. Class, he therefore warned, was a completely inappropriate category of social analysis to use for India.[59] Perhaps seeking to be more authentic by the use of 'indigenous' categories, many outstanding studies of middle-class life in colonial India limited themselves to a single caste community.[60] Precisely because the middle class was so decidedly upper-caste in its composition, yet sought to represent the entire nation, mobilization of lower caste groups had a profound impact on its politics. The mobilization of groups such as the Namashudras of Bengal, the non-Brahmin movement in Madras Presidency, or Jyotiba Phule and then the rise of the Ambedkar-led movement in western India, clearly challenged middle-class hegemony.⁶¹ If one response to this was a mild autocritique and paternalistic 'uplift' movements sponsored by liberal elements among the middle class, an equally significant response was an aggressive championing of Hindu nationalism by the middle class of colonial India.⁶² It is middle-class religiosity, including involvement in Hindu nationalism, that the next two essays in the section explore.

Despite much evidence to the contrary, the notion that somehow an ideal-type middle class must be secular, enlightened, and liberal, persists in writings about the middle class. This is a standard particularly applied to the middle class of non-western or formerly colonized countries. The place of religion in the historiography of colonial India is perhaps even more fraught with problems of reification than the 'career of caste' described by Nicholas Dirks.⁶³ As a result two kinds of approaches predominate. We have, on the one hand, the reduction of religion to politics, the pigs-and-troughs analogy where religion functions merely as a guise for apparently more real economic and political interests. On the other hand, scholars have essentialized religious identities into something primordial and foundational.⁶⁴ Yet, as the essays in this section suggest, such dichotomies are not very useful. My essay about the remaking of Hindu religiosity in Lucknow, and Margrit Pernau's work on the 'secularization' of middle-class Muslims in Delhi, both reveal that religion both shaped and was shaped by the very processes that created a modern middle class in colonial India.

A redefinition of respectability was key to the emergence of the middle class in both Lucknow and Delhi. Margrit Pernau studies a section of Muslim professionals and intellectuals began to reconfigure the meaning of being *sharif*, or respectable, meant. This 'new meaning of sharif' Pernau suggests 'laid less emphasis on birth, noble lineage, and inherited qualities and more on behaviour and achievement.' This allowed for the emergence of a middle class, '[w]ith an identity of its own, clearly demarcated both from the nobility and the lower classes.' Far from a class committed to secularist ideals, religion, new forms of Islamic piety in this case, played a central role in the constitution of the middle class Pernau describes. Sections of the new middle class were drawn from among the *ulama* (religious scholars). But more significant was the reworking of what constituted appropriate religiosity, one that now emphasized 'this-worldly activity as a means to salvation .' Moreover, a focus on the message of revealed texts such as the Quran and the Hadith, reduced the importance of mediatory religious specialists and made personal agency and achievements more significant. A new middle-class Islamic religiosity, Pernau thus argues, was both the product and the producer of the Muslim middle class in nineteenth century Delhi.

Middle-class activists played a central role in the way religiosity came to be imagined and practiced in colonial India. Of course, policies of the colonial state certainly played a significant role in the way religion was reshaped in the period.[65] However, whether Hindu, Muslim, or Sikh, syncretic or sectarian in approach, middle-class activists played a central role in the way religion was deployed in politics, or in the emergence of new forms of piety, and in reworking the relationship between religion and politics during the colonial era.[66] However, as some previous essays in this volume have noted, there was a tremendous variety in the 'middle class' interventions in the area of religion during the colonial era. Middle-class intellectuals manned both the liberal and the conservative, the revivalist and the reformist, sides of the fierce debates that erupted over the place of religion in public life. In some cases, in fact, the same middle-class activists moved from one position to another. Occasionally, this has been read as evidence of middle-class hypocrisy.[67] But, the essays in this volume suggest, such vacillations may well have been integral to the constitution of the middle class in colonial India.

My essay on the middle class of Lucknow, for instance, shows the emergence of a new 'public' religiosity among the Hindu middle class of the city. This was an effort to create a singular kind of 'Hinduism' from multiple strands of beliefs and practices. Liberated from specific devotional beliefs, social and cultural practices, and detached from the world-views from which they emerged, purged of its divisive and hierarchical aspects, this 'republicized religiosity' was easily deployed for a variety of modern projects in which the middle class played a central role. The effort to create a more or less monolithic 'Hinduism' was, of course, largely an upper caste and male effort, and reflected its origins. The contradictions between its claims to inclusiveness and its exclusionary practices is something I take up elsewhere,[68] but can be seen in the efforts of the upper-caste actors M. S. S. Pandian describes in his essay in this volume. What my essay here does is to look at how the middle class recasting of religion created powerful discursive templates which were then deployed in many different ways, for a variety of different political agenda. Not only did a transformed

Hindu religiosity allow for the imagination of an exclusivist Hindu nationalism but, more surprising perhaps, such templates also served the project of a more liberal 'secular' Indian nationalism. In some cases, the same people advocated for both positions in colonial Lucknow. This was not the product of political opportunism or hypocrisy, but rather of the contradictions constitutive of middle-class modernity in colonial India.

Engaging with gender, caste and religion, the essays in this section suggest a complex interaction between class and these other vectors of power and authority. What emerges fairly evidently is that we need to look beyond a paradigm that sees the middle class only as a product of income, occupation and education. Caste, gender, and religion played significant roles in shaping the colonial Indian middle class. But this cannot be used to reject the use of the middle class as a category to understand society or politics in colonial India. Of course there are social and cultural variables that are unique to the Indian context. It is also true that 'class' as a category of analysis developed in the context of understanding western histories and societies and naturally privileges different social and cultural traditions. Nevertheless, class analysis is ultimately about understanding and revealing relationships of power. Without the burden of a colonial and Orientalist legacy, western historiography does not appear to have had too many problems in incorporating race, class, ethnicity and gender into analyses of the middle class.[69] It is high time 'our' difference be equally easily incorporated into class analysis of South Asian history. But it is not so much about the preference for one mode of analysis as it is about the insights into relationships of power that offers the best reason to focus on the middle class. As the essays in this section reveal, not only did religion, gender, and caste shape the middle class, but that middle-class activism, in turn, played a crucial role in configuring gendered, upper caste, and religiously-inflected ideas about the nation, community, and modernity in colonial India. We really cannot understand the politics of caste, religion, and gender without paying close attention to the middle class. Because middle-class ideas have, over time, been normalized and naturalized, it is even more important to reveal and to understand their historical evolution. Lastly, of course, the essays in this section of the book point to the absolute necessity of moving beyond simplistic comparisons of an 'originary' western middle class and a 'derivative' colonial model. In fact, in their rethinking of how the middle class modern was created by middle-class activists in colonial India, these essays compel us to rethink and expand existing models of exploring the meanings of being middle class entailed across the world.

WHITHER MIDDLE CLASS STUDIES?

In the last section of the book I include essays which point us to new and interesting directions toward which the field of middle class studies appears to be headed, and point to others that remain unexplored and need more research. The essays in this section of the volume belong together, for one, because of the way in which they all engage with concerns of everyday life that have not been explored in detail by historians of colonial South Asia. It is studies such as these which point to new, and relatively unexplored, avenues of research which historians of the middle class could profitably engage with in the future. Colonialism and nationalism are hardly absent in any of these essays. Yet, by focusing on issues as diverse as consumption, sport, and popular culture, they are able to decentre the master narratives of modern South Asian historiography, even while enriching our understanding of concerns that were, and remain, central to middle- class lives. I must apologize for not paying more attention to the significant field of music and the middle class. While popular film music has not attracted the attention of historians, outstanding examples of studies on classical music resonate with many strands of the history of middle-class formation in colonial India.[70] For this absence, I can only offer a *mea culpa*, and as an excuse, point to the limitations of space available in volumes such as this one.

The section begins with A.R. Venkatachalapathy's masterly study of coffee-drinking and middle-class culture in colonial Tamilnadu. What can be more basic than food and drink to human society? Like other signs of middle-class modernity, coffee produced its own share of anxieties among the brahmin-dominated Tamil middle class. As in other parts of India, and with other signs of Western modernity, middle-class ideologues were particularly incensed by coffee's 'invasion' of realms hitherto perceived as free of the taints of western modernity. It should come as no surprise to see how the consumption of coffee by women and 'especially the supposedly blemishless, pristine and untainted countryside and its folk,' came under particular surveillance and critique from early opponents of coffee. But over time, coffee's popularity transformed middle-class attitudes, and Venkatachalapathy's essay reveals the very interesting processes through which this formerly alien beverage came to be normalized as the acme of upper caste and middle-class Tamil culture in the twentieth century. In fact, coffee drinking now helped to distinguish the middle class from the plebeian (and the Muslim), who were represented as consumers of tea. Venkatachalapthy's work amply demonstrates how a focus on something ordinary can illuminate the larger processes of middle-class formation and the way in which this class came to shape the world around them.

Just as we need more, and more serious, histories of food,[71] we need historians to turn their talents to exploring other passions of the middle class. Sports (specifically cricket) and films are just two represented in this anthology. Cricket served the interests of empire and was equally well mobilized by those opposing imperialism.[72] The outstanding work on the history of cricket in India, including very interesting insights on the role of the middle class, is by Ramachandra Guha.[73] Boria Majumdar, however, has been even more prolific in detailing the history of the game in colonial and postcolonial India.[74] His essay in this volume focuses on the reasons, and the means through which, the Bengali middle class patronized the sport. Cricket was encouraged by colonial authorities as one of the strategies of 'civilizing' the native population, and also for gaining allies amongst a section of the population—not too different from the intent laid out in the famous 'Minute on Indian Education' by Thomas B. Macaulay in 1835. The products of a Macaulayan educational system did not produce 'a class of persons Indian in blood and colour, but English in tastes, in opinions, in morals and in intellect.' Similarly, exposure to cricket did not necessarily draw Indians closer to their rulers. Majumdar's take on the middle class as patrons and participants in the sport is an explicit attempt at countering the 'bad press' that the middle class receive, particularly in academic forums. His celebration of middle-class efforts makes for a refreshingly different perspective compared to other essays in this volume. Majumdar sees Indian middle-class participation in cricket primarily in terms of contesting colonial dominance. There was, of course, much of that. What Majumdar does not dwell upon is the extent to which participating in the Imperial sport also worked to buttress the social standing of the middle class, distinguishing them from the masses. Given that the

Indian aristocracy also played a significant role in the sport in colonial India,[75] it would have been fascinating to see how the middle class distinguished themselves from the aristocrats in the context of what was to become not just the popular sport, but virtually a religion, in postcolonial India.[76]

If cricket is one modern religion in postcolonial India, cinema is the other. Discussions of both dominate the middle-class media, and from my own observations, most middle-class living rooms as well as street corner conversations. There are some fascinating studies of cinema in colonial India, particularly on imperial representations of India.[77] While the Indian film industry dates its history back to 1913 and Dadasaheb Phalke's *Rajah Harischandra*, we have surprisingly few studies of Indian cinema in the colonial era.[78] That may well be because high costs, strict regulation, and censorship did not allow for overt expressions of nationalism via films during the colonial era. So, perhaps this lacuna in film historiography has roots in Indian historiography's preoccupation with stories about the nation. We do know, however, that early Indian film makers, particularly after the advent of sound, were deeply concerned about social issues such as marriage, family, caste and class.[79] It might be interesting to note the extent to which middle-class concerns permeated and were modified by their involvement in early Indian cinema. Without such analyses available, I have chosen to use a selection from M. Madhava Prasad's seminal work on the history of Indian cinema in the postcolonial era. In this chapter Prasad examines 'Middle-class Cinema,' particularly films that focus on 'the individual in society, faced with the struggle for existence, the locus of desires, fears and hopes.'[80] With its focus on postcolonial India, Prasad's work also reveals the extent to which the anxieties we noted for the Indian middle class in the colonial era continue to be central to the post-colonial Indian middle class. The relationship to modernity remains as fraught with ambivalence, with the middle class both embracing it and yet simultaneously distancing themselves from it through a celebration of the 'real' and 'authentic' rural India, exemplified for instance in Prasad's analysis of films such as *Mere Apne* and *Rajnigandha*. The family, as in colonial times, remains a source of great anxiety. Films such as *Guddi*, Prasad argues, which show the process of the maturing of a schoolgirl into 'responsible middle-class womanhood,' ultimately work to reinforce the ideals of class-based endogamy and, policing female sexuality, ultimately to legitimize middle-class patriarchy.

That there are clear parallels in the themes that Prasad discovers in middle-class cinema in the 1970s and the concerns of the nineteenth century Bengali middle class, is fairly obvious if we were to read Prasad's essay in conjunction with those by Chatterjee, Sarkar and Chakrabarty earlier in the volume. This is not to suggest that there was no change in the constitution of the middle class over a period of almost a hundred years. Rather, these parallels point, first, to contradictory pulls that remain at the heart of the project to be middle class—whether in colonial or postcolonial India. Second, and much more significantly, they also reveal that the project of being middle class is never complete. Certain elements, such as the necessity of maintaining distance from upper, and even more so, the lower classes, have to be reinforced at each historical juncture as they are central to the creation of a middle class. From that distancing emerges the claim to be better than others, and the justification for the leading roles to which the middle class aspire in society, demonstrated in Prasad's essay through his analysis of *Namak Haram*. With its focus on notions of inclusion and exclusion, of contradictions constitutive of the middle-class imagination, this essay draws our attention back to the very paradoxes with which we began this study.

STUDYING THE MIDDLE CLASS OF COLONIAL INDIA

In different ways, contemporary critics are well attuned to the contradictions of the middle class. Let me use a small cross-section of this contemporary critique as an example. The editor of a top news magazine, a politician and political pundit, as well as a bureaucrat (also renowned as an 'expert' on the Indian middle class), all excoriate the Indian middle class for its failings.[81] While Vinod Mehta points to the middle class' hostility to empowering the poor, Mani Shankar Aiyar calls them the 'muddle class' and takes them to task for supporting potentially fascist politics, while Pavan K. Varma reprimands the contemporary middle class for their moral bankruptcy, contrasting their contemporary materialism with the historically progressive role the middle class played earlier in Indian history. While in agreement with elements of the critiques, what is striking about most recent analyses of the Indian middle class is the scant attention paid to the history of the middle class—beyond an idealized view of early nationalists. What historical myopia produces, in turn, is either a superficial, and ultimately grossly ahistorical nostalgia about the 'good old days' of a more noble middle class, or the recourse to easy cliches about the muddleheadedness or hypocrisy of the contemporary middle class. To move beyond such facile analyses, we need to understand the history of this duality.

Essays in this book have highlighted the historical constitution of the middle class in colonial India and the contours of the debates among scholars. While the essays differ in their emphases and their perspectives, the central premise behind their collation is that they illustrate the processes through which this middle class was created. They also reveal the very different ways in which this class has been represented in scholarly writing about modern India. Being middle class in colonial India was a project. Yet, as we see through these essays, it was a project fraught with contradictions and ambivalence. While Dufferin's attempt to paint them as a self-serving elite who only masqueraded as people's representatives evidently reflected the anxieties of colonial rule, we also need to move beyond representations such as the one in *The Bengalee*, which represented the middle class solely as champions of liberalism, social justice and democracy.

As the essay by Kidambi, among others, reveals, the drive toward material success as well as an ethic of public service were constitutive of the making of a middle class in colonial India. That it was a class made aware of its own limitations is quite apparent from Aurobindo's self-critical look at the middle class. The concern with a lack of authenticity that Aurobindo reveals continues to pervade the middle-class imagination. While it sometimes produced a relatively harmless (even admirable) drive to master the domains of the indigenous and the western, in other cases the anxiety about authenticity had more serious consequences for public and private life in colonial and postcolonial India. Ideas about religion, nation, and most significantly, about appropriate gender relations, came to be inflected by this anxiety. Modern nationalism, communalism, as well as many of the more invidious attempts at recasting patriarchy are its products.[82] Equally fraught were the relations between the middle class and the subaltern groups whose interests they claimed to represent, particularly during the nationalist movement. Nehru's essay shows the extent to which the middle class was aware of the social and economic distance between themselves and those on whose behalf they spoke. This distance was negotiated in different ways, depending on time, location and context. There is no doubt that male, upper caste, norms became the foundations of the modern society that the middle class sought to forge in colonial and postcolonial India—as Pandian and Venkatachalapathy show.

Yet, these essays also reveal the extent to which these upper caste norms and practices needed to be justified with a new vocabulary of liberalism, quite different from articulations of a more traditional hierarchical worldview. There are also parallels here with the Bengali bhadralok discussed in the essays by Sarkar and Chakrabarty. It is this vocabulary, this language of (albeit spurious) universalism, that has also allowed for challenges to male, upper caste hegemony. It was not so much the hypocrisy of middle-class individuals, but often the contrary pulls that constituted the middle class that produced the ambivalence of middle-class politics. Understanding this history may well help us better understand the potential as well as limits of middle-class politics in more contemporary times.

NOTES

1. The model for this approach to the study of class formation remains, despite some important critiques, E. P. Thompson's classic, *The Making of the English Working Class* (London: Victor Gollancz, 1964).

2. Pierre Bourdieu, 'What Makes a Social Class? On The Theoretical and Practical Existence of Groups,' *Berkeley Journal of Sociology* (32, 1987).

4. As Veena Naregal argues, the upper caste men managed to secure the public sphere for their own agenda even in colonial western India, where circumstances had allowed for the presence of a strong anti-Brahmanical challenge in the public sphere from people such as Jyotiba Phule. For details, see Veena Naregal, *Language Politics, Elites and the Public Sphere: Western India Under Colonialism,* (New Delhi, Permanent Black, 2001).

5. Raymond Williams, *Keywords: A Vocabulary of Culture and Society* (London: Fontana, 1983), p. 63.

6. See, for instance, Sanjay Joshi, *Fractured Modernity: Making of a Middle Class in Colonial North India* (Delhi: Oxford University Press, 2001), particularly chapter one; Ulrike Stark, *An Empire of Books: The Naval Kishore Press and the Diffusion of the Printed Word in Colonial India, 1858-1895* (New Delhi: Permanent Black, 2007). Christopher Bayly makes a somewhat different argument, later in this volume.

7. Dipesh Chakrabarty, *Provincializing Europe: Postcolonial Thought and Historical Difference* (Princeton: Princeton University Press, 2000), p. 43.

8. Douglas E. Haynes, *Rhetoric and Ritual in Colonial India: The Shaping of a Public Culture in Surat City, 1852-1928* (Berkeley: University of California Press, 1991).

9. Contrast essays by Pernau and Joshi in this volume with Eugene E. Irschick, *Dialogue and History: Constructing South India, 1795-1895* (Berkeley : University of California Press, 1994).

10. For an elaboration of this argument, see Sanjay Joshi, 'The Spectre of Comparisons: Studying the Middle Class of Colonial India' in Amita Baviskar and Raka Ray, eds., *Both Elite and Everyman: The Cultural Politics of the Indian Middle Classes* (Delhi: Routledge, forthcoming 2009).

11. Burton J. Bledstein and Robert D. Johnson ed.s, *The Middling Sorts: Explorations in the History of the American Middle Class* (New York: Routledge, 2001); Stuart M. Blumin, 'The Hypothesis of Middle Class Formation in Nineteenth Century America: A Critique and Some Proposals' *American Historical Review*, 90 (April 1985); Peter N. Stearns, 'The Middle Class: Towards a Precise Definition' *Comparative Studies in Society and History* (21, 1979); Maris A. Vinovskis, 'Stalking the Elusive Middle Class in Nineteenth Century America: A Review Article' *Comparative Studies in Society and History* 33 (July 1991). For an argument contending there was no real bourgeoisie in France, Sarah C. Maza, *The Myth of the French Bourgeoisie : An Essay on the Social Imaginary, 1750-1850* (Cambridge (Mass.): Harvard University Press, 2003).

12. Two of the iconic studies of middle class formation in the western world could be cited in this context, see, Leonore Davidoff and Catherine Hall *Family Fortunes: Men and Women of the English Middle Class, 1780-1850* (Chicago: University of Chicago Press, 1991) and Mary P. Ryan, *Cradle of the Middle Class: The Family in Oneida County, New York, 1790-1865* (Cambridge: Cambridge University Press, 1981).

13. Dror Wahrman, *Imagining the Middle Class: The Political Representation of Class in Britain, c. 1780-1840* (Cambridge: Cambridge University Press, 1995).

14. Wahrman, *Imagining the Middle Class*, p.10.

15. Wahrman, *Imagining the Middle Class*, p.16.

16. Brian P. Owensby, *Intimate Ironies: Modernity and the Making of Middle Class Lives in Brazil* (Stanford: Stanford University Press,1999); Keith David Watenpaugh, *Being Modern in the Middle East: Revolution, Nationalism, Colonialism and the Arab Middle Class* (Princeton: Princeton University Press, 2006).

17. I have made an attempt to be somewhat representative in my selection, taking care to include essays that touch on north, south, east and western regions of India, but I cannot be entirely 'balanced' in the selections. If one task of volumes in this series is to provide readers with a sense of the state of writing on the subject, perhaps this volume may underrepresent Bengal. In the major English language writing on the subject, the history of the Bengali *bhadralok* more or less stands in for the history not just of the middle class in colonial India, but often the history of colonial India itself!

18. For details of Dufferin's relationship with the Indian National Congress, see, Briton Martin Jr., 'Lord Dufferin and the Indian National Congress, 1885-1888.' *The Journal of British Studies*, Vol. 7, No. 1 (Nov., 1967): 68-96.

19. Rudyard Kipling, *Kim* (New York: Viking, 1987); also, 'Head of the District' in *Life's Handicap; Being Stories of Mine Own People* (Garden City: Doubleday, Page and Company, 1899). For other examples of colonial derision of the aspirations of educated Indians, see, Reginald Craddock, *The Dilemma in India* (London: Simpkin, Marshall, & Co, 1867); John Strachey, *India: Its Administration & Progress* (London: Macmillan, 1903); and Valentine Chirol, *Indian Unrest* (London: Macmillan, 1910).

20. See the references under 'Socio-Cultural-Religious Reform and Revival ' in the Annotated Bibliography to this volume.

21. Sudhir Chandra, *The Oppressive Present: Literature and Social Consciousness in Colonial India* (Delhi: Oxford University Press,1992); Sudipta Kaviraj,

The Unhappy Consciousness: Bankimchandra Chattopadhyay and the Formation of Nationalist Discourse in India (Delhi: Oxford University Press,1995); among a host of so many others on Bankim that it led Rukun Advani to pen a satirical piece called 'Bankim's Bunkum' in *Indian History from Above and Below* (Delhi: Don't Press, 1993).

22. Mushirul Hasan, *Wit and Humour in Colonial North India* (Delhi: Niyogi Books, 2007); also, Sanjay Joshi, *Fractured Modernity*.

23. For those who wish to pursue this debate further in primary sources, it may instructive to contrast the view of two doyens of Indian nationalism, Gandhi and Tagore in the 'Nationalism' section of the Annotated Bibliography. Sabyasachi Bhattacharya's compilation of their correspondence also illuminates this issue, *The Mahatma and the Poet: Letters and Debates between Gandhi and Tagore, 1915-1941* (Delhi: National Book Trust, 2001). Also see Wolpert on Tilak and Gokhale in same section of the Bibliography, as well as Tucker on Ranade and Troll on Sir Sayyid in the 'Socio-Cultural-Religious Reform and Revival' section of the Bibliography. All of these explore similar debates between reform, revival, between the proponents of the 'new' light and the 'old.'

24. Though, as Sumit Sarkar points out, newspapers such as *Ananda Bazar Patrika* were using the term '*madhyabitta sreni*' or middle class, as early as 1869. Sumit Sarkar, *Modern India* (Delhi: Macmillan, 1983): 67-68.

25. Jawaharlal Nehru, *The Discovery of India* (Delhi: Oxford University Press, 1982): 312-22. For reasons of space, this is not included in the extract from Nehru's work in the first section of this volume.

26. M. N. Roy, *India in Transition* (Bombay: Nachiketa Publications, 1971 [reprint of 1922 original]), particularly Chapter One;

27. R. C. Dutt, *The Economic History of India* Vol I and II. (Delhi: Publications Division, 1990 [reprint of 1901 and 1903 originals]).

28. Dhurjati Prasad Mukerji *Sociology of Indian Culture* Originally published, 1948. Second edition; reprint. Jaipur: Rawat Publications, 1978.

29. Sumit Sarkar has made this point emphatically in a number of studies in recent years, see for instance, *Writing Social History* (Delhi: Oxford University Press, 1997).

30. See, Dipesh Chakrabarty, *Provincializing Europe*.

31. Chakrabarty, *Provincializing Europe*, and Gyan Prakash, 'Subaltern Studies as Postcolonial Criticism' *American Historical Review* 99, 5 (December 1994).

32. Satish Deshpande, *Contemporary India*: 128.

33. An interesting debate was initiated by Ashok Rudra, a Marxist critic, with, 'Emergence of the Intelligentsia as a Ruling Class in India,' in *The Economic and Political Weekly*, with responses from Andre Betteille, 'Are the Intelligentsia a Ruling Class,' and Pranab Bardhan, 'The Third Dominant Class.' *Economic and Political Weekly of India* (January 21, 1989). Though with potential for an interesting discussion on the definition and role of a middle class, all of the contributors shied away from using that term. It is also telling of the lack of interest in the middle class, that unlike furious and continued debates on modes of production or the composition of the peasantry in *The Economic and Political Weekly*, there was little follow-up to this discussion.

34. And scholars like Bruce McCully before him, see, Bruce T. McCully, *English Education and the Origins of Indian Nationalism* (Gloucester [Mass.]: Peter Smith, 1966).

35. Please look at the section titled 'Nationalism' in the annotated bibliography for detailed citations to these and other important works highlighting the role of the middle class in Indian nationalism.

36. Sumit Sarkar, *Modern India*, is an amazing resource, with original analysis of an incredibly wide body of secondary work that Sarkar manages to synthesize into an engaging larger narrative. I deeply regret that unreasonable demands by the publishers do not allow me to include the section titled, ' "Middle Class" Consciousness and Politics' as part of this volume.

37. See references in the subsection of 'Nationalism' titled 'Cambridge School and their Critics' in the Annotated Bibliography at the end of this volume.

38. Harjot Oberoi, *Construction of Religious Boundaries: Culture, Identity and Diversity in the Sikh Tradition* (Delhi: Oxford University Press, 1994): 260.

39. Joya Chatterjee, *Bengal Divided: Hindu Communalism and Partition, 1932-1947* (Cambridge: Cambridge University Press, 2002): 3-6.

40. Hardiman, 'The Indian "Faction".'

41. See Joshi, *Fractured Modernity*, 24-25 and 32-33.

42. Chatterjee, *Nation and Its Fragments*: 22.

43. See his '"Kaliyuga", "Chakri" and "Bhakti": Ramakrishna and his Times,' for a very different take on Ramakrishna, who also figures prominently in Partha Chatterjee's arguments, also 'Vidyasagar and Brahmanical Society,' both in Sumit Sarkar, *Writing Social History*, pp. 282-357 and 216-281; also 'Identity and Difference: Caste in the Formation of the Ideologies of Nationalism and Hindutva' Ibid.: 358-390. The over-representation of Bengal, although understandable in a collection about the middle class in colonial India, precluded me from including any of these excellent essays in this volume. For another critique of Chatterjee's argument, Tithi Bhattacharya, *The Sentinels of Culture: Class, Education, and the Colonial Intellectual in Bengal* (Delhi: Oxford University Press, 2005).

44. Merchant groups play a central role in Douglas Haynes' analysis of the middle class in colonial Surat, of course, but his is an exceptional study. On the other hand, historical studies of mercantile and entrepreneurial groups make no effort at seeing them as part of the middle class either. See, for instance, David West Rudner, *Caste and Capitalism in Colonial India: The Nattukotai Chettiars* (Berkeley: University of California Press, 1994) and Thomas A. Timberg, *The Marwaris : from Traders to Industrialists* (New Delhi: Vikas Publishing House, 1978). Anne Hardgrove's study might suggest some reasons for this, when she reveals tensions extant between the Bengali *bhadralok* and Marwari communities in Kolkata, see, *Community and Public Culture: The Marwaris in Calcutta, c. 1897–1997* (New York: Columbia University Press, 2004).

45. For just one recent example, see Niall Ferguson, *Empire: The Rise and Fall of the British World Order and the Lessons for Global Power* (New York: Basic Books, 2003); for a more nuanced defense of Orientalist traditions, see John MacKenzie, *Orientalism: History, Theory and the Arts* (Manchester: Manchester University Press, 1995).

46. For a critique of Orientalist traditions, among others, see Carol Breckenridge and Peter van der Veer eds. *Orientalism and the Postcolonial Predicament* (Philadelphia: University of Pennsylvania Press, 1993); Ronald Inden, *Imagining India* (Cambridge, Massachusetts: Basil Blackwell, 1990); Gyanendra Pandey, *The Construction of Communalism in Colonial North India* (Delhi: Oxford University Press, 1990). Also, a special issue of *Journal of Colonialism and Colonial History* 3.1 (Spring 2002) titled, *From Orientalism to Ornamentalism: Empire and Difference in History*, Tony Ballantyne, Guest Editor.

47. Tarabai Shinde's scathing critique of the hypocrisy of middle class male nationalists is well captured in her *Stri-Purush Tulana*. Rosalind O'Hanlon, *A Comparison Between Women and Men : Tarabai Shinde and the Critique of Gender Relations in Colonial India* (Delhi: Oxford University Press, 2000).

48. Reena Handa, *Kamaladevi Chattopadhyaya: A Biography* (Delhi: Oxford University Press, 2002). For Uma Nehru, a surprisingly understudied figure given her family connections and radical feminist politics, see Vir Bharat Talwar, 'Feminist Consciousness in Women's Journals in Hindi: 1910-1920,' in *Recasting Women: Essays in Colonial History*, ed. Kumkum Sangari and Sudesh Vaid (Delhi: Kali for Women, 1989).

49. Perhaps the best known of these remain the essays compiled in Kumkum Sangari and Sudesh Vaid ed.s, *Recasting Women*. Geraldine Forbes' *Women in Modern India* (Cambridge: Cambridge University Press, 1999) contains an excellent bibliographical essay tracking some of the important contributions of feminist historians such as Aparna Basu, Meredith Brothwick, Malavika Karlekar, Gail Minault, Barbara Ramusack, and Bharati Ray to this process.

50. Anshu Malhotra, *Gender, Caste, and Religious Identities: Restructuring Class in Colonial Punjab* (Delhi: Oxford University Press, 2001); Gail Minault, *Secluded Scholars: Women's Education and Muslim Social Reform in Colonial India* (Delhi, Oxford University Press,1998); Judith Walsh, *Domesticity in Colonial India : What Women Learned When Men Gave Them Advice* (Oxford: Rowman & Littlefield Publishers, 2004).

51. Sanjam Ahluwalia, *Reproductive Restraints: Birth Control in India, 1877-1947* (Urbana: University of Illinois Press, 2008); Antoinette Burton, *Burdens of History: British Feminists, Indian Women, and Imperial Culture, 1865-1915* (Chapel Hill: University of North Carolina Press, 1994), also, 'Tongues Untied: Lord Salisbury's 'Black Man' and the Boundaries of Imperial Democracy,' *Comparative Studies in Society and History* 43, 2 (2000), among her other writings; Lata Mani, *Contentious Traditions: The Debate on Sati in Colonial India* (Berkeley: University of California Press, 1998); Mrinalini Sinha, *Specters of Mother India: The Global Restructuring of an Empire* (Durham: Duke University Press, 2006), also her *Colonial Masculinity: The 'Manly Englishman' and the 'Effeminate Bengali' in the Late Nineteenth Century* (Manchester: Manchester University Press, 1995).

52. *Provincializing Europe*, chapter four.

53. See, for instance, G. Arunima, *There Comes Papa: Colonialism and the Transformation of Matriliny in Kerala, Malabar, c. 1850-1940* (Delhi: Orient Longman, 2003); Swapna Banerjee, *Men, Women and Domestics: Articulating Middle Class Identity in Colonial Bengal* (Delhi: Oxford University Press, 2004); some essays in Indrani Chatterjee, ed. *Unfamiliar Relations: Family and History in South Asia* (Delhi: Permanent Black, 2004); Durba Ghosh, *Sex and the Family in*

Colonial India: The Making of Empire (Cambridge: Cambridge University Press, 2006); and Mytheli Sreenivas, *Wives, Widows, Concubines: The Conjugal Family Ideal in Colonial India* (Bloomington: Indiana University Press, 2008).

54. Antoinette Burton has made a forceful case for this in *Dwelling in the Archive: Women Writing, Home, and History in Late Colonial India* (New York: Oxford University Press, 2003). Ironically though, Burton, despite a powerful theoretical argument for use of alternative archives, only uses a limited number of English language texts to make her own case.

55. Chakrabarty, *Provincializing Europe*, 35.

56. For a discussion of some of the problems with bringing the mundanities of middle class family life in colonial India into 'mainstream' historical debates, see Sanjay Joshi, 'Familiarizing History: Writing About the History of the Family in Colonial India.' Unpublished paper presented at the International Association of Historians of Asia meeting, Jawaharlal Nehru University, Nov. 14, 2008.

57. For another perspective, see D.L Sheth 'Secularization of Caste and the Making of a New Middle Class.' *Economic and Political Weekly of India* (August 21-27/August 28-September 3, 1999).

58. Nicholas Dirks, *Castes of Mind: Colonialism and the Making of Modern India* (Princeton: Princeton University Press, 2001).

59. Louis Dumont, *Homo Hierarchicus: An Essay on the Caste System* (Chicago: University of Chicago Press, 1970).

60. To cite just a few examples, J. H. Broomfield, *Elite Conflict in a Plural Society*; Frank Conlon, *Caste in a Changing World: The Chitrapur Saraswat Brahmans, 1700-1935* (Berkeley: University of California Press, 1977); Karen I. Leonard, 'Social History of an Indian Caste: The Kayasthas of Hyderabad.' *Journal of Asian Studies*, 39, 3. (May 1980); Lucy Carroll, 'Colonial Perceptions of Indian Society and the Emergence of Caste(s) Associations.' *Journal of Asian Studies*, Vol. 37, No. 2 (Feb., 1978); Henny Sender, *The Kashmiri Pandits: A Study of Cultural Choice in North India*. Delhi: Oxford University Press, 1988). Studies such as David Rudner's masterly work on the Nattukotai Chettiars that brings together caste, capitalism and community, are rare.

61. On the Namashudras, see Sekhar Bandyopadhyay, *Caste, Protest and Identity in Colonial India: The Namasudras of Bengal, 1872-1947* (London: Curzon Press, 1997). On Phule, among others, Rosalind O'Hanlon, *Caste, Conflict and Ideology: Mahatma Jyotirao Phule and Low Caste Protest in Nineteenth-Century Western India*; Veena Naregal, *Language Politics, Elites and the Public Sphere* explores this specifically in the context of the emergence of a middle class in Western India. For the non-Brahmin movement, see Eugene F. Irschick, *Politics and Social Conflict in South India; the Non-brahman Movement and Tamil Separatism, 1916-1929* (Berkeley: University of California Press, 1969) among much other fine scholarship, especially other works of two of the contributors to this volume, M.S.S. Pandian and A. R. Venkatachalapathy, along with S. Anandhi.

62. Sumit Sarkar has argued this position cogently and forcefully in, 'Intimations of Hindutva: Ideologies, Caste and Class in Post-Swadeshi Bengal' in *Beyond Nationalist Frames: Relocating Postmodernism, Hindutva, History* (Delhi: Permanent Black, 2002).

63. For one discussion of this, see Peter van der Veer, *Religious Nationalism: Hindus and Muslims in India* (Berkeley: University of California Press, 1994).

64. While one continues to see this played out in a variety of contemporary writings, for one example, see the discussion between Paul Brass and Francis Robinson in David Taylor and Malcolm Yapp ed. *Political Identity in South Asia* (London: Curzon Press, 1979).

65. There is a vast body of literature on this subject, for instance, see references to the work of Arjun Appadurai, Ronald Inden, Gregory C. Koslowski, Gyanendra Pandey, Harjot Oberoi, and Peter van der Veer, cited in the 'Socio-Cultural-Religious Reform and Revival' section of the Annotated Bibliography at the end of this volume.

66. Please look at the section titled, 'Socio Religious Reform and Revival' in the Annotated Bibliography of this volume.

67. Tapan Basu, Pradip Datta, Sumit Sarkar, Tanika Sarkar, and Sambudhha Sen, *Khaki Shorts Saffron Flags: A Critique of the Hindu Right* (Delhi: Orient Longman, 1993).

68. Joshi, *Fractured Modernity*, 118-121.

69. In addition to Davidoff and Hall, *Family Fortunes*, see Catherine Hall, *White, Male and Middle Class: Explorations in Feminism and History* (New York: Routledge, 1992).

70. I am particularly disappointed not to have included be able to include the work of scholars as Lakshmi Subramanian or Janaki Bakhle. I would urge readers interested in the subject to see Lakhmi Subramanian, *From the Tanjore Court to the Madras Music Academy: A Social History of Music in South India* (Delhi: Oxford University Press, 2006) and Janaki Bakhle, *Two Men and Music: Nationalism in the Making of an Indian Classical Tradition* (New York: Oxford University Press, 2005).

71. There has been work on the history of food and cuisine of India, of course. Lizzie Collingham, *Curry: A Tale of Cooks and Conquerors* (New York: Oxford University Press, 2007) is an example of recent popular history writing on the subject. K.T. Achaya, *A Historical Dictionary of Indian Food.* (New York: Oxford University Press, 2002) represents another body of work, exceptional in terms of research, though perhaps not as well contextualized as historians might wish. The recent interest in the history of attire, fabrics, and other commodities also indicates growing interest in related areas.

72. The classic work is, C L R James *Beyond a Boundary* (London: Random House, 2005). For a more recent general appraisal, see Richard Cashman, 'Cricket and Colonialism: Colonial Hegemony and Indigenous Subversion?' in J.A.Mangan, ed. *Pleasure, Profit and Proselytism: British Culture and Sport at Home and Abroad 1700-1914* (London: Frank Cass, 1992). Also, Mike Marqusee, *Anyone But England: An Outsider Looks at English Cricket* (London: Aurum Press, 2005).

73. Ramachandra Guha, *Corner Of A Foreign Field: The Indian History Of A British Sport* (London, Pan Macmillan, 2002) Also see, Ashis Nandy, *Tao of Cricket: On Games of Destiny and the Destiny of Games* (Delhi: Oxford University Press, 1989); Arjun Appadurai, 'Playing with Modernity: The Decolonization of Indian Cricket' in Arjun Appadurai ed., *Modernity at Large: Cultural Dimensions of Globalization* (Minneapolis: University of Minnesota Press, 1996).

74. *The Illustrated History of Indian Cricket*, (Delhi: Roli Books, 2006); *Lost Histories of Indian Cricket: Battles of the Pitch* (Routledge, 2005); *Indian Cricket: A Reader* (Delhi: Oxford University Press, 2005); *Twenty-two Yards to Freedom: a Social History of Indian Cricket* (Delhi: Penguin-Viking, 2004); *Once Upon a Furore: Controversies of Indian Cricket* (Delhi: Yoda Press, 2004) in addition to a number of articles on the subject in a variety of scholarly and popular journals.

75. Richard I Cashman, *Patrons, Players, and the Crowd: the Phenomenon of Indian Cricket* (Delhi: Orient Longman, 1980), also Satadru Sen, *Migrant Races: Empire, Identity and K.S. Ranjitsinhji* (Manchester: Manchester University Press, 2005).

76. It is also interesting to note that for once in this volume, the history of Bengal occupies a subaltern position. Just as the Bengal derived paradigm is hegemonic in histories histories of the Indian middle class, in the history of cricket, it is Bombay (now Mumbai) that dominates. Undermining 'Bombay hegemony' is certainly an important part of Majumdar's agenda in this essay.

77. Prem Chowdhry, *Colonial India and the Making of Imperial Cinema: Image, Ideology and Identity* (Manchester: Manchester University Press, 2000).

78. For instance, two of the best recent books about nationalism and Indian cinema, explicitly focus on the post-1947 era. See, Sumita S. Chakravarty, *National Identity in Indian Popular Cinema 1947-1987* (Austin: University of Texas Press, 1993) and Jyotika Virdi, *The Cinematic ImagiNation: Indian Popular Films as Social History* (New Brunswick: Rutgers University Press, 2003). For an important exception, see Priya Jaikumar *Cinema at the End of Empire: A Politics of Transition in Britain and India* (Durham: Duke University Press, 2006).

79. See the discussion of V Shantaram's films in Ashish Rajadhyaksha and Paul Willemen, *Encyclopaedia of Indian Cinema* (London: British Film Institute; Delhi: Oxford University Press, 1994; 2nd ed., OUP, 2001)

80. M. Madhava Prasad, *Ideology of the Hindi Film: A Historical Construction* (Delhi: Oxford University Press, 1998): 162. The quote does not appear in the selection used in this volume.

81. See, Vinod Mehta, 'Eyes, Ears and Minds Closed' *Outlook* (June 5, 2006); Mani Shankar Aiyar, 'A Muddle Class Hero' *India Today* (June 23, 1997), 35; Pavan K. Varma, *The Great Indian Middle Class* (Delhi: Penguin India, 2007).

82. See the essays by Chatterjee, Sarkar, Chakrabarty, and Joshi in this volume.

One
Framing the Middle Class

A Microscopic Minority*

THE MARQUIS OF DUFFERIN AND AVA

[...] Well then, gentlemen, what is India? It is an empire equal in size, if Russia be excluded, to the entire continent of Europe, with a population of 250 million souls. This population is composed of a large number of distinct nationalities, professing various religions, practising diverse rites, speaking different languages—the Census Report says there are 106 different Indian tongues—not dialects, mind you—of which 18 are spoken by more than a million persons—and many of these nationalities are still further separated from each other by discordant prejudices, by conflicting social usages, and even antagonistic material interests. Perhaps the most patent peculiarity of our Indian 'cosmos' is its division into two mighty political communities—the Hindus numbering 190 millions, and the Mahomedans, a nation of 50 millions—whose distinctive characteristics, whether religious, social, or ethnological, it is of course unnecessary for me to refer to before such an audience as the present. But to these two great divisions must be added a host of minor nationalities—though minor is a misleading term, since most of them may be numbered by millions—who, though some are included in the two broader categories I have mentioned, are as completely differentiated from each other as are the Hindus from the Mahomedans. Such are the Sikhs, with their warlike habits and traditions, and their theocratic enthusiasm; the Rohillas, the Pathans, the Assamese, the Biluchees, and the other wild and martial tribes on our frontiers; the hillmen dwelling in the folds of the Himalayas;

---

* Originally published as, 'A Speech at St Andrew's Dinner', 30 November 1888 in Marquis of Dufferin and Ava, *Speeches Delivered in India*:1884-88 (London: John Murray, 1890), pp. 229-48. For the complete text see the original version.

our subjects in Burma, Mongol in race and Buddhist in religion; the Khonds, Mairs, and Bheels, and other non-Aryan peoples in the centre and south of India; and the enterprising Parsees, with their rapidly developing manufactures and commercial interests. Again, amongst these numerous communities may be found at one and the same moment all the various stages of civilization through which mankind has passed from the pre-historic ages to the present day. At one end of the scale we have the naked savage hillman, with his stone weapons, his headhunting, his polyandrous habits, and his childish superstitions; and at the other, the Europeanized native gentleman, with his refinement and polish, his literary culture, his Western philosophy, and his advanced political ideas; while between the two lie, layer upon layer, or in close juxtaposition, wandering communities, with their flocks of goats and moving tents; collections of undisciplined warriors, with their blood feuds, their clan organization and loose tribal government; feudal chiefs and barons, with their picturesque retainers, their seigneuorial jurisdiction, and their mediaeval modes of life; and modernized country gentlemen, and enterprising merchants and manufacturers, with their well-managed estates and prosperous enterprises. Besides all these, who are under our direct administration, the Government of India is required to exercise a certain amount of supervision over the 117 native states, with their princely rulers, their autocratic executives, their independent jurisdictions, and their 50 millions of inhabitants. The mere enumeration of these diversified elements must suggest to the most unimaginative mind a picture of as complicated a social and political organization as ever tasked human ingenuity to govern and administer. (Loud applause.)
[...]
In the earlier stages of England's connection with India, and even after the force of circumstances had transmuted the East India Company of merchants into an Imperial Executive, the ignorance and the disorganization of the peninsula consequent upon the anarchy which followed the collapse of the Mahomedan *régime* necessitated the maintenance of a strong uncompromising despotism, with the view of bringing order out of chaos, and a systematized administration out of the confusion and lawlessness which were then universally prevalent. But such principles of government, however necessary, have never been congenial to the instincts or habits of the English people. (Applause.) As soon as the circumstances of the case permitted, successive statesmen, both at home and in India itself, employed

themselves from time to time in softening the severity of the system under which our dominion was originally established, and strenuous efforts were repeatedly made, not only to extend to Her Majesty's subjects in India the same civil rights and privileges which are enjoyed by Her Majesty's subjects at home, but to admit them, as far as was possible, to a share in the management of their own affairs. (Cheers.) The proof of this is plainly written in our recent history. It is seen in our legal codes, which secure to all Her Majesty's subjects, without distinction of race or creed or class, equality before the law. (Cheers.) It is found in the establishment of local legislative councils a quarter of a century ago, wherein a certain number of leading natives were associated with the Government in enacting measures suitable to local wants. It lies at the basis of the great principle of decentralized finance, which has prepared the way for the establishment of increased local responsibility. It received a most important development in the municipal legislation of Lord Northbrook's administration. It took a still fuller and more perfect expression during the administration of my distinguished predecessor, in the Municipal and Local Boards Acts; and it has acquired a further illustration in the recommendation of the Public Service Commission, recently sent home by the Government of India, in accordance with which more than a hundred offices hitherto reserved to the Covenanted Service would be thrown open to the Provincial Service, and thus placed within the reach of our native fellow subjects in India. (Applause.) And now, gentlemen, some intelligent, loyal, patriotic, and well-meaning men are desirous of taking, I will not say a further step in advance, but a very big jump into the unknown—by the application to India of democratic methods of government, and the adoption of a parliamentary system, which England herself has only reached by slow degrees and through the discipline of many centuries of preparation. (Cheers.) The ideal authoritatively suggested, as I understand, is the creation of a representative body or bodies in which the official element shall be in a minority, who shall have what is called the power of the purse, and who, through this instrumentality, shall be able to bring the British executive into subjection to their will. The organization of battalions of native militia and volunteers for the internal and external defence of the country is the next arrangement suggested, and the first practical result to be obtained would be the reduction of the British army to one half its present numbers. Well, gentlemen, I am afraid that the people of England will not readily be brought to the acceptance of this programme, or to allow such an assembly, or a number of such assemblies, either to interfere with its armies, or to fetter and circumscribe the liberty of action either of the provincial governments or of the Supreme Executive. (Applause.) In the first place, the scheme is eminently unconstitutional; for the essence of constitutional government is that responsibility and power should be committed to the same hands. The idea of irresponsible councils, whose members could arrest the march of Indian legislation, or nullify the policy of the British executive in India, without being liable to be called to account for their acts in a way in which an opposition can be called to account in a constitutional country, must be regarded as an impracticable anomaly. (Applause.) Indeed, so obviously impossible would be the application of any such system in the circumstances of the case, that I do not believe it has been seriously advocated by any native statesman of the slightest weight or importance. I have come into contact, during the last four years with, I imagine, almost all the most distinguished persons in India. I have talked with most of them upon these matters, and I have never heard a suggestion from one of them in the sense I have mentioned. (Cheers.) But if no native statesman of weight or importance, capable of appreciating the true interests of England and of India, is found to defend this programme, who are those who do? Who and what are the persons who seek to assume such great powers—to tempt the fate of Phaeton, and to sit in the chariot of the Sun? (Applause.) Well, they are gentlemen of whom I desire to speak with the greatest courtesy and kindness, for they are, most of them, the product of the system of education which we ourselves have carried on during the last thirty years. But thirty years is a very short time in which to educe a self-governing nation from its primordial elements. At all events, let us measure the extent of educated assistance upon which we could ball at this moment; let us examine the degree of proficiency which the educated classes of India have attained and the relation of their numbers to the rest of the population. Out of the whole population of British India, which may be put at 200 millions in round numbers, not more than five or six per cent can read and write, while less than one per cent have any knowledge of English. Thus, the overwhelming mass of the people, perhaps 190 out of the 200 millions, are still steeped in ignorance, and of the 10 or 12 millions who have acquired education, three-fourths have attained merely the most elementary knowledge. In our recent review of the progress of education, it was pointed out that ninety-four and a half per cent of those attending our schools and colleges were in the primary stage, while the progress made in English education can be measured by the fact that the number of students who have graduated at the universities since their establishment in 1857—that is, during the course of the last thirty-one years—is under eight thousand. During the last twenty-five years probably not more than half a million students have passed out of our schools with a good knowledge of English, and perhaps a million more with a smattering of it. Consequently, it may be said that, out of a population of 200 millions, there are only a very few thousands who may be considered to possess adequate qualifications, so far as education and an acquaintance with Western ideas or even Eastern learning are concerned, for taking an intelligent view of those intricate and complicated economic and political questions affecting the destinies of so many millions of men which are almost daily being presented for the consideration of the Government of India. (Applause.) I would ask, then, how any reasonable man could imagine that the British Government would be content to allow this microscopic minority to control their administration of that majestic and multiform empire for whose safety and welfare they are responsible in the eyes of God and before the face of civilization ? (Cheers.) It has been stated that this minority represents a large and growing class. I am glad to think that it represents a growing class, and I feel very sure that, as time goes on, it is not only the class that will grow, but also the information and experience of its members. At present, however, it appears to me a groundless contention that it represents the people of India. If they had been really representatives of the people of India—that is to say, of the voiceless millions—instead of seeking to circumscribe the incidence of the income tax, as they desired to do, they would probably have received a mandate to decuple it. (Laughter.) Indeed, is it not evident that large sections of the community are already becoming alarmed at the thought of such self-constituted bodies interposing between themselves and the august impartiality of English? These persons ought to know that in the present condition of India there can be no real or effective representation of the people, with their enormous numbers, their multifarious interests, and their tesselated nationalities. They ought to see that all the strength, power, and intelligence of the British Government are applied to the prevention of one race, of one interest, of one class, of one religion, dominating another; and they ought to feel that in their peculiar position there can be no greater blessing to the country than the existence of an external, dispassionate, and immutable authority, whose watchword is Justice, and who alone possesses both the power and the will to weld the rights and status of each separate element of the empire into a peaceful, co-ordinated, and harmonious unity. (Loud cheers.)

[...]

In the speech which I delivered at Calcutta on the occasion of Her Majesty's jubilee, I used the following expression:

Wide and broad, indeed, are the new fields in which the Government of India is called upon to labour, but no longer, as of aforetime, need it labour alone. Within the period we are reviewing, education has done its work, and we are surrounded on all sides by native gentlemen of great attainments and intelligence, from whose hearty, loyal, and honest co-operation we may hope to derive the greatest benefit. In fact, to an administration so peculiarly situated as ours, their advice, assistance, and solidarity are essential to the successful exercise of its functions. Nor do I regard with any other feelings than those of approval and good-will their natural ambition to be more extensively associated with their English rulers in the administration of their own domestic affairs; and glad and happy should I be if, during my sojourn amongst them, circumstances permitted me to extend and to place upon a wider and more logical footing the political status which was so wisely given a generation ago by that great statesman, Lord Halifax, to such Indian gentlemen as by their influence, their acquirements, and the confidence they inspired in their fellow-countrymen, were marked out as useful adjuncts to our Legislative Councils.

To every word which I then spoke I continue to adhere (Cheers); but surely the sensible men of the country cannot imagine that even the most moderate constitutional changes can be effected in such a system as ours by a stroke of the pen, or without the most anxious deliberations, as well as careful discussions in Parliament. (Applause.) If ever a political organization has existed where caution is necessary in dealing with those problems which affect the adjustment of the administrative machine, and where haste and precipitancy are liable to produce deplorable results, it is that which holds together our complex Indian Empire; and the man who stretches forth his hand towards the ark, even with the best intentions, may well dread lest his arm should shrivel up to the shoulder. But growth and development are the rule of the world's history, and from the proofs I have already given of the way in which English statesmanship has perpetually striven gradually to adapt our methods of government in India to the expanding intelligence and capacities of the educated classes amongst our Indian subjects, it may be confidently expected that the legitimate and reasonable aspirations of the responsible heads of native society, whether Hindu or Mahomedan, will in due time receive legitimate satisfaction. (Cheers.) The more we enlarge the surface of our contact with the educated and intelligent public opinion of India, the better; and although I hold it absolutely necessary, not merely for the maintenance of our own power, but for the good government of the country, and for the general content of all classes, and especially of the people at large, that England should never abdicate her supreme control of public affairs, or delegate to a minority or to a class the duty of providing for the welfare of the diversified communities over which she rules, I am not the less convinced that we could, with advantage, draw more largely than we have hitherto done on native intelligence and native assistance in the discharge of our duties. (Loud applause.) I have had ample opportunities of gauging and appreciating to its full extent the measure of good sense, of practical wisdom, and of experience which is possessed by the leading men of India, both among the great nobles on the one hand, and amongst the leisured and professional classes on the other, and I have not submitted officially to the home authorities some personal suggestions in harmony with the foregoing views. (Cheers.)

A Cheap Shoddy Import*

AUROBINDO GHOSH

[...] To begin with, I should a little while ago have had no hesitation in saying that the National Congress was not really national and had not in any way attempted to become *national*. But [...] to deal with this vexed subject, one must tread on very burning ground, and I shall make no apology for treading with great care and circumspection[...] It is therefore incumbent on me to explain what I wish to imply, when I say that the Congress is not really national. Now I do not at all mean to re-echo the Anglo-Indian catchword about the Hindus and Mahomedans. Like most catchwords it is without much force, and has been still further stripped of meaning by the policy of the Congress. The Mahomedans have been as largely represented on that body as any reasonable community could desire, and their susceptibilities, far from being denied respect, have always been most assiduously soothed and flattered. It is entirely futile then to take up the Anglo-Indian refrain; but this at least I should have imagined, that in an era when democracy and similar big words slide so glibly from our tongues, a body like the Congress, which represents not the mass of the population, but a single and very limited class, could not honestly be called national. It is perfectly true that the House of Commons represents not the English nation, but simply the English aristocracy and middle class and yet is none the less national. But the House of Commons is a body legally constituted and empowered to speak and act for the nation, while the Congress is self-created: and it is not justifiable for a self-created body representing only a single and limited class to call itself national. It

---

* Originally published as Aurobindo Ghosh, 'New Lamps for Old—3', *Indu Prakash*, 28 August 1893. For the complete text see the original version.

would be just as absurd if the Liberal Party, because it allows within its limits all sorts and conditions of men, were to hold annual meetings and call itself the English National Congress. When therefore I said that the Congress was not really national, I simply meant that it did not represent the mass of the population.

But Mr Pherozshah Mehta will have nothing to do with this sense of the word. In his very remarkable and instructive Presidential address at Calcutta, he argued that the Congress could justly arrogate this epithet without having any direct support from the proletariate; and he went on to explain his argument with the profound subtlety expected from an experienced advocate. 'It is because the masses are still unable to articulate definite political demands that the functions and duty devolve upon their educated and enlightened compatriots to feel, to understand and to interpret their grievances and requirements, and to suggest and indicate how these can best be redressed and met.'

This formidable sentence is, by the way, typical of Mr Mehta's style and reveals the secret of his oratory, which like all great inventions is exceedingly simple: it is merely to say the same thing twice over in different words. But its more noteworthy feature is the idea implied that because the Congress professes to discharge this duty, it may justly call itself national. Nor is this all; Calcutta comes to the help of Bombay in the person of Mr Manmohan Ghose, who repeats and elucidates Mr Mehta's idea. The Congress, he says, asserting the rights of that body to speak for the masses, represents the thinking portion of the Indian people, whose duty it is to guide the ignorant, and this in his opinion sufficiently justifies the Congress in calling itself national. To differ from a successful barrister and citizen, a man held in high honour by every graduate in India, and above all a future member of the Viceroy's Council, would never have been a very easy task for a timid man like myself. But when he is reinforced by so respectable and weighty a citizen as Mr Manmohan Ghose, I really cannot find the courage to persevere. I shall therefore amend the obnoxious phrase and declare that the National Congress may be as national as you please, but it is not a popular body and has not in any way attempted to become a popular body.

But at this point some one a little less learned than Mr Pherozshah Mehta may interfere and ask how it can be true that the Congress is not a popular body. I can only point his attention to a previous statement of mine that the Congress represents not the mass of the population, but a single and limited class. No doubt the Congress tried very hard in the beginning to believe that it really represented the mass of the population, but if it has not already abandoned, it ought now at least to abandon the pretension as quite untenable. And indeed when Mr Pherozshah Mehta and Mr Manmohan Ghose have admitted this patent fact—not as delegates only, but as officials of the Congress—and have even gone so far as to explain the fact away, it is hardly requisite for me to combat the fallacy. But perhaps the enquirer, not yet satisfied, may go on to ask: what is that single and limited class which I imagine the Congress to represent? Here it may be of help to us to refer again to the speeches of the Congress leaders and more especially to the talented men from whom I have already quoted. In his able official address, Mr Manmohan Ghose asks himself this very question and answers that the Congress represents the thinking portion of the Indian people. 'The delegates present here today,' he goes on, 'are the chosen representatives of that section of the Indian people who have learnt to think, and whose number is daily increasing with marvellous rapidity'. Perhaps Mr Ghose is a little too facile in his use of the word thinking. So much at the mercy of their instincts and prejudices are the generality of mankind, that we hazard a very high estimate when we call even one man out of ten thousand a thinking man. But evidently by the thinking portion Mr Ghose would like to indicate the class to which he himself belongs; I mean those of us who have got some little idea of the machinery of English politics and are eager to import it into India along with cheap Liverpool cloths, shoddy Brummagem wares, and other useful and necessary things which have killed the fine and genuine textures. If this is a true interpretation he is perfectly correct in what he says. For it is really from this class that the Congress movement draws its origin, its support and its most enthusiastic votaries. And if I were asked to describe their class by a single name, I should not hesitate to call it our new middle class. For here too English goods have driven out native goods: our society has lost its old landmarks and is being demarcated on the English model. But of all the brand new articles we have imported, inconceivably the most important is that large class of people—journalists, barristers, doctors, officials, graduates, and traders—who have grown up and are increasing with prurient rapidity under the aegis of the British rule: and this class I call the middle class: for, when we are so proud of our imported English goods, it would be absurd, when we want labels for them, not to import their English names as well. Besides this name which I have chosen is really a more accurate description than phrases like 'thinking men' or 'the educated class' which are merely expressions of our own boundless vanity and self-conceit. However largely we may choose to indulge in vague rhetoric about the all-pervading influence of the Congress, no one can honestly doubt that here is the constituency from which it is really empowered. There is indeed a small contingent of aristocrats and a smaller contingent of the more well-to-do ryots: but these are only two flying-wheels in the great middle-class machine. The fetish-worshipper may declare as loudly as he pleases that it represents all sorts and conditions of people, just as the Anglo-Indians used to insist that it represented no one but the Bengali Babu. Facts have been too strong for the Anglo-Indian and they will be too strong in the end for the fetish-worshipper.

The Carriers of Enlightenment, Freedom, Progress, and Prosperity*

THE BENGALEE

Yesterday we commented upon the official *communique* of the Bengal Government, announcing that among the points referred to the committee appointed in connection with the council regulations is the question of the degree of representation of the educated middle class. We congratulated the government upon this point of reference, for it is a recognition of the fact which has been the subject of persistent complaint that the middle class are not adequately represented on the local council, or that, at any rate, the question of their representation needs reconsideration and revision. We could only wish that when a matter of this kind was to be considered there were more representatives of the middle-class community, though we are bound to admit, in justice to the government, that some of their best representatives have been nominated to the committee. And after all the committee is an advisory board, and the government is not precluded from adopting the recommendations even *of* a minority. We await with some measure of confidence the recommendations of the committee and the decision of the government thereon. In the meantime the official communique has afforded an opportunity to our evening contemporary of the 'Empire' to write one of those luminous articles which from time to time find a place in the columns of that journal. The article deals with the growing importance of the middle class in Bengal and the far-reaching economic and political effects that must follow in the train of this evolution. We reproduce it here so as to give it the prominence which it deserves:

---

* Originally published as 'The Middle Class', *The Bengalee* (Calcutta, 17 February 1911).

The Carriers of Enlightenment, Freedom, Progress, and Prosperity 15

The Bengal Government has just put forth a very interesting communique announcing the appointment of a committee to consider the question of how the middle class in Bengal can best be represented on the Legislative Council. This communique may prove to be an epoch-making document, as it is the first official act of recognition that there is such a thing as a middle class in Bengal. No one who has the least acquaintance with actual conditions will dare to deny that there is such a class, and that its numbers and influence are increasing daily—evidence incidentally of the levelling tendencies of western culture and the solvent process which is attacking India's social institutions right and left. But the phenomenon is something more far-reaching than social change. It promotes economic and political change of infinitely greater import. The rise of a middle class is the indispensable condition of economic and political progress. To what is the prosperity of England due for the last two centuries? To the existence of the middle class. When did France begin to forge ahead economically and industrially? When a middle class came into existence as the result of the revolution. Turning to Germany and Russia we find in the case of the former that the rise of a middle class has been accompanied by the most tremendous advance in industrial productiveness and economic efficiency that Europe has yet seen; in the case of the latter that no middle class has yet emerged, with the result that Russia still lags behind the rest of Europe and is poor, oppressed, and backward. The history of the United States of America compared with the history of Spain points to the same moral. Wherever you have a middle class, you have enlightenment, freedom, progress, and prosperity. Wherever society is sharply divided into upper and lower strata 'et praeterea nihi' you have superstition, reaction, poverty, and decay. The rise of the middle class in Bengal is therefore the most remarkable and the most reassuring of the signs of the times. It is a certain indication that in this part of India our faces are set in the right direction, that progress and not retrogression is the order of the day, and that the whole tendency of present conditions make for an increasing measure of general prosperity.

And this is the class from which come the teachers of our youth, leaders of public opinion, the pioneers of all public movements—social, religious, political, and industrial. This is the class whom the Home Member affected not to know, and to whom a back seat has been assigned on the reformed councils. We trust that so far as Bengal is concerned, Sir Edward Baker, who is in close personal touch with the middle class and their representatives, will remove this anomaly and this injustice. 'Have them on the side of the Government,' said Sir Henry Harrison in an article that he wrote in the *Asiatic Quarterly Review* in 1885, 'and you will have them as useful allies and active cooperators with the Government. If you mistrust them, they will be driven into the opposition and become the severest critics of the Government.' Never was a greater truth uttered, and by one who himself was a prominent member of the bureaucracy, but who at the same time, had the unique advantage of knowing the people well. In Bengal, as in other countries, great representatives of the middle class have been the formers of national ideals, and the guides and leaders of the people. What were Ram Mohun Ray, Keshab Chander Sen, Iswar Chunder Vidyasagar, Ramgopal Ghose, Hurrish Chunder Mookerjee, Kristo Das Pal, Annada Mohan Bose, W.C. Bonnerjea and others? They were all of the middle class; and now that they are dead and gone, their memories are adored by high and low, rich and poor, by the master of broad acres and by the humble peasant who from morning till eve toils for his daily bread. They were the leaders of the great moments which have made India what it is today. The class to which they belonged cannot be ignored. It is growing daily in influence and power, and is making itself felt in every department of national thought and activity. What is this moment for the uplifting of the depressed classes but a movement for self-respect which, emanating from the middle classes, has infected the life of the Hindu community and has penetrated every nook and cranny of the social system? We rejoice to find that an Anglo-Indian contemporary has so frankly recognized the growing importance of the middle class. We trust the Government will take note of it.

A Class in Need of Help*

JAWAHARLAL NEHRU

World War I came. Politics were at low ebb, chiefly because of the split in the Congress between the two sections, the so-called extremists and the moderates, and because of war-time restrictions and regulations. Yet one tendency was marked: the rising middle class among the Moslems was growing more nationally minded and was pushing the Moslem League towards the Congress. They even joined hands.

Industry developed during the war and produced enormous dividends—100 to 200 per cent—from the jute mills of Bengal and the cotton mills of Bombay, Ahmedabad, and elsewhere. Some of these dividends flowed to the owners of foreign capital in Dundee and London, some went to swell the riches of Indian millionaires; and yet the workers who had created these dividends lived at an incredibly low level of existence-in 'filthy, disease-ridden hovels', with no window or chimney, no light, or water supply, no sanitary arrangements. This near the so-called city of palaces, Calcutta, dominated by British capital! In Bombay, where Indian capital was more in evidence, an inquiry commission found in one room, 15 feet by 12, six families, in all, 30 adults and children, living together. Three of these women were expecting a confinement soon, and each family had a separate oven in that one room. These are special cases, but they are not very exceptional. They describe conditions in the 'twenties and thirties of this century when some improvements had already been made. What

---

* Originally published as 'The Last Phase (2) Nationalism Versus Imperialism: Helplessness of the Middle Classes Gandhi Comes', in Jawaharlal Nehru, *Discovery of India* (New Delhi: Oxford University Press, 1981), pp. 356-60. For the complete text see the original version.

these conditions were like previous to these improvements staggers the imagination.[1]

I remember visiting some of these slums and hovels of industrial workers, gasping for breath there, and coming out dazed and full of horror and anger. I remember also going down a coal mine in Jharia and seeing the conditions in which our womenfolk worked there. I can never forget that picture or the shock that came to me that human beings should labour thus. Women were subsequently prohibited from working underground, but now they have been sent back there because, we are told, war needs require additional labour; and yet millions of men are starving and unemployed. There is no lack of men, but the wages are so low and the conditions of work so bad that they do not attract.

A delegation sent by the British Trade Union Congress visited India in 1928. In their report they said that: 'In Assam tea the sweat, hunger, and despair of a million Indians enter year by year.' The Director of Public Health in Bengal, in his report for 1927-8, said that the peasantry of that province were 'taking to a dietary on which even rats could not live for more than five weeks'.

World War I ended at last, and the peace, instead of bringing us relief and progress, brought us repressive legislation and martial law in the Punjab. A bitter sense of humiliation and a passionate anger filled our people. All the unending talk of constitutional reform and Indianization of the services were a mockery and an insult when the manhood of our country was being crushed and the inexorable and continuous process of exploitation was deepening our poverty and sapping our vitality. We had become a derelict nation.

Yet what could we do, how could we change this vicious process? We seemed to be helpless in the grip of some all-powerful monster; our limbs were paralysed, our minds deadened. The peasantry was servile and fear-ridden; the industrial workers were no better. The middle classes, the intelligentsia, who might have been beacon lights in the enveloping darkness, were themselves submerged in this all-pervading gloom. In some ways their condition was even more pitiful than that of the peasantry. Large numbers of them, déclassé intellectuals, cut off from the land and incapable of any kind of manual or technical work, joined the swelling army of the unemployed, and helpless, hopeless, sank ever deeper into the morass. A few successful lawyers or doctors or engineers or clerks made little difference to the mass. The peasant starved, yet centuries of an unequal struggle against his environment had taught him to endure, and even in poverty and starvation he had a certain calm dignity, a feeling of submission to an all-powerful fate. Not so the middle classes, more especially the new petty bourgeoisie, who had no such background. Incompletely developed and frustrated, they did not know where to look, for neither the old nor the new offered them any hope. There was no adjustment to social purpose, no satisfaction of doing something worthwhile, even though suffering came in its train. Custom-ridden, they were born old, yet they were without the old culture. Modern thought attracted then but they lacked its inner content, the modern social and scientific consciousness. Some tried to cling tenaciously to the dead forms of the past, seeking relief from present misery in them. But there could be no relief there, for, as Tagore has said, we must not nourish in our being what is dead, for the dead is death-dealing. Others made themselves pale and ineffectual copies of the west. So, like derelicts, frantically seeking some foothold of security for body and mind and finding none, they floated aimlessly in the murky waters of Indian life.

What could we do? How could we pull India out of this quagmire of poverty and defeatism which sucked her in? Not for a few years of excitement and agony and suspense, but for long generations our people had offered their 'blood and toil, tears and sweat'. And this process had eaten its way deep into the body and soul of India, poisoning every aspect of our corporate life, like that fell disease which consumes the tissues of the lungs and kill slowly but inevitably. Sometimes we thought that some swifter and more obvious process, resembling cholera or the bubonic plague, would have been better; but that was a passing thought, for adventurism leads nowhere, and the quack treatment of deep-seated diseases does not yield results.

And then Gandhi came. He was like a powerful current of fresh air that made us stretch ourselves and take deep breaths; like a beam of light that pierced the darkness and removed the scales from our eyes; like a whirlwind that upset many things, but most of all the working of people's minds. He did not descend from the top; he seemed to emerge from the millions of India, speaking their language and incessantly drawing attention to them and their appalling condition. Get off the backs of these peasants and workers, he told us, all you who live by their exploitation; get rid of the system that produces this poverty and misery. Political freedom took new shape then and acquired a new content. Much that he said we only partially accepted or sometimes did not accept at all. But all this was secondary. The essence of his teaching was fearlessness and truth, and action allied to these, always keeping the welfare of the masses in view. The greatest gift for an individual or a nation, so we had been told in our ancient books, was *abhaya* (fearlessness), not merely bodily courage but the absence of fear from the mind. Janaka and Yajnavalka had said, at the dawn of our history, that it was the function of the leaders of a people to make them fearless. But the dominant impulse in India under British rule was that of fear—pervasive, oppressing, strangling fear; fear of the army, the police, the widespread secret service; fear of the official class; fear of laws meant to suppress and of prison; fear of the landlord's agent; fear of the moneylender; fear of unemployment and starvation, which were always on the threshold. It was against this all-pervading fear that Gandhi's quiet and determined voice was raised: Be not afraid. Was it so simple as all that? Not quite. And yet fear builds its phantoms which are more fearsome than reality itself, and reality, when calmly analysed and its consequences willingly accepted, loses much of its terror.

So, suddenly, as it were, that black pall of fear was lifted from the people's shoulders, not wholly of course, but to an amazing degree. As fear is close companion to falsehood, so truth follows fearlessness. The Indian people did not become much more truthful than they were, nor did they change their essential nature overnight; nevertheless a sea-change was visible as the need for falsehood and furtive behaviour lessened. It was a psychological change, almost as if some expert in psycho-analytical methods had probed deep into the patient's past, found out the origins of his complexes, exposed them to his view, and thus rid him of that burden.

There was that psychological reaction also, a feeling of shame at our long submission to an alien rule that had degraded and humiliated us, and a desire to submit no longer, whatever the consequences might be.

We did not grow much more truthful perhaps than we had been previously, but Gandhi was always there as a symbol of uncompromising truth to pull us up and shame us into truth. What is truth? I do not know for certain, and perhaps our truths are relative and absolute truth is beyond us. Different persons may and do take different views of truth, and each individual is powerfully influenced by his own background, training, and impulses. So also, Gandhi. But truth is at least for an individual what he himself feels and knows to be true. According to this definition I do not know of any person who holds to the truth as Gandhi does. That is a dangerous quality in a politician, for he speaks out his mind and even lets the public see its changing phases.

Gandhi influenced millions of people in India in varying degrees. Some changed the whole texture of their lives, others were only partly affected, or the effect wore off; and yet not quite, for some part of it could not be wholly shaken off. Different people reacted differently and each will give his own answer to this question. Some might well say, almost in the words of Alcibiades:

Besides, when we listen to anyone else talking, however eloquent he is, we don't really care a damn what he says; but when we listen to you, or to someone else repeating what you've said, even if he puts it ever so badly, and never mind whether the person who is listening is man, woman, or child, we're absolutely staggered and bewitched. And speaking for myself, gentlemen, if I wasn't afraid you'd tell me I was completely bottled, I'd swear on oath what an extraordinary effect his words have had on me-and still do, if it comes to that. For the moment I hear him speak I am smitten by a kind of sacred rage, worse than any Corybant, and my heart jumps into my mouth and the tears start into my eyes—Oh, and not only me, but lots of other men.

And there is one thing I've never felt with anybody else—not the kind of thing you would expect to find in me, either—and that is a sense of shame. Socrates is the only man in the world that can make me feel ashamed. Because there's no getting away from it, I know I ought to do the things he tells me to; and yet the moment I'm out of his sight I don't care what I do to keep in with the mob. So I dash off like a runaway slave, and keep out of his way as long as I can: and the next time I meet him I remember all that I had to admit the time before, and naturally I feel ashamed [...].

Yes, I have heard Pericles and all the other great orators, and very eloquent I thought they were; but they never affected me like that; they never turned my whole soul upside down and left me feeling as if I were the lowest of the low; but this latter day Maryas, here, has often left me in such a state of mind that I've fell I simply couldn't go on living the way I did...

Only I've been bitten by something much more poisonous than a snake; in fact, mine is the most painful kind of bite there is. I've been bitten in the heart, or the mind or whatever you like to call it [...].[2]

NOTES

1. Nehru footnotes this as 'These quotations and facts are taken from B. Shiva Rao's *The Industrial Worker in India* (London, 1939) which deals with labour problems and workers' conditions in India.'

2. Nehru footnotes this as, 'From 'The Five Dialogues of Plato', *Everyman's Library.*' [Ed: This is all the information Nehru provides. In all probability, he refers to: Plato. Sydenham, Floyer. *Five Dialogues of Plato Bearing on Poetic Inspiration.* Shelley, Percy Bysshe, 1792–1822, ; Tr. Everyman's library, ed. by Ernest Rhys. London, New York, 1910.]

Two

Debating the Middle Class

The Bourgeoisie Comes of Age*

D.D. KOSAMBI

The long-awaited publication of Jawaharlal Nehru's tremendous book[1] on India, past and present, has in many ways justified the great hopes raised by the author's distinguished record in the struggle for India's freedom, and by his active share in the struggle against war. His career is too well known for further comment here; those who do not know it would be well advised to read his *Autobiography* as well as this book. No person knows India better than Pandit Jawaharlal. He is able to express himself brilliantly both in Hindi and Urdu, as friends and admirers among Hindus as well as Muslims will admit. Most important of all, he has an intimate acquaintance with the British ruling class because of his education in England. The book in question is, therefore, a damning indictment of British rule in India; but more than that, its ambitious scope includes the history of India, culturally as well as politically, in a single perspective. The performance is all the more remarkable when it is considered that the work was essentially completed in jail under the most distressing circumstances with full consciousness on the part of the author that a struggle against Hitlerism was being waged without his help, though he himself had always been an unswerving opponent of fascism and all that fascism represents. The very fact that so able a personality should be jailed without trial while a considerable number of British agents were foisted upon India to fight the war from the safety of office chairs had an unfortunate result for the Indian population; for while the British officials and a considerable number of Indian businessmen filled their

---

* Originally published as 'The Bourgeoisie Comes of Age in India', *Science and Society*, vol. X (New York, 1946), pp. 392-8. For the complete text see the original version.

pockets with vast quantities of paper currency, the people at large had the benefit of inflation, famine, epidemics, and shortages [...].

The book cannot be too strongly recommended to the general reader. The present writer wishes to make it clear that he himself is a humble admirer of the author. This is to prevent misunderstanding, for the bulk of this communication is necessarily devoted to pointing out a certain number of flaws. For the ancient history of India little need be said because such sources as we possess are extremely meagre and their interpretation puzzles even those who have devoted a lifetime to their study; on this score we need not hold the author responsible. In some ways it is unfortunate that he has not had the leisure to study Indian sources more critically and that he has relied so heavily upon comparatively popular accounts by British authors. This, however, may be condoned on the ground that Indian political prisoners hardly have reference libraries at their disposal.

One feature that may strike the reader as rather surprising is a curious attitude towards the much abused term 'race'; denunciation of racialism and of imperialism occurs on p. 386f. [all the page numbers cited here are from the *Discovery of India* (for details see endnote 1 in this chapter)], but on p. 387 we read: 'psychology counts and racial memories are long.' Just what racial memory means is not clear, particularly in the case of a country that has forgotten the splendid Mauryan and Gupta periods, including the very script of those times; that ascribes almost every cave of any date to the mythical Pandavas; and is capable of pointing out as prince Pratap Sinha, the statue of Outram (a butcher of the 1857 revolt) on the Esplanade at Calcutta. It was noticeable, on the contrary, that class memories are extremely short or at any rate strikingly different from what Nehru imagines to be race memories. For example, the British Commissioner of Police in Bombay whose name was execrated for his incompetent or deliberately provocative handling of popular discontent at the end of January and February, 1946 (ending in a real bloodbath in the working-class areas of Bombay) was nevertheless a guest of honour in May, along with the Congress ministers, at the richest Indian weddings of the year in Bombay. On p. 431 we read: 'old races develop that attitude [of quietism] to life.' Just what this means is also not clear, for ethnologically there is no evidence that any race is older than any other. In fact if the sentence can be taken as applying to the Indian races, it is quite impossible to explain why quietism has been on the wane since 1940 at least, and has given place to the constant ferment of political activity in this country.

Far more serious to the present reviewer is the absence of the question 'why'. No attempt at history can be regarded as mature which does not, within the framework, of the author's ideology, make some attempt at analysis. For the ancient period we find considerable difficulty in explaining certain facts for the simple reason that the facts themselves are not always clear; but for the modern period it seems to me that the author's present approach cannot stand unchallenged. I may go further and venture the statement that this vague use of the term 'race', the absence of the question as to why certain changes take place at certain times, are intimately bound up with another striking feature of the book, the absence of a class analysis. The author could have asked himself one question with the greatest of advantage, namely, *cui bono*; what is the *class* that called for or benefited by a certain change at a certain period of history? This might have clarified one issue noted by the author, that the British have fought desperately and till now effectively against granting India the same kind of social and political rights of which the English themselves are so proud in England. It is quite obvious that the class of Englishmen who fought for the suppression of local governments and civil liberties in India have also fought desperately against the lower classes in England; but when the pressure of the working class in India became too great, the bourgeois front was breached in some one place and a local amelioration won; the losing section of the bourgeoisie necessarily fought for the imposition of the same restriction against all other owners of means of production and ultimately put a good face on the whole matter, proclaiming that they, the rulers, had granted certain reforms of their own sweet free will. There was little class opposition from India as the British had taken every care to preserve as much feudal and religious prerogative as possible.

It may be further suggested that the absence of developed modern capital in the Muslim community as well as the great relative poverty of the Muslims in India might explain both the case against the Muslim League (p. 466) and Muslim backwardness (p. 468) as well as the reactionary attitude of the Muslim upper classes in India. Nehru has himself pointed out (p. 437) that Indian businessmen demand exactly the same kind of protection in Ceylon which they rightly resent having given to British business interests in India. He is undoubtedly aware of the fact that Indians in South Africa, backed wholeheartedly by the Indian trading community there, are fighting hard for equality; but for equality with the whites and not equality with the Negroes also. The absence of class analysis vitiates the peculiar presentation of provincial differences and growth of industry (pp. 392-8). We read that the people of Gujarat, Kathiawar, and Kutch were traders, manufacturers, merchants, and seafarers from ancient times. Now it is undeniable that the great majority of people in just those districts are definitely not traders, although people from the localities mentioned occupy so prominent a place in the capitalistic section of India today. The reason is that early contact with Mahometan traders enabled this small fraction to develop early contact with the British and thereby introduced them to a new system of production: that is, production based on machinery and modern capital. The best example of this perhaps is the Parsi community which, in its original situation in Gujarat, was one the most oppressed of refugee minorities and is today one of the most advanced and powerful of communities in India because of their adoption of modern industrial and finance capitalism. On the other hand, the case is totally different with the Marwaris of Rajputana (pp. 394-6) who did control finance and moneylending in the old days but had no political rights whatsoever. If Nehru will take the trouble to look up the records he will see how often such moneylenders backed the British in the days of British expansion in India. Of course that may not lead him to realize a basic contemporary phenomenon: the change of pseudo-capital thus accumulated to modern productive money. The change-over is now actually so rapid that even the most backward and degenerate of Indians, the feudal princelings, are now becoming shareholders on a large scale. The days are gone when shares were issued at a face value of Rs 30 to be quoted today at well over Rs 3,000 or when a stock was issued at Rs 100, of which Rs 99 was given back as a capital repayment, to give a dividend of over Rs 150 today, being quoted at Rs 2,300. Those stocks had a much longer start in the race for modernization of industry, but the total volume of such capital was negligible and has now been enormously increased by the conversion of primitive accumulation as well as by the tremendous inflation and profiteering of the war period.

Not only has Nehru neglected to take note of this accumulation, but he has also been unable to grasp just what this quantitative change has done collectively to the character of the Indian middle class, a class which may now be said to be firmly in the saddle. A few drops from the banquet (generally from the excess profits) have been scattered in the direction of education, scientific research, and charity; a considerable slackening of the ancient rigidity of manners, and unfortunately of morals also, is duly noticeable. Yet this is nothing compared to the principal characteristic of this class, the ravening greed which is now so obvious in the black market, in enormous bribes spent in making still more enormous profits, in speculation in shares, and an increasingly callous disregard for the misery and even the lives of their fellow Indians. The progressive deterioration in the living conditions of our peasant workers (over 50 per cent of the population), of our factory labour and even the lower-paid office workers and intellectuals affords a striking contrast with the wealth that flows into the pockets of the upper middle class, though the gain may be camouflaged by the ostentatious simplicity of white *khaddar* (homespun) and the eternal Gandhi cap. The new constitution for India, in the gaining of which Nehru and his friends have spent so many of the finest years of their lives in jail, will come only as a recognition of the power of this newly expanded Indian middle class.

Actually the negotiations of the British Cabinet Mission are nothing if not recognition of the position of the new bourgeoisie in India. The old trusteeship theory no longer yields profits either by investment or by export; the British bourgeoisie which must export and invest has admitted the necessity of coming to terms with their Indian counterpart which needs capital goods. It is surely not without significance that the modern industrialists and financiers contribute to Congress (by which I mean the Indian National Congress Party in this note) funds, while the leadership of the Muslim League is on strikingly good terms with the Mohammedan owners of money in India; it may be suggested that one reason for the conflict between these two middle-class political organizations is not only the fact that the Muslim minority forms one-third of the population of the country with less than one-tenth of its wealth, but further that the wealth in Muslim hands is based predominantly on barter pseudo-capital or semi-feudal agrarian production, both of which look for protection to the British.

In the light of all this, which Nehru does not acknowledge explicitly, it is interesting to note his comments on the Indian Communist Party (pp. 524 and 629). Nehru does not realize that the Indian Communist Party (never ideologically powerful) had in 1941 been suppressed to the point of ineffectiveness and that their increasing force in Indian politics today, though still virtually negligible as against that of the bourgeoisie, is due solely to their having really gone down to the peasant workers and the very small industrial proletariat—two sections of the Indian population among which the Congress and the Muslim League both have much less influence today than they did before 1943. In speaking of the Congress Planning Committee (pp. 482-4) it is curious to note that the findings of the Committee had apparently no influence whatsoever on the provincial Congress governments then functioning. Nehru might have studied with profit the differences between the Congress programme and the actual performance of the Congress ministries. There is no evidence whatsoever that the Congress as constituted today is in the remotest danger of drifting (like its planning committee) towards socialism. With the Muslim League leadership, of course, it is difficult to observe anything except pure opportunism and reaction. Without going deeper into the statistics of capital investments, it may be stated—and verified by a reference to the newspapers advertisements of the period—that the years 1937-9, when the Congress ministries ruled, show in their particular provinces a considerable number of new enterprises being started. The investor certainly demonstrated his confidence in the Congress, whether or not the British and the Congress Planning Commission gave any attention to that aspect of the matter. Of course this cannot compare with the almost explosive increase in capital today.

In dealing with the stirring events of August 1942 (p. 579f.), Nehru has given the parliamentary side of the question in a straightforward manner. To the external observer, however, there seems one very striking point which has not even been visualized in the book. When the All India Congress Committee met at Bombay, the members knew that arrest was imminent and most of them had prepared for the event by setting their family affairs and personal finances in excellent order against all contingencies that might arise for the next year or two. What strikes this writer as remarkable is that not one of these worthy and able delegates, though aware that the British adversary was about to strike, ever thought of a plan of action for the Congress and for the nation as a whole. The general idea was 'the Mahatma will give us a plan', yet no special impression was made by the Mahatma's speech just before the arrests—though that address to the assembled delegates on the eve of an anticipated popular explosion is not only not revolutionary in character, nor a plan of action of any sort, but seems, when taken objectively, to be on the same level as a comfortable after-dinner speech. Why is it that knowledge of popular dissatisfaction went hand in hand with the absence of a real plan of action? Does it mean, for example, that the characteristic thought then current among the Indian bourgeoisie had in effect permeated the Congress leadership? One may note that on a class basis the action was quite brilliant, no matter how futile it may have seemed on a national revolutionary scale. The panic of the British government and jailing of all leaders absolved the Congress from any responsibility for the happenings of the ensuing year; at the same time the glamour of jail and concentration camp served to wipe out the so-so record of the Congress ministries in office, thereby restoring the full popularity of the organization among the masses. If the British won the war it was quite clear that the Congress had not favoured Japan; if on the other hand, the Japanese succeeded in conquering India (and they had only to attack immediately in force for the whole of the so-called defence system to crumble) they could certainly not accuse the Congress of having helped the British. Finally, the hatred for the mass repression fell upon the thick heads of the bureaucracy, while having the discontent brought to a head and smashed wide open would certainly not injure the Indian bourgeoisie.

In this connection we may again recall Lenin's words that 'only when the lower classes don't want the old and when the upper class cannot continue in the old way then only can the revolution be victorious. Its truth may be expressed in other words: 'Revolution is impossible without a national crisis affecting both the exploited and the exploiters.' You look in vain in Nehru's book for any recognition of the undeniable fact that in 1942, while the toiling masses had begun to taste the utmost depths of misery and degradation, the Indian bourgeoisie was flourishing as never before. War contracts, high prices, the ability to do extensive black-marketing, had given the financiers and industrialists what they wanted; furthermore even the lower middle classes who had normally been the spearhead of discontent in India had begun to experience an amelioration because of the great number of new clerical and office jobs created by the war and the expanding war economy. Taking cognizance of this and of the further truth that the British in India had consistently allowed investors to make an increasing amount of profit in this country, one may be able to account for the lack of a plan in 1942 and for the successive deadlocks that followed in spite of mass pressure in the direction of revolution.

History has thrust upon Nehru the mantle of leadership of a very powerful organization which still commands a greater mass support than any other in India, and which has shown by its unremitting and painful struggle that it is determined to capture political control of the entire subcontinent. But will Nehru's orientation towards Marxism change when the interests of the class which now backs Congress so heavily diverge from the interests of the poorer classes; or will his lack of a class analysis lead only to disillusionment? It would be silly to proclaim that Mahatma Gandhi, than whom no more sincere person exists, is a tool of the capitalists in India. But there is no other class in India today, except the new bourgeoisie, so strong, so powerfully organized, and so clever as to exploit for its own purposes whatever is profitable in the Mahatma's teachings and to reduce all dangerous enunciations to negative philosophical points. This bourgeoisie needs Nehru's leadership, just as India has needed the class itself. As I read the omens, the parting of the ways is clearly visible; what is not clear is the path Nehru himself will choose in that moment of agony.

NOTE

1. Ed: In this essay D.D. Kosambi reviews Jawaharlal Nehru, *The Discovery of India* (Calcutta, 1946).

The Middle Class of Colonial India*
A Product of British Benevolence

B.B. MISRA

This work [...] is an attempt to trace the growth of the Indian middle classes from about the middle of the eighteenth century to modern times. It is in the main a story of the social policy and changes that occurred in the course of about 200 years of British rule, largely as a consequence of Western education and modern capitalist enterprise, of improved communications and commercial progress, of land reforms and legal administration. [...] My object is to produce a social history, a historical survey of the composition, character, and role of the Indian middle classes. This is a difficult task, since it demands an appreciation of three of the main disciplines immediately involved: history, economics, and sociology. I have some knowledge of the first, but not of the remaining two. Yet in the absence of a work on this subject I have ventured to undertake this as a pioneering project.

CONCEPT OF THE MIDDLE CLASS

The term middle class is frequently used and since most of us, without the aid of a specialist, understand what we mean when we use it in our everyday conversation, I am not attempting a meticulous definition. While it may be of interest to note the features of the Indian middle classes, and while it may be necessary broadly to know their composition in order to be able to assess their historical role, to

---

* Originally published as, 'Introduction', in B.B. Misra, *The Indian Middle Classes: Their Growth in Modern Times* (London: Royal Institute of International Affairs, 1961; reprint New Delhi: Oxford University Press, 1983), pp. 1–17. For the complete text see the original version.

attempt to draw the precise limits of the middle class, a heterogeneous social layer, is, in the words of Lewis and Maude, to get 'lured into an almost interminable discussion of the social sciences; and the result, while probably failing to satisfy the expert, would certainly weary the layman.'[1]

The concept of a single social class implies social division which proceeds from the inequalities and differences of man in society, which may be natural or economic. It is chiefly the economic inequality of man that influences, if it does not wholly determine, social differentiation. It arises basically from the difference of relationship which a person or a group bears to property or the means of production and distribution. If an individual is an owner of land, for example, he tends to exercise a relatively superior social significance. But if, on the contrary, he is a mere tiller of the soil that does not belong to him, he finds himself socially scaled down. This is a general principle which applies to all fields of economic production. This principle of relationship to property is qualitative in character in that it determines the quality of social honour, or lack of it, which we call 'status'. Income, earned or unearned, forms part of the total economic factor, but the concept is quantitative rather than qualitative in character. It relates to the physical size of the means capable of acquiring interests in property. A difference of income produces a hierarchy of prestige and power according to variations in its size. It produces qualitative change in the status of an individual or group only when it is converted into a form affecting relationship to property.

Income is, in fact, a means to the creation of wealth. For instance salary receipts if allowed to accumulate unproductively would remain a pure quantitative entity, but the moment they are invested in the purchase of land or an industry, the position changes. The transaction brings about a qualitative change that varies according to the nature and size of the interest so purchased. [...]

The civil and political inequality of man is distinct from natural inequality. It consists in the different privileges which some men enjoy to the exclusion of others. Some, for example, are rich, honoured, and powerful, while others are not in spite of there being no difference in natural qualities. That is because of the operation of the economic and social factors. Society is thus divided into classes or groups of people joined together from motives of common economic interest, common ways of behaviour, and common traits of character. Each such class forms a hierarchy of status according to the varying quality of social prestige and power expressed through the standard of living, nature of occupation, and wealth. A social class is in fact a complex phenomenon whose complexity grows with the existence or emergence of a wide range of interests connected with the ownership and management of economic and social institutions.

For most of human history the social inequality of man was regarded as something immutable, an invariable order of things founded on the religious consent of man himself. The Renaissance and the Protestant movements of Europe questioned the validity of a social order based on religious sanction. The American and the French Revolutions went farther. They put this principle into practice. These were middle-class bourgeois revolutions, anti-feudal and secular in their approach to civil and political institutions. They appealed to certain natural rights due to man as man. They introduced laissez-faire as the principle of trade and broke the monopoly of political privileges which the owners of feudal estates enjoyed before. The new groups of people, for example, the élite and the business classes who came to share these rights, did so from no religious sanction. They rose into higher social and political grades merely by virtue of their wealth, education, and power. [...] It meant equality of opportunity to improve one's lot in society. It was a dynamic concept which left the individual to move freely in social space. It became a principle of economic law and social philosophy which guided the conduct of the western middle-class societies.

Another important element that emerged from the eighteenth-century revolutions was that of self-consciousness. It was a result of the intellectual thinking and progress of secular education that preceded these revolutions. It emphasized the importance of the 'natural rights' of man regardless of the 'estate' to which he might belong. It was the principle of human dignity which formed the basis of struggle against feudalism. It signified adherence to certain liberal values which received the general acceptance of the nation in time. To become a member of a middle-class group it was usual not only for the individual on the basis of these values to feel himself to be so, but likewise to be felt so by others. Thus while the element of social mobility was conducive to progress, the factor of socially accepted consciousness involved fulfilment of conditions precedent to that progress. While one was dynamic, the other was static. Together they constituted an important principle of social mechanics. It was under the influence of this principle that the social history of the democracies proceeded.

THE GROWTH OF THE MIDDLE CLASSES IN ENGLAND

The dynamic concept of a social class is basically an economic concept, for new classes and groups emerge initially from changes in the size and mode of production. [...] In England in the fourteenth century the emergence of the trader as a separate social and functional category formed the first step in the rise of a middle class. In the course of the Hundred Years War which stimulated production, especially of cloth, the trading element gradually separated itself from the ranks of the well-to-do master-craftsmen, monopolized certain specific spheres of trade, and organized trade associations which dominated the government of towns. This new element became a distinct group of merchant capitalists who financed the craftsmen, supplied raw materials, introduced new designs, improved quality, and marketed the goods so produced. Every augmentation in the size of their business was a step forward in the degree of urbanization. Before the emergence of joint-stock companies, they united both proprietary and managerial functions in business.

From his earliest urban association the trader was in fact the first burgher or bourgeois, who obtained royal charters and influenced urban governments to protect his trading rights against the inroads of the aristocracy on one hand and the wage demands of the craftsmen on the other. He represented the antithesis of the old regime based on feudal dues and personal service. 'The trading, travelling, money-making middle class', Lewis and Maude justly say, 'is presented to us as the antithesis of feudalism, that stable pyramid of society in which each man owed allegiance to his overlord, paying him with services in kind in return for his rule and protection.'

The English merchant capitalists of the fifteenth and sixteenth centuries established schools with an emphasis on the education of the laity to suit their growing requirements of geographical and scientific knowledge. These in time broke down the ecclesiastical monopoly of the educated professions. The trading entrepreneurs navigated the uncharted seas and carried on commerce with the distant parts of the globe. To share the risk of large-scale trading in foreign lands, they introduced a system of joint-stock companies which necessitated an increased division of labour, a separation of proprietary, directional, and managerial groups. The establishment of the English East India Company under the royal charter of 31 December 1600 was perhaps the biggest of the early examples of joint-stock trading.

But since, on account of technological backwardness, production remained essentially domestic in character, social stratification was limited. [...] Indeed it was the exigencies of large-scale mechanical production that really heralded a new social order, distinct from feudalism and founded not on bondage but free relations. It took time for that revolution to stabilize itself, but generally speaking its first phase of development ushered in an era of laissez-faire which broke down the barriers of mercantilism and stimulated trade and industry to an extent never known before. [...] Each step in the advancement of technology was accompanied by a birth and extension of new skills, by acceleration in the increase of professional groups in both urban and rural areas. Already the establishment of joint-stock companies had resulted in a separation of proprietary and managerial functions in business. The increasing pace of industrial development produced a more complex division of labour, and added to the old directional group a hierarchy of managerial and financial as well as technical and supervisory elements, not only in key industries but also in ever-increasing ancillary branches. Technological advance led to the establishment of a diversified system of education, and with increasing demand for varying degrees of applied and professional skills remunerated at different levels, there arose a much wider range of differentiation between the classes of employed persons.

The increasing number of new groups and categories emerging, as they did, from the expansion of trade and industry, education and professions, added to the complexity of social structure and relationship. History did not march in the direction Marx had indicated during the first phase of capitalist development. Instead of a growing concentration of wealth, the progress of technology and capitalist enterprise brought about a gradual diffusion of its ownership and control. It was in fact large-scale business enterprise that created an ever-increasing class of technicians, administrators, and supervisors remunerated at various levels for the most part well above those of manual and clerical workers. It was again the growth of capitalist enterprise that from its complexity produced in other fields a large body of professionals specialized in various branches of knowledge, such as law and medicine, education and journalism. They added to the number of the middle classes.

Capitalism made the middle classes an integral part of a unitary social order. The old trading middle class was called 'middle' because it was situated in between the baronage and the peasant or artisan class. But something more than this was implied by the new middle-class social order; it was not simply that they stood between the capitalist and the worker. There were two other important factors. First, they formed a composite intermediate layer consisting of a wide range of occupational interests but bound together by a common style of living and behaviour pattern. Secondly, they stood for certain liberal, democratic values which they expressed in their social and political conduct. They showed respect for the individual and gave less weight to a religious sanction of authority. Ideologically, the new order stood for intellectual freedom and social mobility, liberal individualism, and political democracy. A middle-class society thus became identified with a stratified social order representing a new standard of values which its members or groups impressed upon the entire societies in which they lived.

THE INDIAN SITUATION

Institutions conducive to capitalist growth were not lacking in India before British rule. Indian artisan industry and occupational specialization were very highly developed. [...] [T]here existed in addition a separate class of merchants whom the accounts of foreign travellers admired for the great extent of their foreign trade, the quality of their goods, and the magnitude of their wealth. They were organized in guilds designed to regulate prices and to protect trading rights against the interference of royal officials and landed magnates. These were comparable to medieval European trade associations which exercised a great measure of autonomy in the regulation of commerce. India had no joint-stock companies, but Indian traders employed what might be called a sort of managing agency which operated throughout the country. It consisted of a class of middlemen who managed the business of mercantile and banking houses, made advances to producers, and supplied finished goods to merchants.

A money economy had developed in India at an early period of her history. The coining of money was a royal privilege held by certain private families of traders specializing in currency. [...] The shroffs, a class of money-changers, were an ancient community who specialized in coinage and issued drafts (*hundi*s) or letters of credit against the money deposited with them—a system which greatly facilitated the movement of trade. 'Yet modern capitalism,' Max Weber rightly observes, 'did not develop indigenously before or during the English rule. It was taken over as a finished artifact without autonomous beginnings.'²

The political and social systems of the country were to a large extent responsible for this. The royal officials and priesthood often combined against the bourgeois plutocrats. It is true that such combinations were not peculiar to India; they occurred also in the West. But in the West the mercantile control of municipal governments, especially of the police, rendered them ineffectual. The guild power in India remained purely money power, unsupported by any authority of a political or military nature. It collapsed as soon as the king found it convenient to call in the aid of priestly and knightly elements.

The limitations arising from the existence of caste, the foundation of the Hindu social system, were no less menacing to a merchant guild. Consisting, as it did, of members belonging to different castes, the observance of its rules depended upon the sanction of the caste council (panchayat) concerned. That is where the Brahman and the king stepped in as final arbiters. They played off the superior caste organization against the guild by the threat of punishing recalcitrant members by excommunication. The priesthood thus assisted the king and his officials in the preservation of their dominance over the class of merchants.

[...] The Indian political and social systems as a whole were authoritarian and despotic in nature, highly prejudicial to the growth of an independent bourgeois class. Indian merchants were known for their fabulous wealth, but generally they were royal monopolists appointed after the collapse of merchant guilds and dependent for their prosperity upon palace officials or provincial governors.

Ideologically too their situation was equally unfavourable. The priestly and knightly classes regarded trade and industry as inferior callings. The literary classes who followed intellectual professions were ignorant of crafts. The artisans who had the monopoly of craftsmanship received no education. The shrewdness of business classes was proverbial, but their education was limited to commercial accounts. Their knowledge was empirical, descending from the father to the son. Occupational specialization arose from hereditary callings, not from higher education or research, which remained literary in emphasis and divorced from the pursuits of applied skills and sciences.

In spite of the potential of a middle-class bourgeois development, therefore, the immobility of the caste organization and the despotism of bureaucracy precluded such a development. The middle-class elements in society could not become a stratified order, each individual or group having the freedom to move in social space and being conscious of a superior status based on the superiority of the values acquired. They remained divided into water-tight status groups according to the caste to which they belonged. They could not form themselves into a unitary middle-class social order comparable to that of western countries. Cases of caste schisms did arise from time to time to oppose the exercise of hereditary privileges, but they were exceptions. The religious movements of Buddhism and Jainism which supported such schisms, for instance, were pacifist in their approach like the devotional (*bhakti*) movements of the middle ages. They degenerated into sects which later came to be absorbed into the caste system.

Moreover, the caste system was related to the law of property. It formed an integral part of the prevailing land economy. Under the law of inheritance, for example, succession depended upon the performance of caste obligations. And since land constituted a more or less exclusive means of livelihood, except for the artisans who in part earned their living from handicrafts, starvation became the only alternative to the observance of caste rules.

The emergence of a stratified social order depended on occupational and educational diversification. Land economy and limited education were both obstructive to social stratification, but more important still was the backwardness of technology, the existence of a domestic system of production, from which no stratified order could emerge. This small-scale handicraft production afforded little or no scope for a multiplicity of economic functions, such as arose from an increased division of labour under joint-stock business, in large-scale mechanical production or diversified national education. None of these conditions existed prior to British rule. Society was divided into fixed status groups. There were intermediate categories as well but no middle classes of the type described above.

THE RISE OF AN INDIAN MIDDLE CLASS UNDER BRITISH RULE

Radical changes accompanied the advent of the British in India. In the absence of an adequate political and economic system, they transplanted into India their own form and principles of government and economic organization which they modified only to suit local conditions.

As between European business and British government in India, the relationship differed little from its home pattern. The former exercised considerable influence over the latter. As for Indians, they could join British firms as junior partners, for the membership of a European trade organization was not exclusive, and although the size of the stock held by an individual was significant, the rule of law made no distinction between a European or Indian businessman.

The number of Indians able to carry on business on modern European lines was negligible in the beginning. The British attempted as part of their educational policy to create a class comparable to their own, so that it might assist them in the administration of the country and help in the development of its internal resources, necessary for the payment of the increasing imports of British manufactures. In Macaulay's words, this was to be a 'class, Indian in blood and colour, but English in tastes, in opinions, in morals and intellect'.[3]

These ideas and institutions of a middle-class social order were imported into India. They did not grow from within. They were implanted in the country without a comparable development in its economy and social institutions. The Indian middle class that the British aimed at creating was to be a class of imitators, not the originators of new values and methods. The West proceeded to develop education so as to satisfy the needs of an already developed economy. India under the British proceeded to develop education so as to form a class to develop its economy. That was the British theory of 'infiltration' which was to apply to both educational and economic fields.

It was to put the cart before the horse. The traditional Hindu bias against industrial occupation and the administrative requirements of Government led to the whole educational machinery being geared to satisfy the needs of the public service and had the effect of perpetuating the old emphasis on literary education as a virtual monopoly of the upper castes of Hindu society. The development of the country's economy thus long remained the main concern of Europeans. The educated class of Indians who emerged as a result of British educational policy cared more for position and influence in the civil service and councils than for mass education or economic development. New business classes did grow, but not so rapidly as the literary classes. By virtue of their traditional superiority of caste, intellectual pursuits, and political influence, the latter continued to dominate the former except in recent decades during which Indian business had begun to assume a professional character. The respect attaching to higher education and professional skill was gradually imparting to money power a social status which it did not enjoy before.

COMPOSITION OF THE INDIAN MIDDLE CLASSES

The progress of education and the advancement of technology, even though delayed, were tending towards the goal of a middle-class society. India's industrially developed cities produced a social order which, in its complexity, compared favourably with its European counterpart. Its component parts, though heterogeneous and even mutually conflicting at times, exhibited in great measure an element of uniformity not only in their behaviour pattern and style of life, but also in their mode of thinking and social values. From the circumstances of their growth the members of the educated professions, such as government servants and lawyers, college teachers and doctors, constitute the bulk of the Indian middle classes. The mercantile and industrial elements which dominate the composition of the western middle classes are still a minority, limited for the most part to cities like Calcutta and Bombay, Madras and Cawnpore (Kanpur), Ahmedabad, and Jamshedpur. But since they form the rising classes, the advanced section of a middle-class bourgeois society, I have given them priority in the following analysis of the Indian middle classes, which consist in the main of the following groups:

1. The body of merchants, agents, and proprietors of modern trading firms [...].
2. The bulk of salaried executives [...] in banking, trading, and manufacturing businesses [...].
3. The higher salaried officers of a wide group of institutions and societies ranging from the chambers of commerce and other trade associations to political organizations, trade unions, philanthropic, cultural, and educational bodies.
4. The main body of civil servants and other [high ranking] public servants. [...]
5. The members of the principal recognized professions [...] such as lawyers and doctors, lecturers and professors, the upper and middle ranges of writers and journalists, musicians and artists, religious preachers and priests.

6. The holders of the middle grades of proprietary tenures of land, such as joint and peasant proprietors, rentiers, and farmers of revenue [...] exclusive of the largest and some of the smallest holders of estates.
7. The body of well-to-do shopkeepers and hotel keepers including the managers, accountants, and other officers employed in the joint-stock concerns operating in such fields.
8. The group of rural entrepreneurs engaged in plantation industry, with a number of salaried managerial hands employed on landed estates.
9. The main body of the full-time students engaged in higher education at a university or comparable level.
10. The main body of clerks, assistants, and other non-manual workers below the managerial and the recognized professional levels.
11. The upper range of secondary school-teachers and the officers of the local bodies, social, and political workers.

[...]

The ending of the Company's rule in 1858 resulted in a steep and steady rise in India's external trade, which created capital resources for industrialization, paying for loans incurred on government account for the construction of railways, irrigation, and other public works, as well as maintaining the entire establishment of the India Office and Indian Civil Service. The flow of British capital and skill contributed to the agricultural and manufacturing industries and also led to the introduction of the managing agency system, which provided a pattern of industrial organization which shaped the character of India's economic development. [...] A limited number of managing agents thus came to control the bulk of the country's economic power. This financial integration restricted the growth of the Indian industrial middle classes, while the administrative integration reduced the number of superior executives, especially directors. The Indian managing houses such as the Birlas, the Tatas, the Dalmias, and the Thapars, not only adopted this model but added to it regional and caste prejudices affecting the appointment of directors and managers, secretaries, and engineers. Thus was perpetuated a tendency towards limiting the selection of business administrators to persons belonging to the caste or community controlling the businesses concerned.

With the spread of higher education among the traditional business communities of India, unless their concerns come under public control industrial administration may become their exclusive sphere of influence, and the dominance of the old literary classes may continue by virtue of the lead they gained in the early phases of British rule. Another consequence of the managing agency system was the concentration of capital in Calcutta and Bombay which, together with the growth of education in the Presidency towns, concentrated the growth of the middle classes in these towns, tending to cause social instability.

Founded on the rule of law and the principle of laissez faire, sociologically speaking British rule produced a gradual elevation of the Indian bourgeoisie as controllers of money power, whose influence became more widespread with the growth of modern towns and cities. Moreover the gradual substitution of custom by law and the growth of a highly centralized administrative apparatus, which took over such duties that had traditionally been performed by village communities or large landholders, encouraged the growth of the middle classes. What shook the foundations of the old society even more were the British land reforms, the cumulative effect of which was to reduce the power of the landholders, to give tenants legal recognition and a prestige they had never enjoyed before, and to transform society from a basis of status to one of contract. Moreover the creation of property in land and the freedom with which that property could be alienated resulted in the growth of a class of moneylenders or rural financiers, and the revenue laws and tenancy reforms led to an unprecedented increase in the volume of litigation to validate disputed claims. This produced a corresponding increase in public business, which necessitated on the one hand hierarchies of officials and on the other professional hierarchies of lawyers. Both swelled the middle classes, who were tending to supplant the influence previously exercised by chief proprietors or village headmen. The extent to which the old social order was facing dissolution towards the end of the nineteenth century is reflected in a telling passage in a report on the condition of the lower classes in 1881-91:

In rural, as in urban, life changes are taking place of which the result is to bring new men to the surface, and to relegate to comparative obscurity the classes on whom the public attention has been up to recent times concentrated ... There can be no doubt that, one by one, the forces which have hitherto held native society together are being loosened, and that the whole masses of the community are being melted as in a crucible, and are gradually losing the form and colour which have hitherto distinguished them, to take what new shape or to reappear in what combinations, it is premature to conjecture.[4]

While it was the bureaucracy that in fact became the most powerful of the new social forces, the growth of the independent professions, especially of law, was at the same time tending to the creation of a counterweight to the bureaucracy. These new men came forward as the representatives of the citizenry, and claimed to step into the social vacuum caused by the disintegration of the old order. With the help of the rising Indian bourgeoisie, the educated classes were enabled to become successful rivals of an officialdom controlled by alien rule and not rooted in the land.

[...] A by-product of the British educational policy of promoting vernacular education in order to spread European knowledge and culture was the revival of Oriental studies on the one hand and the translation into Indian regional languages of English books on the other. The subjection of Oriental studies to western methods of analysis and scrutiny led to their critical revaluation. The depth of Indian scholarship, the flexibility of Hindu philosophy, and the superiority of its ethics enabled Indians to interpret their traditions so as to make them ideologically conformable to the demands of western liberalism, but the Hindu social system could not be made to conform to a liberalism that was the product of mechanized technology and industrial revolution, of social mobility and a belief in the natural rights of man. In India, this conflict emphasized two main trends already present in Indian cultural development—liberal reformism and reactionary revivalism. The spirit of the new age was represented by the Brahma Samaj in Bengal and the Prarthana Samaj in Bombay, but these middle-class reformist movements had no mass backing, for the bulk of the population was rural, illiterate, steeped in superstition, and profoundly suspicious of the pro-western educated classes, whom they regarded as Christian. These movements in fact stimulated the spirit of reaction, epitomized in Swami Dayanand Saraswati's Arya Samaj, whose appeal was much wider and whose leader was the first to decry foreign rule and its influence. Men such as Bal Gangadhar Tilak and Lala Lajpat Rai, carrying their revivalist convictions into the political field, ushered in an era of violence which Gandhi had to fight against. But there could be no going back to the Vedas, for the Hindus had become well advanced in western education and capitalist enterprise, two of the main props of liberalism. They could no longer afford to live in the past, and the most enlightened worked for a cultural synthesis. But the traditional orthodoxy of Islam and the time-lag in the western education of Muhammadans made revivalism a relatively stronger force in that community, and this was reinforced by the economic decline of the Muslim community. In consequence, the Muslim traditionalists dominated the politics of even the educated class of Muslims. The British refusal to extend recognition to Indian aspirations inevitably discredited the moderates, or the liberals, the first champions of constitutional advance in India. Religious bias and political violence followed, and the radical or extremist elements of the Congress tried to produce a mass movement through religious and socially reactionary propaganda. But the religious approach to politics accentuated communal differences, and by the time the goal of responsible government came to be recognized in principle, the situation had got out of control. Thus, India became independent but divided in 1947.

NOTES

1. Roy Lewis and Angus Maude, *The English Middle Classes* (London, 1949), p. 13.

2. Max Weber, *The Religion of India*, tr. and ed. H.H. Gerth and Don Martindale (New York, 1958), p. 4.

3. H. Sharp, *Selections from the Educational Records*, pt I, 1781-1839 (Calcutta, 1920), p. 116.

4. Quoted in J.O. Miller, *On the Condition of the Agricultural and Labouring Classes, in Condition of Lower Classes in India, 1881–91* (P.B. Coll. 220).

The Myth of a 'Westernized Middle Class'*

MICHELGUGLIELMO TORRI

[...]

THE RISE AND APOGEE OF THE CONCEPT OF 'WESTERNIZED MIDDLE CLASS'

In its most general form, the concept of 'westernized middle class' is simple enough. It defines those Indians who, during the colonial era, particularly since the 1820s and 1830s, acquired an education based on English language and culture. The concept itself has an illustrious pedigree, as it can be related to Thomas Babington Macaulay's famous Minute on Education (2 February 1835) and the hopes there expressed that, through a diffusion throughout India of English language and culture, 'a class of persons, Indian in blood and colour, but English in taste, in opinions, in morals, and in intellect' would come into being.[1] By the end of the nineteenth century, the first theorists of the rising nationalist movement, especially Surendranath Banerjea, gave currency to the concept of a 'new middle class' which was born from the impact of western culture on Indian society and which was the carrier of 'enlightenment, freedom, progress and prosperity'.[2]

It is easy to see how the use of this concept carried an obvious polemical advantage for the first Indian nationalists. As members of a modern middle class, the westernized Indians could claim that, according to key principles of the English political tradition, they were entitled to a growing role in the government of their own country, along the path already taken by the white dominions.[3]

---

* Originally published as 'Westernized Middle Class: Intellectuals and Society in Late Colonial India', in John L. Hill (ed.), *The Congress and Indian Nationalism: Historical Perspectives* (London : Curzon Press, 1991), pp. 18-55. For the complete text see the original. In the present version, some portions of the essay have been removed and notes rearranged accordingly.

On their part, the British rulers reacted strongly to the nationalists' polemical challenge. They pointed out that the westernized Indians, far from being a new class, formed an élite whose members belonged to those high castes, especially the Brahmanical castes, which traditionally filled the bureaucracies of any existing Indian state. Besides, the British claimed that, after all, the westernized Indians were not as westernized as they made themselves out to be and, anyway, not enough to be able to wield power according to adequate—namely British—standards of fairness and justice. At the same time, and rather contradictorily (but when has the strength of a polemical onslaught ever been diminished by its lack of internal consistency), the British rulers asserted that the westernized Indians, being westernized, had cut themselves off from the traditional society, namely from 'true India'. That meant that they represented only themselves, which was not much, as in the words of that very liberal Viceroy, Lord Dufferin, the westernized middle class formed 'a microscopic minority'.[4]

In spite of their deep differences when assessing the role of the westernized Indians, nationalist politicians and colonial rulers were agreed on a fundamentally important point. This was the fact that the westernized Indians formed an autonomous social group, which was internally consistent and differentiated from the other component parts of the social body. As a result, terms such as 'westernized middle class' or 'westernized élite' became, in everyday usage, interchangeable and synonymous.

Those two interpretations—the westernized Indians as coincident with a new professional and bureaucratic bourgeoisie or as members of a caste élite—were the extremes between which historians continued to move in their attempt to assess the role of the western-educated Indians. The categories of 'westernized middle class' and 'westernized élite' were made use of as interchangeable terms that defined a sociological entity which, according to the convenience of the author, could be either the intersection or the sum or simply one of the two definitions elaborated by British rulers and Indian nationalists.

It goes without saying that such an unembarrassed utilization of the concept was not without ambiguities. However, even if there was some limited discussion, an in-depth debate on the subject never got started.[5] A possible explanation is that, in spite of its ambiguities, or may be because of them, the concept itself appeared a methodological tool capable of producing conspicuous results. Therefore it was a master key for interpreting the late colonial period, which was seen as dominated by the clash between the British Raj and the 'new class', or the 'new élite', bearer of the ideals of nationalism. [...]

THE FALL OF THE CONCEPT OF 'WESTERNIZED MIDDLE CLASS'

The book which marked both the apogee in the utilization of the concept of westernized middle class and, quite suddenly and unexpectedly, its swan song was Judith Brown's first monograph on Gandhi. Not by chance, the essay which put an end to the time when —in Eric Stoke's ironic words—one could 'unblushingly' talk of the 'modern English-educated Indian middle class'[6] was published as a review article of her book. The author, David Washbrook, one of the young lions of the then rising Cambridge school of Indian historians, [...] unleashed a devastating attack on her 'extensive analysis of the structure of Indian politics between 1915 and 1922'.[7] He argued that Brown's analysis was 'very wrong' precisely because it was based on 'such vast and unwieldy categories as Western educated presidency elites, or even their regional constituents'. In other words, [...] the category of the westernized middle class/élite was unable to explain 'the minutiae—and therefore the substance—of politics'. Accordingly, it was unable to make head or tail of the peculiar phenomenon according to which, in 1920, in the Madras Presidency, the Congress broke up into three factions, each going its own separate way. [...] In Washbrook's opinion, this was a rather peculiar outcome, as the leaders of the three different factions 'were all Western educated lawyers, all Tamilians, all Sri Vaishnava Brahmins and, indeed, all active in the pre-1915 Congress'. The problem was, according to Washbrook, that 'if we begin to examine the kind of people behind each leader it rapidly becomes apparent that each had a constituency which extended far beyond members of the elite.' [...] :

The political wrangling between the three (leaders) represented not just a localized conflict within a small culturally defined group but a major clash in society, affecting an improbably wide range of connexions, over the distribution of power under the Montagu-Chelmsford reforms. There were, no doubt, senses in which the three would stand together—as lawyers, Brahmins, Tamilians, or Vaishnavites—but these were of little importance when compared to the practical differences, based on the membership of different factions and networks, which kept them apart.[8]

Apart from this, the westernized Indians did not even enjoy a paramount position in the factions which they formally led. Washbrook points out that, in Madras, 'the Western educated as a group controlled relatively few means of production and hence possessed relatively little economic power in the presidency'.[9] [...] In Washbrook's opinion:

[...] In function, the Western educated of Madras provide us with a classical example of the middle-man, essentially alike both to the British administration and to Indians with local influence, *yet ultimately dependent upon being accepted by both and, individually, capable of being destroyed by the withdrawal of the confidence of either*. Of course, the extraordinarily convoluted and dislocated system of government in India gave the middle-man great room for manoeuvre. [...]. But, however he came to acquire his importance, he still needed some support from above and from below and had to tailor his individual policies to these ends. A great many of the actions of Western educated politicians were, therefore, dictated not by their own wishes, [...] but by their need to gain personal support from the leader of society and from the government. Thus it makes no sense to regard them as a permanently unified category standing against the rest of society, nor indeed as an elite in the world of politics.[10]

I have used this long quotation because it is not only the death warrant of the former master concept of the historiography of India in the age of nationalism but because in it an alternative category is forcefully put forward. The westernized middle class wanes like a nightmare at the moment of awakening and the attention of the analyst shifts to the interaction between the British and those indigenous magnates who, according to Washbrook, dominated Indian society at the local level. A by-product of this shift is the sudden disappearance of the Indian National Congress, namely the all-India organization of the westernized middle class, as a key political structure in late colonial India. In Washbrook's own words, 'politics is about the control and organization of power and the Congress, quite simply, was not an institution which, of itself, controlled very much power.'[11] Others were the institutions which exerted power in India: 'the bureaucracy, municipalities, rural boards, temples, universities, charities, etc., which were changing and expanding rapidly from the 1880s.'[12] Accordingly, it is on these organizations—and not on the Congress, which was little more than an empty box which could occasionally be useful to certain notables as a stump from which to orate—that the attention of the historian must be focused.

The ideas put forward by Washbrook were taken up by Anil Seal and inserted in a brilliant article in which Seal summed up and systematized the result of the research work of some of his students and colleagues. In so doing, Seal produced what came to be regarded as the manifesto of the new Cambridge school of Indian historians.[13]

[...] Accordingly, following Washbrook's indications, Seal depicted the westernized Indians as clients and spokesmen of the notables who controlled Indian society, and intermediaries between the latter and the British Raj. [...] Indeed the campaign to dispose of the old concept and to replace it with that of middleman was so effective that, by the time she wrote her second book on Gandhi, even Judith Brown had been converted. The Mahatma, seen in her first book as a kind of demonic figure who, from a politically inchoate chaos, conjured up and moulded powerful new social forces, in her second book is cut down to the rather modest size of a go-between. [...]¹⁴

OF LINGERING DOUBTS AND CONTRADICTIONS

If even Judith Brown—as Paul on his way to Damascus—had seen the light, must we conclude that Washbrook's word had triumphed? As a matter of fact, the answer is less than an unqualified yes. Among the Cambridgeites themselves one can notice some uncertainties and contradictions when one comes to peruse closely their position on the problem. Let us take the example of John Gallagher [...] [who] although careful in not making use of such *démodé* terms as 'westernized middle class' or 'westernized élite' conveniently substituting less compromising labels such as 'the politicians of Calcutta', the 'oligarchs', 'the Hindu politicians'—is really talking about that same political group that J.H. Broomfield called 'the *bhadralok*', namely the Bengal westernized middle class.¹⁵

Another Cambridgeite who, although cautiously and somehow tentatively, differentiates himself from David Washbrook is Christopher Bayly. In his 1973 article on Allahabad, Bayly firmly shared his colleague's revisionist position.¹⁶ However, in his book on the same topic, published in 1975, Bayly seems to arrive at a somewhat different position. According to him, by 1920, namely at the end of the period which he analyses, the situation in Allahabad was characterized by the emergence, besides the notables who dominated the economic and social life of the city, of at least a section of westernized Indians wielding a comparable and autonomous power. This process was the by-product of 'the general development of association, publicity, and regional organs of representation' and the coming into being of 'new arenas of town-wide politics associated with housing improvement, a more consolidated labour market, and new mercantile associations'. As the power of this group of 'professional men and local publicists' was a function of new and developing socio-political institutions and political techniques, it is only logical to assume—as Bayly himself does—that the importance of these men was bound to gradually rise in the post-1920 period. Yet, the influence of this group of westernized Indians was still ultimately dependant on their ability at playing the role of intermediaries—although, of course, not between the notables and the colonial authorities, but between the latter and certain sectors of the local population, formerly controlled by the notables.[17]

Sharper, even if still somewhat muted, is the contrast between Washbrook's thesis and the conclusions reached by another Cambridgeite, B.R. Tomlinson. [...] Tomlinson portrays the Congress as the necessary ladder to be used by nationalist politicians to climb the walls of the political-administrative citadel that the British—for their own imperial reasons—were in the process of turning over to the Indians. [...] Even more importantly for the present discussion, the political personnel of the Congress (namely the westernized élite) is seen as engaged in an active and autonomous role, which is not in any way dependent on the *placet* by the notables. The politicians of the Congress appear deeply involved in all-out confrontations among themselves with the aim of taking over both the Congress organization and the self-governing bodies created by the British. Tomlinson shows how as a consequence, they were inevitably driven to widen their contacts with the external world in an effort to augment their political leverage inside the Congress, and to bring inside the Congress as wide a range of social forces as possible.[18]

THE WESTERNIZED MIDDLE CLASS'S COME-BACK

So, after all, on the particular problem of the status and role of the westernized Indians, the Cambridge school's assessment is far from being homogeneous. Such a situation could not but invite a rebuttal. This has come from a brilliant Bengali scholar, himself a former pupil of Cambridge University, Dr Rajat K. Ray.

Ray's departing hypothesis is that the contradiction between the picture of the Indian social system given by the Cambridgeites—based on cross-caste and cross-class vertical structures—and that painted by other historians—where horizontal social formations, such as the westernized middle class, are prominent—is only apparent. Or rather this difference is a function of the different speed of the process of modernization in different areas of the subcontinent.[19]

According to Ray, the kind of social organization which Washbrook and Baker portray as dominant in the Madras Presidency, up to the mid-1930s, was already typical, once the necessary adjustments are made, of both the Mughal Empire and its successor states. On the basis of the work by Satish Chandra and Athar Ali on the Mughal Empire and Cohn, Calkins and Leonard on the successor states, Ray claims that in all cases analysed by those scholars, the social system appears articulated in vertical structures controlled by powerful patrons.[20] Such structures cut through castes and classes, linking together their segments.[21] When the English took over the subcontinent, they tried to disrupt as little as possible the existing social organization and made use of it in order to administer 'economically'—in the wider meaning of the term—their Indian Empire. However, in spite of all other similarities, there was a crucial difference between the British Raj and other Mughal successor states. This difference was the necessity on the part of the colonial state to subordinate Indian convenience to British interests.

The necessity to promote and protect these alien interests—among which Ray stresses the need to create 'a congenial field of operation' for British capital—was the engine behind 'the process of administrative centralization from the late nineteenth century, which has figured so prominently in recent analysis of political change'.[22] In spite of the desire of the British administrators of the subcontinent not to disturb the existing social order, the colonial connection implied a dynamic made of ever-growing economic and administrative interference vis-à-vis Indian society. Cause and effect of this dynamic was the widening and thickening of the state apparatus. [....] The result of this 'process of structurally distorted, partial modernization' was 'a shift in social influence from ruling noble, chief, and warrior elements' (namely the powerful patrons who lorded over the cross-class, cross-caste vertical structures which had hitherto been the stuff of Indian society) to 'bureaucratic and professional communities formally tied to the ruling elements'.[23] This was because the members of these bureaucratic and professional communities filled the ranks and files of the colonial bureaucracy.

If I am allowed a slightly unbecoming rhetorical figure, I will try to sum up Ray's thinking by saying that the gradual unfolding of the tentacles of imperialism through the ports of Calcutta and Bombay brought about the parallel and gradual withering away of the vertical structures of social control, increasingly substituted in their functions by the widening state apparatus. In turn, this process liberated the various horizontal segments formerly linked and subordinate to a patron and caused their coalescing in wider horizontal strata or—as Ray calls them, following Kaleki and K.N. Raj's usage—'intermediate strata'.[24] According to Ray, these intermediate strata, 'identified neither with a propertied class owning the means of production, nor with a property-less class living by physical labour', did not have any definite class alignment.[25]

Ray points out that the intermediate strata were subdivided into two main sectors: urban and rural. From what he says it is not difficult to realize that, behind the label of urban intermediate strata is disguised a social formation including the westernized middle class/élite plus the vernacular literati. Analogously, behind the label of rural intermediate strata appears another old warhorse of Indian historiography (and sociology), namely that social formation variously described as 'rich peasants' or 'dominant peasant castes'. In sum, once again, we are regaled with the good old theory that Indian nationalism can best be explained by the anti-imperialist alliance between the westernized middle class—plus vernacular literati—and the peasantry. Any former partisan of the westernized middle class/élite as a key historiographical concept should rejoice at Ray's bold counter-revisionist attempt.

THE FINAL DEFEAT OF THE WESTERNIZED MIDDLE CLASS

However, is Ray's counter-revision really so well-grounded as to withstand any serious criticism? [...] First of all, Ray's two main components of the 'intermediate strata' can be classified under the same label only through a semantic mystification. As a matter of fact, according to Ray's own analysis, at least in those parts of India in which the rural 'intermediate strata' were really an intermediate social formation, existing in between 'sharecroppers and bonded labour' on one side and zamindars and talukdars on the other, there was a basic contradiction between urban and rural intermediate strata. [....]

Here, one could object that Ray's analysis [...] could be maintained once it is limited to its urban component. However, even by doing so, one is rapidly confronted by additional problems. The first is the evanescence of the concept of urban 'intermediate strata'. Not only did they have no 'defined role in the production system' but, more important, according to Ray's description, they were able to wield some kind of political weight only when acting in connection with other social forces: capital, labour and, in particular, the dominant peasant castes.[26] [....]

But the more substantial objection to the usefulness of Ray's concept is, quite simply, that Washbrook's criticism of the category of westernized élite still holds true for the urban intermediate strata. The latter was a social formation which, as soon as it had to deal with any major or minor political problem, showed an irrepressible tendency to break up into two or more warring parties or factions, call them what you will. [....]

TURNING TO A DIFFERENT CULTURAL TRADITION

At this point the fog of war has settled on the methodological battlefield. The old key reference point—the westernized middle class/élite—has disappeared from sight; the others are hazy and considered by most as untrustworthy. [...] All this has brought about a great deal of confusion and some rather queer results. We have Indian scholars who go on discussing the westernized Indians and the Congress just as if Washbrook and his colleagues had never written a single line related to these questions. On the other hand, there are British historians who, in the same essay, light-heartedly switch from the concept of westernized Indians as an autonomous social group, endowed of its own class interests, to that of westernized Indians as middlemen, apparently without realizing that the two categories are mutually exclusive.[27] [...]

This being the situation, a possible way out can be offered by the realization that the problem under examination, namely the role of the so-called 'educated class', is far from being an exclusive problem of Indian historiography. The role of this social formation has been scrutinized and solutions have been offered by other cultural traditions. It is by drawing on that peculiarly Italian version of Marxism whose author is Antonio Gramsci that I will now put forward my proposal for a new solution of the problem.[28]

Gramsci came to grips with the role of the 'educated class' as part and parcel of his reinterpretation of Italian history and cultural tradition. Gramsci put the problem of the members of the 'educated class', namely, the intellectuals, in its proper context by the question which opens his notes on the intellectuals. He writes: 'Are intellectuals an autonomous and independent social group, or does every social group have its own particular specialized category of intellectuals?'[29] Although claiming that the problem is a complex one, Gramsci's answer to his own question is clear-cut: intellectuals are not an autonomous social group.

Gramsci acknowledges that historically intellectuals mostly hail from certain social classes, such as 'the petty and middle landed bourgeoisie and certain strata of the petty and middle urban bourgeoisie'.[30] However, the class origin of the intellectuals is irrelevant. What matters is that they, as a 'professional category', namely as a set of persons whose common denominator is their professional role, acquire social and political weight only by acting as theorists, organizers, strategists, and spokesmen on behalf of autonomous social groups, that is, social classes, either existing or in the process of formation. It goes without saying that these social classes are not necessarily those from which the intellectuals hail. [...]

It is the presence of [...] intellectuals, whom Gramsci calls 'traditional intellectuals', which has given rise to 'that social utopia, by which the intellectuals think of themselves as "independent", autonomous, endowed with a character of their own.'[31].[...] According to Gramsci, the most typical of these categories of traditional intellectuals is that of the ecclesiastics, who, in the past, performed a crucial role by wielding the monopoly of religious ideology, education, justice, and charity. This category of intellectuals 'had equal status juridically with the aristocracy, with which it shared the exercise of feudal ownership of land, and the use of state privileges connected with property.'[32] [...] Now, according to Gramsci: 'Since these various categories of traditional intellectuals are characterized by an *"esprit de corps"* which stresses their uninterrupted historical continuity and their professional qualifications, they claim to be autonomous and independent of the dominant social group.'

As already indicated, for Gramsci this claim is groundless. But, interestingly enough, he concedes that this pretension on the part of the traditional intellectuals 'is not without consequences in the ideological and political field, consequences of wide-ranging import'.[33] Gramsci is less than exhaustive in characterizing and discussing these wide-ranging consequences. However, by developing logically what he writes and drawing on the whole Marxist intellectual tradition, one can easily contend that the traditional intellectuals, both because of their tendency to consider themselves as independent of the dominant social group and their skills as political theorists and strategists, can discern more easily than most people the long-term trend of the historical process in the making. Accordingly, they may sometimes shift their allegiance to new social classes on the rise. It is precisely this shift of loyalties that, in Gramsci's thinking, marks the turning point in the struggle on the part of a new rising class which is developing towards dominance.[34]

THE WESTERNIZED INDIANS AND THE VERNACULAR LITERATI AS INTELLECTUALS

Armed with the insight offered by Gramsci, we can now return to our original problem. My contention is that the concept of 'intellectuals', as defined by Gramsci, has a closer correspondence to reality and, therefore, is a sharper and more useful methodological tool than either the concept of westernized middle class/élite—including its various avatars—or that of middlemen. It defines those Indians who, quite independently from their class and caste origin, were politically aware and active as theorists, strategists, organizers, and spokesmen on behalf of existing or emerging autonomous social groups. The set of persons thus defined is partially coincident with both the so-called westernized middle class/élite and Washbrook's middlemen. However, the boundaries of the old and new categories are not identical.

When compared to Washbrook's, the concept that I am now putting forward includes a somewhat wider group, as not all the politically aware and politically active Indians were middlemen in Washbrook's sense. Certainly, people who performed such a crucially important political role as Dayananda and Romesh Chandra Dutt never acted as middlemen. [....] But, of course, all these people easily fit in the category of 'intellectuals' as defined by Gramsci.

Analogously, westernized middle class/élite and Gramsci's intellectuals are concepts which define two overlapping but not identical sets of people. Not all the westernized Indians can be considered as Gramscian intellectuals but only those who were politically aware and politically active. On the other hand, the concept of intellectuals has the advantage of including the politically aware and politically active vernacular literati, whose great importance in the political evolution of late colonial India is now universally acknowledged.

Using Gramsci's notes as a foil, we can better understand the shortcomings of the former key methodological concepts. Turning first to the concept of intermediaries or middlemen, the problem with Washbrook's categorization—quite apart from his total, and quite clearly ideological, disregard for the importance of nationalist ideology—seems to originate from his chronological and geographical area of inquiry. The Madras Presidency in the decades from the 1860s up to the First World War was characterized by a stagnant society, where the process of change was almost non-existent. [...] In sum this was a situation which was economically and socially static, where the politics of the indigenous dominant classes were factional politics, and where a racial and linguistic cleavage existed between the people who controlled the base and those who controlled the apex of the political system. No doubt, in this context, Indian intellectuals acted also, or seemed to act, in the way summarized by Washbrook. However, as soon as the winds of change started to blow, both the situation of the indigenous notables and the role of the westernized Indians appeared in a radically different light. In order to weather the challenges represented by the growing interference of the colonial state and the rise of newly-organized social groups, eager for their share of political power and economic resources, the notables had to organize themselves along class lines. [...] Although a limited number of Indian politicians went on acting as freelance ambassadors between the foreign rulers and Indian social groups, this was a limited and diminishing role.[35] By the early 1920s, the political stage came to be dominated by Indian politicians who acted in the way suggested by Gramsci. They were far from being simple go-betweens and, accordingly, their political standing could not be destroyed by the displeasure of the colonial rulers.[36]

We can now discuss the crucial ambiguity which weakens the concept of westernized middle class/elite and its various avatars, Ray's 'intermediate strata' included. This ambiguity flows from the confusion between the urban non-capitalist bourgeoisie, considered in Marxist terms as an autonomous sort at group, and the politically aware and politically active intellectuals hailing from this class. This confusion has two origins. The first is, quite simply, that in the nineteenth century, practically all the politically aware Indian intellectuals came from the urban petty bourgeoisie. One of those social strata specialized, according to Gramsci, in 'producing' intellectuals. The second, and possibly more important, source of confusion is that in the crucial period in which Indian nationalism took its shape—let us say from the 1860s to the First World War—Indian intellectuals both claimed and believed themselves to be a new middle class.

As we have seen, this attitude, far from being exceptional or surprising, is characteristic of that group of intellectuals whom Gramsci calls traditional intellectuals. No doubt, the westernized

Indians, who mostly hailed from a limited number of high-ranking castes whose members traditionally served the ruling élites and often shared their privileges, were 'traditional' intellectuals. In their case, the normal syndrome according to which the traditional intellectuals 'think of themselves as "independent", autonomous, endowed with a character of their own, etc.' could not but be powerfully strengthened by the revolutionary intellectual upheaval brought about by the acquisition of a totally new culture against a background in which the old culture remained dominant. It is my contention that while, eventually, the new culture furnished the westernized Indians with both a keener perception of historical reality and additional tools for their political armoury, at first this change of their mental categories somewhat blurred their political perception. As a consequence, before being able to take stock of their real position, many westernized Indians tried to act as if part of an autonomous social group, and one potentially endowed with a relevant political weight of its own.

It is in this perspective that we can re-read the history of the social reform movement and its failure in the nineteenth century. Undoubtedly, many westernized intellectuals became convinced that the successful promotion of radical social reforms would be proof of the 'modernity' of the new class to which they claimed to belong and, implicitly, of the existence of a new class able to take the place of the European ruling class. However, in a situation in which Indian society was completely dominated by deeply conservative classes, such as the old landed aristocracy and merchant groups, the social reform policy of the westernized intellectuals was largely unrealistic and self-defeating. Of course, if a modern and politically dominant middle class had existed, the social reforms could have been implemented as an expression of the cultural outlook—Gramsci would say of the cultural hegemony—of the new dominant class. The problem was that, at that stage of the economic development of India, no modern middle class had yet taken shape, let alone staked its claim to political dominance. [...] By 1885, with the foundation of the Congress, even the most 'progressively minded among the social reformers left the social reforms in the background in favour of a strategy aimed at political reforms'.[37]

This shift has usually been seen, both by contemporaries and historians, as resulting from a failure in the moral strength of the individual reformers. My contention is that, on the contrary, it was proof of realism and political maturity. [...] By espousing the cause of political reforms, the 'microscopic minority' which had fancied itself to be a new and crucially important social class found a way out from the political wilderness and began to relate, or try to relate, to its potential constituencies.

THE INDIAN INTELLECTUALS AS STRATEGISTS AND ORGANIZERS

The shift of emphasis on the part of the bulk of the intellectuals from social to political reforms and the individuation of the overthrow of colonialism—sometimes seen as a short-term process, sometimes as a long-term struggle, but always as the main task ahead—[38] came with the realization that the desired objective could be reached only by putting together a wide-ranging alliance, reuniting all the live forces present in Indian society. [...]

In turn, this had three consequences. The first was the mutation of the role of the intellectuals vis-à-vis the old dominant groups. As we have already seen, by the end of the nineteenth century the main role of the traditional intellectuals became [...] that of spokesmen, theorists, strategists, and organizers of the whole class to which the individual notables belonged.

Secondly, while the mutation of the role of the traditional intellectual vis-à-vis the old dominant classes was taking place, a part of the intellectuals—who, sometimes, were the same individuals active in the process described above—began to act as organizers of new and rising social classes or sections of social classes (the latter sometimes defined by ethnic elements, such as religion, caste, or language). Logically enough—and this could be listed as the third reason for the persistent confusion between the class origin and the political role of the westernized Indians—they first got busy in organizing the class from which they hailed, namely the non-capitalist urban bourgeoisie. However, the westernized Indians did not limit their activities, as Gramscian intellectuals, to their origin. Soon enough they began to act as organizers, theorists, and representatives for the modern entrepreneurial class, the industrial workers and, more important, certain sectors of the peasantry. The anti-partition movement in Bengal and the 1919 satyagraha movement at the all-India level exemplify both the remarkable success of the efforts of the Indian intellectuals and its limitations. [...] As a rule, they were successful only as they were able to collaborate with 'organic' intellectuals, namely intellectuals hailing from the new, rising social groups.[39]

The third crucial role performed by the intellectuals was the attempt to devise a strategy which could accommodate all the organized social groups and the groups in the process of getting organized. Certainly, it was not easy to forge and maintain a working coalition of entrepreneurs and working class, zamindars and dominant peasant castes, wealthy professionals and impoverished urban petty bourgeoisie, and so on. Yet, as anybody knows, even allowing for the major qualification that this 'grand alliance' was unable to encompass the bulk of the Indian Muslims, this apparently hopeless task of coalition-building was a resounding success. Of course, it could not have been attained without the remarkable political skills of the Indian nationalist intellectuals. However, it is worth stressing that the *sine qua non* of the 'grand alliance' was the fact that the colonial regime was or became inimical to the interests of all Indian social groups or, in other words, of the Indian people as a whole. [...]

[A]s has most recently been shown by Tomlinson (a historian whom nobody would dare accuse of being over-sympathetic towards Indian nationalism), the imperial commitment, that is, the necessity to subordinate Indian to English interests, increasingly forced the colonial Government to siphon off Indian resources and prevented the implementation of policies favourable to Indian interests.[40] This was a gradual process, which was started in the 1870s by the changing international situation and the beginning of the slow but unstoppable decline of the English economy vis-à-vis those of her main competitors: the USA and Germany.[41] The British, particularly the 'men on the spot', namely the Indian Government, tried their best to cushion or reward their Indian collaborators. However, the imperial commitment eroded slowly but irreversibly the very bases of the colonial regime. [...] [E]ven those indigenous groups whose rise had been made possible by the *pax britannica*, such as the new industrial entrepreneurs, and those other groups whose conservation or power seemed strictly tied to the permanence of British rule, such as the big landlords, had to look out for alternatives to the colonial ruling class and its policies or, better, lack of policies. It was at that point that even the most politically conservative social groups accepted the lead of the nationalist intellectuals or the spokesmen and theorists of these groups espoused the cause of nationalism.

When examined in depth, the process summarized above highlights two important aspects of the role of the intellectuals. The first is that the intellectuals, although able to foresee the evolution of the political setting and plan out a strategy accordingly, were heavily conditioned by the extant political reality. [...] The second point which must be stressed is the following. As mentioned before, the early efforts of the traditional intellectuals, grouped in the Congress, to act as the organizers and representatives of new social groups on the rise were largely fruitless. [....] Very often, the 'organic' intellectuals of these new groups articulated this hostility through the non-Brahman ideology, namely the scathing criticism of the social customs and social pretensions of those Brahmanical castes from which the bulk of the traditional intellectuals hailed. [...] Then in a major turning point in the history of Indian nationalism, during the 1930s most of the former constituencies of these non-Brahman movements and the organic intellectuals of these social groups radically revised their positions and entered the Congress.[42] By doing so, they gave a powerful boost to the Congress by substantiating its long-standing claim to be the true representative of the Indian people as a whole.

This crucial political shift has sometimes been explained as being mainly the product of factional squabbles and opportunistic policies engineered by ruthless politicians who disguised their self-interest under the cloak of a high sounding nationalist rhetoric.[43] We should be highly sceptical of such an explanation, remembering that this turn-about coincided with the devastation of the Indian economy and society made possible by the colonial government's inability to cope with the impact of the world crisis—an inability which was the necessary by-product of the subordinate position of India in the British colonial empire. [...]

INTELLECTUALS AND THE SOCIAL SYSTEM

As a conclusion to our discussion, we must now turn our attention to the relationship between Indian intellectuals and the social system as a whole.

First of all, let us recall the well-known fact that Indian society in the late colonial period was extremely complex, heterogeneous, and segmented. The usual contradictions, to be observed in any society in which capitalism is gradually emerging as the dominant mode of production, were compounded by divisions arising from caste, religious, and linguistic factors. A result of this situation was the absence of any single class able to exercise its hegemony over the whole Indian society. What existed was a heterogeneous cluster of dominant groups characterized by widely divergent interests and outlooks. This made easier the upward mobility of new social formations aiming at becoming part of this loose conglomerate of dominant social groups.

The lack of either a single dominant class or a homogeneous dominant social block resulted in an uneasy balance of power. [...] In this situation any important politician was the representative of an extremely wide and heterogeneous network of interests. Accordingly, his role was not only to represent these interests, but to mediate among them. [...] Clearly, there were physical limits to the size and heterogeneity of the social following which any single politician could manage. Such limits could best be overcome by making use of political organizations. By far the most successful of these organizations was the Congress. Since its foundation, the Congress set as its goal that of representing the whole Indian people. As has already been noticed, this meant the elaboration of policies which could be seen as an acceptable compromise by all the organized and organizing social groups, no matter how heterogeneous their interests were. During the colonial era, this strategy on the part of the Congress reached its highest point in the years 1937 to 1939. [...]

From that period the countdown to the end of British Empire in India began, even if the changed relationship of power between the nationalist movement and the Raj remained concealed up to the moment when the Quit India crisis revealed it suddenly and dramatically.[44] However, what does matter here is that it was the presence inside the Congress of these heterogeneous interests which at the same time set the limits and opened a vast room for manoeuvre to the Congress as a political organization and to its political leadership. Men such as Mohandas Gandhi and, after him, Jawaharlal Nehru were not primarily the representatives of certain class or group interests. Nor were they simple umpires who supervised the observers of certain fixed rules of the political game and sanctioned the victory of the strongest team. They were politicians who, because of their technical skill in reconciling divergent interests and the personal prestige which they enjoyed, in part because of this ability, could wield an autonomous power and act as independent centres of power.[45]

So, after having begun by denying any autonomous role to the politically aware intellectuals, we have ended up by acknowledging that, within limits, they sometimes were able to play such a role. I admit that this is not fully consistent. But, as Bertrand Russell claims when speaking of Locke's philosophy, 'no one has yet succeeded in inventing a philosophy at once credible and self-consistent' and 'there is no reason to suppose that a self-consistent system contains more truth than one which...is more or less wrong'.[46] I do hope that my methodological proposal, in spite of its rather paradoxical conclusion, might be accepted by my fellow scholars as a useful methodological tool.

NOTES

1. The key passages of Macaulay's 'Minute' are available in W.M. Theodore de Bary (ed.), *Sources of Indian Tradition* (New York, 1966) vol. II, p. 49.

2. Sir Surendranath Banerjea, *A Nation in Making* (1925; Bombay, 1963), *passim*. Banerjea's quotation is from *The Bengalee*, 17 February 1921 [sic. 1911]. It is cited in Rajat K. Ray, 'Three Interpretations of Indian Nationalism', in B.R. Nanda (ed.), *Essays in Modern Indian History* (Delhi, 1980), p. 1. Another nationalist theorist who played a relevant role in giving currency to the concept of a new middle class was Aurobindo Ghose in his essays entitled *New Lamps for Old*, originally published in the *Indu Prakash* in 1893/94. For an assessment of Aurobindo's contribution see B.N. Ganguli, 'Conceptualizing the Indian Middle Class', in K.S. Krishnaswamy and Ashok Mitra, (eds), *Society and Change: Essays in Honour of Sachin Chaudhuri* (Bombay, 1977).

3. For two among many examples of the official way of thinking on the subject see Sir Valentine Chirol, *Indian Unrest* (London, 1910) and Sir Reginald Craddock, *The Dilemma in India* (London, 1929).

4. Dufferin's notorious statement was delivered in his farewell speech, on the 30 November 1888. See John R. McLane, *Indian Nationalism and the Early Congress* (Princeton, 1977), pp. 116-17. For Dufferin's conviction that Indian society was horizontally divided between 'the educated Babus, and the uneducated masses' see Bipan Chandra, *Nationalism and Colonialism in Modern India* (New Delhi, 1979), pp. 275 ff.

5. That limited discussion which did take place hinged on the definition of the term *bhadralok*, first used by J.H. Broomfield, in his *Elite Conflict in a Plural Society* (Berkeley, 1968) in order to define the Bengali westernized middle class. See Sumit Sarkar, *The Swadeshi Movement in Bengal 1903-8* (New Delhi, 1973), pp. 509ff. and L.A. Gordon, *Bengal: The Nationalist Movement 1876-1940* (New York, 1974), pp. 7ff.

6. Eric Stokes, 'The Return of the Peasant to South Asian History' *South Asia*, 6, (December 1976), p. 98.

7. David Washbrook, 'Gandhian Politics', *Modern Asian Studies*, 7, (1973), p. 107; Washbrook drew on his own and C.A. Bayly's, C.J. Baker's, and R.A. Gordon's dissertations. All these dissertations, with the exception of the latter (R.A. Gordon, 'Aspects in the History of the Indian National Congress, with special reference to the Swarajya Party', Oxford University, 1970), were soon to be published.

8. Washbrook, 'Gandhian Politics', p. 109. The previous quotations are from pp. 107-9.

9. Ibid., p. 110.
10. Ibid. (emphasis added)
11. Ibid.
12. Ibid.
13. By now, the term 'Cambridge school' has become part of the jargon of Indian historians. However, there is considerable confusion about who belongs to that school, what are its distinctive features, or even if that school has ever existed (a fact which is denied by some of its members). Throughout this article, when speaking of 'Cambridge school', I designate those scholars whose research, one way or another, went to building and developing the interpretative model whose main features were summed up by Anil Seal in the essay 'Imperialism and Nationalism in India', which opened the monographic issue of *Modern Asian Studies*, 7, 3, (1973) later reprinted as John Gallagher, Gordon Johnson and Anil Seal (eds), *Locality, Province and Nation: Essays on Indian Politics*, 1870 to 1940 (Cambridge, 1973).
14. Judith M. Brown, *Gandhi and Civil Disobedience: the Mahatma in Indian Politics, 1928–34* (Cambridge, 1977).
15. John Gallagher, 'Congress in Decline: Bengal, 1930 to 1939', *Modern Asian Studies*, 7, (1973), pp. 589–645.
16. C.A. Bayly, 'Patrons and Politics in Northern India', *Modern Asian Studies*, 7, (1973), pp. 349–88.
17. Bayly, *The Local Roots of Indian Politics: Allahabad, 1880–1920*, (Oxford, 1975); the quotations are from p. 273.
18. B.R. Tomlinson, *The Indian National Congress and the Raj, 1929–42: The Penultimate Phase* (London, 1976). See also his 'Congress and the Raj: Political Mobilization in Late Colonial India', in *Modern Asian Studies*, 16, 1982, pp. 334–49.
19. Rajat K. Ray, 'Political Change in British India', *The Indian Economic and Social History Review*, XIV, (1977), pp. 493–513.
20. Ray bases his thesis on Satish Chandra, *Parties and Politics at the Mughal Court 1707–40* (New Delhi, 1959); M. Athar Ali, *The Mughal Nobility under Aurangzeb* (Bombay, 1968); and the articles by Bernard S. Cohn, Philip B. Calkins, and Karen Leonard *The Journal of Asian Studies*, XIX, (August 1960), pp. 418–31, XXIX, August 1970, pp.799–806, and XXX, (May 1971), pp. 569–82.
21. Ray makes the important point that in pre-colonial Indian society not only class solidarity but also caste and community ties did not have an existence of their own at the super-local level. Accordingly, 'the activation not only of class forces but also of caste sentiments and communal passions in the twentieth-century mass politics must be sought in a relatively modern process of social and political change.' Ray, 'Political Change', p. 500. My own research on Surat in the second half of the eighteenth century shows that caste and religious ties were as often elements of solidarity as factors of division among the members of any given religious/caste community. Accordingly, even at the local level, communal solidarity cannot be considered as an important factor of social mobilization. See my 'Surat during the Second Half of the Eighteenth Century. What Kind of Social Order?– A Rejoinder to Lakshmi Subramanian', *Modern Asian Studies*, 21, 4 (1987).

22. Ray, 'Political Change', pp. 506-7.
23. Ibid., pp. 509-10.
24. On the concept of 'intermediate strata' see Michail Kaleki, 'Social and Economic Aspects of "Intermediate Regimes"', in *Essays on the Economic Growth of the Socialist and the Mixed Economy*, (Cambridge, 1972) and K.N. Raj, 'The Politics and Economics of "Intermediate Regimes"', *Economic and Political Weekly*, 7 July 1973.
25. Ray, 'Political Change', p. 510.
26. Ibid., pp. 511-13.
27. Either the westernized Indians were a social group or, as Washbrook implies, they were members of a cultural category. In the former case they were bound to act mainly according to their own group/class interest; in the latter case they would not have an overriding group/class interest, whereas their common cultural/educational interests would be of lesser import. This, in turn would allow the individual members of the 'westernized Indians' cultural category to perform their most significant political role as intermediaries among the existing power groups.
28. The striking analogies between the Italian Risorgimento and the Indian nationalist era have first been remarked on by Sumit Sarkar. As far as I know, Sarkar is the first Indian historian to point out the potential usefulness of Gramsci's reflections on Italian history in general and the Risorgimento in particular as a methodological compass which could be employed in analysing Indian history during the nationalist era. See the conclusion of his *The Swadeshi Movement*. Since then, several historians, either contributing to the publication of Ranajit Guha (ed.) *Subaltern Studies* (Delhi: vol. I, 1982, vol. II, 1983, vol. III, 1984) or working under the leadership of Professor Bipan Chandra (see his 'Presidential Address: The Long-Term Dynamics of the Indian National Congress, Indian History Congress': Forty-Sixth Session, Amritsar, 1985) have made large use of Gramscian categories. In my own case, the stimulus to make use of Gramscian concepts is a natural result of my own Italian cultural background.
29. Quintin Hoare and Geoffrey Nowell Smith (eds), *Selections from the Prison Notebooks of Antonio Gramsci* (New York, 1983; first edn, 1971), p. 5. The original of this and the other quotations made hereafter in Antonio Gramsci, *Gli intellettuali e l'organizzazione della cultura* (Torino, 1949).
30. Hoare and Smith, *Selections from...Gramsci*, p. 11.
31. Ibid., p.7.
32. Ibid.
33. Ibid.
34. Ibid., p. 10. See also 'Bellettristica storica' in Antonio Gramsci, *Passato e presente* (Torino, 1951), pp. 29-32.
35. Sir Tej Bahadur Sapru can be pointed out as one of the few examples of Indian politicians who, in the 1920s and 1930s, while limiting their political role to that of go-between, were nevertheless able to exercise some influence on the unfolding of the events.
36. So, for example, Gandhi's defeat and eclipse at the end of the civil disobedience movement of 1930-4 was not the result of the unwillingness of part of the Raj to accept him as a go-between but the outcome of the

The Myth of a 'Westernized Middle Class'   67

heavy disproportion of strength then existing between the colonial state the nationalist movement. After all, that was still the time when the Raj, in the words of B.N. Gupta, who was just then beginning his career as a future Congress boss, 'filled the sky' like a giant. See the interview with B.N. Gupta quoted in James Manor, 'Anomie in Indian Politics', *Economic and Political Weekly*, Annual Number: (January 1983), p. 725.

37. Of course, some individual intellectuals went on working mainly as social reformers. But, by doing so, they cut themselves off from the mainstream of Indian politics. On the whole question of the social reform movement see Charles H. Heimsath, *Indian Nationalism and Hindu Social Reform* (Princeton, 1964). See also Sudhir Chandra, 'Hindu Conservatism in the Nineteenth Century' in *Economic and Political Weekly*, 12 December 1970, and Tarashkar Banerjee, 'Social Movement in Bengal in the Nineteenth Century—an Assessment', *Indo-British Review*, 5, d.n., pp. 39-47.

38. On this point see Bipan Chandra's stimulating remarks in his 'Presidential Address: The Long-Term Dynamics of the Indian National Congress'.

39. This is implicitly shown by much research work. See, for example, Eugene F. Irshick, *Politics and Social Conflict[in South India: the non-Brahman Movement and Tamil Separatism, 1916-29* (Berkeley, 1969); David Arnold, 'The Gounders and Congress: Political Recruitment in South India, 1920-37', *South Asia*, no. 4, (October 1974), pp. 1-20; and Rosalind O'Hanlon, 'Acts of appropriation: non-Brahman radicals and the Congress in early twentieth-century Maharashtra', Paper presented at the Canadian Conference on the Centenary of the Indian National Congress, Concordia University, Montreal, 16-18 May 1986.

40. See the series of excellent studies by B.R. Tomlinson on the growing contradiction between England and the British Empire on one hand and India on the other, namely: 'India and the British Empire 1880-1935' and 'India and the British Empire 1935-47', *Indian Economic and Social History Review*, XII, (1975), pp. 337-80, and XIII, (1976), pp. 331-52; *The Political Economy of the Raj 1914-47* (London, 1979); 'The Contradiction of England', *The Journal of Imperial and Commonwealth History*, XI, (1982), pp. 58-72. On the same subject see also John Gallagher and Anil Seal, 'Britain and India between the Wars', *Modern Asian Studies*, 15, (1981), pp. 387-414.

41. On the initial phase of this process and India's role in cushioning British economy against its adverse effects see Marcello De Cecco, *Economia e finanza internazionale dal 1890 al 1914* (Bari, 1971), chs II and IV.

42. For a description of this process in Maharashtra, see O'Hanlon, 'Acts of appropriation'...

43. For example, C.J. Baker, *The Politics of South India, 1870-1920* (Cambridge, 1976).

44. Francis G. Hutchins, *India's Revolution: Gandhi and the Quit India Movement* (Cambridge, Mass. 1973), chs 9 and 10. For an alternative view see Gowher Rizvi, 'The Congress Revolt of 1942: A Historical Revision', *Indo-British Review*, Xl, (December 1984), pp. 28-45.

45. Of course even powerful leaders such as Gandhi and Nehru could not

hope to take on the whole party victoriously by themselves. But, within limits, they had the strength to push through policies which were judged superfluous or even harmful by influential sectors of the party and the social groups which they represented. My contention is that the same was true at the lower levels of the party organization in the case of provincial/state or local leaders. In other words, the politicians, although conditioned in their actions by their following, could come to enjoy substantial room for autonomous action. All the story of Nehru's partially successful attempt at planned economic development can be seen in this light.

46. Bertrand Russell, *History of the Western Philosophy* (London, 1979), 3, P I, ch. XIII, p. 592.

A Pre-History of the Middle Class?*

C.A. BAYLY

[...] Indian nationalism of the later nineteenth century needs a longer perspective. We need to soften the sharp break between tradition and nationalist modernity, and between east and west, which still impoverishes the historical literature. Excellent studies have shown that Indians passionately debated religion before the mid-nineteenth century.[1] Other histories reveal how Indians represented shifts in political power through festivals and cultural performances,[2] but historians, following anthropologists have often over-emphasized the importance of broad ideological principles such as segmentation and hierarchy; this has blighted intellectual historiography. Public opinion—the weight of reasoned debate—was not the preserve of modern or western polities. Ironically, as European observers occasionally admitted, the support of British military detachments tended to make Indian magnates less, not more, amenable to the opinion of their subjects. The Indian versions of degenerate Roman emperors—the 'Caligulas and Commoduses'[3] whom Sir Henry Elliot scornfully denounced—were products of British tutelage rather than avatars of the Indian past. Many publicists of the later nineteenth century were drawing on techniques of communication, debate, and persuasion which owed as much to Indian norms as they did to Comte or Mazzini. Even after 1885 western public debates had not

---

* Originally published as 'The Indian Ecumene: An Indigenous Public Sphere', in C.A. Bayly *Empire and Information: Intelligence Gathering and Social Communication in India, 1780–1870* (Cambridge: Cambridge University Press, 2000), pp. 180–211. For the complete text see the original. In the present version, some portions of the essay have been removed and notes rearranged accordingly.

altogether subsumed indigenous discourse about rights, duties, and good kingship as some studies have argued.[4] Recent polemics against the 'derivative' character of modern Indian political ideology have not even begun to characterize indigenous political theory and practice. This chapter considers political theory, individuality, rationality, and social communication in the Indian context. These, of course, are all essential elements in the concept of critical politics which developed in the west and they all find a place in Jurgen Habermas's influential discussion of the 'public sphere'.[5] All had analogues within the north Indian *ecumene*.

I use the word ecumene to describe the form of cultural and political debate which was typical of north India before the emergence of the newspaper and public association, yet persisted in conjunction with the press and new form of publicity into the age of nationalism. For classical writers, ecumene conveyed the sense of the inhabited or civilized world. In Christian times it came to mean a universal, godly civilization embodied in a community of affection and constantly renovated through a discourse of worship, rights, and obligations. Thus, according to the Oxford English Dictionary, 'the head of the Christian family or *oikoumene* was the Emperor in Constantinople'. Similar critical ecumenes existed in most complex civilizations of the era before print as an ideal of the 'godly city' and as a set of actual political processes. Their relationships to the later imagined communities of print and nationhood need to be examined with greater care.[6]

The ecumene of Hindustani-writing literati, Indo-Islamic notables and officers of state (which included many Hindus) fought its battles with a well-tested arsenal of handwritten media. The guardians of the ecumene represented the views of bazaar people and artisans when urban communities came under pressure. Their connections spread across religious, sectarian, and caste boundaries, though they never dissolved them. A common background in the Indo-Persian and, to a lesser extent, Hindu classics enlightened them. The theme of high-minded friendship animated the poets, scholars, and officials who conversed along these networks and set the tone for them. Though suffused with pride of country, the ecumene remained cosmopolitan, receiving information and ideas from central and west Asia as well as from within a dimly defined 'Hindustan'.[7] In this sense, it was closer in spirit to the groupings of philosophers, urban notables and officials in the world of late antiquity—the Christian-Greek ecumene—

than it was to Habermas' modern public. His public sphere is more sharply separated from the world of intimate social relations; people's judgement is represented through marketed print in an almost mechanical way. The Indian ecumene, however, does bear comparison to the modern European public in the sense that its leaders were able to mount a critical surveillance of government and society. How was this possible in a world supposedly encompassed by religious principles and despotic kingship?

IDEOLOGIES AND SOCIAL CRITIQUE

In political theory, the western public emerged from ideological debates which had contested and confirmed authority since the beginnings of Christendom. The dual inheritance of Roman Law and feudal liberties blunted the authority of both King and Pope. The Reformation encouraged personal interpretation of scripture in accordance with conscience. Superficially, 'Islam' and 'Hinduism' appear to weave seamless webs of authority, leaving no ideological space for the emergence of any species of critical public. Islamic Law was both canon and secular law, pre-empting the kind of contestation which developed inside Christendom. The Hindu order, at least as it is interpreted by Louis Dumont, subsumed the political order.[8] The individual will was subjected to the collectivity through the institution of caste and the pragmatics of purity and pollution.

Yet even in theory, still more in practice, authority within these Indian conceptual systems was actually quite friable and ambiguous. In Muslim thought the authority of the sultan was most uncertain and in the Twelver Shia tradition even verged on the illegitimate.[9] The sultan's power was limited by Islamic Law and the interpretation of the learned, but also by the collective authority of the tribe and the general assembly of believers. [...] Many Sufis distanced themselves from political power. Their tomb-shrines, headquarters of spiritual provinces, became alternative sources of social power.[10] [...]

Though little is made of this in studies of the western public, the notion of individual property right (as an electoral qualification, for instance) lies close to the idea of the public. In India, hereditable proprietary right (*watan*, *zamindari*, *milkiyat*) was not subject to appropriation by the state as Enlightenment thinkers averred. This error was a consequence of the European obsession with Oriental Despotism, which confused the rights of office-holders with the rights of patrimony.[11] Religious donations also functioned as a realm of liberties outside the state's purview in a manner not unlike 'mortmain' in Christendom. It is within the religious corporation that some latter-day Weberians see the beginnings of both transcendent bureaucracy and civil society in Europe.[12] India does not seem to be an exception here. Most important, the notion of government (*sarkar*) came to hold a virtue beyond the will of the king of the moment, so becoming an equivalent to European 'public authority'.[13] This Indo-Muslim conception of government embodied sophisticated concepts of just and unjust rule, *zulum* ('oppression'), which could be introduced into popular debate on the merits of rulers through poetic satire, handbills, speeches and by ironic visual displays during popular festivals.

Even the authority of Islamic Law (Shariat) was ambiguous enough to leave room for personal judgement. The 'doors of interpretation' (*idjtihad*) of the Koran and Sayings of the Prophet were thrust ajar on many occasions in Islamic history. As more rationalistic and legalistic schools of jurisconsult emerged, the independent judgement of the massed doctors of law came to take precedence over both traditional interpretations and charismatic authority. [...]

The monolithic appearance of Islamic Law was also limited by the concept of custom (*dastur*). This could be extended to the customary law of Muslim tribes, the *kanun* or royal law, or even the customs of the infidel subjects.[14] In India, the local law officers adjudicated cases according to Islamic precepts, but Hindus were not bound to submit to their jurisdiction. [...]

The theory of the Hindu Dharmic order was fragile to a similar degree. The purity of the Brahmin and hence his authority was compromised by his position in society. He could withdraw and preserve his purity, like the Sannyasi or renouncer,[15] or he could participate in society and its rituals and risk pollution. Both in theory and in practice, therefore, the Brahmin became a tricky, dangerous commodity, a thorn in the flesh of both king and layman. The non-Brahminism of the late nineteenth-century public possessed a deep historical lineage in the popular critique of Brahmin pretensions in earlier centuries.[16] [...] Many verses written in interpretation of the classic political theories are implicit warnings to the king not to transgress the very limited bounds of his authority.[17] The king's authority, as Heesterman argues, was a conundrum; it was also friable.

These structural ambiguities of the key figures in the Indian hierarchy were compounded by two more general concepts which compromised the coherence of authority in general. First, there was the notion of Apadharma, or those conditions under which the ideal, righteous Dharmic order ceases to function. [...] Apadharma could be introduced to legitimate violations of caste rules, the suspension of religious ceremonies, the abandonment of hereditary occupation or the commission of unrighteous deeds by kings and Brahmins. Secondly, influential teachers preached personal devotion to God (*bhakti*) and proclaimed the irrelevance of all worldly hierarchies.[18] Though they were not 'revolutionary' in a modern sense, bhakti movements encouraged people to question social and political authority, and in many cases they prescribed rational rules for social life.[19] Since all power in India was ideologically compromised, the learned and respectable 'middling sort' took it upon themselves to maintain a constant critical vigilance over the doings of state and society.

NORMS AND CONTEXTS OF DEBATE

Though authority and sanctity weighed heavily in these Indian debates they might still reflect 'the critical judgement of a public making use of its reason'.[20] Some Europeans saw India as a 'dream society'. Others, however, noticed the existence of rational sciences and modes of debate within Indian traditions.[21] [...] Several scholars have [...] noted the steady rise of the rational sciences of jurisprudence, medicine, and mathematics among the international Indo-Muslim intelligentsia during the seventeenth and eighteenth centuries.[22] Finally, what Peter Burke has called 'literal-mindedness' even seems to permeate the world of theology in the eighteenth and nineteenth centuries when matter-of-fact, but authoritative Persian and Urdu began to oust the prolix and flowery writing of earlier periods in works such as Muhammad Ismail's key text for the 'Wahhabi' reformers, the 'Refuge of the Faith' (*Taqwiyat al-Iman*).[23]

What was the context for these debates on politics and society? Assemblies and places of debate (*sabha*s, *katha*s, *panchayat*s, and *samaj*s) represented more than the blind sense of collectivities denominated as tribes, castes, or religious sects.[24] [...] A similar point has been made forcefully by Mattison Mines in his recent critique of Dumont.[25] Mines argues that the politics of south India from early times should be understood in terms of the interplay of the 'public reputations' of 'big men' among peasants and commercial people, in competition with each other and sometimes in conflict with the authorities. Even the fabled temple-building of the south represents, in Mines' analysis, not the agency of castes and corporations, but the individual aspirations of patrons expressed through institutions. Thus the words for association—samaj and sabha—which become part of the western-style debate of the later nineteenth century were not simply communities. Such words could be used to designate collectivities which spilled over the boundaries of social and religious groupings and represented temporary collections of individuals engaged in debate or judgement. [...] This was a formula which guaranteed a kind of political representation to influential local people, not to mobilized castes or religious communities.

In the cities of north India, the office-holders, jurists, Sufi elders and community counsellors were the key people who represented the 'opinion of the locality' to the authorities. They also acted as a critical audience for the rulers' policies. For instance, the judge (*kazi*) of Banaras led Muslim protests against unlawful changes in city government in the mid-eighteenth century.[26] In 1816 it was the mufti of Bareilly, also a Sufi teacher, who led the popular movement of both Hindus and Muslims against the British authorities when they attempted to introduce house taxation into northern Indian cities.[27] Historically the learned, the local office-holders and the 'honourable' (*ashraf*) had acted as a check on the ephemeral ruling elites of the Muslim world. [...]

These officers were Islamic in form but non-Muslim people referred to them for adjudication and leadership, and they continued to flourish even in regions where Mughal rule had given way to Hindu or Sikh dynasties in the eighteenth century. Without doubt the question of the representation of Hindus within the ecumene is a complex one. But the model of two opposed 'religious communities' is certainly wrong. Though the religious establishments of the two major religions continued to keep their distance from one another, well-tried procedures of arbitration, joint representation and mutual consultation between Hindus and Muslims had evolved over a long period. Imbalances and asymmetries there were, but the same can be said of the participation of Catholics, Protestants, and Jews in the emerging western European public sphere.

The learned and respectable elites kept up a constant conversation on matters of religious wisdom through ritual and official *darbar*s, mosque schools, the Sufi orders, and private homes. In early nineteenth-century Delhi bodies of scholars and gentlemen met in the houses of local officers such as the kazi and the *sadr-ul-sudr* to debate matters as apparently trivial as the licitness of eating mangoes (a fruit not mentioned in the scriptures).[28] There also was a long tradition of free-thinking and debate about the status of non-Islamic religion and culture.[29] Congregational meetings among the Muslim community during the nights of the month of Ramadan provided a forum for wider discussions on matters concerning the community, and the consensus of these meetings might be conveyed to the rulers.[30] Alongside this, the educated maintained a debate on literature, language, and aesthetics through poetry-reading circles or *mushairah*s. The chapter now turns to three forms of public debate centring on public religion, history, and literary propriety.

PUBLIC DOCTRINE AND THE ECUMENE

The guardians of the ecumene among the Muslim gentlefolk were concerned to detect violations in religious law and custom. To an extent, Hindu leaders associated with elite Muslim circles sought to protect and explain the role of their coreligionists within the polity. This was not the blind clash of religious communities, rather a series of transactions about the public face of religious observation. The debate over the rights and privileges of Shias and Hindus among Sunni Muslims was often literate and measured.[31] Even orthodox Sunni participants, for example, allowed that it was legitimate for Shias and 'polytheists' to participate in debates about public doctrine, though they might detest their beliefs. [...]

The disintegration of the Mughal Empire after 700 set the scene for the sharpening of debates between Sunnis, Shias, and Hindus. These had political, social, and ethnic, as well as doctrinal implications. [...] Conflict within the ruling cliques of Delhi and Hyderabad during the eighteenth century was often expressed in terms of doctrinal difference, while sarcastic comment attributed the political failings of notables to their religious and racial backgrounds.[32] Moreover, these controversies spilled over into political and social matters— luxury, debt, and the decline of manufacture as well as 'religion'.[33] [...] These debates (*munazarah*) were governed by certain standards of conduct which implicitly acknowledged the existence of a critical public sphere.[34] Thus Dildar Ali, champion of Shi'ism, religiously sent copies of his works to the Delhi Sunni jurists (although the latter only responded with denunciations).[35] Social and political changes concurrently encouraged Muslim literati to take a greater interest in the newly powerful Hindu rulers and merchants. For example, the historian and administrator, Khairuddin Khan Illahabadi, followed the tradition of Akbar and debated with the Banaras pandits on matters of history and cosmology, showing deep knowledge of their scriptures.[36] [...]

Insistent doctrinal debate and campaigns of purification amongst urban citizens therefore preceded and accompanied the Christian missionary and the 'reform' campaigns of the early nineteenth century.[37] Controversy about public doctrine was in the air. Missionaries found 'the Mahomedan mind in a state of considerable enquiry'.[38] They targeted towns such as Lucknow or Jaunpur where 'party feeling' between Sunnis and Shias, or between Wahhabis and broad-church Muslims, had already taken root. Muslims, moreover, were already strengthening their popular base before Christian missionaries and the supposedly secular colonial government confronted them. By 1845, Urdu translations of the Koran were in use among the reformist Muslims.[39]

The appearance of print added a powerful new weapon to the arsenal of debate within the ecumene. When Christian missionaries began to pour printed propaganda into north India, its guardians responded vigorously, initiating formal logical contests and written refutations.[40] Missionaries were often surprised by the vehemence with which not only the religious teachers, but also local officers, *thanadars* (superintendents) and *kotwals*,[41] engaged them in debate. These were not cowed victims of colonial power. These were trustees of a public doctrine which seemed under threat. [...]

In the Hindu world, too, the activities of Brahmins and ruling-caste men had long transcended their ascribed functions as priests and warriors. Brahmins filled a similar role to Sheikhs and Sayyids as local justiciars, counsellors, literary arbiters, astronomers, and doctors. The late eighteenth and early nineteenth centuries saw continuing formal debates between different schools of the Hindu learned about scripture and philosophy.[42] But, faced with direct attacks on their spiritual clienteles by Christians, priestly Brahmins had now to defend, to rationalize, to preach, and to grasp the new tools of publicity. Some missionaries resorted to physical violence and coercion, such as 'shaking' the fakirs out of their spiritual trance.[43] More often, they found themselves drawn into complex and inconclusive debates which raged around the nature of godhead, the age of the universe, and the qualities of good kingship, so touching directly on the political realm and claims to truth of western science. [...] A generation before the modernist Arya Samaj stepped in to defend ancient religion with print, north Indian Hindu scholars were employing their skills of logical debate to refute, rebuff, or incorporate the missionaries. This was no simple Hindu 'reaction' to western 'impact'; instead, the headstrong Westerners plunged into a torrent of controversy which had for centuries pitted Vaishnavite scholars against Buddhists and Jains, Siddhantists against the Puranas, and devotional gurus against the orthodox. All these formally doctrinal issues, however, bore on the question of good kingship and social propriety.

SPEECH AND CRITICAL AESTHETIC COMMENT

An important precondition for the development of this widespread debate on religion and politics was the flexibility and accessibility of the Hindustani or Urdu language itself (Urdu is used here to mean the more refined and Persianized form of the common north Indian language, Hindustani). Urdu came to impart to the discussions of the ecumene a popular character which was difficult when Arabic and Persian totally dominated them. The turn towards Urdu in the courts and camps of north India in the eighteenth and nineteenth centuries represented a deliberate populist strategy on the part of the elite. [...]

Urdu/Hindustani itself had not taken on the character of the public tongue of the ecumene. It was a popular language spread by Sufi saints and Hindu devotees and a language of the court and a discerning literati. [...] Outside centres of high Urdu court culture some Muslims continued to use the Devanagari character. The devotional poetry of the fifteenth- and sixteenth-century Sufi teachers was as likely to be found in the Devanagari as in the Persian script. [...] Thus regional versions of Hindustani appear to have carried overtones of community and harmony. [...]

Poetic assemblies held in the court, in the houses of notables and in the shops of bazaar people, spread common standards of aesthetic judgement and common forms of language across the country. Urdu writing was not confined to a self-conscious realm of literature. Instead, it was a discourse among men of weight on matters of aesthetics, health, religion, and politics. Aristocratic writers were honoured in this world, but their rank did not exempt their ideas, their forms of letter-writing or their calligraphy, from critical scrutiny.[44] The poet Mir is alleged to have ridiculed the Emperor Shah Alam for his poetry. The Emperor had claimed that he was such a good poet that he could dash off several poems while he was doing his ablutions in the morning; 'Yes, and they smell like it,' said Mir.[45]

Aesthetic issues could become more directly political. The debate between the advocates of Persian and those of Urdu had ethnic, class, and religious undertones.[46] Though they enjoyed the patronage of the royal family, by the 1840s the proponents of Urdu were often less consciously aristocratic than the champions of Persian and were more influenced by Indian forms.[47]

One literary form which reflected and perpetuated the memory of the ecumene was the *tazkirah*, or collective literary biography. Literature here went beyond poetry to topics as diverse as medicine and topography. Through such works literary lineage and styles of endeavour could be traced over many generations. Having one's name entered in a major tazkirah guaranteed some degree of literary immortality, and individuality. These collective biographies demonstrate the diverse origins of the people who were known to the Indian critical public. [...] Among the noted poets were sons of washermen, water-carriers, tailors, an 'occulist and chess-player', a 'talented man who have himself up to profligacy', 'a great drunkard', and so on. Just as Islam was supposed to pay no attention to class in matters of faith, so in matters of style and literary excellence, men from humble backgrounds could achieve great fame.

In the 1840s Alois Sprenger carried out a detailed analysis of a number of literary biographies, including one of the Persian poets of Calcutta and Banaras, which paints a complex picture of social communication and the geography of the ecumene.[48] The literary men were often drawn from the old officers of the towns and *qasbah*s, such as the kazi and the King of Awadh's newswriter at Banaras.[49] [...] Others were dispersed remnants of the Delhi royal house, the Shahzadas of Banaras. Imperial family members who had been exiled or who had fled to Lucknow and Patna became the hubs of patterns of cultural patronage. Many of the people honoured worked in British government offices. They included residency *munshi*s, clerks to the Calcutta Court of Appeal, clerks of the customs department at Banaras, and others in more lowly official positions who still cultivated Persian and Hindustan letters. [...]

People of poor background were not as evident here. [...] Sprenger, however, listed many humbler authors in a comprehensive listing of tazkirahs, accounting for more than 1,800 literary people. Here, for instance, there were druggists,[50] a serving woman,[51] a Hazrat (one who had memorized the Koran) who kept an apothecary's shop in the Nakhas cattle market of Banaras,[52] a common writer,[53] a tailor skilled in *marsiya*s (lamentations on the Shia martyrs),[54] a Hyderabad 'dancing woman'[55] and many others. Hindus accounted for a small but significant percentage of the list. Most of these were from the Kashmiri Brahmin, Khattri, or Kayastha communities and were traditionally associated with Persian and Urdu through Mughal service. There were, however, occasional entries for men of the Hindu commercial castes. One Eurasian even appeared: John Thomas, a 'soldier-like man',[56] son of George Thomas, who had founded a small state in Hariana at the end of the eighteenth century.

So it was not only men of power who participated in the literary activities of the ecumene. The egalitarian traditions of the Islamic lands and the community sensibilities of Indian cities encouraged ordinary artisans and people of the bazaars to aspire to eminence as poets or commentators. The form of the language was inclusive; it mirrored and even helped to stimulate the rapid social mobility which was characteristic of post-Mughal north India. Even women wrote and circulated poems.[57] In Lucknow, noblewomen, courtesans, musicians, dancers, and other cultural performers from poor backgrounds achieved power in court and urban politics. This gravely offended evangelical Christian commentators and some later Indian purists, who saw corruption and decadence in what was actually striking social mobility.

HISTORY, LIBRARIES, AND SOCIAL MEMORY

Alongwith questions of public doctrine and literary aesthetics, 'history' and topography played an important role in maintaining the identity of the ecumene. History in the Indo-Muslim tradition was, as Peter Hardy has written, a protean form which merged into poetry, moral and political instruction, and theology.[58] Amir Khusrau's poetic and panegyric history of the fourteenth century began a tradition which still had its imitators in the eighteenth century when court historians rendered the deeds of the founders of the successor states into ornate Persian. More influential yet in our period was the historical work of Abul Fazl. The 'Ain' and the 'Akbarnamah' were read and discussed extensively by the literati of the successor states and the munshis of the British offices. [...] They represented the strain of historical and moral philosophy which inspired Mirza Jan-i Janan to reaffirm the theology of Ibn-i Arabi, and the doctrine of the immanence of God, against the more exclusive doctrines of the Delhi theologians, Shah Waliullah and Shah Abdul Aziz. It inspired that archetypical denizen of the ecumene, Ghali, to describe ecstatically the sight of the festival of lights, Diwali, at Banaras, 'the Mecca of India'.[59] Despite his earlier adherence to a purist creed, Sayyid Ahmad's description of Delhi displays similar affection for the Hindu and Jain temples which had arisen in the city.[60]

This sense of the luminosity of place, and of the pleasures and ease of the erstwhile great and culturally diverse empire of Hindustan, was a compelling motif for much of the poetic-cum-historical work of the eighteenth and early nineteenth centuries. Hindus and Muslims, peasant and poet, were united in a wistful remembrance of what was and what might have been. This mode of elegiac historiography reached its fullest expression in the works of 'social poets' such as Sauda and Nazir who elaborated the form called *ashob sheher*,[61] 'bewailing the fallen greatness of the city', that is, the civilization of Mughal India. It also expressed itself in what is conventionally called 'history' (though the word *tarikh* does not quite mean history). [...]

Libraries, or rather 'book houses' provided the resources from which this social memory in the fields of history, literature, and theology was drawn. Indian libraries were no doubt highly unstable by European standards. Often they were built up out of patterns of princely gift-exchange[62] or plunder,[63] as annexes to royal treasuries. Royal and noble libraries were looted by their guardians as well as by external enemies.[64] Many Indian libraries were also exclusive. Temple libraries among Hindus and Jains were generally available only to priests; sacred knowledge was dangerous and had to be stored in safe places.[65] This literary memory, however, was neither negligible nor sealed off from the debates of the ecumene. The largest libraries comprised tens of thousands of volumes,[66] while many thousands of families had smaller collections amounting to a handful of manuscripts. There is some evidence, too, that a more specialist understanding of the library was developing among the elites even before the colonial period; in Jaipur, for example, Raja Jai Singh separated off a study collection from his treasury and this was used by the king and his officials in adjudications on religious and social issues.[67] Though never public, these collections could sometimes serve as a resource for the wider learned community. On occasion the Lucknow Royal Library was asked to produce a text when a controversy between the Muslim learned and Christian missionaries took place.[68] Scholars from outside princely families were allowed to see and copy texts. Sayyid Ahmad

Khan, for example, was one person who was allowed to work in the Delhi Royal Library.[69]

COMMUNICATIONS AND POLITICAL DEBATE

Historians agree that in the west the public sphere was a domain of communication given form by printed media and the market.[70] Evidently, this key component was lacking from the north Indian scene before the introduction of lithography in the 1830s and 1840s, but the reasons for this remain obscure. Politics may have played a part; several Indian rulers at the turn of the nineteenth century continued to discourage the use of the printing press because it threatened their authority.[71] Rather than being testimony to passivity and the absence of political debate, however, our evidence suggests exactly the opposite conclusion: that royal authority was already too fragile to support this further dissemination of ridicule and *lèse majesté*. [...] In the ecumene, written media and oral communication complemented each other. Francis Robinson[72] has made a strong case for the dominance of oral exposition and importance of the physical presence of the reputed teacher within the pre-print culture of Islamic north India. [...] Written media were, nevertheless, an essential part of north Indian critical debate, and could create eddies and flurries, of opinion distant from the immediate presence of their authors. Ghalib's proficiency as a letter-writer was as striking as his memory. [...]

The north Indian case indicates that critical debate within a broad political class could be spread through personal and institutional letter-writing, through placarding and public congregation. In Rajasthan and adjoining areas, the bardic tradition and the written stories to which it gave rise also proved capable of carrying subversive political messages. James Tod noted the prevalence of 'licence' and satire, the dissemination of 'truths unpalatable' and 'the absence of all mystery and reserve with regard to public affairs'[73] in the Rajput principalities. All this gives a picture of a lively social and political debate whose existence was reluctantly acknowledged when colonial officials made disparaging references to 'bazaar rumour'.

A similar point was made by Garcin de Tassy on the basis of a lifetime's study of Hindustani literature. It was common to argue that politics and rational discourse had no part in a society dominated by fable. On the contrary, he argued, the western distinctions between politics, literature, and history did not really apply. Many so-called 'fables' were strongly political in tone [...]. For instance one such story is a fable about diplomacy. A herd of deer hired a jackal to make a compact with a lion, but the jackal betrayed the deer to be eaten because he was the usual recipient of the lion's pickings.[74] This story must have seemed particularly timely in the savage politics of eighteenth-century India.

In contemporary west Asia, political debate was carried on in smoking dens and coffee shops.[75] The same was true in India, though here druggists' stalls, selling betel nut, tobacco, or medicaments,[76] and sweetshops[77] served as more important forums of gossip and news. In west Asia, again, more resolute protests were made by seizing control of that pre-eminently public place, the mosque, at a time just before the muezzin's call to prayer and making statements critical of the authorities from the minaret. The regularity of this procedure suggests that it was sanctioned by the community, and even reluctantly tolerated by rulers. In India, too, political demonstrations were made at or near mosques. The shrines of saints, or of deceased rulers popularly revered as just men, were also the venue of demonstrations—an indication of the relative importance for the subcontinent of tomb worship and Sufism in both elite and popular life. In Lucknow, at the beginning of the nineteenth century, for example, 'oppressions' by the police chief of the city brought together thousands in the garden of the tomb of the late ruler, Shuja-ud Daulah. The crowd called out '*andhera! andhera!*' 'darkness!, darkness!', that is 'tyranny!'[78] In other incidents, people affixed handbills to points on or near the Friday mosque or royal temple. [...]

Political debates over a wider geographical area were carried on by the Indo-Muslim literati through recognized newsletters and also by private correspondence, still often delivered by covert indigenous postal systems. The literature associated with popular Sufi teachers sometimes contained critical comment on rulers, or on various ethnic groups.[79] Hindu sages crafted similar comments on contemporary politics. The poet Kavindracarya wrote verses in honour of the emperor Shahjahan who had facilitated pilgrimage to Banaras.[80] They were recorded and used on later occasions when pilgrimage rights came under pressure. Shah Waliullah wrote letters to contemporary rulers urging a more strenuously Islamic policy.[81] Such epistles were, of course, destined for the readers of the wider critical ecumene; they were not 'private' letters.[82]

The practice of personal letter-writing also kept the ecumene informed. Figures for the early nineteenth century produced by the nascent British postal authorities suggest that even quite small towns produced a surprisingly large number of letters, perhaps as many as two hundred per annum per head for the literates and people who could afford to have letters written.[83] For men of the pen such as the poet Ghalib, letter-writing was viewed as a necessity of life. [...] Outside scholarly circles, most towns had substantial communities of bazaar writers acting for ordinary people who could pay them. Village schoolmasters also helped people communicate with their folk 'in distant parts'.[84] [...]

As we have seen, the newsletters written from the courts of rulers all across the country were copied by hand in relatively limited numbers. As in the case of later printed newspapers which were read to large groups of people and handed around in the bazaar for several days, the information they purveyed seems to have become public property very quickly. Pages of newspapers were lent by one family to another.[85] Whole copies of newspapers were read out to crowds in the streets in the evening.[86] Professional newswriters moved between the world of the written newsletter and the printed newspaper. Some of these writers also kept lists of subscribers to whose houses they would repair daily in order to read the news from their own manuscript compilations.[87] A combination of these instruments could create a formidable blast of publicity even before the rise of the press. [...]

The ecumene was led by respectable men who could draw limits to the actions of government and also seek to impose their standards of belief and practice on the populace. Meanwhile, dense networks of social communication could bring butchers, flower-sellers, bazaar merchants, and artisans into political debates and demonstrations. This has been thoroughly demonstrated by the many studies of the taxation riots and religious disputes of the early nineteenth century.[88] These events, however, are evidence of a continuing ecumenical critique; they should not be seen as sudden upsurges of resistance from tyrannized and voiceless subalterns. In 1779 in Lucknow, for instance, there was a celebrated debate between learned physicians who had newly arrived in town,[89] and resident savants who were trying to protect their livelihoods against the newcomers. [...] Professional clerics contended with lay literati. Perhaps the most important aspect was the way in which the debate attracted the attention of the whole city with huge throngs of people of all persuasions, numbering more than 1,500, clustering around the house where the contest took place. [...]

Such standard patterns of political representation and debate embraced Hindus as well as Muslims. Several historians have given us analyses of the political movement at Banaras in 1810 against the new British system of house taxation, emphasizing its popular character.[90] From our perspective what is striking is that a vigorous and effective public opinion could express itself in the public arena across the boundaries of caste and religion. Here the ecumene spoke in a Hindu idiom, though Muslims were also active. The protesters presented petitions against the assessment as discrete communities. One particular market-gardener caste leadership sent a 'letter of righteousness' (*dharmapatra*) to mobilize its rural supporters, in what was probably an adaptation of the normal method of raising temple funds or seeking adjudication in cases of infringements of caste rules.[91] The action of the Banaras citizens was, however, carefully coordinated between groups. The demonstrators all took a common oath of resistance and congregated in a single spot. Petitions argued the case against taxation in terms of the sanctity of Banaras but also the past and present usage of 'the country of Hindoostan, preferable to the kingdom of the seven climes', acknowledging a sense both in charismatic place and of wider patria.[92] Ultimately, too, they accepted the good offices of the Maharaja of Banaras as an intermediary with the British. Abdul Kadir Khan and another 'faithful old government servant', Akbar Ali Khan, also played the part of intermediaries. Although one historian has denounced them as 'spies' for the British,[93] and they certainly worked to end the uprising, these men had high status within both communities. They continued to resemble the munshis and advisers of the eighteenth century rather than the police informers of the nationalist period.

Finally, one should beware of the assumption that, even in cases where religious communities were pitted against each other, rational argument and social communication was totally abandoned. A few months earlier than the house tax affair, Banaras had been convulsed by a riot between Hindus and Muslims over the status of a holy place. In this case the petitioners on the part of the Hindus argued from history and current information. All had been well in Banaras, they said, until the Emperor Aurangzeb had destroyed the harmony between the communities by demolishing a temple; but the Emperor was so powerful that the Hindus had 'necessarily submitted with patience'.⁹⁴ Now the Muslim weavers had become 'more bigotted' than Aurangzeb, and the Hindus were forced to respond. Showing an acute awareness of current affairs, they argued that Muslims should concentrate on protecting the holy places of the Middle East against the Arabian Wahhabis who had recently sacked them, killing, it appears, the agent in Iraq of the late Ali Ibrahim Khan.⁹⁵

ELITE AND MASS IN CULTURAL PERFORMANCE

In addition to these set-piece demonstrations of discontent, strong political messages could be conveyed through cultural performance which linked elite and populace in enjoyment. Historians have been interested in recent years in the symbolism of festivals such as Ramlila, Holi or, amongst Muslims, Mohurrum and Id.⁹⁶ Well before the intervention of nationalist politicians at the end of the nineteenth century, these festivals had become the scene of attempts by magnates to claim new status or bodies of people attempting to asset cohesion or identity. In this sense, the Ramlila festival, which increased in importance and size in most parts of north Indian in the eighteenth and nineteenth centuries, should itself be seen as a widening arena of public communication.⁹⁷ Garcin de Tassy listed many different types of popular literature for recitation at these festivals, including songs, chants, homilies, and prayers, all of which could be used to promote cohesion and mutual knowledge.⁹⁸ These ranged from laments on the death of the Shia martyrs, through didactic treatises (*risalas*) to what he called, as early as the 1840s, 'national-musical' performances in Indian-owned premises in Calcutta and other cities.⁹⁹ This flexible range of media, part-written and part-oral, added up to a wide array of procedures for spreading information, subversion, parody, and biting political comment.

A number of different styles stand out. The heroic ballads of warrior heroes conveyed not only tales of ancient valour but observations on right kingship and religious conduct. The 'Prithvi Raja ki Kahani' which told of the last Hindu king of Delhi was a kind of foundation-legend for the high-caste warrior communities. [...] These legends had a definite reactive and community dimension. The epic of Pabuji, for instance, was circulated throughout Rajasthan by travelling story-tellers with elaborate cloth panels depicting the hero's exploits. In it the Muslim ('Turk') Mirza Khan is anathematized as a cow-killer: 'Oh king of Patan, in your kingdom calves and white cows are slain; at daybreak are slain the frogs and peacocks of the gardens.'¹⁰⁰ [...]

Another version of popular communication was the didactic debate between pupil and master which was found both in the Sufi tradition and in its Hindu form. All these written media and their 'shadow' verbal forms could be used to propagate critical comment and debates on the conduct of both the rulers and society as a whole.

Alongside these, finally, should be placed the performances of wandering cultural specialists: bards, puppeteers, actors, and jugglers. Bands of these artistes moved rapidly around India often from bases at the major pilgrimage places. They conveyed political and social messages which might originate in either the literate or the non-literate spheres. In Rajasthan and adjoining areas of the Agra Province, for instance, traditional bards (Bhats and Charans), singers of family pride and the heroic exploits of the Rajput rulers, introduced into their repertoire tales of the resistance of the Jats of Bharatpur against Mughal and British. Rather lower down the social scale, courtesans and prostitutes were famous purveyors of music and popular song. Some of their stock in trade were the *ghazals* [101] or musical versions of poems which had been written by noted satirists, or even by popular and munificent rulers such as Nawab Asaf-ud Daulah of Awadh.[102] While the British garnered their fair share of sycophantic ditties, they were often the target of attack too. For decades after 1799, any European traveller who wandered into the red light district of Banaras was serenaded from the roof gardens of the courtesans' houses by songs praising the exploits of the deposed Nawab Vazir Ali, who had killed the British judge of Banaras and chief intelligence expert, George Cherry, during the abortive uprising of that year.[103]

Travelling puppet shows and theatrical performances also helped spread subversive political ideas. Thus, in the months before the Vellore mutiny of 1806, it was puppeteers that carried the message that Tipu Sultan's sons were about to regain their power, aided by the French. Several decades later an observer investigated the bodies of actors who took improvised comedies around north India to all the major festivals. [...] One group was attached to a body of irregular Indian cavalry, but was hired from time to time by rich magnates who wanted to entertain their guests. Captain Bevan recorded one such performance which satirized the proceedings in a British criminal court. In the drama the magistrate appeared whistling and striking his riding boots with a cane. The prisoner was brought in, but the magistrate paid no attention to him as he was flirting with a young Indian woman among the witnesses.[104] During the deposition he continued to make signs and leer at her. Finally, the bearer appeared saying *'tiffin taiyar hai'* ('tea is ready') and the magistrate got up. When the officers of the court asked what to do with the prisoner, he replied 'Dam [sic] his eyes, hang him!' This subversive assault on the white man's justice and lecherousness was, Bevan reported, greatly enjoyed both by the Indian troops and the British army officers present.

THE LIMITS OF THE ECUMENE

The north Indian critical ecumene as we have described it spilled over the bounds of caste, community, and sect; it encompassed a dialogue between elite and popular political culture. It stands as a reminder that Indian minds and Indian social life cannot be reduced to the behaviourist simplicities of hierarchy and segmentation. It takes us beyond the limited and monolithic concept of 'resistance' to the realm of political critique and intellectual history. Yet this is not to say that the ecumene was a seamless web. On the contrary, there were significant breaks and discontinuities in it. For example, while Hindu noblemen, poets, and specialists took part in the wider debate and wrote in its languages, Persian and Urdu, the Brahmin establishments stood relatively aloof.[105] Ghalib could say that 'Benares was the Mecca of India', but it is difficult to imagine him participating in the pandits' ritual debates (*shastrartha*s) in the same way that Khattri Hindus participated in the Persian poetry circles. Even Ghalib had relatively few Hindu literary correspondents. In the case of one of the most prominent, Munshi Hargopal Tafta, it seems that the poet hoped to touch him for money;[106] elsewhere he says he employed '*bunya*-language' (shopkeeper talk) with a leading Delhi banker.[107] As a token of the assimilative power of public doctrinal debate, some learned Hindus became Muslims, but the process did not take place in reverse even though poor and unlettered Muslims sometimes venerated Hindu deities.[108] [...] An overlapping debate did not mean equal participation. In fact, when a critical public sphere using the newspaper finally emerged, these inequalities of participation were reinforced by the desire of editors to grasp and hold abstract constituencies of readers' opinions, now more distant from the face-to-face, or pen-to-pen, relations of the ecumene.

Amongst the less privileged, too, social and even economic discourse was still to some extent constricted within what was called the 'opinion of the caste', even if, as in the Peshwa's territories, the authorities intervened to adjudicate and advise.[109] Among the upper castes, extra-caste opinion and debate appears to have influenced these insider debates. So, for instance, social transgressions by an Agarwal banker might have been dealt with by the caste assembly, but it had severe repercussions within the wider multi-caste arena of the market and its rumours, since social and commercial credit were closely bound up. But nobody worried much about what went on amongst the leather workers or liquor distillers. Only bhakti devotion bridged these divides of status, and the sects were becoming increasingly respectable and market-centred in the eighteenth and nineteenth centuries.[110] The ecumene had always worked unevenly beneath the network of the most enlightened intelligentsia. In this, India was not qualitatively different from other societies with emergent public spheres.[111] Nevertheless, the ecumene did display a range of fractures which were widened by the powerful pressures of later colonial politics.

NOTES

1. Kenneth W. Jones, (ed.), *Religious Controversy in British India. Dialogues in South Asian Languages* (Albany, New York, 1992).

2. See the contributions in S. Freitag, (ed.), 'Aspects of the public in colonial South Asia', *South Asia*, 14, i, June 1991.

3. *Friend of India*, 26 April 1849, extracts from *Biographical Index to the Historians of Mahomedan India*.

4. cf. D. Daynes, *Rhetoric and Ritual in Colonial India. The shaping of public culture in Surat city, 1852–1928* (Berkeley, 1991).

5. cf. J. Habermas, *The Structural Transformation of the Public Sphere*, tr. T. Burger (Cambridge, Mass., 1992); cf. A.L. Kroeber, 'The ancient Oikoumene as a historical culture aggregate', *The Nature of Culture* (Chicago, 1952), pp. 379–95. For Byzantium, the term ecumene denotes an aesthetic, religious, and political community. It expanded the ideal of *oikos* (household) into *koine* (commonalty) (cf. ibid., pp. 4–5). While retaining some sense of patrimonial power derived from the emperor and patriarch, it came to mean 'our common home'. Power here was 'representationaly public' (ibid., p. 13), but this does not exhaust the meaning of public, because there was also public, political debate between clerics, philosophers, and administrators. This was 'critical' and 'reasoned' in Habermas's sense (ibid., p. 24), though within broad cosmological assumptions (this is also true of the 'modern' West). In some ways the Indo-Islamic world had a clearer sense of 'public'. The ulama and other learned acted as public 'jurisconsults' and 'censors' giving a sense of public beyond the medieval Christian priesthood which was more 'corporate' and introverted in character. In India, however, no single word encapsulated this notion of ecumene; instead it is a composite of communities and groupings of male adults and their dependents: *shura* or lain *umma*, the body of 'believers'; *dar*, 'homeland' (as in dar-ul Islam), *badshahi* (the common home of the emperor's subjects), or sarkar which implies 'public authority' (ibid., pp.

18-20), but comes to mean 'commonweal', implying an entity independent of the incumbent dynasty.

6. B. Anderson, *Imagined Communities. An Inquiry into the Origin of Nations* (Cambridge, Mass., 1993).

7. F. Robinson, 'Scholarship and Mysticism in early eighteenth century Awadh', in A.L. Dallapiccola and S.Z. Lallemant, *Islam and Indian Regions* (Stuttgart, 1994), pp. 377-98.

8. L. Dumont, *Homo Hierarchicus. The Caste System and Its Implications* (London, 1970).

9. S.A. Arjomand, *The Shadow of God and the Hidden Imam* (Chicago, 1984).

10. R.M. Eaton, *Sufis of Bijapur 1300-1700: Social Roles in Medieval India* (Princeton, 1978).

11. B.R. Grover, 'Land rights in Mughal India', *The Indian Economic and Social History Review*, I, 1, 1963, 1-23.

12. Randall Collins, *Weberian Sociological Theory* (Cambridge, 1986).

13. Habermas, *Public*, pp. 18-21.

14. 'Kanun', *Encyclopaedia of Islam*. New edn, IV, pp. 556-62.

15. J.C. Heesterman, *The Inner Conflict of Tradition. Essays on Indian ritual, kingship and society* (Chicago, 1985).

16. E.F. Irschick, *Tamil Revivalism in the 1930s* (Madras, 1986), pp. 13-20; R. O'Hanlon, *Caste, Conflict and Ideology* (Cambridge, 1985), pp. 16-35.

17. Professor Heesterman remarked that *slokas* in commentaries on shastric texts on kingship often limited the role of kings even more closely than the rules of the Arthashastra; personal communication, 1992.

18. Jayant K. Lele, *Tradition and Modernisation in Bhakti Movements* (Leiden, 1981).

19. A sect such as the Sadhs outlawed the use of astrology and the concept of auspicious and inauspicious times. Their 'creed' was set out in a number of *hukm* or *adhikar* (rules or orders), see, M. Garcin de Tassy, *Historie de la litterature hindouie et Hindoustanie* (Paris, 1870), I, 342ff.; W. Allison, *The Sadhs* (Calcutta, 1934).

20. Habermas, *Public*, p. 24.

21. B. Matilal, *Nyaya-Vaisesika, A History of Indian Literature*, (ed.), J. Gonda, (Wiesbaden 1977), vol. VI, 2; cf. L. Wilkinson, 'The use of the Siddhantas in native education', *Journal of the Asiatic Society of Bengal*, 3, 1834, pp. 504-19. *Panchangs* included astronomical and astrological observations, all the major calendars (Christian, Muslim, Hindu, revenue); later, details of charges and postal services, moral tales, advertisements, and political propaganda, see C.A. Bayly, *Empire and Information: Intelligence Gathering and Social Communication in India, 1780-1870* (Cambridge, 2000), pp. 249, 262-3.

22. Francis Robinson, 'Ottomans-Safavids-Mughals: shared knowledge and connective systems', unpublished Ms. [Ed. Since the original publication of this chapter, the essay cited here appears to have been published as Francis Robinson, 'Ottomans-Safavids-Mughals: Shared Knowledge and Connective Systems', *Journal of Islamic Studies,* 1998 (2). pp. 151-84]

23. C. Troll, 'A note on an early topographical work of Sayyid Ahmad Khan: Asar-al Sanadid', *Journal of the Royal Asiatic Society*, 1972, 143.

24. R. Inden, *Imagining India* (Oxford, 1991), passim.

25. Mattison Mines, 'Individuality and achievement in south Asian social history', *Modern Asian Studies*, 26, i, 1992, 129-56.
26. 'Gyanbaffee Mosque' file, bundle 50, file 97, Judl. 1866, Comr Banaras, Post Mutiny Records, UPCRO.
27. Address of Md Ewaz, 27 Rabi-us sanee 1231 Hijree, Bengal Criminal Judicial Procs, 25 October 1816, 29 enc. 3, 132/48, OIOC.
28. Troll, 'Sayyid Ahmad', p. 41 (the sadr-ul-sudr was a judge with particular cognizance of matters of religious endowment).
29. S.A.A. Rizvi, *Shah Wali-Allah and His Times* (Canberra, 1980), pp. 317-42.
30. Extract Bengal Pol. Letter 19 June 1807, 'Disturbances at Delhi', BC 217/4758.
31. S.A.A. Rizvi, *A Socio-intellectual History of Isna 'Ashari Shi'is in India* (Canberra, 1986), Vol. II, pp. 19-24, 35-7; A. Powell, *Muslims and Missionaries in Pre-Mutiny India* (Richmond, 1993), p. 43-75; Hermann Ethé, *Catalogue of Persian Manuscripts in the Library of the India Office* (London, 1903), p. 1335.
32. Rizvi, *Shi'is*, II, 88-9.
33. Rizvi, *Wali-Allah*, pp. 298-9, 304.
34. 'munazarah', *Encyclopaedia of Islam*. New edn VII (Leiden, 1990), pp. 565-8; Abdul Halim Sharar, *Lucknow: The Last Phase of an Oriental Culture* (London, 1974), p. 95.
35. Rizvi, *Shi'is*, II, 137.
36. Khairuddin Khan Illahabadi, 'Tuhfa-i-Tazah', trans. F. Curwen, *Bulwuntnamah* (Allahabad, 1875), pp. 87-92.
37. This began with the series of Urdu, Hindi, and Persian pamphlets denouncing Indian religion released by Serampore missionaries in 1804-6, for example, 'An address from the missionaries of Serampore to all persons professing the Mohumadan religion', HM 690.
38. *Church Missionary Record*, I, 2, 1830, 45 (Jaunpur); F. Nizami, 'Madrasahs, scholars and saints: Muslim responses to the British presence in Delhi and the Upper Doab, 1803-1857', unpublished, DPhil. dissertation, Oxford University, 1983; W. Fusfeld, *The Shaping of Sufi Leadership in Delhi. The Naqshbandiyya Mujaddidiyya, 1750-1920* (Ann Arbor, 1981), pp. 1-52; 116-98.
39. For the history of Urdu translations of the Koran, *LH*, I, 76-87; cf. *Friend of India*, 28 January 1841.
40. Powell, *Missionaries*, pp. 43-75; *Church Missionary Record (CMR)*, I, 3, 1830, 59, 62; I, 6, 1830, 120-2, 133, 137; I, 10, 1830, 217-19.
41. For example, the Sadr Amin and 'The chief native judge' near Lucknow refutes Christianity, *CMR*, 6, 7, 1836, 137-8; ditto, the office manager of the Collector of Ghazipur, ibid., 9, 1, 1838, 15.
42. See for example., the description of a western Indian debate between Advaita Vedantists and their opponents, J. Howison, *European Colonies in Various Parts of the World* (London, 1834), II, 52-4.
43. C.B. Leupolt, *Recollections of an Indian Missionary* (London, 1856), p. 56.
44. A vivid picture of the world of the mushairah is given in Akhtar Qamber, *The Last Mushairah of Delhi* (Delhi, 1979).

45. R. Russell and K. Islam, *Three Mughal Poets. Mir, Sauda, Mir Hasan* (London, 1969) p. 6; cf. pp. 55-8; S.A.I. Tirmizi, *Persian Letters of Ghalib* (Delhi, 1969), p. xxiii.
46. Daud Rahbar (tr., ed.), *Urdu Letters of Mirza Asadu'llah Khan Ghalib* (Albany, New York, 1987), p. xxvii; Tirmizi, *Persian Letters of Ghalib*, p. xxvii-xxx.
47. cf. R. Russell and K. Islam, *Ghalib, 1797-1969*, I, *Life and Letters* (London, 1969), pp. 79-81.
48. A. Sprenger, *A Catalogue of the Arabic, Persian and Hindustani Manuscripts of the Libraries of the King of Oudh* (Calcutta, 1854), pp. 195-306; we have used the term ecumene to describe a *style* of communication but tazkirahs could be used to demonstrate the *geography* of social communication in the sense used by Deutsch. The relative decline of literary and social comment in the western cities, Lahore, Delhi, and others., would be matched in the late eighteenth century by the rise of Lucknow, Banaras, Patna, Hyderabad, and their associated qasbahs. Calcutta would become significant for Persian and Urdu scholarship.
49. Ibid., pp. 165-75.
50. Ibid., p. 207.
51. Ibid., p. 217.
52. Ibid., p. 234.
53. Ibid., p. 282.
54. Ibid., p. 289.
55. Ibid., p. 217.
56. Ibid., p. 299.
57. *LH*, I, 69-72; cf. Garcin de Tassy, 'Les femmes poetes de l'Inde', *Revue de l'Orient*, May 1854; Sprenger, *Catalogue of Libraries of Oudh*, p. 11
58. P. Hardy, *Historians of Medieval India. Studies in Indo-Muslim Historical Writing* (London, 1960), pp. 122-31.
59. Tirmizi, *Persian Letters of Ghalib*, p. xxiii.
60. Sayyid Ahmad Khan, 'Asar-us Sanadid', trans. as 'Description des Monuments de Delhi en 1852', *Journal Asiatique*, January 1861, 80, 87, 91, passim.
61. Fritz Lehman, 'Urdu Literature and Mughal Decline', *Mahfil*, 6, 2, 1970, pp. 125- 31; Russell and Islam, *Three Mughal Poets*, pp. 1-68.
62. I.A. Arshi, *Catalogue of the Arabic Manuscripts in Raza Library, Rampur*, 6 vols (Rampur, 1963-77).
63. Datta, B.K., *Libraries and Librarianship of Ancient and Medieval India* (Delhi, 1970) p. 84.
64. Also note the lack of catalogues, A. Sprenger to H. Elliot, 25 June 1847, Elliot Papers, Add. 30, 789, BL.
65. D.C. Dasgupta, *The Jaina System of Education* (Calcutta, 1944), pp. 36-40; John E. Cort, 'The Jain knowledge warehouses: traditional libraries in India', *Journal of the American Oriental Society*, 115, 1, 1995, pp. 77-88.
66. Sprenger to Elliot, 25 June 1847, Elliot Papers, Add. 30, 789; cf. Sprenger, *Report of the Researches into the Muhammadan Librareis of Lucknow. Selections from the Records of the Government of India*, no. 28 (Calcutta, 1896)

which records 6,000 volumes in the Topkhana Library and about 1,000 in the Farah Baksh; the private library of Sheikh Mahomed Hazin's family had 5,000 volumes, Belfour, *Hazin*, p. 10; Datta, *Libraries*, pp. 69, 73, 85.

67. G.N. Bahura, 'Glimpses of historical information from manuscripts in the Pothikhana of Jaipur', in J.N. Asopa (ed.), *Cultural Heritage of Jaipur* (Jodhpur, 1982), pp. 104–5; cf. Arshi, *Rampur*, I, preface p. 1.

68. *Miss. Reg.*, August 1826, p. 395.

69. Troll, *Sayyid Ahmad*, p. 104.

70. Habermas, *Public*, pp. 57ff.

71. For example,, the case in 1849 where the King of Awadh destroyed the Lucknow presses because they had displeased him. A. Sprenger, *A Catalogue of the Arabic, Persian and Hindustani Manuscripts in the Libraries of the King of Oudh*, (Calcutta, 1854), p. vi, or an equivalent case in Punjab, Emmet Davis, *The Press and Politics in British West Punjab, 1836–47* (Delhi, 1983), p. 184.

72. F. Robinson, 'Technology and religious change. Islam and the impact of print', *MAS*, 27, i, 1993, pp. 229–51.

73. J. Tod, *Annals and Antiquities of Rajast'han or the Central and Western Rajpoot States of India* (London, 1829–32, reprt, 1950), introduction, p. 16; cf. V.N. Rao, D. Shulman, and S. Subrahmanyam, *Symbols of Substance. Court and State in Nayaka Period Tamilnadu* (Delhi, 1992), pp. 1–22 and passim.

74. C. Bendall, 'The Tantrakhyana. A collection of Indian tales', *Journal of Royal Asiatic Society*, 2, 4, 1890, 484; cf. *The Panchatantra*.

75. Note by Prof. Halil Inalcik in author's possession.

76. An observation of Prof. Ravinder Kumar.

77. 'Bankas and swindlers', *Delhi Gazette*, 18 December 1839.

78. Faiz Baksh, Muhammad, 'Tarikh-i Farah Baksh' trans. W. Hoey *Memoirs of Delhi and Faizabad* (Allahabad, 1889), II, pp. 285–7.

79. S. H. Askari, 'Mirat-ul-Muluk: A Contemporary Work Containing Reflections on Later Mughal Government', *Indica, Indian Historical Research Institute Silver Jubilee Commemoration Volume* (Bombay, 1953) pp. 44ff.

80. V. Raghavan, 'The Kavindrakalpalatika of Kavindracarya Sarasvati', ibid., pp. 336–7.

81. Rizvi, *Wali-allah*, pp. 302–3.

82. cf. David Lelyveld, reported by S. Freitag, 'Introduction' *South Asia*, n.s., 14, 1, 1991, p. 9 and fn. 19.

83. 'District Dawks', *Friend of India*, 18 July 1850.

84. For example., the case in Westmacott, 'Travels', Mss. Eur. C26, f. 173.

85. Rahbar, *Ghalib*, pp. 94, 205.

86. *Friend of India*, 4 April 1850.

87. Evidence of Chuni Lal, newswriter 'for the public', 'Trial of the King of Delhi', pp. 1859, 1st session, xviii, 84.

88. See, K.H. Prior, 'The British administration of Hinduism in north India, 1780–1900', unpublished PhD thesis, Cambridge University, 1990.

89. Cole, *Roots of North Indian Shi'ism*, pp. 55–8.

90. R. Heitler, 'The Varanasi house-tax hartal of 1810–11', *Indian Economic and Social History Review*, 9, 3, 1972, pp. 239–57; G. Pandey, *The Construction of Communalism in Colonial North India* (Delhi, 1990) pp. 24–50; S. Freitag,

A Pre-History of the Middle Class? 93

Collective Action and Community. Public arenas and the emergence of communalism in north India (Berkeley, 1989), pp. 19-52.

91. Actg Magt. to Govt, 8 January 1811, Bengal Criminal Judl Procs, 8 February 1811, 1, 130/28, OIOC.

92. Petition of Mohulla Seedhestree, Bengal Criminal Judl Procs, 5 January 1811, 25, 130/27, OIOC.

93. Heitler, 'Hartal', p. 251; cf. Actg Magt. to Govt, 28 January 1811, Bengal Crim. Judl, 8 February 1811, 5, 130/28, OIOC.

94. 'Memorial of the Hindoos of the City of Benares', 20 November 1809, 'Disturbances at Benares', BC 365, OIOC; the British were peeved that another important old 'native informant', Bishambhar Pandit, had been involved in fomenting the Hindus.

95. Ibid.

96. S. Freitag, *Culture and Power in Banaras. Community, performance and environment, 1800-1980* (Berkeley, 1989).

97. S. Pollock, 'Ramayana and political imagination in India', *Journal of Asian Studies*, 52, 2, 1993, pp. 261-97.

98. *LH*, I, 24-50.

99. *LH*, I, 41.

100. J.D. Smith, *The Epic of Pabuji. A study in transcription and translation* (Cambridge, 1991), pp. 290-1.

101. See A. Bansani, 'Ghazal', *Encyclopaedia of Islam*, 2nd edn, II, 1036.

102. *LH*, I, 103-4.

103. Bholanauth Chunder, *The Travels of a Hindoo to Various Parts of Bengal and Upper India* (London, 1869), pp. i, 283; cf. *LH*, I, 103-4, on Asaf-ud Daulah; for the use of another ghazal in a contemporary dispute, Judge Banaras to register Nizamat Adalat, 12 January 1813, Bengal Criminal Judicial, 12 July 1816, 18, 132/43, OIOC; for use of popular theatre in a political cause, de Tassy, *LH*, I, 24-5.

104. Ibid., 27.

105. 'Mahommedan Festivals in India', ibid., 16, 1835, 52.

106. Rahbar, *Ghalib*, p. 380, n. 1.

107. Ghalib to Nawab Husain Mirza, 29 October 1859, ibid., p. 207.

108. *LH*, I, 63-4.

109. G.C. Vad (ed.), *Selections from the Satara Rajas' and the Peshwas' Diaries* (Bombay, 1907-11) makes it clear that the rulers' courts acted a role as a kind of 'public tribunal' for intra-caste disputes.

110. D. Gold, 'What the merchant-guru sold; social and literary types in Hindi devotional verse', *Journal of the American Oriental Society*, 112, 1, 1992, pp. 22-36.

111. As is made clear by C. Calhoun (ed.), *Habermas and the Public Sphere* (Cambridge, Mass., 1992).

The Subalternity of a Nationalist Elite*

PARTHA CHATTERJEE

The terms *middle class*, *literati*, and *intelligentsia* all have been used to describe it. Marxists have called it a petty bourgeoisie, the English rendering of *petit* marking its character with the unmistakable taint of historical insufficiency. A favourite target of the colonizer's ridicule, it was once famously described as 'an oligarchy of caste tempered by matriculation'. More recently, historians inspired by the well-meaning dogmas of American cultural anthropology called it by the name the class had given to itself—the *bhadralok*, 'respectable folk'; the latter interpreted the attempt as a sinister plot to malign its character. Whichever the name, the object of description has, however, rarely been misunderstood: in the curious context of colonial Bengal, all of these terms meant more or less the same thing.

Needless to say, much has been written about the sociological characteristics of the new middle class in colonial Bengal.[1] I do not wish to intervene in that discussion. My concern in this book is with social agency. In this particular chapter, my problem is that of mediation, in the sense of the action of a subject who stands 'in the middle', working upon and transforming one term of a relation into the other. It is more than simply a problem of 'leadership', for I will be talking about social agents who are preoccupied not only with leading their followers but who are also conscious of doing so as a

---

* Originally published as 'The Nationalist Elite', in Partha Chatterjee, *Nation and Its Fragments: Colonial and Postcolonial Histories* (Princeton: Princeton University Press, 1999), pp. 35-75 (and notes). For the complete text see the original. In the present version, some portions of the essay have been removed and notes rearranged accordingly.

'middle term' in a social relationship. In fact, it is this 'middleness' and the consciousness of middleness that I wish to problematize. Of all its appellations, therefore, I will mostly use the term 'middle class' to describe the principal agents of nationalism in colonial Bengal.

THE 'MIDDLENESS' OF THE CALCUTTA MIDDLE CLASS

Like middle classes elsewhere in their relation to the rise of nationalist ideologies and politics, the Calcutta middle class too has been generally acknowledged as having played a pre-eminent role in the last century and a half in creating the dominant forms of nationalist culture and social institutions in Bengal. It was this class that constructed through a modern vernacular the new forms of public discourse, laid down new criteria of social respectability, set new aesthetic and moral standards of judgement, and, suffused with its spirit of nationalism, fashioned the new forms of political mobilization that were to have such a decisive impact on the political history of the province in the twentieth century.

All this has also been written about at length. But this literature adopts, albeit necessarily, a standpoint external to the object of its inquiry. It does not let us into that vital zone of belief and practice that straddles the domains of the individual and the collective, the private and the public, the home and the world, where the new disciplinary culture of a modernizing elite has to turn itself into an exercise in self-discipline. This, however, is the investigation we need to make.

I propose to do this by taking up the question of middle-class religion.[2] As a point of entry, I will consider the phenomenon of Sri Ramakrishna (1836–86), which will afford us an access into a discursive domain where 'middleness' can be talked about, explored, problematized, lived out, and, in keeping with the role of cultural leadership that the middle class gave to itself, normalized.

The colonial middle class, in Calcutta no less than in other centres of colonial power, was simultaneously placed in a position of subordination in one relation and a position of dominance in another. The construction of hegemonic ideologies typically involves the cultural efforts of classes placed precisely in such situation. To identify the possibilities and limits of nationalism as a hegemonic movement, therefore, we need to look into this specific process of ideological construction and disentangle the web in which the experiences of simultaneous subordination and domination are apparently reconciled.

For the Calcutta middle class of the late nineteenth century, political and economic domination by a British colonial élite was a fact. The class was created in a relation of subordination. But its contestation of this relation was to be premised upon its cultural leadership of the indigenous colonized people. The nationalist project was in principle a hegemonic project. Our task is to probe into the history of this project, to assess its historical possibility or impossibility, to identify its origins, extent, and limits. The method, in other words, is the method of critique.

I will concentrate on a single text, the *Rāmkr̥ṣṇa kathāmr̥ta*,³ and look specifically at the construction there of a new religion for urban domestic life. The biographical question of Ramakrishna in relation to the middle class of Bengal has been studied from new historiographical premises by Sumit Sarkar:⁴ I will not address this question. Rather, I will read the *Kathāmr̥ta* not so much as a text that tells us about Ramakrishna as one that tells us a great deal about the Bengali middle class. The *Kathāmr̥ta*, it seems to me, is a document of the fears and anxieties of a class aspiring to hegemony. It is, if I may put this in a somewhat paradoxical form, a text that reveals to us the subalternity of an elite. [...]

DOUBTS

[...] The Brahmo religion, influential as it had been in the social life of urban Bengal, was undoubtedly restricted in its appeal to a very small section of the new middle class. In the 1870s there were scarcely more than a hundred Brahmo families in Calcutta; fewer than a thousand persons in the city declared themselves as Brahmos in the 1881 census.⁵ Keshab [Chandra Sen, 1838–84] was beginning to feel that there was something inherently limiting in the strict rationalism of the new faith. In his writings and speeches of the mid-1870s, Keshab talked frequently of the importance of a faith that was not shackled by the debilitating doubts of cold reason. [... and] was deeply concerned that the rationalist ideal which he and his predecessors had pursued was alien to the traditions of his country and its people. [...]

It is also significant that in his search for a path of reform in consonance with Eastern spirituality, Keshab was looking for an inspired messenger through whom God makes his appearance in human history. The idea was repugnant to many enlightened brahmos, for it smacked of the age-old Hindu belief in the *avatāra* (divine incarnation); Debendranath Tagore is said to have remarked that in a country where even fish and turtles were regarded as incarnations of God, he found it strange that Keshab should aspire to be one.[6] But Keshab's doubts were of a different sort: he had become skeptical about the powers of the human intellect and will. [...]

This was roughly Keshab Sen's frame of mind when, one day in the middle of March 1875, he retired as usual to the quiet of the garden house in Belgharia and had a visitor.

THE MEETING

[...] Ramakrishna was at this time entirely unknown among the Calcutta middle class. True, he had been patronized by Rani Rasmani of Janbazar, and she along with several members of her family regarded Ramakrishna with much veneration. But Rasmani's family, largely because of its lower-caste background, was not a part of the culturally dominant elite of Calcutta, although she herself was well known as a spirited and philanthropic woman. [...]

What might be called the official biography of Ramakrishna, the *Rāmkrṣṇa-līlāprasaṅga*, describes Ramakrishna on this day as clothed in 'a dhoti with a red border, one end thrown across the left shoulder'. On being introduced, he said, 'Babu, I am told that you people have seen God. I have come to hear what you have seen.' This is how the conversation began. [...][7]

The same incident is described by Pratap Mozoomdar from the point of view of Keshab's followers. 'Soon he began to discourse in a sort of half-delirious state, becoming now and then quite unconscious. What he said, however, was so profound and beautiful that we soon perceived he was no ordinary man.'[8] [...]

THE DISCOVERY

Keshab Sen ran two newspapers. The English paper, the *Indian Mirror*, began as a weekly and in 1871 became a daily. The Bengali weekly, *Sulabh Samācār*, was started in November 1870 and in three months reached a peak circulation of twenty-seven thousand. Even in 1877 when its circulation had dropped somewhat because of competition from other publications it was still the most widely circulated paper in Bengali.[9]

Two weeks after the meeting between Keshab Sen and Ramakrishna, the *Indian Mirror* published an article entitled 'A Hindu Saint'. After describing the great Hindu devotees talked about in the religious literature of India and still revered in popular memory, it continued: We met one not long ago, and were charmed by the depth, penetration and simplicity of his spirit. The never-ceasing metaphors and analogies in which he indulged are, most of them, as apt as they are beautiful. The characteristics of the mind are the very opposite of those of Pandit Dayanand Saraswati, the former being gentle, tender and contemplative as the latter is sturdy, masculine and polemical. Hinduism must have in it a deep source of beauty, truth and goodness to inspire such men as these.[10]

It is more than likely that the article was written by Keshab himself and a few weeks later something along the same lines appeared in *Sulabh Samācār*, the first of several articles on Ramakrishna published in that paper.

Suddenly Ramakrishna became an object of great curiosity among the educated young men of Calcutta. [...]

Balaram Bose, who came from a wealthy family of landlords and was one of Ramakrishna's principal patrons in the last years of his life, first read about him in Keshab Sen's newspapers.[11] So did Girishchandra Ghosh, the foremost personality in the Calcutta theatre at this time.[12] By the early years of the 1880s, when most of the men who would form the closest circle of disciples around Ramakrishna had gathered in Dakshineswar,[13] he was a frequently discussed personality in the schools, colleges, and newspapers of Calcutta.

Remarkably, the enormous legend that would be built around Ramakrishna's name in the words and thoughts of the Calcutta middle class was the result of a fairly short acquaintance, beginning only eleven years before his death. Only in those last years of his life did he cast his spell over so many distinguished men, who would make his name a household word among educated Bengalis.

The followers of Keshabchandra and Ramakrishna have, of course, never managed to agree on which of the two great leaders influenced the other. The hagiographers of Ramakrishna write as though Keshab, a determined seeker after truth who roamed aimlessly for the greater part of his life, finally found salvation at the feet of the Master. [...] A biographer of Keshab, on the other hand, complains: 'It is sad to contemplate that such friendship should be misunderstood, misinterpreted. It has even been suggested that Keshub borrowed his religion of Harmony, the New Dispensation, from Ramakrishna.'[14]

With the advantage of a hundred years of hindsight, we have no need to take sides in this quarrel. But, for precisely that reason—the fact that we are prisoners of an incorrigibly historical vision of our selves and the world—we had to begin our story with the meeting in Belgharia on a spring afternoon in 1875.

DIVINE PLAY

This, however, is not how the story is supposed to begin. Those who tell the story of Ramakrishna remind us that the Master's life was not the life of any ordinary man, not even that of an extraordinary man. The Absolute being, in one of his inscrutable, playful decisions, appears on earth from time to time in the guise of a human being to act out an exemplary life for the edification of the world. According to the authorized version, therefore, the story of Ramakrishna's life must be told as one more episode in an eternal *līlā*. [...]

In the *Līlāprasaṅga*, Saradananda [Ramakrishna's biographer] takes great pains to explain to what he presumes will be a skeptical readership the significance of...extraordinary and miraculous happenings surrounding Ramakrishna's birth.[15] He argues, for instance, that such events are common to the life stories of all great souls 'who sanctify the earth by their birth,' stories that 'are recorded in the religious books of all races.' Similar events portray 'the unique spiritual experience and visions' of the parents of Rama, Krishna, the Buddha, Jesus, Śaṅkara and Caitanya.[16] [...] Miraculousness, it would seem, is the aura that surrounds the life histories of those who are the incarnations of God and marks out their lives as different from history itself.

But Saradananda also has other arguments to offer. India, he thinks, has been particularly blessed by the Almighty Being in the matter of incarnations. This explains the spirituality of Indian culture.

When we make a comparative study of the spiritual beliefs and ideals of India and of other countries, we notice a vast difference between them. From very ancient times India has taken entities beyond the senses, namely, God, the self, the next world, etc., to be real, and has employed all its efforts towards their direct realization. ... All its activities have accordingly been coloured by intense spirituality throughout the ages. ... The source of this absorbing interest in things beyond the senses is due to the frequent birth in India of men possessing a direct knowledge of these things and endowed with divine qualities.[17]

Knowledge of a similar kind, Saradananda is sure, is denied to the West, for the procedures of Western knowledge are 'attracted only by external objects.'

Although capable of achieving great progress in physical science, the [Western] procedure...could not lead men to the knowledge of the Atman. For the only way to attain that knowledge is through self-control, selflessness and introspection, and the only instrument for attaining it is the mind, with all its functions brought under absolute control.

Western knowledge could not accomplish this. Consequently, Western people 'missed the path to Self-knowledge and became materialists, identifying themselves with the body'.[18]

We have here the familiar nationalist problematic of the material and the spiritual, the identification of an incompleteness in the claims of the modern West to a superior culture and asserting the sovereignty of the nation over the domain of spirituality. In itself, this is not surprising because Saradananda himself was very much a part of the middle-class culture of Bengal that had, by the turn of the century, come to accept these criteria as fundamental in the framing of questions of cultural choice. What is curious is that instead of 'cleaning up' the layers of myth and legend from the life story of someone like Ramakrishna and presenting it as the rational history of human exemplariness, as in Bankim's *Kṛṣṇacaritra*, for instance, Saradananda seeks to do the very opposite: he authenticates the myth by declaring that the life of Ramakrishna is not to be read as human history but as divine play.[19]

Indeed, Saradananda is forthright in stating his purpose. Why does he feel called upon to write the story of Ramakrishna's life for his educated readership? The reason has to do with 'the occupation of India by the West'.

Coming more and more under the spell of the West, India rejected the ideal of renunciation and self-control and began to run after worldly pleasures. This attitude brought with it the decay of the ancient system of education and training, and there arose atheism, love of imitation and lack of self-confidence. [...] The influence of the west had brought about its fall. Would it not be futile, then, to look to the atheistic West for its resurrection? Being itself imperfect, how could the West make another part of the world perfect?[20]

The conditions of the problem were clear. The assertion of spirituality would have to rest on an essential difference between East and West, and the domain of autonomy thus defined would have to be ordered on one's own terms, not on those set by the conqueror in the material world. If myth is the form in which the truth is miraculously revealed in the domain of Eastern spirituality, then it is myth that must be affirmed and the quibbles of a skeptical rationalism declared out of bounds.

[...]

Thus it was that Ramakrishna decided to gather around him a circle of young disciples and to initiate them into his religion. In each case, the Master had a yogic vision of the disciple before he actually arrived in Dakshineswar.[21] From the beginning of 1881, 'the all-renouncing devotees, the eternal playmates of the Master in his Lila, began coming to him one by one'.[22] By 1884, they had all arrived. It was only then that Ramakrishna finally took up his *divyabhāva*, 'the attitude of the divine'.

The purpose of all this is clear to Saradananda. Had not the Divine Lord promised in the *Gita* that whenever religion declines, he would assume a human body and manifest his powers?[23] Now, when the nation lay enslaved and its brightest minds confused and frustrated, had not such a time arrived?

[...]

But although the *Līlāprasaṅga* claims to be something like an official biography, it is not the text that is most familiar to generations of avid readers of Ramakrishna literature. That honour is reserved for the *Rāmkṛṣṇa kathāmṛta*. Circulated now in several editions and virtually annual reprints, it is a collection of the Master's 'sayings'. Ever since its publication in the early years of this century, its five volumes have acted as the principal sourcebook on Ramakrishna.

LANGUAGE

Sumit Sarkar has noted the stylistic peculiarity of the *Kathāmṛta* in the way it combines two radically different linguistic idioms—one, the rustic colloquial idiom spoken by Ramakrishna, and the other, the chaste formality of the new written prose of nineteenth-century Calcutta.[24] The former, for all its rusticity (a 'rusticity', we must remember, itself produced by the difference created in the nineteenth century between the new high culture of urban sophistication and everything else that became marked as coarse, rustic, or merely local), was by no means a language that any villager in nineteenth-century Bengal would have spoken, for its use by Ramakrishna shows great conceptual richness, metaphoric power, and dialectical skill. It was the language of preachers and poets in pre-colonial Bengal, and even when used by someone without much formal learning (such as Ramakrishna), it was able to draw upon the conceptual and rhetorical resources of a vast body of literate tradition. By contrast, the new written prose of late nineteenth-century Calcutta, in what may be called its post-Bankim phase, was distinct not so much as a 'development' of earlier narrative forms but fundamentally by virtue of its adoption of a wholly different, that is, modern European, discursive framework. Recent studies have identified the ways in which grammatical models borrowed from the modern European languages shaped the 'standard' syntactic forms of modern Bengali prose; other studies have shown similar 'modular' influences of rhetorical forms borrowed from English in particular.[25]

The appearance of these formal differences between the two idioms was of course intricately tied to another difference—a difference in the very conceptual and logical apparatus articulated in language. The users of the new Bengali prose not only said things in a new way, they also had new things to say. This was the principal intellectual impetus that led to the rapid flourishing of the modern Bengali prose literature; by the 1880s, when Mahendranath Gupta (1854-1932) was recording his diary entries of Ramakrishna's sayings for what was to become the *Kathāmṛta*, a considerable printing and publishing industry operated in Calcutta (in fact, one of the more important industrial activities in the city), testifying to the creation of both a modern 'high culture' and a 'print-capitalism', the two sociological conditions that are supposed to activate the nationalist imagination.[26] What is nevertheless intriguing is the quite rapid 'standardization' of this prose. The 1850s was still a time when a 'standard' form had not appeared; by the 1880s, the 'standard' form had come to stay. It is worth speculating whether the sheer proximity of European discursive models—available, palpable, already standardized by more momentous historical processes and hence unquestionably worthy of emulation—had something to do with the astonishing speed with which the entirely new form of narrative prose came to be accepted as 'normal' by the English-educated Bengali middle class.

The modular influence was strongest when written prose was employed to discuss subjects that were explicitly theoretical or philosophical. The *Kathāmṛta* is marked not only by the divergence between the 'rustic' and the 'urban' idioms in Bengali; it is an even more explicitly bilingual text in its repeated employment of English terms, phrases, and quotations. It is remarkable how often Mahendranath introduces with a heading in English sections in which Ramakrishna discusses questions of a philosophical nature: there must be some fifty sections with titles such as 'Reconciliation of free Will and God's Will—of Liberty and Necessity', or 'Identity of the Absolute or

Universal Ego and the Phenomenal World', or 'Problems of Evil and the Immortality of the Soul', or 'Philosophy and Scepticism', and so on. Each heading of this kind is followed by a recording of Ramakrishna's own words or a conversation, directly reported, between him and his disciples. Mahendranath, in his self-appointed role of narrator, does not attempt to explicate the sayings of his preceptor, and yet this form of introducing sections serves to create the impression that Ramakrishna is dealing with the same questions that are discussed in European philosophy. Mahendranath also repeatedly translates various philosophical concepts used by Ramakrishna with English terms and inserts them into the text in parentheses or in footnotes. Thus, for instance, when Ramakrishna describes his state of trance as one in which he is unable to count things—*ek duier pār* (literally, 'beyond ones and twos')—Mahendranath adds a footnote in English: 'The absolute as distinguished from the relative.' [...] A section entitled 'Perception of the Infinite' has a footnote saying, 'Compare discussion about the order of perception of the Infinite and of the Finite in Max Müller's Hibbert Lectures and Gifford Lectures.'

This bilingual dialogue runs through the text, translating the terms of an Indian philosophical discourse into those of nineteenth-century European logic and metaphysics. It is as though the wisdom of an ancient speculative tradition of the East, sustained for centuries not only in philosophical texts composed by the learned but through debates and disquisitions among preachers and mystics, is being made available to minds shaped by the modes of European speculative philosophy. (The invocation of Max Müller is significant.) This dialogue also expresses the desire to assert that the 'common' philosophy of 'rustic' Indian preachers is no less sophisticated, no less 'classical' in its intellectual heritage, than the learned speculations of modern European philosophers: in fact, the former is shown as providing different, and perhaps better, answers to the same philosophical problems posed in European philosophy.[27] [...] But for both narrator and reader of the *Kathāmṛta*, the terrain of European thought is familiar ground—familiar, yet foreign—from which they set out to discover (or perhaps, rediscover) the terrain of the indigenous and the popular, a home from which they have been wrenched. The bilingual discourse takes place within the same consciousness, where both lord and bondsman reside. Contestation and mediation have taken root within the new middle-class mind, a mind split in two. [...]

THE PRISONHOUSE OF REASON

For the colonized middle-class mind, caught in its 'middleness', the discourse of Reason was not unequivocally liberating. The invariable implication it carried of the historical necessity of colonial rule and its condemnation of indigenous culture as the storehouse of unreason, or (in a stage-of-civilization argument) of reason yet unborn, which only colonial rule would bring to birth (as father, mother, or midwife—which?), made the discourse of Reason oppressive. It was an oppression that the middle-class mind often sought to escape. Bankimchandra Chattopadhyay (1838–94), unquestionably the most brilliant rationalist essayist of the time, escaped into the world not of mythic time but of imaginary history, sliding imperceptibly from the past-as-it-might-have-been to the past-as-it-should-have-been to an invocation of the past-as-it-will-be.[28] So did the most brilliant rationalist defender of 'orthodox' tradition—Bhudeb Mukhopadhyay (1827–94), in that remarkable piece of utopian history *Svapnalabdha bhāratbarṣer itihās* (The history of India as revealed in a dream). More common was the escape from the oppressive rigidities of the new discursive prose into the semantic richness and polyphony of ordinary, uncolonized speech. [...]Even more striking is the communicative power of the modern Bengali drama, the least commended on aesthetic grounds by the critics of modern Bengali literature (certainly so in comparison with the novel or the short story or poetry) and yet arguably the most effective cultural form through which the English-educated literati of Calcutta commanded a popular audience (and the one cultural form subjected to the most rigorous and sustained police censorship by the colonial government). Reborn in the middle of the nineteenth century in the shapes prescribed by European theatre, the modern Bengali drama found its strength not so much in the carefully structured directedness of dramatic action and conflict as in the rhetorical power of speech. Where written prose marked a domain already surrendered to the colonizer, common speech thrived within its zealously guarded zone of autonomy and freedom.

FEAR

It is important to note that the subordination of the Bengali middle class to the colonial power was based on much more than a mental construct. Hegemonic power is always a combination of force and the persuasive self-evidence of ideology. To the extent that the persuasive apparatus of colonial ideology necessarily and invariably fails to match the requirements of justifying direct political domination, colonial rule is always marked by the palpable, indeed openly demonstrated, presence of physical force.

For the middle-class Bengali babu of late nineteenth-century Calcutta, the figures of the white boss in a mercantile office or a jute mill, the magistrate in court, the officer in the district, the police sergeant or uniformed soldiers and sailors roaming the streets of Calcutta (invariably, it seems, in a state of drunkenness) were not objects of respect and emulation: they were objects of fear.

Consider the following episode from a skit written by Girishchandra Ghosh (1844-1912), the most eminent playwright and producer on the nineteenth-century Calcutta stage and a close disciple of Ramakrishna. This minor farce, *Bellik-bājār*, was first performed at the Star theatre on Christmas Eve of 1886, only a few months after Ramakrishna's death.[29]

The opening scene is set, not without reason, in the Death Registration office at the Nimtala cremation ground in Calcutta. We meet first a doctor and then a lawyer inquiring from a *murdāpharās* (whose business it is to burn dead bodies) about recent cremations. They are practitioners of the new arts of commercialization of death: the first works upon bodies in a state of sickness, prolonging the disease while holding death at bay; the second begins his work after death, entangling surviving relatives in an endless chain of litigation. The colonial city is where people come to make money out of death. The sole official representative here—the registration clerk (who, when we meet him, is, suitably enough, asleep)—has the job of putting into the official accounts the details of every death.

Enter Dokari, himself a recent and lowly entrant into the world of the Calcutta babus, learning to survive by his wits in a city of worldly opportunities. He tells the two gentlemen about the death of a wealthy trader whose only son, Lalit, would be an easy prey for all of them. The three strike a deal and proceed to lure the moneyed young man into the path of expensive living, dubious property deals, and lawsuits. In time, Dokari is predictably outmaneuvered by his more accomplished partners and, thrown out by is wealthy patron, finds himself back on the street. It is Christmas Eve, and the lawyer and doctor have arranged a lavish party, at Lalit's expense, of course, where they are to deliver upon their unsuspecting victim the coup de grâce.

Dokari, roaming the streets, suddenly comes upon three Englishmen and, instinctively, turns around and runs. (The italicized words in the following extracts are in English in the original.)

ENG. 1: *Not so fast, not so fast...*
They catch hold of Dokari.
DOKARI: Please, saheb! *Poor man!...License have, thief not.*
ENG 1: *Hold the ankle, Dick. Darkee wants a swing...*
They lift him up and swing him in the air.
DOKARI: My bones *all another place*, my insides *up down, head making thus thus*. [Falls]

....

ENG 2: *Grog-shop?*
DOKARI: Curse in English as much as you please. I don't understand it, so it doesn't touch me.
ENG 2: *A good ale house?*
DOKARI: Let me give it back to you in Bengali. My great-grandson is married to your sister, I'm married to your sister, I'm her bastard. ...
ENG 3: *Wine shop...*sharab ghar...
Dokari now realizes what the Englishmen want and remembers the party in Lalit's gardenhouse.
DOKARI: *Yes, sir, your servant, sir. Wine shop here not. Master eat wine? Come garden, very near.* ... *Brandy, whiskey, champagne, all, all, fowl, cutlet...free, free, come garden, come my back, back me, not beat, come from my back.*

    The party is a travesty of 'enlightened' sociability, with a couple of hired dancing girls posing as the liberated wives of our friends the lawyer and the doctor. A social reformer delivers an impassioned speech on the ignorance and irrationality of his countrymen. As he ends his speech with the words '*Oh! Poor India, where art thou, come to your own country,*' Dokari enters with the three Englishmen. The sight of the white men causes immediate panic, the party breaks up in confusion, and the Englishmen settle down to a hearty meal.
    A mortal fear of the Englishman and of the world over which he dominated was a constituent element in the consciousness of the Calcutta middle class—in its obsequious homages in pidgin English and foul-mouthed denunciations in Bengali no less than in the measured rhetoric of enlightened social reformers. But fear can also be the source of new strategies of survival and resistance.

WITHDRAWAL FROM KARMA

[...] MASTER: [...] In the Kaliyuga the best way is bhaktiyoga, the path of devotion singing the praises of the Lord, and prayer. The path of devotion is the religion [dharma] of this age.[30]

This recurrent message runs through the *Kathāmṛta*. Worldly pursuits occupy a domain of selfish and particular interests. It is a domain of conflict, of domination and submission, of social norms, legal regulations, disciplinary rules enforced by the institutions of power. It is a domain of constant flux, ups and downs of fortune, a domain of greed and of humiliation. It is a domain that the worldly householder cannot do without, but it is one he has to enter because of the force of circumstances over which he has no control. But he can always escape into his own world of consciousness, where worldly pursuits are forgotten, where they have no essential existence. This is the inner world of devotion, a personal relation of *bhakti* (devotion) with the Supreme Being. [...]

OF WOMAN AND GOLD

What is it that stands between the family man and his quest for God? It is a double impediment, fused into one. *Kāminī-kāñcan*, 'woman and gold', 'woman-gold': one stands for the other. Together they represent *māyā*, man's attachment to and greed for things particular and transient, the fickle pursuit of immediate worldly interest. Together they stand as figures of the bondage of man. [...]

This woman who stands as a sign of man's bondage in the world is the woman of flesh and blood, woman in the immediacy of everyday life, with a fearsome sexuality that lures, ensnares, and imprisons the true self of man. It binds him to a pursuit of worldly interests that can only destroy him. The figure of this woman is typically that of the seductress.

[...] Master: [...] You must be extremely careful about women. Gopala bhava! Pay no attention to such things. The proverb says: 'Woman devours the three worlds.' Many women, when they see handsome and healthy young men, lay snares for them. That's gopala bhava! 31 [...]

The only path for survival for the householder is to reduce one's attachments in the world, to sever oneself and withdraw from the ties of worldly interest, escape into the freedom of a personal relationship of devotion to an absolute power that stands above all temporal and transient powers. [...]

The creation of this autonomous domain of freedom in consciousness impels the family man to an everyday routine of non-attached performance of worldly activities, guided by duty (*kartavya*) and compassion (*dayā*), not by the sensual pursuit of *kāma* (desire) or the interested pursuit of *artha* (wealth). [...]

MASTER: When one has true love for God [*rāgabhakti*], there are no ties of attachment with one's wife or child or kin. There is only compassion. The world becomes a foreign land, a land where one comes to work. Just as one's home is in the village, Calcutta is only a place where one works.[32] [...]

MASTER: [...] So I say to those who visit me: 'Live in the world by all means. There is no harm in that. But always keep your mind on God. Know for certain that this house, family and property are not yours. They are God's. Your real home is beside god.'[33]

In fact, with an attitude of non-attachment, the family man can turn his home into a haven for his spiritual pursuits.

MASTER: [...]Why should you leave the world? In fact, there are advantages at home. You don't have to worry about food. Live with your wife—nothing wrong in that. Whatever you need for your physical comforts, you have them at home. If you are ill, you have people to look after you.[34]

[...] For the most part, the life of a householder can be ordered by means of a suitable *aśramadharma*.

MASTER: The renunciation of woman-and-gold is meant for the sannyasi. ... [It] is not meant for householders like you. ... As for you, live with woman in an unattached way, as far as possible. From time to time, go away to a quiet place and think of God. Women must not be present there. If you acquire faith and devotion in God, you can remain unattached. [...] [35]

THE ASSERTION OF MASCULINITY

The figure of woman often acts as a sign in discursive formations, standing for concepts or entities that have little to do with women in actuality. Each signification of this kind also implies a corresponding sign in which the figure of man is made to stand for other concepts or entities, opposed to and contrasted with the first. However, signs can be operated upon—connected to, transposed with, differentiated from other signs in a semantic field where new meanings are produced.

The figure of woman as *kāminī* and the identification of this figure with *kāñcan* (gold) produced a combination that signified a social world of everyday transactions in which the family man was held in bondage. In terms of genealogy, the specific semantic content of this idea in Ramakrishna's sayings could well be traced to a very influential lineage in popular religious beliefs in Bengal, in which the female, in her essence of *prakṛti*, the principle of motion or change, is conceived of as unleashing the forces of *pravṛtti*, or desire, to bring about degeneration and death in the male, whose essence of *puruṣa* represents the principle of stasis or rest.[36] (One must, however, be careful, first, not to attribute to this any essentialist meaning characteristic of 'Hindu tradition' or 'Indian tradition' or even 'popular tradition', for it is only one strand in pre-colonial religious and philosophical thought. Second, we must bear in mind that even this idea of the male and female principles operated within a rich semantic field and was capable of producing in religious doctrines and literary traditions a wide variety of specific meanings.)

But in the particular context of the *Kathāmṛta* in relation to middle-class culture, the figure of woman-and-gold could acquire the status of a much more specific sign: the sign of the economic and political subordination of the respectable male householder in colonial Calcutta. It connoted humiliation and fear, the constant troubles and anxieties of maintaining a life of respectability and dignity, the sense of intellectual confusion and spiritual crisis in which neither the traditional prescriptions of ritual practice nor the unconcretized principles of enlightened rationality could provide adequate guidance in regulating one's daily life in a situation that, after all, was unprecedented in 'tradition'. The sign, therefore, was loaded with negative meanings: greed, venality, deception, immorality, aggression, violence—the qualifications of success in the worlds both of commerce and of statecraft. The signification, in other words, could work toward a moral condemnation of the wealthy and the powerful. It would also produce a searing condemnation in nationalist mythography of the British imperialist—the unscrupulous trader turned ruthless conqueror.

The figure of woman-and-gold also signified the enemy within: that part of one's own self which was susceptible to the temptations of an ever-unreliable worldly success. From this signification stemmed a strategy of survival, of the stoical defence of the autonomy of the weak encountered in the 'message' of Ramakrishna. It involved, as we have seen, an essentialization of the 'inner' self of the man-in-the-world and an essentialization of womanhood in the protective and nurturing figure of the mother. This inner sanctum was to be valorized as a haven of mental peace, spiritual security, and emotional comfort: woman as mother, safe, comforting, indulgent, playful, and man as child, innocent, vulnerable, ever in need of care and protection.

But we are dealing here with a middle class whose 'middleness' would never let its consciousness rest in stoical passivity. The 'hypermasculinity' of imperialist ideology made the figure of the weak, irresolute, effeminate babu a special target of contempt and ridicule.[37] The colonized literati reacted with rage and indignation, inflicting upon itself a fierce assault of self-ridicule and self-irony. No one was more unsparing in this than Bankimchandra.[38]

[...] [C]onsider the following, purportedly a prediction by the sage Vaisampayana, the all-seeing reciter of the *Mahabharata*:
The word 'babu' will have many meanings. Those who will rule India in the Kali age and be known as Englishmen will understand by the word a common clerk or superintendent of provisions; to the poor it will mean those wealthier than themselves, to servants the master. [...] He who has one word in his mind, which becomes ten when he speaks, hundred when he writes and thousands when he quarrels is a babu. He whose strength is one-time in his hands, ten-times in his mouth, a hundred times behind the back and absent at the time of action is a babu. He whose deity is the Englishman, preceptor the Brahmo preacher, scriptures the newspapers and pilgrimage the National Theater is a babu. He who declares himself a Christian to missionaries, a Brahmo to Keshabchandra, a Hindu to his father and an atheist to the Brahman beggar is a babu. One who drinks water at home, alcohol at his friend's, receives abuse from the prostitute and kicks from his boss is a babu. He who hates oil when he bathes, his own fingers when he eats and his mother tongue when he speaks is indeed a babu. [...]
O King, the people whose virtues I have recited to you will come to believe that by chewing *pan*, lying prone on the bed, making bilingual conversation and smoking tobacco, they will reconquer India.[39]

The mode of self-ridicule became a major literary form of expressing the bhadralok's view of himself. And once the moral premises of the auto-critique had been stated publicly—the valorization, that is to say, of courage, achievement, control, and just power as the essence of true manliness—the critique of babu effeminacy could be legitimately voiced even by the babu's indigenous 'others', that is, by the women in their families and by both men and women of the lower classes. Fiction and drama in late nineteenth-century Bengal are replete with instances of women, from 'respectable' families as well as from the urban poor, showing up the pretentiousness, cowardice, and effeminacy of the educated male.

We have then, simultaneously with the enchantment of the middle class with Ramakrishna's mystical play upon the theme of the feminization of the male, an invocation of physical strength as the true history of the nation, an exhortation to educated men to live up to their responsibilities as leaders of the nation, as courageous sons of a mother humiliated by a foreign intruder. Narendranath transformed into Swami Vivekananda is the most dramatic example of this switching of signs, converting Ramakrishna's message of inner devotion into a passionate plea for moral action in the world, turning the attitude of defensive stoicism into a call for vanguardist social and, by implication, political activism. Bankim too used the inherently polysomic possibilities of the construction of social entities as gendered categories by classicizing, in an entirely 'modern' way, the ideal of masculinity as standing for the virtues of self-respect, justice, ethical conduct, responsibility, and enlightened leadership, and of feminity as courage, sacrifice, inspiration, and source of strength.

Ramakrishna was hardly appreciative of these exhortations of hyper-masculinity in the male or of the supposed activization of the masculine-in-the-female. [...][40] More interesting is a report on Mahendranath's reading passages from Bankim's novel *Debī Caudhurānī* to Ramakrishna. [...] [and] then read from the novel the section on Praphulla's education, on how she read grammar, poetry, Sankhya, Vedanta, logic.
MASTER: Do you know what this means? That you cannot have knowledge without learning. This writer and people like him think, 'Learning first, God later. To find God you must first have knowledge of books!'[41]

Ramakrishna was thoroughly unconvinced by the emerging middle-class ideal of the 'new' woman who would fulfil her vocation as daughter, wife, or mother in respectable urban homes precisely by means of an education that had been denied to 'traditional' women or to women of the lower classes. [...]

What is rational and realistic to Bankim becomes immoral worldliness to Ramakrishna; what is true devotion to Ramakrishna becomes hypocrisy to Bankim. Both attitudes were, however, parts of the same consciousness. They came to be reconciled in curious ways, most importantly by an ingenious and not always comfortable separation between, on one plane, the outer and the inner selves, and on another plane, the public and the private selves. The public self of the intelligentsia was its political self—rationalist, modern, expressing itself within the hegemonic discursive domain of enlightened nationalism. The private self was where it retreated from the humiliation of a failed hegemony. [...]

TO RETURN TO MEDIATION

There are three themes in this reading of the *Kathāmṛta* that I will pursue [...]. All of them have to do with nationalism as a project of mediation.

First is the appropriation of the popular. Mahendranath's favourite description of Ramakrishna is that of the child—laughing, innocent, mischievous, playful. This innocence is not quite pre-adult, but an innocence that has passed through the anxieties and misfortunes of adulthood to return to itself. It is an innocence that contains within itself a wisdom far richer and more resilient than the worldly cunning of worldly adults.

We know this to be the preferred form in which middle-class-consciousness desires to appropriate the popular. The popular becomes the repository of natural truth, naturally self-sustaining and therefore timeless. It has to be approached not by the calculating analytic of rational reasoning but by 'feelings of the heart', by lyrical compassion. The popular is also the timeless truth of the national culture, uncontaminated by colonial reason. In poetry, music, drama, painting, and now in film and the commercial arts of decorative design, this is the form in which a middle-class culture, constantly seeking to 'nationalize' itself, finds nourishment in the popular.

The popular is also appropriated in a sanitized form, carefully erased of all marks of vulgarity, coarseness, localism, and sectarian identity. The very timelessness of its 'structure' opens itself to normalization.

The popular enters hegemonic national discourse as a gendered category. In its immediate being, it is made to carry the negative marks of concrete sexualized femininity. Immediately, therefore, what is popular is unthinking, ignorant, superstitious, scheming, quarrelsome, and also potentially dangerous and uncontrollable. But with the mediation of enlightened leadership, its true essence is made to shine forth in its natural strength and beauty: its capacity for resolute endurance and sacrifice and its ability to protect and nourish.

The second theme is that of the classicization of tradition. A nation, or so at least the nationalist believes, must have a past. If nineteenth-century Englishmen could claim, with scant regard for the particularities of geography or anthropology, a cultural ancestry in classical Greece, there was no reason why nineteenth-century Bengalis could not claim one in the Vedic age. All that was necessary was a classicization of tradition. Orientalist scholarship had already done the groundwork for this. A classicization of modern Bengali high culture—its language, literature, aesthetics, religion, philosophy—preceded the birth of political nationalism and worked alongside it well into the present century.

A mode of classicization could comfortably incorporate as particulars the diverse identities in 'Indian tradition', including such overtly anti-Brahmanical movements as Buddhism, Jainism, and the various deviant popular sects. A classicization of tradition was, in any case, a prior requirement for the vertical appropriation of sanitized popular traditions.

The real difficulty was with Islam in India, which could claim, within the same classicizing mode, an alternative classical tradition. The national past had been constructed by the early generation of the Bengali intelligentsia as a 'Hindu' past, regardless of the fact that the appellation itself was of recent vintage and that the revivalism chose to define itself by a name given to it by 'others'. This history of the nation could accommodate Islam only as a foreign element, domesticated by shearing its own lineage of a classical past. Popular Islam could then be incorporated in the national culture in the doubly sanitized form of syncretism.

The middle-class culture we have spoken of here was, and still is, in its overwhelming cultural content, 'Hindu'. Its ability and willingness to extend its hegemonic boundaries to include what was distinctly Islamic became a matter of much contention in nineteenth- and twentieth-century Bengal, giving rise to alternative hegemonic efforts at both the classicization of the Islamic tradition and the appropriation of a sanitized popular Islam.

The third theme concerns the structure of the hegemonic domain of nationalism. Nationalism inserted itself into a new public sphere where it sought to overcome the subordination of the colonized middle class. In that sphere, nationalism insisted on eradicating all signs of colonial difference by which the colonized people had been marked as incorrigibly inferior and therefore undeserving of the status of self-governing citizens of a modern society. Thus, the legal-institutional forms of political authority that nationalists subscribed to were entirely in conformity with the principles of a modern regime of power and were often modelled on specific examples supplied by western Europe and North America. In this public sphere created by the political processes of the colonial state, therefore, the nationalist criticism was not that colonial rule was imposing alien institutions of state on indigenous society but rather that it was restricting and even violating the true principles of modern government. Through the nineteenth century and into the twentieth, accompanied by the spread of the institutions of capitalist production and exchange, these legal and administrative institutions of the modern state penetrated deeper and deeper into colonial society and touched upon the lives of greater and greater sections of the people. In this aspect of the political domain, therefore, the project of nationalist hegemony was, and in its postcolonial phase, continues to be, to institute and ramify the characteristically modern forms of disciplinary power.

But there was another aspect of the new political domain in which this hegemonic project involved an entirely contrary movement. Here, unlike in Europe in the eighteenth and nineteenth centuries, the public sphere in the political domain, and its literary precursors in the debating societies and learned bodies, did not emerge out of the discursive construction of a social world peopled by 'individuals'. Nor was there an 'audience-oriented subjectivity', by which the new conjugal family's intimate domain became publicly transparent and thus consistent with and amenable to the discursive controls of the public sphere in the political domain.[42] In Europe, even as the distinction was drawn between the spheres of the private and the public, of 'man' and 'bourgeois' and later of 'man' and 'citizen', the two spheres were nevertheless united within a single political domain and made entirely consistent with its universalist discourse. In colonial society, the political domain was under alien control and the colonized excluded from its decisive zones by a rule of colonial difference. Here for the colonized to allow the intimate domain of the family to become amenable to the discursive regulations of the political domain inevitably meant a surrender of autonomy. The nationalist response was to constitute a new sphere of the private in a domain marked by cultural difference: the domain of the 'national' was defined as one that was different from the 'Western'. The new subjectivity that was constructed here was premised not on a conception of universal humanity, but rather on particularity and difference: the identity of the 'national' community as against other communities.[43] In this aspect of the political domain, then, the hegemonic movement of nationalism was not to promote but rather, in a quite fundamental sense, to resist the sway of the modern institutions of disciplinary power. The contradictory implications of these two movements in the hegemonic domain of nationalism have been active right through its career and continue to affect the course of postcolonial politics. The process could be described, in Gramscian terms, as 'passive revolution' and contains, I think, a demonstration of both the relevance and the insurmountable limits of a Foucauldian notion of the modern regime of disciplinary power.[44] The search for a postcolonial modernity has been tied, from its very birth, with its struggle against modernity. [...]

NOTES

1. To mention only a few of the more notable works: J.H. Broomfield, *Elite Conflict in a Plural Society: Twentieth-Century Bengal* (Berkeley, 1968); Anil Seal, *The Emergence of Indian Nationalism* (Cambridge, 1971); Pradip Sinha, *Calcutta in Urban History* (Calcutta, 1978); Sumit Sarkar, *The Swadeshi Movement in Bengal* (New Delhi, 1973); Rajat K. Ray, *Social Conflict and Political Unrest in Bengal, 1875–1914* (Delhi, 1984).

2. A recent work that raises this question is Tapan Raychaudhuri, *Europe Reconsidered: Perceptions of the West in Nineteenth-Century Bengal* (Delhi, 1988).

3. Ma [Mahendranath Gupta], *Śrīśrīrāmkṛṣṇa kathāmṛta*, 5 vols (Calcutta: 1902–32). For this study, I have used the single-volume complete edition (Calcutta, 1983). [...]

4. Sumit Sarkar, '"Kaliyuga," "Chakri" and "Bhakti": Ramkrishna and His Times', *Economic and Political Weekly* 27, 29 (18 July 1992), pp. 1543–66.

5. In 1931, there were a total of 1,544 Brahmos in Calcutta, nearly two-thirds of them concentrated in the single municipal ward of Sukea's Street. *Census of India, 1931*, vol. 6 (Calcutta), pts 1 and 2 (Calcutta, 1933), imperial table 13, pp. 169–71.

6. Rajnarayan Basu, *Ātmacarit* (1909), in Nareschandra Jana, Manu Jana, and Kamalkumar Sanyal, (eds), *Ātmakathā* (Calcutta, 1981), 1, p. 72.

7. Swami Saradananda, *Śrīśrīrāmkṛṣṇalīlāprasaṅga* (1908–20; reprint, Calcutta, 1965), 2, pp. 398–9 [...].

8. P.C. Mozoomdar, *The Life and Teachings of Keshub Chunder Sen* (1887; reprint, Calcutta, 1931), p. 227.

9. Meredith Borthwick, *Keshub Chunder Sen: A Search for Cultural Synthesis* (Calcutta, 1977), pp. 140–1. Anil Seal, quoting Grierson, gives much lower figures: in 1882–3 there were, according to this government source, only two Bengali papers, the *Baṅgabāsī* and *Sulabh samācār*, with circulations of 4,000. Seal, *Emergence*, p. 366.

10. Nanda Mookerjee, (ed.), *Sri Ramakrishna in the Eyes of Brahma and Christian Admirers* (Calcutta, 1976), p. 2.

11. Christopher Isherwood, *Ramakrishna and His Disciples* (New York, 1965), p. 240.

12. Ibid., p. 248.
13. The closest devotees all arrived between 1879 and 1884. Saradananda, *Sri Ramakrishna the Great Master*, trans. Swami Jagadananda, p. 811. A recent study of Ramakrishna's disciples is Swami Chetanananda, *They Lived with God: Life Stories of Some Devotees of Sri Ramakrishna* (St Louis, Mo., 1989).
14. Prosanto Kumar Sen, *Keshub Chunder Sen* (Calcutta, 1938), p. 119.
15. Saratchandra Chakrabarti (1865–1927), who with the founding of the monastic order after Ramakrishna's death adopted the name Swami Saradananda, was the secretary of the Ramakrishna Math and Mission from 1898 to his death. Between 1908 and 1920 he wrote the series of articles that were later compiled to from the *Līlāprasaṅga*, the authorized account of the Master's life, of which *Sri Ramakrishna the Great Master* is a translation.
16. Saradananda, *Sri Ramakrishna the Great Master*, trans. Swami Jagadananda, p. 33.
17. Ibid., p. 5.
18. Ibid., p. 13.
19. See Partha Chatterjee, *Nationalist Thought and the Colonial World: A Derivative Discourse?* (London, 1986), pp. 58–60.
20. Saradananda, *Sri Ramakrishna the Great Master*, trans. Swami Jagadananda, p. 15.
21. Ibid., p. 811.
22. Ibid., p. 711.
23. Ibid., p. 16.
24. Sarkar, '"Kaliyuga," "Chakri" and "Bhakti".'
25. I have in mind the researches of Sisirkumar Das, Tarapada Mukhopadhyay, Anisuzzaman, Pradyumna Bhattacharya, Debes Ray, and Prabal Dasgupta. For a recent survey of the questions surrounding the development of the new Bengali prose, see Pradyumna Bhattacharya, 'Rammohan ray ebam banla gadya', *Baromas* 11, no. 2 (April 1990), pp. 1–22.
26. Ernest Gellner, *Nations and Nationalism* (Oxford, 1983); Benedict Anderson, *Imagined Communities: Reflections on the Origin and Spread of Nationalism* (London, 1983).
27. There have been many attempts in the last hundred years to place Ramakrishna in the tradition of classical Indian philosophy. One of the most erudite of these is Satis Chandra Chatterjee, *Classical Indian Philosophies: Their Synthesis in the Philosophy of Sri Ramakrishna* (Calcutta, 1963).
28. Sudipta Kaviraj, 'Bankimchandra and the Making of Nationalist Consciousness. IV: Imaginary History', manuscript.
29. Girishchandra Ghosh, *Giriś racanābalī*, vol. 1, (eds), Rathindranath Ray and Debipada Bhattacharya (Calcutta, 1969), pp. 113–28.
30. Ma [Mahendranath Gupta], *Śrīśrīrāmkṛṣṇa kathāmṛta*, pp. 41–2; [Mahendranath Gupta] *The Gospel of Sri Ramakrishna*, trans. Swami Nikhilananda (New York, 1942), pp. 142–3 [...]. Unless otherwise specified, I will quote from this translation of the *Kathāmṛta*. I must, however, point out that there is a quite deliberate attempt in the *Gospel* to 'Christianize' Ramakrishna's language: the translation into English provides the opportunity to put yet another gloss on the language of the *Kathāmṛta*.

The Subalternity of a Nationalist Elite   117

31. Gupta, Śrīśrīrāmkṛṣṇa kathāmṛta, pp. 334-5; *The Gospel of Sri Ramakrishna*, trans. Swami Nikhilananda (New York, 1942), p. 603 [...]. Unless otherwise specified, I will quote from this translation of the Kathāmṛta. I must, however, point out that there is a quite deliberate attempt in the *Gospel* to 'Christianize' Ramakrishna's language: the translation into English provides the opportunity to put yet another gloss on the language of the Kathāmṛta.

32. Gupta, Śrīśrīrāmkṛṣṇa kathāmṛta, pp. 64-65; *The Gospel of Sri Ramakrishna*, p. 173.

33. Gupta, Śrīśrīrāmkṛṣṇa kathāmṛta, pp. 104-5; *The Gospel of Sri Ramakrishna*, pp. 456-7.

34. Gupta, Śrīśrīrāmkṛṣṇa kathāmṛta, p. 122; *The Gospel of Sri Ramakrishna*, p. 627.

35. Gupta, Śrīśrīrāmkṛṣṇa kathāmṛta, p. 177; *The Gospel of Sri Ramakrishna*, p. 866.

36. A useful account of these religious ideas will be found in Sashibhusan Das Gupta, *Obscure Religious Cults* (Calcutta, 1969).

37. Ashis Nandy, *The Intimate Enemy: Loss and Recovery of Self under Colonialism* (Delhi, 1983).

38. See Sudipta Kaviraj, 'Bankimchandra and the making of Nationalist Consciousness: I. Signs of Madness; II. The Self-Ironical Tradition; III. A Critique of Colonial Reason,' Occasional Papers 108, 109, and 110 (Calcutta, 1989).

39. Bankimchandra Chattopadhyay, *Baṅkim racanābalī* (Calcutta, 1965), 2, pp. 11-12 [...].

40. Gupta, Śrīśrīrāmkṛṣṇa kathāmṛta, p. 191; *The Gospel of Sri Ramakrishna*, p. 891.

41. Gupta, Śrīśrīrāmkṛṣṇa kathāmṛta, pp. 362-6; *The Gospel of Sri Ramakrishna*, pp. 683-6.

42. The classic analysis of this process in western Europe is in Jürgen Habermas, *The Structural Transformation of the Public Sphere: An Inquiry into a Category of Bourgeois Society*, trans. Thomas Burger (Cambridge, 1991).

43. Homi Bhabha points out an interesting distinction in nationalist narratives between the people as 'a pedagogical object' and the people 'constructed in the performance of the narrative'. The former produces a self-generating tradition for the nation, while the latter 'intervenes in the sovereignty of the nation's *self-generation* by casting a shadow between the people as 'image' and its signification as a differential sign of Self, distinct from the Other or the Outside.' 'DissemiNation: Time, Narrative, and the Margins of the Modern Nation', in Bhabha, (ed.), *Nation and Narration* (London, 1990), pp. 291-322. I am trying to explore a similar disjunctive process in anti-colonial nationalist encounters with the narrative of modernity.

44. I have attempted to trace the course of anti-colonial nationalist politics in India in these terms in *Nationalist Thought and the Colonial World*.

What about the Merchants?*
A Mercantile Perspective on the Middle Class of Colonial India

CLAUDE MARKOVITS

The notion of a unified and large Indian middle class is a fairly recent construct, the product of the ongoing liberalization, and of the unreasonable expectations of market analysts and multinational firms regarding the size of the Indian market. A recent author underlines that, even understood solely in terms of consumption, the Indian middle class 'cuts a rather pathetic figure'.[1] This is, however, a view which has been formed by a comparison with the developed West. In relation to other developing countries, and even more so to the mass of the poor and the ordinary working population in India itself, the figure it cuts is not that pathetic. But there remains the problem of where to locate this vast and fairly undifferentiated group on the social map of India. Prior to the 1990s, social scientists generally preferred to talk of the middle classes to take into account the extreme diversity of the middle strata of the Indian society. Whether singular or plural, the two dominant narratives of the rise and growth of this group in India have been a 'Macaulayan' one and a 'Kaleckian' one. In the former, pride of place was undoubtedly given to the English educated professionals as forming the core group in the Indian middle class, while in the latter, merchants and entrepreneurs occupied a more central position. In this paper, I seek to present an alternative narrative, in which Macaulay

---

* Originally published as 'Merchants, Entrepreneurs and the Middle Classes in Twentieth Century India', in Claude Markovits, *Merchants, Traders, Entrepreneurs: Indian Business in the Colonial Era* (New Delhi: Permanent Black, 2008), pp. 167-83. For the complete text see the original. In the present version, some portions of the essay have been removed and notes rearranged accordingly.

and his kind play no role, but which also takes some distance vis-à-vis the Kaleckian model, a narrative of the slow emergence, from within a merchant world, of a strata of entrepreneurs who have become an important component of the Indian middle classes. In the first part, I take a quick look at these two dominant narratives.

A CRITIQUE OF TWO DOMINANT NARRATIVES

Although the rise of an Indian middle class is generally traced to the colonial period, in particular to the middle decades of the nineteenth century, when Macaulay's programme outlined in his famous 'Minute on Indian education' of creating a 'class of persons, Indian in blood and colour, but English in taste, in opinions, in morals and in intellect'[2] started being implemented by the colonial state with the creation of universities and more generally the encouragement given to the expansion of Western education in the major cities of India. However, it should be noted that neither Macaulay nor other colonial luminaries used the term 'middle class' in conjunction with the emerging new social group of Indian English-educated literati. Actually it could be argued that the use of the term 'middle class' in the Indian context was fundamentally an anathema to them. It was a basic assumption of Western 'orientalism' that one of the major differences between European and 'Oriental' societies was precisely the absence in the latter of a 'middle estate', of an intermediate class between the tiny dominant elite and the mass of the subject population. Recognizing the existence of an Indian 'middle class' would have amounted to acknowledging a certain degree of similarity between the English and Indian societies, which would have endangered the colonial project itself. Macaulay himself thought in terms of a class of intermediaries, of cultural brokers, who were basically clerks, but not 'middle class', with the connotations of respectability and affluence which the term had in the nineteenth century. As Indian nationalism emerged in the late nineteenth century, British colonial administrators were careful not to define it as a 'middle class' movement, but tended to dismiss it as reflecting the views of a 'microscopic minority' of elite individuals totally cut off from the masses of India. The early Indian nationalists in their turn, in spite of the fact that they undoubtedly belonged to the middle strata of society (they were mostly lawyers and professionals) were wary of defining their movement and aspirations as 'middle class' and preferred to present themselves either as an aspiring elite or, in a more populist fashion, as the vanguard of the people.

The theme of the rise of an Indian middle class or rather a petty bourgeoisie was first elaborated upon only in the 1930s, mostly by Marxist authors, such as Rajani Palme Dutt,[3] but, in 'orthodox' Marxist fashion (although there is some ambiguity as to Marx's own position on the question), they saw this class as doomed to be squeezed by the growing polarization between a big bourgeoisie and an emerging proletariat. A slightly modified form of the classical Marxist position was articulated by D.D. Kosambi in the 'introduction' to his celebrated book, *Culture and Civilization of Ancient India*[4]. [...]

The first academic author to deal in a systematic way with the question of the Indian middle class, B.B. Misra, however, came from a completely different ideological horizon.[5] He offered a broad-ranging historical survey [...] of the rise and growth of the middle class in India which he equated with a phenomenon of modernization induced by colonialism and the impact of the West. This kind of approach sounds rather obsolete 40 years later, but one of Misra's merits was his alertness to the great empirical diversity of the Indian middle classes. In particular he was careful to distinguish among a commercial middle class, an industrial middle class, a landed middle class and an educated middle class, in which he gave particular attention to the practitioners of what he called 'the learned professions', and not to reify any of these categories as constituting the Indian middle class. In spite of his empirical caution, in the 1960s the dominant narrative of the Indian middle class was nevertheless undoubtedly 'Macaulayan', inasmuch as it put at the centre of the stage those who were the English-educated, and directly linked the Indian middle class to modernization theory which was then the fashionable paradigm. This view was challenged in the late 1960s and early 1970s by the rise of the so-called 'Cambridge school', which tended to dismiss the link between Western education and political consciousness, especially in accounting for the emergence of the Indian nationalist movement, but did not come forward with an alternative sociological formulation.

In the following decades, the burgeoning sociological literature about India paid relatively little detailed attention to the middle class, preoccupied as it was with grander questions regarding caste and class, and discussions of the Dumontian and other paradigms. It was left to economists and historians operating within a broad Marxist framework to put forward an alternative view which I call 'Kaleckian' because it derived its original inspiration from a short article on 'intermediate regimes' by the famous Polish economist.[6] It had been written in the 1950s but was translated into English in the early 1970s and attracted the attention of K.N. Raj, who applied Kalecki's insight to the Indian case in a well-known article.[7] [...] Burton Stein elaborated on Kalecki's and Raj's contributions to put forward a *longue durée* view of India as an 'intermediate regime' centred on a characterization of the 'petty bourgeoisie' as a particularly significant category in both economic and political terms.[8] The rise of this petty bourgeoisie was related to a particular form of the transition to capitalism which started in the eighteenth century before colonization but remained largely unrealized till the late twentieth century. Far from being a sign of triumphant modernity, the rise of this class was perceived by Stein as emblematic of an arrested transition and of the kind of populist politics that it bred. This class was seen by Stein and others as a class in itself and not as a section of the bourgeoisie: it often frontally opposed the latter, but it was also in an exploitative relationship vis-à-vis the mass of the people. Stein's view, which was couched in a somewhat dogmatic language, never gained wide acceptance in an academic community which was increasingly steeped in culturalism and post-modernism, and the 'Kaleckian' paradigm, with its clear Marxist connotations, largely fell into disuse during the 1990s. It is interesting to note that a recent widely-celebrated essay on the Indian middle class,[9] ignores Kalecki altogether, and basically goes back to a Macaulayan narrative of the origins of the middle class.

These two narratives, while addressing different concerns and adopting different angles of vision, attempt to locate the middle class into some broad historical scheme, but give little detailed attention to the historical process of formation of a class of merchants and entrepreneurs. In this paper I shall focus exclusively on the latter group and shall not preoccupy myself primarily with definitional problems [...] For the purpose of this paper, I shall adopt a largely pragmatic and empirical definition. The section I shall be looking at will be those merchants, traders, and entrepreneurs who are not, strictly speaking, shopkeepers (the latter constituting a very large category on which there exists practically no empirical work in the Indian context), but at the same time do not belong to the very top echelons of the business world either. I will thus deliberately exclude from my area of inquiry the Birlas, the Tatas, and other big capitalists, who are certainly not 'middle class' and about whom I have written at length elsewhere.[10] The people I am going to talk about are 'middle' in terms of their incomes, in the sense that they do not belong to the low income majority or to the tiny elite of the really rich, but range from the moderately well-off to the conspicuously affluent ... .They are merchants, traders, and medium or small-scale industrialists. They obviously account for a significant chunk of the overall middle classes in terms of numbers, but there remains a big question as to whether they constitute a separate social group or can be seen as part of a broader sociological category. My approach to them will be decidedly historical, because there is a certain lack of readily available historical literature on the subject.

THE MERCANTILE AND ENTREPRENEURIAL SECTOR OF INDIAN SOCIETY SINCE THE MIDDLE OF THE NINETEENTH CENTURY

[...] The middle decades of the nineteenth century saw a series of concomitant developments which concurred to reshape to a significant extent the profile of the mercantile world of India, although they did not amount to a complete revolution. These developments were on the one hand of an economic nature: the beginning of a transport revolution with the building of the first railways, the birth of a mechanized textile industry (cotton in Bombay, jute in Calcutta), and the reorganization of banks (with the passing of the Presidency Banks Act of 1876) and financial markets (with the gradual emergence of stock markets in Calcutta and Bombay) along 'modern' lines. On the other hand these developments were of a political and legal nature: the completion of the British conquest of India and the political reorganization following the end of the 1857 Revolt, with the introduction of British company law and more generally a British-inspired legal system into India. The mercantile world felt the impact of those developments only gradually but they reinforced trends which were already at work from the 1830s. One of the main outcomes of these decades of reorganization was the definitive eclipse of the elite indigenous merchant bankers who still dominated the scene in most of northern India in the first half of the nineteenth century. As British power sought to reorganize itself along modern financial principles, Indian bankers were totally deprived of their functions as state bankers, which survived only in the princely states, and the 'new men' who emerged had a different kind of link with the British. The collapse, in the 1880s, of the last great house of traditional north Indian bankers, the Mathura Seths, was emblematic of the new dispensation. It should also be noted that the 1857 Revolt itself had a significant impact on the map of wealth in India, as many landowners who had supported the Revolt or had been perceived as too lukewarm in their support to the British saw their estates confiscated, while those who had been conspicuously loyal were rewarded. An important transfer of wealth occurred in the wake of the Revolt and it helped to propel forward a new type of merchants and men of business. The increasing commodification of agriculture linked to the growth of exports produced by the limited transport revolution provided this set of operators with new opportunities. They were mostly 'upcountry merchants' who migrated from some of the princely states to the colonial port cities. In Calcutta, they came mostly from Bikaner, Marwar, and the Shekawat area of Jaipur State, the so-called 'Marwaris'.[11] They displaced the Bengali traders, the Gandhavaniks and the Suvarnavaniks, who had become the intermediaries of the British in the eighteenth century. In Bombay, there was a similar influx of traders from Kutch (Memons, Khojas, and Bhatias) and from the Kathiawar states, and a decline of the 'indigenous' Konkani Muslims who had played a significant role in the first half of the nineteenth century. These new men were pushed out by the poverty prevalent in the princely states of the 'dry zone' of northwestern India (Gujarat, Rajasthan), and the decreased opportunities linked to the decline of old trade routes caused by the domination of colonial capital. They were also, more positively, drawn by the beckoning opportunities in the port cities and were adept at exploiting residual political differences between British India and the Indian states, particularly in the matter of taxation law. The absence of income tax in the princely states made it advantageous to regularly remit there a part of the profits earned in British India. There began thus, a regular stream of remittances from Bengal and the Bombay Presidency to the princely states of Rajputana, Kutch, and Kathiawar, and many great *havelis* were built in small towns and villages of these areas thanks to the profits earned from the sweat and labour of the peasantry of Mymensingh and other areas of jute and cotton cultivation in eastern and central India. The 'new men', some of whom also hailed from the Punjab, Sind, and other semi-arid areas of British India, were mostly traders, moneylenders, and brokers of different kinds, who played the role of intermediaries between the mass of peasant cultivators and the mostly British export firms operating from a few colonial port-cities. The chain of intermediation found its concrete translation in the rise of merchant networks which linked the brokers in the port-cities (known as the banians to the big British firms), with the traders in the market towns and the moneylenders in the rural areas through a web of family, caste, and community relationships. Some of these men of business also played a major role in the growth of the new mechanized industries, in particular of the cotton textile industry. While the original entrepreneurs had often been people from outside the world of trading (such as Ranchhodlal Chhotalal, a Nagar Brahmin who created the first cotton mill in Ahmedabad), very quickly merchants seized the new opportunities and, through the managing agency system, established their domination over much of industry. While an upper stratum of big merchants accumulated significant fortunes, the majority of these traders definitely remained in the middle income brackets. Altogether this mercantile wealth probably accounted for only a small share of the landed wealth of the big zamindars and maharajahs, even if the latter were often heavily in debt.

The growth of an entrepreneurial group was further accelerated after 1920, by the granting of fiscal autonomy to India and the adoption of a limited policy of discriminative protection which de facto reserved for local entrepreneurs a share of the domestic market in steel, cotton textiles, sugar, and other basic industrial commodities.[12] The coming of independence and the rise of the 'licence raj' from 1960 onwards gave further impetus to the growth of this section, which came to occupy an important position in the political economy of India. As the industrial sector grew in both size and complexity, small and medium-scale industrialists exploited specific niches, especially after the banning of imports of manufactured consumer goods in 1957.[13] They came from various backgrounds, but many were importers who converted themselves into industrialists and therefore had a trading background. In spite of the rise of a significant industrial sector in India from 1920 onwards, it would still be difficult to argue for the emergence of a class of industrialists separate from the vast mercantile world which spawned it in the first place. Marketing and financial skills were always at a premium in Indian industry as compared to 'technical' skills, a situation which has perhaps, started to change only very recently.

The mercantile world of India in the pre-independence period, in spite of its own great internal diversity, remained largely separate from the world of the English-educated middle classes which were more conspicuous and influential, politically and culturally. Merchant communities, with the notable exception of the Bombay Parsis, did not pay great attention to English education, which was of limited interest to them. Its main use was in the legal arena, and there were enough competent English-educated lawyers available for hire by mercantile interests, Gandhi being only one case in point. They remained steeped in vernacular regional cultures, to which they often contributed significantly through the patronage of writers, journalists, and musicians. Another factor responsible for separateness was ethnic differences. In eastern India for instance and particularly in Bengal, the commercial middle class was overwhelmingly dominated, from the late nineteenth century onwards, by the Marwari and other north Indian elements. The Bengali commercial element was largely displaced or confined to the lower rungs of mercantile activity and the separation between the educated Bengali middle class and the 'new' commercial middle class was complete. In Maharashtra likewise there was a wide gulf between the Marathi-speaking, largely Pune-based, educated middle class and the Gujarati-speaking commercial middle class based in Bombay. Even in south India, particularly in Tamil Nadu, where such ethnic differences were absent as both the Nattukottai Chettiars, who dominated the world of financial, mercantile, and industrial enterprise, as well as the educated Brahmin and non-Brahmin middle class were Tamil speaking, there remained a certain amount of social distance, in particular between Chettiars and Brahmins. With the coming of independence and the economic development it helped nurture, there occurred a limited rapprochement between the mercantile world and that of the educated middle classes through the medium of the state and the role it played in furthering industrialization. But it is only with the advent of consumerism as a dominant ideology in the 1990s that these two universes can be said to have engaged in a process of fusion which, however, remains far from complete. I shall now focus more specifically on the problem of values.

MERCHANT VALUES AND MIDDLE-CLASS VALUES

Do middle classes have values? It would be easy to give this question a cynical answer, which one could couch in the language of the Frankfurt school ('minima moralia') and stress that the central value for middle-class people is making money, while their mode of thinking favours social conformism (keeping up with the Jones'). In India, it has become fashionable to deplore the 'moral vacuum' of the present day middle class and its lack of social responsibility, as it remains apparently unconcerned by the persistence of mass poverty on an enormous scale. Such moral condemnations are facile, especially when they come from middle-class westerners who do not face the same kind of ethical dilemmas as their Indian counterparts. In a different vein, it should be noted that sociologists of the Bourdieu school have emphasized the importance of cultural assets, the so-called 'symbolic capital' to the constitution of social elites, and the area of values deserves an exploration. The merchant world of India, particularly the dominant Hindu and Jain merchant communities of northern and northwestern India, was characterized by the existence of a set of values which amounted to a 'moral economy', and could be seen as a well constituted 'habitus' already by the eighteenth century. On the other hand, the 'new' educated middle classes that developed in India in the second half of the nineteenth century were more uncertain as to what constituted their core values. Although strongly influenced by the kind of Victorian values which were then dominant in Britain, they sought at the same time to preserve a domain of 'indigenous values' which, as has been often pointed out, they located largely in the sphere of 'domesticity'. On the contradictions this dichotomy between public sphere and domestic sphere could entail, Satyajit Ray provides an illuminating and ironical commentary in *Charulata*. Merchants precisely did not have to contend to the same extent with a contradiction between two spheres, since the world of business, thanks to the dominance of the family firm, was largely coeval with the world of domesticity and did not entail entering into a 'public sphere'. Most businessmen raised capital from within their own family, kin, caste, or community and did not go 'public'. If they operated in the market place, the latter was so segmented as not to constitute a 'public arena' in any significant sense. Even nowadays, it is only a minority of large-scale firms which raise capital from the public at large. Most small and medium-scale firms rely on family and kin resources for their managerial staff and permanent capital and on borrowings from state banks for their working capital. This gives the business sector a wide measure of autonomy vis-à-vis other sections of the middle class, such as professionals, who tend to invest only in the big publicly quoted companies.

One difficulty in pursuing a comparative exercise regarding value systems is the existence of a certain degree of asymmetry in terms of information. While members of the educated middle classes were prone to express themselves orally and in writing to leave traces of their views, merchants were a more inward-looking group, which rarely expressed itself in public. For the modern and contemporary period, there is no equivalent of the *Ardhakathanak*[14], the autobiography of the seventeenth-century north Indian Jain merchant Banarsidas which is a precious source of information on the mentality of late medieval or early modern merchants. We are left to deduct merchant values from an examination of the behaviour of the merchants rather than from texts written by them. This behaviourist approach has its limitations of course, but, in the absence of direct expressions, it is the only course open to the researcher.

As a point of departure, we can take the view of the late eighteenth-century north Indian merchant world presented by the historian Christopher Bayly in his well-known *Rulers, Townsmen and Bazaars*,[15] a world which appears to have remained largely unchanged till the twentieth century. It is a broadly 'Chayanovian' view which stresses the similarities between the merchant family and the peasant family inasmuch as it makes reproduction of the family rather than enlargement of its assets, its primary goal, leading to behaviour which could be 'anti-accumulationist'. The central notion for merchants was that of credit which was largely equated with honour and social prestige: its preservation was deemed more precious than any aggrandizement. Great store was set on austerity and conspicuous consumption was looked down upon as unworthy as well as economically counter-productive. Whether merchants actually conformed to this set of norms is of course open to question and it would be only too easy to find instances of non-conforming behaviour. It appears nevertheless also fatuous to totally dismiss norms to which there was undoubtedly deeply-felt adherence, in spite of lapses in actual conduct. Were these norms very different from those which guided the 'English-educated' section of the middle classes? Some common features would be immediately apparent, such as the devaluation of conspicuous consumption and the emphasis put on thrift and self-denial. In matters of sexual morality, there would also be a lot of common ground, a markedly 'puritanical' ethic, although on the question of female education, merchants would for a long period be characterized by a very cautious attitude, which would leave them open to accusations of 'backwardness'. An area of both difference and commonality would be that of 'service', the typical Indian middle-class notion of *seva* which was popularized by organizations such as the 'Servants of India Society' and given central place by Gandhi who made it the basis of his teachings. Seva implied a certain distancing vis-à-vis family and community to encompass a notion of society at large, and that is where the ways of the merchants and of some members of the educated classes tended to diverge. While the latter often aspired to make 'service' the central vocation of their lives, merchants were too embedded in the universe of family and caste to conceive of such a devotion. They often financed liberally these 'service' activities but rarely engaged in them very deeply. Their sociability remained bound by notions of caste and family, which prevented them from interacting with society at large. This is one factor of explanation for the support given to Gandhian movements by many merchants. By financing these movements, often on a generous scale, the merchants could assuage their consciences without having to engage too openly with a public arena. Gandhi imported into the sphere of public action notions of honour (*abru*) and trust which were directly borrowed from the world of the Gujarati *banias*,[16] to which his family belonged. However, the Gandhian attempt at a synthesis between the values of the merchant world and the more 'Victorian' values of the educated classes did not succeed in completely bridging the gap between those two sections of the middle classes and its long-term impact remains a matter for speculation.

Independence and the increased role played by the state in the economy tended to result in some measure of further rapprochement between different middle-class sections. In the heydays of the 'licence raj', aspiring capitalists had to develop a rapport with bureaucrats if they wanted to enjoy the bounties of the state, and a certain closeness ensued, although one would need detailed empirical data on topics such as matrimonial alliances to know how far it all went. Prior to the recent reforms, there was nevertheless no clear trend of integration between different middle- class sections and the idea of one 'great Indian middle class' remained largely a fantasy. Since 1991, the exponential growth of consumerism (though it already existed) has tended to provide a unifying ideological cement to the diverse components of the middle class. However it is not certain as to whether the growth of consumerism is sufficient to keep together such an unstable conglomeration of groups.

Merchants and entrepreneurs constitute a numerically important section of the Indian middle class, but their place in its overall configuration remains uncertain. One durable characteristic which sets them apart from other middle class sections is their fairly narrow base of recruitment in terms of caste. While the middle class intelligentsia is drawn from a fairly large conspect of caste and regional groups, albeit mostly from upper castes, most merchants and entrepreneurs still belong to a limited number of castes, the bania and assimilated castes, and are drawn disproportionately from specific areas of the subcontinent, mostly the northwest (Gujarat, Sind, Rajasthan, Punjab). This situation has its roots in certain specific historical developments going back at least to the sixteenth century, which I have analysed elsewhere,[17] and which I shall not evoke here. Pan-Indian merchant networks such as those of the Marwaris have entrenched themselves in many areas and are not perceived any more as forming 'immigrant communities'. It is even said that in Assam it was the Marwari merchants, whose presence in the region goes back to the beginning of the nineteenth century, who were partly behind the anti-Bengali agitation of the 1970s and 1980s. They continue to give preference in employment in their firms to members of their family, kin, caste, and community, even if they are less competent than 'outsiders' (although probably to a lesser extent, now, than in earlier periods). Whether the ongoing 'liberalization' will result in breaking the hold of the bania castes on the mercantile and industrial sector is an open question. A new breed of entrepreneurs, not belonging to these castes, is undoubtedly present on the one hand in the agro-industrial sector (where they often come from peasant castes), and on the other hand in the so-called 'new economy' such as the computer software sector (where there are many Brahmins and members of other upper castes), but the overall importance of these high-tech activities should not be exaggerated. The 'old economy', where the merchant castes are still solidly entrenched, weighs more in the balance in terms of assets (once the present-day bubble bursts, as it has already started doing) as well as of employment. Notice should, however, be taken of significant changes in the way the members of the 'traditional' merchant castes relate to education and politics. They have taken to English education to a greater extent than before, often have MBAs from American universities, and some of them have developed more permanent links with political parties, particularly, in northern and western India, to the Bharatiya Janata Party (BJP). In view of the recent rise of the Sangh Parivar, it is sometimes suggested that, through their privileged links to the Hindu right, the merchant castes have been able to acquire a kind of hegemonic position and that they have imposed their values on the middle class at large. This raises two kinds of questions: first, that of the exact type of relationship which the merchant castes have with the Hindu nationalists, about which little serious empirical work has been done and second, that of the 'hegemonic' nature of Hindutva ideology, which seems to be very much open to debate.[18]

To conclude, it is not obvious to me that the merchant and entrepreneurial classes are as yet getting subsumed into an ensemble which could be called 'the great Indian middle class'. In spite of a rapprochement between this group and the professional and technical intelligentsia at the level of education and lifestyle, there remain significant differences. The universe of the merchants and small and medium-scale entrepreneurs is still centred more around the family, which remains the basic economic unit, than that of other sections of the middle class which are more dependent either on the state or on the market at large. This might partly explain the apparent paradox that while, in theory, the entrepreneurs should be the driving force behind the ongoing liberalization process, in fact large sections of this group have various reservations vis-à-vis the process and tend to act as a brake rather than as an accelerator. Many of its members are still too deeply steeped in the structure of entitlements linked to the old economy to fully embrace a liberalization which could result in a complete reshuffle and redistribution of cards. As a result, they cannot be expected to give a clear direction to the process, and it will be left largely to the bureaucrats and politicians, constrained as they are by the compulsions of populist politics, to define its pace.

NOTES

1. Gupta, 2000, p. 95
2. Macaulay 1835 quoted in Varma, 1998, p. 2
3. Dutt, 1940
4. Kosambi, 1964, p. 2
5. Misra, 1961
6. Kalecki, 1972
7. Raj, 1973
8. Stein, 1991
9. Varma, 1998
10. Markovits, 1985, 1996
11. Timberg, 1978
12. Ray, 1979
13. Jha, 1984
14. Sharma 1970
15. Bayly, 1983
16. Haynes, 1991
17. Markovits, forthcoming.
18. Hansen, 1999

REFERENCES

Bayly, C.A., *Rulers, Townsmen and Bazaars: North Indian Society-in the Age of British Expansion, 1770–1870* (Cambridge, 1983)

Dutt, R.P., *India Today*, (London, 1940).

Fox, R.G., 'Urban Class and Communal Consciousness in Colonial Punjab: The Genesis of India's Intermediate Regime', *Modern Asian Studies*, vol. 18, no. 3 (Cambridge 1984), pp. 459–89,

Gupta, D., 'India's Unmodern Modernity', in R. Thapar (ed.), *India: Another Millenium?* (Delhi, 2000), pp. 85–107.

Hansen, T., *The Saffron Wave: Democracy and Hindu Nationalism in Modern India*, (Princeton, 1999).

Haynes, D., *Rhetoric and Ritual in Colonial India: The Shaping of a Public Culture in Surat City, 1852–1928* (Berkeley, 1991).

Jha, P.S., *India: A Political Economy of Stagnation* (Bombay 1980).

Kalecki, M., 'Social and Economic Aspects of "Intermediate Regimes"', in *Selected Essays on the Economic Growth of the Socialist and Mixed Economy*, (Cambridge, 1972).

Kosambi, D.D., *The Culture and Civilisation of Ancient India in Historical Outline*, (London, 1964).

Markovits, C., *Indian Business and Nationalist Politics 1931–1939: The Indigenous Capitalist Class and the Rise of the Congress Party* (Cambridge, 1985).

—— 'The Tata Paradox' in B. Stein and S. Subrahmanyam (eds), *Institutions and Economic Change in South Asia* (Delhi, 1996), pp. 237–48.

—— (forthcoming), 'Merchant Circulations in South Asia (XVIIIth–XXth centuries), ' in Markovits, C, J. Pouchepadass, and S. Subrahmanyam (eds), *Circulation and Society in South Asia c. 1750–1950* (Delhi).

Misra, B.B., *The Indian Middle Classes: Their Growth in Modern Times* (London, , New York, Bombay, 1961).

Mitra, A., *Terms of Trade and Class Relations: An Essay in Political Economy*, (London, 1977).

Raj, K.N., 'The Politics and Economics of "Intermediate Regimes"', *Economic and Political Weekly*, vol. VIII, no. 27 (27 July 1973) pp. 1189–98.

Ray, R.K., *Industrialization in India 1914–1947: Growth and Conflict in the Private Corporate Sector* (Delhi, 1979).

Sharma, R.G., 'The Arda-Kathanak: A Neglected Source of Mughal History', *Indica*, 106–20, vol. VII, no. 1 (1970), pp. 49–73.

Stein, B., Towards an Indian Petty Bourgeoisie: Outline of an Approach', *Economic and Political Weekly*, pp. PE 9–20, vol. XXVI, no. 4 (1991) January.

Timberg, T.A., *The Marwaris: From Traders to Industrialists* (Delhi, 1978).

Varma, P., *The Great Indian Middle Class* (Delhi, 1998).

Consumption, Domestic Economy, and the Idea of 'Middle Class' in Late Colonial Bombay*

PRASHANT KIDAMBI

INTRODUCTION

There has been of late a surge of scholarly interest in the Indian middle class. The far-reaching transformation within contemporary Indian society and politics triggered by economic liberalization and globalization has turned the spotlight on the changing character of the 'Great Indian middle class'.[1] In particular, recent writings have highlighted the centrality of public discourses about market relations and consumption in the constitution of the 'new middle class' since the early 1990s.

According to Leela Fernandes, both defenders and opponents of economic liberalization have converged in 'their discursive production of the urban middle class as the site of commodity consumption and as the recipients of the benefits of economic liberalization'. On the one hand, the print and visual media have been instrumental in fashioning images of a 'new' middle class, 'one that has left behind its dependence on austerity and state protection and has embraced an open India that is at ease with broader processes of globalization'. On the other hand, critics of economic liberalization have emphasized the deleterious social and political consequences of the consumerist ethos

---

* Originally published in Douglas Haynes, Abigail McGowan, Tirthankar Roy, and Haruka Yanagisawa (eds), *Towards a History of Consumption in South Asia* (New Delhi: Oxford University Press, 2009). For the complete text see the original. In the present version, some portions of the essay have been removed and notes rearranged accordingly.

embraced by the middle class. However, Fernandes argues, 'the public debate on the new middle class has had less to do with a shifting or expanding social basis of the middle class than it has with the new cultural standard which has been projected onto the urban middle classes, a standard which is inextricably linked to India's policies of economic liberalization.'[2]

The significance of consumption in the making of middle-class culture and social identity has also been underscored in a number of recent studies of contemporary Indian society. Some writers have dwelt on this theme in exploring the interplay between class, gender, national identity, and post-colonial modernity.[3] Yet others have explored middle-class attitudes towards consumption. One ethnographic account of Baroda during the late 1990s notes that 'members of the middle class understand consumption in moral terms, and that this understanding is shaped through the operationalization of ideals of sociality, set against the everyday experience of urban middle-class life.' As a consequence, it has been argued, middle-class Indians view contemporary consumer culture with ambivalence and often characterize it as 'debased materialism'.[4]

These studies raise some interesting questions about the social and cultural history of the Indian middle class. For instance, when did discourses about the middle class couched in terms of material indices of income, expenditure, and patterns of consumption, historically emerge in modern India? What were the political and intellectual contexts in which such representations first took root? How significant were discourses about market relations and consumption in the constitution of middle-class social identities? Can one discern internal tensions and contradictions in the interplay between moral discourses about, and quotidian practices of, consumption among those who identified themselves as 'middle class'?

This essay represents a preliminary attempt to grapple with such questions. Focusing on empirical evidence pertaining to Bombay City, it highlights the significance of the late colonial period (c. 1920s–1940s) in the articulation of urban middle-class identity. The first part of the essay suggests that in the period following the First World War, the material context of everyday life became increasingly central to public discourse about the middle class in Bombay. The impetus for this development, it is argued, emanated principally from white-collar salaried employees drawn from the city's upper-caste 'service communities' who invoked the discursive category of the 'middle class' in seeking to legitimate their demands for economic entitlements in a context of rising inflation, unemployment, and deteriorating living standards.

The volatile economic conditions of the late colonial period also inflected discourses about the everyday practices of middle-class life. The second part of the essay focuses on a growing interest in 'domestic economy', especially the efficient management of household consumption, on the part of those who identified themselves as belonging to the 'middle class'. In an era characterized simultaneously by economic flux and a growing range of consumer goods, many contemporaries within Bombay's upper-caste service communities sought to emphasize the need for more efficient management of household income and expenditure in order to maintain the middle-class way of life. In the process, these men and women expressed a moral ambivalence towards modern consumption not entirely dissimilar to that highlighted by recent ethnographic writings about contemporary South Asian society.

My analytical approach to this empirical material draws upon new perspectives that have informed recent historical scholarship on the middle class. In particular, it builds on the suggestion that the category of the 'middle class', far from being a straightforward sociological 'given', was a historically contingent ideological construct of the modern public sphere. Furthermore, as Simon Gunn has noted, 'the precise identity and meaning of the term "middle class" at any time was always a matter of cultural construction'.[5]

Sanjay Joshi's monograph on the making of the middle class in colonial Lucknow during the late nineteenth and early twentieth centuries illustrates the salience of this analytical framework in the South Asian context. Joshi's book critiques a long-standing sociologically-informed tradition of Indian scholarship on the middle class, which identifies it in terms of clearly defined criteria of occupation and income and traces its historical origins and seamless evolution under British colonial rule. He argues that the Indian middle class during the colonial period should not be viewed in terms of 'traditional sociological indicators of income and occupation'. As he points out, such accounts tended to reify the middle class as a 'self-evident' and 'bounded' sociological entity. Instead, he suggests, the middle class is better understood as a process of collective 'self-fashioning' carried out within the colonial public sphere. 'Though its economic background was important,' Joshi notes, 'the power, indeed, the constitution of the middle class in India, as perhaps over much of the world, was based not on economic power it wielded, which was minimal, but from the abilities of its members to be cultural entrepreneurs.' Middle-class formation, in this view, was a 'cultural project', constantly 'in the making', rather than a 'flat sociological fact'. Joshi's book shows how 'a hitherto politically insignificant group of men from "service communities" were able to emerge as the new arbiters of appropriate social conduct and establish new modes of political activity that empowered them at the expense of the traditional elites of the city, less powerful social groups, and ultimately also the British rulers'.[6]

Joshi's account yields many insights into the social history of the Indian middle class during the colonial period. There is no denying the centrality of the public sphere in the discursive construction of the middle class. However, this essay argues that 'simple economic indicators of income and occupation', and the material context more broadly conceived, were integral to this process.[7] It thus contests the assumption that there was a clear-cut distinction between the 'material' and 'cultural' domains in the ideological articulation of middle-class identity.

Furthermore, the essay suggests (although implicitly) that historians have not paid sufficient attention to the material aspects of middle-class lives in the twentieth century. Existing studies of the Indian middle class tend mostly to focus on the intellectual and political strivings of the late nineteenth (and, to an extent, early twentieth) century intelligentsia. As a result, contemporary pronouncements regarding the changing orientations and values of the Indian middle class derive much of their force from idealized images of a pre-Independence middle class that abjured material aspirations. Such assertions are also based on the questionable assumption that the 'middle class' in India was a stable category prior to the era of economic liberalization. Neither of these notions is sustainable. Material pursuits were far from marginal in middle-class lives in earlier periods. And the category of the 'middle class' itself acquired new social referents and meanings as it changed over time.

This essay has also benefited from the insights offered by recent writings on the history of the European, Asian, and Latin American middle classes. British historians, for instance, have drawn attention to the significance of the 'new consumerism' of the early twentieth century, which increasingly came to be associated with an expanding 'lower middle class'. Indeed, the predominance of the Conservative party during the inter-war period owed much to the discursive identification of this new 'lower middle class' with the 'public'. At the same time, it has been argued, the 'new consumerism' also generated 'a wider series of anxieties about the loss of patriarchal control within and beyond the family'.[8]

Similarly, a recent account of Japanese bourgeois culture in the early twentieth century has shown how material factors, especially consumption, became integral to the constitution of middle-class identity amongst a growing class of white-collar workers in cities like Tokyo. Indeed, it is argued, 'despite the failure of the majority of the salaried employees to prosper or to organize politically, there is no question that a distinct salaryman lifestyle emerged in the inter-war years and that it was seen by many young men as desirable'. Importantly, it has been noted, much of 'the positive appeal was consumption-based'.[9] Likewise, the Chinese historian Wen-hsin Yeh has linked the modern culture of consumption that emerged in Republican Shanghai to the rise of a white-collar salariat that constituted the social basis of a 'new urban middle-class society'.[10]

The place of consumption in the articulation of middle-class identity has also figured prominently in recent Latin American historiography.[11] To cite just one example: in a delicately etched study Brian Owensby has drawn attention to the centrality of market relations and the material context of everyday life in the fashioning of middle-class social identities in Brazil during the early twentieth century. Patterns of consumption became both a crucial marker of status, enabling Brazilian middle-class men and women to distinguish themselves from those below in a culture that continued to lay great store by hierarchy, as well as a source of perennial domestic anxiety as they confronted the pressures of a society ordered along class lines.[12] Importantly, by creatively integrating the insights generated by the 'linguistic turn' with the materialist concerns of social history, many of these writings have breathed new life into the study of the middle class.

I

On a sultry Saturday afternoon in late February of 1920 a large audience gathered in the hall of the Marwadi Vidyalaya on Bombay's Sandhurst Road. The occasion was the inaugural session of the first Bombay Clerks' Conference. In his address of welcome, the chairman of the Reception Committee noted that it was 'the first Conference of its kind, first at least in India'. He went on enumerate many of the problems confronting Bombay's large clerical community: rampant inflation, high unemployment, and a growing shortage of affordable housing. 'The grievances of the clerical community under these hard times were thus doubled,' he declared, 'and in order to consider how the same could be alleviated or minimized the Conference was convened.'[13]

The Clerks' Conference was organized by the Bombay Clerks' Union, an association founded in January 1918 to advance the interests of the city's clerical community. The first annual report of the Union stated that the Union had 463 registered members on its rolls belonging to 'no less than a hundred offices of this city'.[14] [...] The founding of the Bombay Clerks' Union and the subsequent organization of the Clerks' Conference occurred during a particularly tumultuous period in the city's history. As scholars have noted, the years after the end of the First World War were a tumultuous period in Bombay's history. Rampant inflation and severe shortages in many items of everyday consumption resulted in heightened political tensions.[15] Most notably, many sections of the city's vast working-class population began to grow increasingly restive and belligerent. In January 1918, grain riots broke out in the city's mill districts as workers attacked grain shops, cloth shops, and wood depots, in an attempt to destroy the account books of their creditors. Strikes became endemic in all the industrial establishments of the city as workers in the textile mills, railway and municipal workshops, postal services, and dockyards, sought increased wages and special allowances in the face of the rising cost of living. In the last week of 1918 a dispute between employers and workers in a Bombay textile mill sparked off the first ever general strike by the workers of the city. An estimated 150,000 workers, employed both in the city's 85 textile mills and other industrial establishements, took part in this demonstration of labour solidarity.

Contemporary observers were quick to note the significance of the collective mobilization by the workers. For employers the sight of thousands of workers massed on the streets signalled the onset of a new era in industrial relations and forced upon them the urgency of a united front. For the colonial state on the other hand other spectres loomed large, not least that of a 'Bolshevik conspiracy'. The events of January 1919 and its sequel, the general strike of January 1920, appeared to pose a threat which was serious enough to trigger the setting up of a Labour Office in the city to collect information on the working classes [...] But perhaps the most far-reaching consequence of the rising tide of working-class protest was the emergence of a new social vocabulary of class war and class conflict. Newspaper reports, as well as other contemporary accounts, of the general strikes of 1919 and 1920 were full of the impending conflict between 'Capital' and 'Labour'.

White-collar collective organization in Bombay in the years that immediately followed upon the First World War thus emerged in the context of a new political conjuncture. In a political climate where labour was becomingly increasingly strident in articulating its grievances, Bombay's clerks began to recognize the need to make their own voices heard [...] Even prior to the Clerks' Conference, some white-collar workers had already engaged in overt forms of protest. Thus, in the midst of the general strike of 1919, the *Mehta*s (the term refers to book-keepers, clerks, and salesmen) employed in the Gujarati-dominated Mulji Jetha, Laximidas Khimji, and Mangaldas cloth markets had gone on strike protesting against the rising cost of living and demanding a 35 per cent increase in their salaries.[16] [...] In all 10,000 *Mehta*s were reported to have taken part in the 1919 strike.[17]

Many of the grievances expressed by Bombay's clerical classes bore remarkable similarities to those that were concurrently being expressed by the city's manual working classes. Like the latter, Bombay's clerks demanded an improvement both in the material aspects of their everyday life and in their working conditions. The Bombay Clerks' Conference sought to draw the attention of the state and their employers to three pressing issues. First, the clerks demanded that the government redress the housing problem by expediting schemes 'which would make it possible for the clerical and other middle-class communities, to obtain healthy quarters in Bombay and suburbs at reasonable rents'. Second, they contended that in the prevailing economic context they were entitled to a 'substantial increase' in their salaries. At the same time, they argued that it was the government's moral duty to combat rising inflation. Finally, the clerks called for changes in the terms and conditions of employment, remuneration, and benefits of clerical workers. Thus, the conference recommended the introduction in 'all offices in Bombay' of provident, gratuity, and pension schemes for clerical workers, which would serve to 'cement more closely the relations between the employers and the employees'. The clerks also registered their protest against 'the practice prevalent in some Offices of filling higher vacancies by the appointment of outsiders, without giving chance to the existing clerical staff though fit to fill the vacancies'. [...] The resolution passed at the Clerks' Conference also drew attention to the 'physical breakdown and want of vitality in the majority of clerks in this City, one of the causes of which is the system of exacting work from the staff for a longer time than is advisable' and appealed for a seven-hour work day with an hour's recess as well as pay for over-time work. It noted too that 'in a number of private Offices in Bombay clerks are denied the privilege of leave', and therefore called on employers to standardize the rules pertaining to absence from work.[18]

In many respects, then, the demands of Bombay's white-collar workers resembled the grievances about wages and work conditions that were being aired at the time by the city's manual workers. Yet, in the arguments that they deployed in pursuit of their demands, these white-collar workers were at pains to distance themselves from the working classes. In particular, Bombay's clerks and their supporters insistently invoked the idea of the 'middle class' in differentiating themselves from the latter. Speaking at the inaugural meeting of the Bombay Clerks' Union, Sir Narayan Chandavarkar, a prominent figure in the city's public life, undoubtedly expressed the sentiments of a majority of his listeners, when he noted:

The profession of a clerk was a respectable profession. They might get very much less pay than a chauffeur, a labourer, or a shoe-maker, but after all they must remember that it was not the pay that made a profession respectable. What made the profession of a clerk respectable was the fact that he had the mental culture, and he had the power to think for himself; and secondly, because clerks generally come from that class, which was really the intellectual power of a country, namely, the middle class. [...][19]

Most notably, white-collar workers and their supporters emphasized the distinctive material needs that distinguished them from the manual working classes. They argued that as members of a 'respectable' class, white-collar workers had no choice but to engage in forms of consumption that were intrinsic to their social position. In turn, it was suggested, their status obligations had rendered the plight of white-collar workers even more pitiable than that of the working classes, who faced no such pressures on their resources. As J.K. Mehta of the Indian Merchants' Chamber noted in his presidential address to the Bombay Clerks' Conference:

No one can say that the lot of the working classes is at all enviable and yet the lot of the clerical community, especially the low grade portion of it, is particularly the hardest lot of any human being. Their salary ranges from Rs 30 to Rs 100 and with this they have to maintain themselves, their wives and children and even sometimes their poor dependents. There are again Mehtas or clerks, employed by a large number of Indian merchants and traders, who draw even a less salary than their brother-clerks in commercial offices conducted on Western lines. All of these belong to a certain status in society and have certain appearances to keep up. They have to provide decent clothing for their wives and children and a decent education to the latter. Not only this, but they have to live in decent quarters and have faithfully to keep up certain social engagements. With all this they happen to be the only earning members of their family, for while all the members of the family of a working man are co-operating with him in adding to the family exchequer a clerk's family is entirely dependent on him for all its expenditure.[20]

Significantly, the issue here was not simply about the low levels of clerical pay. Rather, the contention was that because of the *innate* differences in the consumption needs of a middle-class person and a manual worker, the former suffered more on account of rising inflation. Underlying such assertions was the notion that the logic of market relations ought not to outweigh other determinants of social status. Indeed, Bombay's clerks and their sympathizers reverted to an older idiom of ascribed identities and status entitlements in seeking to justify their modern class demands. For instance, in the speech quoted above, Mehta argued:

Though the analogy is just very close between clerks and working men, it ceases, if we compare their social and economic conditions, especially in their country. We may or may not believe in castes and classes, but we have to view things as they are and the position is that clerks are considered a class superior to the working men. It is these social ideals and economic conditions which make the lot of the low grade clerks far harder than even the lot of the working classes living in the slums and working for ten hours a day.[21]

The invocation of longstanding notions of social hierarchy within a modern taxonomy of class bears significant affinities with the 'contradictions' constitutive of the middle class that Joshi has recently highlighted in his study of colonial North India. Indeed, such contradictions were integral to the social formation of Bombay's white-collar middle class during the late colonial period. At the same time, it is also worth emphasizing that the interplay between traditional notions of hierarchy and modern taxonomies of class were not unique to the Indian middle class. Recent research has shown, for instance, how very similar tendencies were also at work in the context of middle-class formation in early twentieth century Latin America. For instance, in his nuanced account of the Brazilian middle class,

Brian Owensby had shown how 'the market mentalities, meritocracy and egalitarianism, professionalization, consumer culture, and social identities typically connected with the notion of the traditional notion of the middle class' were intimately bound up with 'a disdain for manual labour, an insistence on social hierarchy, and the presumed naturalness of patronage, time-tested values and practices constantly renewed and folded into modern social life'.[22] Likewise, David Parker's fascinating account of the politics of white-collar workers in Peru in the early twentieth century shows how the protagonists of his study began to employ 'a language of class, superficially echoing demands and vocabulary that working-class militants had brought to the eight-hour day movement'.[23] Like the country's labouring classes, Peruvian white-collar workers were driven by high inflation and straitened economic circumstances to protest against their employers as well as the state. At the same time, however, an 'imported vocabulary of class and class conflict did not replace longstanding traditions of caste and hierarchy'. On the contrary, the new words and ideas associated with the modern language of class were intertwined with older ideological notions of rank and status. Thus, 'by asserting that their middle-class birth gave them, by definition, the right to a respectable living standard, Peru's *empleados* turned a largely archaic vision of the social order into a very modern demand for higher salaries and better working conditions'.[24] Engaged in a similar quest, their contemporary counterparts in Bombay would have recognized and understood the argument perfectly well.

II

The material context of everyday life in late colonial India was also central to the idea of the 'middle class' in other ways. The period after the First World War was marked by an expansion in the range of goods, services, and mass entertainments available to city dwellers. Equally, the deepening of market relations also led to a proliferation in the choices that lay before consumers. However, during the 1920s and 1930s such choices amongst those who identified themselves as 'middle class' had to be made in a context of considerable economic uncertainty and financial hardship. Thus, the emergence of an incipient mass culture and new sources of consumption combined with the rising cost of living and growing unemployment to produce among members of upper-caste 'service communities' a new concern about quotidian 'domestic economy'. The reflections of these contemporary observers shed light on the pressures and dilemmas confronting families within the city's service communities as they struggled to negotiate a new climate of economic flux and rapid social change. On the one hand, those who claimed to belong to the 'middle class' were conscious of the fact that consumption had become an essential measure of status in a modernizing urban context where the traditional markers of the caste hierarchy were no longer adequate guarantors of social standing. On the other hand, their insecure economic situation consistently forced these men and women to weigh up their quotidian spending choices.

This part of the essay seeks to illustrate these themes with special reference to the Kanara Saraswats of Bombay, a traditional Brahman 'service community', whose members were largely to be found employed in white-collar occupations in the city's commercial establishments, legal firms, and government offices.[25] The members of this community had been migrating to Bombay from the Kanara region in southern India since the late nineteenth century and by the early 1920s there were over 2,000 Saraswats in Bombay.[26] Over 90 per cent of the community was said at this time to be employed as clerks in various commercial and government offices in the city. Like others of their ilk, the Kanara Saraswats were badly affected both by the rising cost of living as well as the fluctuations in Bombay's economic fortunes that resulted in high unemployment amongst white-collar workers during the 1920s and 1930s. One consequence of these developments was a growing sense of urgency within the community about the need to balance the competing demands of status and solvency. The intense debates over these issues were regularly published in the pages of the *Kanara Saraswat*, the monthly journal of the Kanara Saraswat Association in Bombay. The articles contributed to this journal offer an insight into the ways in which the men and women of traditional upper-caste service communities, who explicitly identified themselves as 'middle class', responded to the pressures and anxieties generated by the onset of the age of mass consumption.

The dangers inherent in 'living beyond one's means' was a recurring theme in the articles published in the Kanara Saraswat community's journal during the 1920s and 1930s. The 'wicked habit of living beyond one's means', it was argued, had pauperized many well-to-do families, 'while exercise of proper economy has made comparatively poor families self-reliant, happy and contented'.[27] The ideal family, in this view, was one that adopted a simple lifestyle and abjured all forms of conspicuous consumption.

Some Saraswats argued that the tendency to live beyond one's means was an outcome of the changing urban environment and its many new enticements such as the cinema, which had caused men of moderate means to lose their self-restraint. Thus,

In spite of themselves the young and the old of Bombay feel themselves inextricably encircled in the general and indiscriminate scramble for the ignoble and vicious pleasures of life, and a considerable number of them is actually stranded in the plague-spots of Bombay misnamed her pleasure-resorts.[28]

For others, however, it was the essential psychological characteristics of 'modern man', rather than the urban environment, which was at the root of the problem. In the words of one writer [...] 'The problem of poverty is solved not by the gaining of wealth, but by the attainment of an inner wealth which makes external poverty or wealth insignificant.' This 'inner joy' could only be achieved by eschewing the desire to strive for things that were beyond one's reach and to reject the competitive modern social order.

It is very simple: we must be ourselves; we must accept ourselves completely. Most of us try to be something more than ourselves, other than ourselves. To learn to be content with oneself, to accept our limitations of capacity is to throw a great burden off our back. Just try to realise what an enormous waste of effort and energy is involved in keeping up appearances.[29]

Yet, whatever the perceived cause, most contemporaries agreed that rapidly changing social mores had eroded the 'traditional' values of the Saraswat community. [...] [A]n account of the history of the Kanara Club (established in 1874 by the first generation of Kanara Saraswat immigrants in Bombay) recalled with nostalgia the austere lifestyle of an earlier generation.

Life in the club at Shantaram's Chawl (tenement) was on the whole simple and agreeable. While the monotony of the local food was relieved twice a week by *tamblie*s and *kadie*s ... there was nothing of extravagance of luxury... There were few chairs, and most of us sat on a mat to study. As for the dress,—alas! those days have gone, perhaps never to return,—it was simple in quality and small in quantity. Two *dhotar*s to be used on alternate days in the course of a whole year, and two *pairan*s with two coats to be washed alternately by the washerman, formed the whole wardrobe of a student ... Collars and neckties were quite unknown. As regards the head-dress, the seniors wore a turban, while the juniors were content with a cap ... The wearing of a turban was then regarded as a sign of gentlemanliness. But what a difference now! At present a booking clerk at a railway station or steamer office is more courteous to a *hatwalla* asking for a third class ticket than to a gentleman in a turban asking for a first or second class ticket.[30]

These observations cannot, of course, be taken as a straightforward reflection of the changing material conditions of middle-class Saraswat lives in Bombay. [...] Such representations are better understood as a 'local appellation of the narrative of loss of order, morality, authenticity, and community that seems intrinsic to most experiences of urban modernity'.[31] It was the disillusionment with the content of their modernity that prompted a deep-seated yearning among contemporary Saraswats for 'days bygone' that were ostensibly untainted by the existential tensions and anxieties of the urban competitive social order.

The perception that the 'wicked habit of living beyond one's means' was one of the most pressing problems facing the community prompted many Bombay Saraswats during the inter-war years to emphasize the need for personal thrift. [...] Interestingly, some observers believed that the urban salaried classes, far from being innately thrifty, were *naturally* prone to be more profligate in their patterns of expenditure. In his welcome address to the Kanara Saraswat Conference in December 1926, S.S. Talmaki, one of the leading lights of the Saraswat community in Bombay, remarked:

Of all the professions in life, the service of employment on a monthly salary breeds the habit of thriftlessness. The receipt of salary month after month [...] lead a man into a state of mind that even if the expenditure of every month absorbed all his earnings, the future months will be able to take care of themselves [...] But when any unforeseen event happens, like sickness leading to doctors' bills, then the trouble begins [...] Once a man postpones the idea of saving, ten to one he will not begin at all [...] Unfortunately for us we readily copy the various Western methods of spending, but not of saving, to be met with especially among the middle and the lower middle classes.[32]

But what exactly did contemporaries mean when they called for 'thrift'? This is how one Saraswat defined it:

Thrift is the habit of saving something out of our earnings so that we may be able to use it at some future time when it will be of greater benefit to us than it is at present. Thrift therefore presupposes discrimination as well as foresight [...] Many people confound thrift with miserliness, though the two are poles apart. If a person stints himself or his children of the necessary food and clothing or proper shelter when he has the means of supplying them, he is really unthrifty [...] On the other hand it would be equally unthrifty to spend on showy dress, on dainty dishes, on overfeeding, or on such like luxuries. In fact use of anything in excess of moderation may do positive harm.[33]

Thus thrift, in this view, did not entail abstaining from consumption altogether; rather, it called for judicious discrimination in one's patterns of expenditure. Central to the cultivation of thrift, as the above quote suggests, was the need to distinguish between 'necessities' and 'luxuries' [...]. The problem, as some Saraswat writers saw it, was that increasingly the desire for a comfortable lifestyle as well as the demands of middle-class status had begun to blur the traditional distinctions between 'necessities' and 'luxuries'. [...]

Contemporary Saraswats also regarded the elimination of waste and excess in patterns of consumption as being integral to the cultivation of thrift. As one observer wrote in 1928, 'The greatest hindrance to thrift is waste. Extravagance as such as may fall to the share of only a few. But there are numerous abuses leading to waste which the generality of us care little to stop, either through ignorance or carelessness, leading later on to a habit.'[34] [...] Significantly, contemporary reflections on the topic of thrift point to the tensions experienced by Saraswats seeking to negotiate the competing demands of two parallel systems of social hierarchy. On the one hand, they were obliged to perform rituals and ceremonies that were essential to the maintenance of their upper-caste status and identity. On the other hand, the expenditure incurred on these 'traditional' practices constrained their ability to engage in forms of consumption that were an important marker of urban middle-class status. Indeed, ceremonial rituals increasingly came to be perceived by many middle-class Saraswats as 'needless' expenditure. Such views prompted numerous articles in the *Kanara Saraswat* calling for a reform of caste rituals and marriage ceremonies in order to reduce the financial burden that they imposed on those who had to undertake them. [...]

However, some Saraswats argued that it was anxieties about their status within the modern social order, rather than an adherence to the old way of life, that impelled middle-class men and women to engage in ostentatious festivities. In other words, the expenditure on traditional ceremonies was being driven increasingly by a shallow desire to 'keep up appearances'. Thus, it was argued,

The roots of 'needless expenditure' lies in the fact that human beings are subject to one great frailty, namely, love of admiration. The desire that others should call us rich and liberal is a weakness that we can hardly overcome. The fear of what people might say if we do not do this thing or that, naturally lies at the bottom of much of our extravagance; but it is of great importance that we should learn to control our feelings of false dignity and our fear of public opinion.[35]

Contributors to the *Kanara Saraswat* in the 1920s and 1930s dwelt frequently on the need for efficient 'domestic economy'. Indeed, following the inquiry into middle-class family budgets published in 1928 by the newly-established Bombay Labour Office, some contemporary Saraswats urged their brethren to practise diligent household budgeting, rationalize their patterns of consumption and harness their scarce financial resources with discretion and discipline.[36]

The most sustained and systematic attempt in this regard was by H. Shankar Rau, a prominent member of the community in Bombay, who expounded the virtues of sound budgetary management in a series of articles. [...] In order to illustrate the benefits of proper household management, Rau constructed the 'family budget' of an average '*Bombay middle class family* of three adults and two children, a family with a gross monthly income of Rs 175'.[37] (Italics in original) If this family was careful in balancing its budget, he conjectured, it would probably spend its incomes as follows. Food: sixty rupees; fuel and lighting: eight rupees; clothing: twelve rupees; bedding: three rupees; house rent: thirty-five rupees; and miscellaneous expenditure: fifty-seven rupees. The scope for domestic thrift for such a 'typical' middle-class household, he admitted, was decidedly limited. In particular, the first five items 'do not admit of much curtailment', since any retrenchment might 'tell on the health of the family and increase medical charges.'[38]

For instance, his 'typical' middle-class family engaged no cook and could not afford to do so. In his view, the sixty rupees that it spent on food consumption was just about right and indeed, at six annas per head 'happens to be no more than twice the cost of the daily rations allowed to the C class prisoner in an Indian Jail!' In these circumstances, he argued, it was 'not possible for an ordinary middle class family to reduce this scale without impairing health or upsetting convention'. But, he suggested, a careful middle-class family ought nonetheless to consider measures that might bring about small economies. This could be effected by buying household items through co-operative schemes; minimizing needless expenditure on visitors; stopping 'altogether the habit of taking tea, coffee etc., either in the house or out of it', given that it was 'a habit of comparatively recent growth which does a great deal of harm when repeated too often'; 'the gradual elimination of salt, spices, and condiments out from dietary'; undertaking steam cooking instead of 'ordinary boiling and frying', which, in turn, by avoiding 'over-boiling of rice or boiling over of milk' would eliminate the 'untidy cook' and the 'elaborate kitchen'; and, finally, not serving 'what is not at all needed, or more than is needed'.[39]

Rau buttressed his case for greater economy in food consumption in the middle-class Saraswat household by pointing to practices in Europe that he regarded as exemplary. For instance,

The European would not think of dining, lunching or taking tea with a friend unless the friend invited him, usually several days beforehand. And then, he is at liberty to take just what he wants and is seldom pressed, if ever. It is such conventions as these that we must copy from the West with advantage.[40]

At the same time, he drew on indigenous ideas that embodied 'the wisdom of the East'. In particular, invoking Brahmanical notions of bodily humours, Rau argued that it was 'the clear duty of the Saraswat Brahman, of all people...not to cultivate the quality of *rajas* ... or that of *tamas* which is worse' [...]. Adhering to these suggestions, he contended, was 'desirable not only from the higher point of view of ethics, but also from the practical point of view of health, and ... from the lower one of thrift'[...].

Rau suggested various ways in which the average middle-class family could trim its expenditure on those non-food items that could not be eliminated without triggering serious status repercussions. For instance, Saraswat householders were advised that fuel and lighting costs could be reduced by restricting the number of visitors; 'accustoming themselves to the use of tepid or cold water for the bath in preference to hot water'; and 'suitably regulating the use of electric light'. Likewise, expenditure on clothing could be reduced if, like Europeans, one relied 'on regular washing and ironing and on personal gait and posture rather than on the expensive nature of the material [...]'.[41] On the other hand, the expenditure on house rent did not allow for any saving to be effected. The difficulties faced by the middle-class family in Bombay were 'special' in that it spent a higher proportion of its income on house rent than those living elsewhere.

[...]

Yet, closer scrutiny revealed that...there were many items of expenditure that were unavoidable given the status requirements of a middle-class household. For instance, for a majority of salaried employees there was 'no getting away' from paying income tax. Similarly,

The servant cleans the vessels, washes the clothes and sweeps the rooms, and would strike if you reduced his wages; the ladies in our middle-class families are not accustomed to this sort of work. Even in these days of self-shaving, the barber of the saloon or of the visiting fraternity, is required to rear the only crop of which most of us are now the proud possessors; and so is the washerman who must needs split the recalcitrant stone with the humble shirt. The earning member has perforce to get his season ticket to go to work and cannot walk it out. Postage, stationery, soap and toilet requisites offer little scope for the retrenchment axe. These items thus represent charges which are more or less fixed and obligatory.[42]

Nor was it easy to reduce expenditure on education which 'is as expensive as it is necessary'. While reforms were needed in this area, there was very little prospect of a reduction in the expenditure in this regard. Likewise, medical charges, 'generally a very fluctuating quantity', did not permit of any savings either. Nonetheless, Rau had a suggestion for the readers of his 'family budgets':
As many of our girls as possible should receive a course in first aid, home hygiene, home nursing and simple treatment of diseases by the homeopathic or the biochemic system [...] I do not suggest that the qualified doctor should be replaced by the ignorant quack, but the knowledge is a boon where the doctor is not available, and, in any case, it should enable timely preventive, palliative or even remedial measures to be taken [...].[43]

Finally, the 'miscellaneous' category also included expenditure incurred on account of personal vices or the urge to sample the mass entertainments available to the modern city-dweller. [...] However, unlike the other items of 'miscellaneous' expenditure, which did not permit of any major reduction on account of their status connotations, Rau argued that the inducements of urban mass culture could be avoided by adopting a more 'pure' lifestyle. In other words, the remedy lay in 'healthy occupation of leisure hours—good company, wholesome reading, useful honorary work, a determined attempt, through devotional exercises in particular, to attain purity of thought, word and deed'. Thus, he suggested, by avoiding the urge to give into the temptations of urban mass culture and adopting a more spiritual way of life the middle-class household could 'enjoy better health and truer happiness'.[44]

Rau believed that his proposed economies would enable the middle-class Saraswat family in Bombay 'to exchange rajas and tamas for *satva*, ill-health for health, debt for savings, and worry for peace'. Moreover, adhering to his suggestions would better equip such a family to cope with unforeseen contingencies, such as accidents or deaths to the earning members, as well as the expenditure entailed during special occasions like marriages or thread ceremonies[...] Rau ended by acknowledging that a 'typical budget is not an ideal budget any more than a typical family is an ideal family'. He accepted that 'each individual might have his or her own ideal'. His ideal family was 'one which made use of its faculty of discrimination and lives a life of purity and simplicity'; his ideal budget 'one which reflects such a life, and succeeds not only in avoiding debt, but also in effecting a reasonable provision for the future'. But the reality was that 'no two families were alike in their circumstances, environment or temperament'. Consequently, 'quite a number of budgets could be framed according as this, that or the other aspect of the expenditure position was emphasised'.

Notwithstanding this diversity, however, Rau sought to advance some generalizations that would be valid for all families. Thus, he argued, household expenditure would automatically increase if a family lived in the city, if it grew in size, if it moved up the social scale, and if, correspondingly, there was a change in its ideas about what constituted an acceptable standard of living. On the basis of these generalizations, Rau drew four conclusions. First, middle-class Saraswats ought to abandon the city and return to the village. Second, the size of the family should be determined by the economic means at its disposal. Third, the proportion allocated to each category of expenditure ought to be adjusted in accordance with the financial circumstances of the family. And, he ended, 'do not raise your standard of living to an extent which may prove embarrassing'.[45]

Thus, rather like many middle-class Indian men and women at the end of the twentieth century, Rau viewed consumption with ambivalence. His account recognized that consumption was a key marker of social worth in the modern world. Indeed, he took it for granted that the demands of middle-class status imposed certain inescapable forms of expenditure on the average Saraswat household. At the same time, Rau exalted the values of 'purity' and 'simplicity' and was sharply critical of the hedonistic logic of modern consumer culture. He regarded the unrestrained pursuit of material possessions and pleasures as being inimical not only to the physical and moral well-being of individuals but also to the values of sociality within the community.

The 'ambivalent consumer' is by no means a singularly Indian phenomenon. Historians working on different regions have begun lately to undermine the triumphal narratives spawned by the seemingly unchallenged dominance of 'American-led global trends that privilege the consumer and consumption'. Recent scholarship has queried 'the assumption that all consumer revolutions are fundamentally alike or are converging toward the endpoint of the American model' and highlighted the 'discontents, ambivalence, and dilemmas' provoked by the rise of modern mass consumption in diverse cultural contexts.[46] A significant feature of this shift in perspective is that consumption is no longer viewed, as in the 'Americanization' model, primarily in terms of the self-interested, utility-maximizing individual. 'Instead of a breakthrough of one particular mode of individualistic consumerism,' it has been argued, 'modernity appears marked by the gaps and tensions between consumption as practice, the identity of the consumer, and social systems and values.' Narratives of 'linear convergence' have thus begun to give way to more complex and nuanced accounts documenting the resilience of 'parallel moralities of consumption' that emphasized 'restraint'.[47]

CONCLUSION

This essay is a preliminary attempt at exploring the relationship between material life and middle-class identity in late colonial India. As such, the points made here are necessarily provisional. The principal aim of the exercise has been to suggest that the material context of quotidian life became integral to the discursive construction of the 'middle class' in inter-war Bombay. On the one hand, embattled white-collar workers drew attention to their distinctive consumption requirements in seeking to press their demands on the colonial state and their employers. On the other hand, the efficient management of household consumption in a context of rising inflation, financial hardship, and economic fluctuations, was also central to internal debates within Bombay's service communities about the middle-class way of life.

The shortcomings of the essay will be readily apparent. It has, for the most part, focused on discourses about consumption and has not sought to probe at length the empirical reality that these claimed to represent. Nor has this essay explored the impact of these discourses on the quotidian practices of consumption in middle-class households. Furthermore, it has made no attempt to trace the intellectual genealogy of the arguments that were deployed or the ways in which such discourses differed from those articulated by other middling social groups (for instance, traders and shopkeepers) or intermediate castes (especially non-Brahman ones like the Marathas) in Bombay.

And most importantly, the essay has not considered at length the gendered nature of Saraswat representations of consumption. These important issues are the focus of another essay.

NOTES

1. Pavan K. Varma, *The Great Indian Middle Class* (Delhi, 1998).
2. Leela Fernandes, 'Restructuring the Middle Class in Liberalizing India', *Comparative Studies of South Asia, Africa and the Middle East*, XX: 1 and 2, 2000, pp. 88–91.
3. Purnima Mankekar, *Screening Culture, Viewing Politics: An Ethnography of Television, Womanhood and Nation in Postcolonial India* (Durham, NC, and London, 1999); Arvind Rajagopal, *Politics after Television: Hindu Nationalism and the Reshaping of the Public in India* (Cambridge, 2001); Leela Fernandes, 'Nationalizing the "Global": Media Images, Cultural Politics and the Middle Class in India', *Media, Culture and Society*, 22, 2000, pp. 611-28.
4. Margit van Wessel, 'Talking About Consumption: How an Indian Middle Class Dissociates from Middle-Class Life', *Cultural Dynamics*, 16:1, 2004, pp. 94–5.
5. Simon Gunn, 'The Public Sphere, Modernity and Consumption: New Perspectives on the History of the English Middle Class', in Alan Kidd and David Nicholls (eds), *Gender, Civic Culture and Consumerism* (Manchester, 1999), p. 24.
6. Sanjay Joshi, *Fractured Modernity: Making of a Middle Class in Colonial North India* (New Delhi, 2001), pp. 1–10.
7. Indeed, Joshi's own evidence suggests that the struggle 'to make ends meet' was integral to the lives of middle-class men striving to maintain 'the increasingly expensive signs of respectability in their social lives'. Joshi, *Fractured Modernity*, pp. 69–74.
8. Gunn, 'The Public Sphere', pp. 20–3.
9. Jordan Sand, *House and Home in Modern Japan: Architecture, Domestic Space, and Bourgeois Culture, 1880–1930* (Cambridge: Massachusetts, 2003), pp. 225-6. See also, Sheldon Garon, 'Japan's Post-War "Consumer Revolution", or Striking a "Balance" between Consumption and Saving', in John Brewer and Frank Trentmann (eds), *Consuming Cultures, Global Perspectives: Historical Trajectories, Transnational Exchanges* (Oxford, 2006), pp. 191–2.
10. Wen-hsin Yeh, 'Shanghai Modernity: Commerce and Culture in a Republican City', *The China Quarterly*, 150, June 1997, pp. 393–4.
11. David Parker, *The Idea of the Middle Class: White-Collar Workers and Peruvian Society, 1900–1950* (Pennsylvania, 1998), pp. 376–7.
12. Brian Owensby, *Intimate Ironies: Modernity and the Making of Middle-Class Lives in Brazil* (Stanford, 1999).
13. *Bombay Chronicle*, 1 March 1920.
14. *Times of India*, 5 March 1919.
15. J.C. Masselos, 'Some Aspects of Bombay City Politics in 1919', in Ravinder Kumar (ed.), *Essays in Gandhian Politics* (Oxford, 1971), pp. 145–88.
16. *Times of India*, 13 January 1919.
17. *Times of India*, 14 January 1919.

18. *Bombay Chronicle*, 2 March 1920.
19. *Times of India*, 8 April 1918.
20. *Bombay Chronicle*, 1 March 1920.
21. Ibid.
22. Owensby, *Intimate Ironies*, p. 7.
23. Parker (1998), p. 77
24. Ibid., p. 236.
25. On the history of this caste, see Frank F. Conlon, *A Caste in a Changing World: The Chitrapur Saraswat Brahmans, 1700–1935* (Berkeley, 1977).
26. *Kanara Saraswat* [...] (October 1922), pp. 107–17.
27. *The Saraswat Quarterly* [...] (April 1919), pp. 23–4. The journal was renamed the *Kanara Saraswat* in January 1922.
28. *Kanara Saraswat* (October 1925), p. 8.
29. Ibid. (October 1939), pp. 254–6.
30. V.V. Kalyanpurkar and S.N. Koppikar, 'The Kanara Club, Bombay, 1874–1892', in H. Shankar Rau (compiled and edited), *A Chitrapur Saraswat Miscellany* (Bombay, 1939), p. 91.
31. Thomas Blom Hansen, *Violence in Urban India: Identity Politics, 'Mumbai' and the Postcolonial City* (Delhi, 2001), p. 5.
32. *Kanara Saraswat* (January 1927), p. 13.
33. Ibid. (April 1928), p. 7.
34. Ibid.
35. Ibid. (July 1937), p. 8.
36. Of course, middle-class discourses about 'domestic economy' were by no means a new development. As scholars have shown, the need for thrift was a common theme in the *modern* didactic literature that emerged in the subcontinent from the mid to late nineteenth century. Many of the texts in this genre 'focused on training women to run a household efficiently on a limited budget'. Joshi, *Fractured Modernity*, p. 70. A well-known example here is Khwaja Altaf Husain Hali's novel *Majalis un-Nissa*, first published in 1874. The story of Zubaida Khatun, the heroine of Hali's novel, is an 'example of the triumph of virtue and skill over the multiple trials of family life'. Educated at home by her father, Zubaida learns from her mother 'all the arts of household management. She is taught to be thrifty and pious, to shun unnecessary household rituals, and to reject a variety of superstitious customs.' Gail Minault, *Secluded Scholars: Women's Education and Muslim Social Reform in Colonial India* (New Delhi, 1998), p. 38. Joshi has similarly drawn attention to the writings of Sannulal Gupta, the author of a 'domestic manual' entitled *Strisubodhini*, published in 1905. Gupta's treatise emphasized 'the importance of maintaining domestic economies through careful budgeting, savings, and preventing waste'. Joshi, *Fractured Modernity*, pp. 70–1.
37. In estimating the notional size of the 'typical' middle-class Saraswat family in Bombay, Rau drew upon two existing reports. In its enquiry into middle-class 'family budgets', the Bombay Labour Office had suggested that the average household size was 5.09. Likewise, the community census conducted by the Kanara Saraswat Association in Bombay in 1932 had established that 'the average Chitrapur Saraswat family consists of 5.4

members, and the average income per head per month is Rs 31'. H. Shankar Rau, 'Family Budgets', in Rau, *Chitrapur Saraswat Miscellany*, pp. 15-16.
38. Ibid, pp. 16-17.
39. Ibid., pp. 19-20.
40. Ibid.
41. Ibid., pp. 22-3.
42. Ibid., p. 24.
43. Ibid. pp. 25-6.
44. Ibid.
45. Ibid., pp. 29-30.
46. Sheldon Garon and Patricia L. Maclachlan (eds), *The Ambivalent Consumer: Questioning Consumption in East Asia and the West* (Cornell: Ithaca, 2006), pp. 2-3.
47. Garon, 'Japan's Post-War "Consumer Revolution"', pp. 190-1.

Three

Gender, Caste, and Religion
in the Making of
Middle-class Modernity

Domesticity and Middle-class Nationalism in Nineteenth-century Bengal*

TANIKA SARKAR

In nineteenth-century Bengal the intelligentsia was engaged in a convoluted critical exercise. This exercise involved interrogating power relationships within indigenous customs and traditions—especially gender norms within such customs—though there were definite patriarchal limits to this interrogation. The exercise involved, simultaneously, questioning the connections established between the local and the metropolitan—in short Bengal's overall colonial connection. The problems so interanimated and complicated one another that, far from reaching a resolution, Bengal's intelligentsia was unable to set itself an agenda with any absolute certainty. Emergent nationalist consciousness, which straddled a complex range of forms and possibilities, posed yet more questions and doubts to settled convictions instead of offering any clear answers.

It is perhaps time to remind ourselves that colonization did not necessarily simplify the range of questions and problems for the colonized. Recent historiographical and cultural studies sometimes tend to reduce the whole complex enterprise of colonialism to the manageable yet impoverished proportions of a crude binary framework: whether the local assented to or refused the structures of colonialism. Further surgeries displace these structures from the realm of colonial

---

* Originally published as 'Hindu Wife, Hindu Nation: Domesticity and Nationalism in Nineteenth-century Bengal', in Tanika Sarkar, *Hindu Wife, Hindu Nation: Community, Religion, and Cultural Nationalism* (Delhi: Permanent Black, 2001), pp. 23–52. For the complete text see the original. In the present version, some portions of the essay have been removed and notes rearranged accordingly.

political economy into a conveniently attenuated rump of the epistemological and ontological aspects of colonial mastery—these are now to be regarded as the *real* structures. The recent historiographical shift further simplifies its task by locating these structures in a single form of Western power-knowledge with monolithic and fixed signs. A flat, uninflected, deductive, structural determinism then reads the consciousness of the colonized mechanically off these signs. Moreover, since these signs are vested with totalitarian powers, the consciousness of the colonized is divested of all claims to an autonomous life and made parasitic upon the master discourse of colonialism. This discourse supposedly constitutes the iron cage of language and meaning within which the colonized mind may only perform mimetic gestures.[1]

There is no denying that colonialism spawned the nineteenth-century intelligentsia. It is equally true that the history of the new middle classes was marked by many absences and voids—the absence of economic and political leadership being dominant and constitutive. The aftermath of 1857 left little doubt about the coercive and violent aspects of colonial rule. The sense of racial discrimination was heightened steadily through Lyttonian repression in the 1870s: the vernacular press and the theatre were muzzled, the Indian population was forcibly disarmed. The rabidly racist rhetoric during the Ilbert Bill agitation of the 1880s and a relatively moderate government's capitulation to it constituted crowning proof. Given the new political conditions, which largely demystified colonial myths about their non-discriminating fairness and the existence of a rule of law, Bengal's earlier reformism soon got over its hopeful youth. The Brahmos were split right down the middle and Vidyasagar spent his law few days in bitter disillusionment over his own agenda.[2] Earlier creative innovations within the new arena of education lost their initiative: a standardized and officialized uniform education policy proceeded to unfold itself from the 1880s.[3] The initiative would not be recovered till the time of the Swadeshi movement.

The formation of a nineteenth-century political sphere is usually located within the religious and political associations that began to acquire pan-Indian aspirations from the 1870s. [...] In the late-nineteenth-century middle-class context, however, the politics of associations, of self-government bodies and of lower-class protest acquired immediacy and substance largely through the mediation of vernacular printed journals which described these developments in close and vivid detail, and opened up such activity to widespread debate and comment.[4] The debate did not stop there. The public sphere, at this stage, remained integrally linked to domestic issues. A substantial number of journals and newspapers came into existence to debate issues of sati, kulin marriage, and widow remarriage[5]— domestic issues which generated a wide range of authors and readers, from Bankimchandra to Battala farces. [...]

Not only were there very substantial popular writing traditions even before the entry of print, the fact is that print itself stimulated new expressions of urban popular culture—the theatre, woodcut prints, Battala literature. [...] These were written by and for a literate but little-educated, sprawling readership and authorship which rarely read or wrote anything else. [...] Cheap woodcut prints, and later oleographs, similarly carried pictures of religious matters, of current scandal, and of the new city elite into a much larger number of lower-middle-class and even rural homes.[6]

The new Calcutta theatre, again, boomed largely through lower-middle-class patronage, and, in its turn, stimulated the growth of print through the continuous turnout of play scripts. [...] The red light area of Chitpur Road borders on it and this, in the nineteenth century, was the main source for the supply of actresses. The success of the theatre depended significantly upon lower-middle-class themes and preferences. While the classical themes and chaste language of Madhusudan Dutt's early plays were displayed to depressingly empty halls, the fortunes of the lately established Bengal Theatre picked up and flourished in the early 1870s with the performance of a popular farce—*Mohanter Ei Ki Kaj*. This play enacted a scandal that had rocked the popular imagination when the *mohunt* of the Tarakeswar pilgrimage seduced a young girl who was, later, murdered by her husband—an employee, interestingly, at a printing press.[7]

Print revolutionized reading habits and possibilities. It penetrated into all sorts of times and spaces within everyday life by its sheer portability. Earlier, manuscripts were extremely rare commodities with a slow and thinly spread-out circulation. [...] Each page had to be carefully extracted from between the wooden *patta*s, read, and then restored to its proper place. This whole complicated, delicate, and time-consuming reading exercise could be carried out only at special times and places and involved fixed postures. The new, plentiful, cheap, portable, and replicable printed books, in contrast, inserted themselves into all kinds of times and spaces effortlessly. This unprecedented and easy availability was augmented by the introduction of primers and textbooks in school and *pathshalas*. [...] Within the confines of a limited class, reading became a non-specialized, fluid, pervasive, everyday activity. This is why vernacular presses developed and proliferated, provoking comment from many observers of contemporary society.

The growth of vernacular prose and the press made possible the incorporation of a new range of themes within literate culture which neither the English works, nor classical Sanskrit/Persian education, nor theological and imaginative literature could have included within their scope: themes concerning everyday life. In the Bengali language catalogues of the Imperial Library holdings, for the three decades between the 1870s and the 1890s roughly half of all prose works deal with problems pertaining to the organization of everyday living. Simultaneous with the entry of these new themes, an extended range of new authors was created. A cross-section of thinking men, and even a few exceptionally fortunate women, could, without formal learning, develop and express ideas within a public debate over the shape of their own daily lives. A vast range of 'non-authors' could at least follow the debates on themes involving themselves. Within this shared yet contested enterprise, the middle class could recuperate something of what it lacked, in terms of an articulated position, within the production process and the power structure. By marking out an autonomous discursive field of force, which drew within its orbit men as well as a few women, highly educated professionals as well as petty clerks, artists, artisans, hack writers, and theatre persons, the Bengali middle class was certainly present at its own making.

This autonomy was expressed primarily through a paradox. A deep, pervasive awareness of political subjection did not elicit from this class of people, for a long time, any direct or explicit demand for independence. What it did was to make the middle class dourly deny its own energies, to refuse any description of itself except those that were deeply negative and bleak. [...] The general run of popular observation as well as more erudite literary production would equally characterize present time as degenerate, recasting the old trope of kaliyug to express new kinds of anxiety about a modernity ushered in under alien direction.[8]

For a long time, unease about foreign rule would be obliquely expressed through a critique of modern times. Spectacular changes, technological growth, and breakthroughs that were revolutionizing their own life and experiences—railways, electricity, telegraph, urban growth, city crowds, street scenes—were steadfastly refused recognition into the symbolic order of these sections of people, except in a tangential and negative sense. It is disconcerting to find how scantily Calcutta was being represented as a city, whether in Bankim's novels, or in bazaar paintings, or in woodcut pictures which dwell on domestic situations and interior scenes. [...] In 1829, the newspaper *Bangadoot* had pioneered one of the first definitions of the new middle class. It was then described in terms of a marked increase in the size and circulation of wealth.[9] During the last few decades of the century, vernacular journals were unanimous in their description of a diseased, unproductive, morally decaying bhadralok.

II

Middle-class Bengalis chose to read certain features of their physical and economic environment obsessively, as symptomatic elements, as metaphors of their larger condition. It seems useful to point out some of the physical and economic changes which particularly engaged their attention, and the ways in which these were used as narrative devices to describe their lives and times.

Concrete physical reasons shaped much of the bleak mental landscape which the nineteenth-century middle class inhabited. The Hindu nationalists of these times belonged largely to Calcutta or to the western, southern, and central parts of the province which had been, for the past several centuries, the key cultural zones of the region. [...] Large zamindari estates provided patronage to art and manufacture, while the growth of foreign trade from the seventeenth century stimulated local artisanal, commercial, and peasant economies.[10] The rise of the port of Hooghly bore testimony to the growth of new commerce.[11] Political turbulence and economic disasters over the eighteenth century, however, combined to fearfully destabilize the entire region. Eighteenth-century Shakta devotional poetry expressed these experiences in terms of existential uncertainties: coming back again and again to the unknowable countenance and the inscrutable intentions of the Divine Mother.[12]

From the late seventeenth century, and especially throughout the eighteenth century, the very land itself went through a major crisis.[13] The western arm of the Ganga, which bore most of the river's waterflow, gradually silted up, leading to the formation of a moribund delta in this region.[14] Productivity was lowered markedly due to frequent inundation: by the 1830s, some of the land which had yielded two crops a year was producing a harvest only every three or four years.[15] Low food supply weakened the Bengali constitution and made it vulnerable to the fevers and epidemics of stagnant waters: the Burdwan or Hooghly fever which was a great killer; cholera epidemics from 1817; and the smallpox that raged once very seven years.[16] [...]

A dread of prolonged and fatally weakening fevers, and of sudden and unexpected epidemics, structured the self-awareness of Bengalis. Enough ecological information had come in by the first three decades of the century[17] to build up a pessimistic picture of the land, the air, and the people. Contrasts between an earlier era and present times were most often made in terms of impaired health.[18] The woman in much of nineteenth-century literature presides over the sick bed.[19] Interestingly even though children, young women, and agricultural labourers were the worst victims of fevers and epidemics, it was the vulnerability and degeneration of the body of the Hindu male babu which became the most significant sign of the times. One might even say that this is how the Bengali middle class sought to express its hegemonic aspirations; not by attributing to itself political or economic leadership roles, not through claims to power, but through ascribing to itself all the ills and deprivations that marked nineteenth-century Bengali society as a whole.

As the volume of water flowing down the Hooghly branch of the Ganga shrank, and as early colonial depredations shattered established economic and political patterns, a number of flourishing commercial, manufacturing, and administrative centres went into decline. The decay, of the great port of Hooghly was dramatic. The ruin of Dacca—though this did not lie on the moribund delta—caused extensive comment. Malda, Murshidabad, Krishnanagore, Vishnupur—all were broken cities.[20] [...] Mid-century famines and ravages caused by forced indigo cultivation by white planters led to havoc and panic in rural areas. Bengali journalists agitated extensively over these issues.[21] The sense of depression produced by such sights and news came to make larger sense when they were fitted into a framework of systematic, critical knowledge shaped by theories of drain, de-industrialization and poverty.

The growth of the colonial urban sector provided little comfort or hope. The higher reaches of the new liberal professions were racially structured and congested. The massive tertiary sector provided scope only for very small-scale investment. The larger part of the middle class found employment as petty clerks in foreign administrative or commercial establishments. In the discourse of the master race, manhood was defined not just through financial solvency but by the nature of relationship to property. A passive and subordinate working life produced, therefore, a deep sense of emasculation.

Yet, in the early decades, the bhadralok had seemed poised on the brink of a major entrepreneurial breakthrough when several wealthy Calcutta houses began to make substantial fortunes from shipping, insurance, mining, and some foreign trade.[22] The boom was over by the 1840s, and after the 1860s hardly any new fortunes were made that way. Hopes of business success had already formed a new economic vocabulary. Debendranath Tagore talks in his autobiography about the failure of their business enterprise as the time 'when we lost all our property',[23] even though the Jorasanko Tagores still retained substantial rural estates and a solid Calcutta establishment. Property, for some time at least, meant a specific kind of activity, that is, business. [...]

Bengali capital was to be tied up largely in urban real estate and rural landholding, which did not require much acumen or entrepreneurship, and in local trade, which had little potential for growth.[24] By the late nineteenth century the second rung in business activities had been monopolized by Marwaris, the top rung having already long been an European preserve. By the mid-nineteenth-century Bengalis had only a marginal presence in Burrabazaar—the heart of indigenous business in Calcutta.[25]

[...] *Sambad Prabhakar* complained in 1892: 'The Lakshmi of sound commerce has abandoned Bengal. Mother Bengal now produces coolies and clerks alone.' The tragedy was caused, said the paper, by a self-destructive inclination towards easier or more luxurious foreign alternatives.[26]

Women were primarily responsible for deciding household purchases. They, therefore, served as the target of both nationalist appeal and blame. A large body of tracts and folk art depicted the modern woman as a self-indulgent, spoilt, and lazy creature who cared nothing for family or national fortune. This charge encompasses the triadic relationship between women, gold, and servitude—*kamini, kanchan, dasatva*—that the nineteenth-century saint Ramakrishna was to engrave so deeply upon the Bengali moral order.[27] The archetypal evil woman of these times was not the immoral or the economically independent one, but one who, inspired by modern education, had exchanged sacred ritual objects (the conchshell bangle, the ritually pure fabric, sindur) for foreign luxury ones.[28] There was thus an interchange between economic compulsions and pleas for feminine commitment to ritual.

The rent-revenue gap that the Permanent Settlement had generated and guaranteed had constituted the major security area for Bengal's middle-class bhadralok. It had ensured a whole spectrum of fairly comfortable rentier incomes at many levels. Certainties of absolute manipulative power over rent began to be breached—though in a very limited sense—from the mid-nineteenth century by the Rent Acts of 1859 and 1885. They intended to give a measure of security to upper tenants and curb some of the arbitrary coercive powers exercised by the landlord's kutcheries on unofficial courts-cum-dungeons. The Rent Act of 1859 had come about partly as a result of missionary pleas on behalf of the tenant.[29] Missionary-inspired colonial interference into the hitherto closed world of largely upper-caste Hindu zamindar and the lower-caste or Muslim peasant was curiously coextensive with very similar intrusions into the closed world of Hindu domestic practices. Both aroused a keen sense of the fragility of economic and domestic arrangements that had cushioned some of the traumas of the Hindu bhadralok. After the 1859 Act, landlords had been complaining that the loss of disciplinary power had eroded their moral authority and affected rent collection. The grievance closely parallels the dirges that were composed over each colonial or reformist suggestion for new conjugal laws. Clearly, the moral order of Hindu patriarchy was in peril.

If an alien, imposed modernity was represented as a series of deprivations, then nationalism could situate its emancipatory project only by enclosing a space that was still understood as inviolate, autonomous. Much of nineteenth-century nationalism identified this space as the 'Hindu way of life'. The fundamental distinction between reformers and Hindu nationalists of the nineteenth century did not lie in the fact that the former were less patriotic or that the latter were more rooted in indigenous tradition. It stemmed from two different readings of Hindu domestic practices and custom. While liberal reformers described them as a distortion of earlier purity and a major symptom of present decay, Hindu nationalists celebrated them as an excess reserved over and above colonization, any change in which would signify the surrender of the last bastion of freedom. [...] Colonization had made it imperative to introduce an absolute distinction between the Self and the Other, while emergent nationalism made it equally imperative to stake out claims to sole representational authority over the self. [...]

The concern with domestic practice initiated much discussion and debate. The consequent transparency of concrete practices demystified the self-legitimizing arguments around custom and, eventually, put far too many strains on the commitment to it. The Hindu nationalist agenda consequently moved out of the area of human relationships into the more public and reified domain of social service and patriotism towards the turn of the century. I would, then, relocate some of the vital beginnings of Bengali nationalism away from the recognized issues in the political sphere and into the politics of relationships within the family.

III

The Hindu home was the one sphere where improvement could be made through personal initiative, and changes wrought whereby education would bring forth concrete, manipulable, desired results.[30] The home, then, had to substitute for the world outside and for all the work and relations there that lay beyond personal comprehension and control. 'Just as the King reigns over his dominion, so the head of the household (*karta*) rules over his household'[31]—began a mid-nineteenth-century tract on domestic management. 'The karta sometimes rules like a King, sometimes needs to legislate like the lawgiver and sometimes he adjudicates like the chief justice,'[32] said another. 'Whoever can run a Hindu family can administer a whole realm'[33] was an assertion frequently made within this body of writing. Yet another tract advised the karta on how to marshal his forces to face a rebellious woman within the family.[34] The karta, therefore, becomes within the home what he can never aspire to be outside it—a ruler, an administrator, a legislator, or a chief justice, a general marshalling his troops. Apart from compensatory functions, the strategic placement of the home assumes other functions as well. The management of household relations becomes a political and administrative capability, providing training in governance that one no longer attains in the political sphere. The intention is to establish a claim to a share of power in the world, a political role that the Hindu is entitled to, via successful governance of the household. A possibly unintended consequence, however, is that in the process this renders household relations into political ones.

This was an unintended consequence because the Hindu nationalist strategy centred its critique of colonialism primarily on the loveless, purely deprivational, unrequited nature of its political arrangement, an arrangement which endowed the dominant group with absolute power and profits and the subject people with helpless surrender—with no possibility of self-fulfilment. If the home was not merely an escape from this world but its critique and an alternative order in itself, then love and affect had to be the organizing principle of this inner, hidden nation, and the exercise of power needed to be replaced with the notion of self-surrender and general self-fulfilment. Household relations had to be shown as supra-political ones, relations of power represented as purely emotional states.

Out of the entire gamut of household relations, conjugality was found to be ideally relevant to this project. Conjugality was based on the apparent absolutism of one partner and the total subordination of the other. As such, it was the one relationship that seemed most precisely to replicate colonial arrangements. Hence, this would best constitute the grounds for challenging and contesting colonial arrangements—that is, by showing the supposedly real and radical difference between the two sets of relationships despite their apparently similar basis, and by establishing where the moral superiority of the one lay over the other. [...]

[...] Hindu nationalists needed to naturalize love as the basis for Hindu marriage, a higher form of love that excelled allegedly utilitarian, materialist and narrowly contractual western arrangements. They argued that non-consensual Hindu marriages could, indeed, be more loving than the western pattern of courtship based on class and property qualifications more than on love. In the Hindu case, a lifetime of togetherness beginning with infancy guaranteed a superior and more certain compatibility. Nationalists denied that the production of sons was the sole aim of Hindu marriage: they argued it was a complete spiritual union through perfect love. It was also kinder to women since it ensured not just a hold on the husband's affection but an integration with the family which gave her greater security. While the entire system of non-consensual, indissoluble, infant marriage was to be preserved intact and inviolate, each aspect of the Hindu marriage needed to be written as a love story with a happy ending.[35]

Let us look at a very typical description of a child bride.

People in this country take great pleasure in infant marriage. The little bit of a woman, the infant bride, clad in red silk.[...] Drums are beating and men, women and children are running in order to have a glimpse of that lovely face. From time to time she breaks forth into little ravishing smiles. She looks like a little lovely doll.

The key words are 'little, lovely, ravishing, pleasure, infant, doll'— inserted at carefully chosen selected intervals.[36] The community of 'men, women, and children' formed round this figure is bonded together by great visual pleasure, by happiness. Loveableness bathes the trauma of patrilocality in warm sensuousness and grounds non-consensual indissoluble infant marriage in mutual desire alone.

Given this sensual starting point, the absolute and unconditional chastity of the Hindu wife, extending beyond the death of the husband, was equally strongly grounded by this discourse in her own desire. This purity, since it is supposedly a conscious moral choice, becomes at once a sign of difference and of superiority, a Hindu claim to power. The politics of women's monogamy then is the condition of the possible Hindu nation: the one is often explicitly made to stand in for the other. 'We are but a half civilised, poor, sorrowful, subjected, despised nation. We have but one jewel and for us that is the treasure of seven realms, a priceless gem.'[37] [...] Woman's chastity, then, has a real and stated, not merely symbolic, political value.

Willed chastity enables the widow to desire the austerities and sacrifices that her condition imposes on her. Since she still belongs spiritually to her husband in a transcendental sort of way, worldly comforts have actually ceased to matter and her body and soul draw pleasure, not pain, from the rigours of material existence. Her life is not marked by loss or absence but by surfeit because her voluntary abdication of an earthly life is a form of sanyas within the household.[38] It not only gives her moral and spiritual energy but also ensures a reservoir of spirituality in each home and for the Hindu order as a whole. Also, strict ritual observances root the widow's body in ancient India, thus miraculously enabling her to escape foreign domination. The cloth she wears is necessarily indigenous, the water she drinks is to be carried from the sacred river and not through foreign water pipes, and the salt that goes into her food is special rock salt untouched by machines. Ergo, the nation needs ascetic widowhood.[39]

The final and highest test of the supremacy of Hindu conjugality was the proven past capacity for self-immolation by widows.[40] The sati was an adored nationalist symbol, her figure representing the moment of climax in expositions of Hindu nationalism. Bankimchandra saw in it the last hope of a doomed nation.[41] [...]

Rabindranath's writing of the early Swadeshi period recall her glory.[42] An immense body of patriotic tracts routinely invoked the act as an unfailing source of nationalist inspiration and pride. [...]

It was the nature of the woman's commitment to the conjugal order that bound the system together. Moral initiative therefore passes on to the woman, uniquely privileging her activism. If the household was the embryonic nation, then the woman was the true patriotic subject. The male body, having passed through the grind of western education, office, routine, and forced urbanization, having been marked with the loss of traditional sports and martial activities, was supposedly remade in an attenuated, emasculated form by colonialism.[43] The female body, on the other hand, was still pure and unmarked, loyal to the rule of the *shastras*.

This construction of the Hindu wife could also bind wide-ranging social segments around her practices and norms in order to formulate a middle class which, in colonial Bengal, lacked a clearly articulated economic base. [...] Since the new economic man did not appear in Bengal, it would be the new domestic woman who had to carry the image of a class.

IV

The image of the loving heart of Hindu conjugality was, understandably, more an act of heroic imagination and conviction than of lived experience. Paradoxically, the stronger the expression of conviction in the vision, the more strongly critical attention would focus on concrete aspects of the reality and render the project enormously complicated. Four developments problematized the Hindu nationalist discourse on conjugality in the last two decades of the nineteenth century. There was already an old and deeply influential counter-tradition of folklore and verse that described marriage and domesticity as a source of profound unhappiness for the woman.[44] Nineteenth-century discursive prose would extend these desperate sobs into critical argument, interrogation, and frontal challenge: into a movement for change. From the 1860 women's own writings began to appear, further confirming this tradition.[45] And finally, there were reformist campaigns for change that, from the mid-1880s under Malabari assiduously picked up and wove together all the material evidence on force and coercion within Hindu marriage. Two sensational events—Rukmabai's demand to be released from a marriage contracted at her infancy, and a little girl Phulmani being raped to death by her husband—seemed to abundantly vindicate the reformist critique and added strength and urgency to their campaign.[46]

Women's voices had frequently been borrowed by male authors to express a profound sense of bleakness about her existence. Jayadev's Radha had remained implacably angry about sexual double standards.[47] A particular stream within eighteenth-century Shakta devotional poetry—the Agamani songs—would use the mother's voice to mourn Durga's imminent parting at the end of her annual visit to her parent's home: 'Do not pass away the night of Nawami, leave her with me just a little longer.'[48] These songs, enormously popular throughout the nineteenth century, would find a double resonance from within a very wide-ranging age group among Bengali women. Thanks to the widespread custom of infant marriage, women, by their early twenties, might be daughters longing for their mothers, and, simultaneously, young mothers pining for their married daughters. In lullabies and folk verses, probably composed largely by women themselves, married sisters threatened to drown themselves unless their brothers came and took them away from 'this place of torture'. A little girl would plead with her playmate to play a last game with her, 'for the son of a stranger is coming to take me away and I shall never play again'. A young mother, hungry for the sight of her baby—from whom the endless duties of a joint family routine separate her—plans thus: 'I'll run away to the forest with my baby, and there, in solitude, I'll gaze upon the face of my treasure.'[49] A complicated variety of female rites—*vrats*—were evolved to eliminate the threat of the co-wife.[50]

The experience of their own subjection, however, gave to colonized men a fresh and acute sensitivity in relation to bondage. *Adhinata* became a peculiarly loaded word, fraught with a double guilt: the sin of submitting to foreign domination, which necessarily conjured up the associated guilt of submitting the woman to a state of subjection. The two senses of the word would continuously flow into each other, interanimate each other. They would sometimes be posed as cause and effect. 'When our white masters kick us, we return home and soothe ourselves by kicking our wives.'[51] Or, 'Our women lost their freedom when we lost ours.'[52] [...]

Occasionally one kind of subjection was so closely linked to the other that they interchanged as metaphors. There is a poem on the caged bird and the title of this poem refers to the incarceration of women within the home:

Free bird, how do you hope to be happy within the cage?
Imprisoned, you have forgotten your own speech.
And you repeat the words of others mindlessly.[53]

Loss of one's language was also the most familiar trope for describing political subjection.

A whole alternative, contestatory description developed from the extended guilt over subjection, representing the Hindu home as the very antithesis of pleasure. [...]

The interrogation was not restricted to reformers. Hindu nationalists themselves, by relentlessly focusing on conjugality, problematized the entire arena. Even the most status-quoist tracts, which conclude with very orthodox prescriptions, do so not with confidence and certainty but after a compulsive and obsessive probing of all the tension spots.[54] This endless preoccupation reveals continuous doubts rather than any final resolution, since excessive speech points at anxiety just as surely as silence does.

The alternative, challenging description gained in authenticity once Hindu women began to write about themselves from the 1860s. They wrote about the trauma and not the beauty of infant marriage, the deprivations of the widow, the absence of love in the lives of wives. 'Conjugal love has disappeared from our country,' wrote a Hindu woman in 1863. She also claimed that Hindu women suffered more than anyone else in the world.[55] The Hindu household was described as 'a most terrible mountain range, infested with wild beasts.'[56] [...]

All varieties of women's writings unanimously identified and condemned two problem spots within the Hindu woman's existence—the pain of patrilocality and the longing for knowledge. Whatever the format and whatever the basic political stance towards patriarchy, women's writings at this time agreed on these points of criticism. The longing for systematic learning was not a desire implanted by male reformers, missionaries, and colonialists. A pious Hindu housewife, spending her life in a non-reformed domestic environment where no woman ever learnt to read, was so driven by this sharp desire that she taught herself the letters in great secrecy and with difficulty. When she finally started reading, a measure of her triumph was conveyed by her coining of a magnificent new word to describe her own achievement and 'mastery over the word'—*jitakshara*.[57] [...]

In 1884 Rukmabai, a low-caste, educated Maharashtrian girl sought to repudiate an unconsummated marriage contracted at her infancy with an illiterate, dissolute, sick husband.[58] Over this sensational challenge, Malabari mobilized reformers and renewed his campaign for the introduction of divorce and for a higher age of consent—demands that seriously eroded the principles of indissolubility and of infant marriage. A higher age of consent for the girl would also jeopardize the fundamental Hindu tenet of *garbhadhan*, that is, the obligatory ritual cohabitation as soon as the wife attains puberty—for otherwise her womb is tainted and her sons lose the right to serve up ancestral offering.[59] Since in the hot climate of Bengal puberty may occur fairly early, a higher age of consent, it was feared, would interfere with this injunction.

For some time, in Hindu nationalist circles, Rukmabai became a name more dreaded than Malabari's or those of colonial legislators.[60] They would still valiantly argue that a true Hindu wife must find the husband desirable, irrespective of external circumstances [...]. Already, however, the basis of conjugality had shifted from love to prescription as soon as the imperative 'must' was introduced in the statement. A structured duality thus complicated the representation of conjugality. The two compulsions and possibilities of construction—preservation of conjugal discipline and accent on love—would inevitably prove incompatible.

Reformers had an easier time of it since they were willing to surrender the principle of sacrament to the principle of willed and regularly consummated conjugal love. Widows could remarry because the physical relationship was over for them and hence the marriage was over as well. Similarly, wives of endlessly polygamous Kulin Brahmins were really not married since, in their case, consummation was rare, if not impossible. Infant wives, thrown into a relationship not chosen by them, could similarly repudiate their marriage tie. Hindu nationalists, on the other hand, fused love into sacrament which, once performed, must reign supreme, irrespective of absence of consummation or consent. There were no gradations within marriage—a child widow who had not seen her husband was as meaningfully married to him as the wife of a monogamous, loving husband. Once love and willed surrender were separated out from the sacrament, however, Hindu nationalists had to take their stand on the latter alone in order to preserve the totality of the conjugal system.

They continued to sensualize the discipline of the sacrament—up to 1889 at least, when a more severe jolt occurred. Phulmani, a girl of ten, was raped to death by her twenty-nine-year-old husband, Hari Maiti. Since she was beyond the statutory minimum age of ten, Hari Maiti could not be punished under existing Penal Code provisions. The event seemed to fully justify Malabari's allegations and a very hesitant government was at last inclined to give in to proposals for a higher age of consent.[61]

The narrative of Hindu marriage could no longer use the language of love; it had to be rewritten in terms of force and pain. If the element of difference from other systems was so obviously seen to lie in discipline, then Hinduism had to be celebrated as a superior coercive power. 'The Hindu is truly very severe, even cruel,' exulted Chandranath Basu in 1892 in his rejoinder to Rabindranath on the question of 'Hinduvivaha'.[62] Self-fulfilment and pleasure were now demoted to a rather lower order of values. If infant marriage led to violence, even to bloody death, then it was the unique privilege and strength of the Hindu woman to accept the risk. Its practice could lead to weakened progeny and racial degeneration. But 'the Hindu prizes his religion above his life and short-lived children.'[63] Hindu scriptures did impose harsh injunctions on the wife as well as the widow. Yet 'this discipline is the prize and glory of chaste women and it prevails only in Hindu society.'[64] [...]

Yet the grounding of an imagined nation upon sheer pain could not proceed beyond this point. Hinduism has come far too close to its own description of the perspective, loveless, disciplinary regime that is colonialism. The discourse reaches its breaking point and begins to collapse into self-travesty, the beginnings of self-disgust. When Joygobinda Shome said in 1891: what if infant wives die in childbirth since female scorpions always do in any case—the limits of this discourse had been reached.[65] Rajendralal Mitra had earlier raised a laugh at a Shobhabazaar Raj palace meeting when he described the Hindu wife as 'an article of gift...she is given away even as a cow or any other chattel.'[66] I suspect that the laugh was uneasy. The hegemonic desires of Hindu nationalism clashed too violently with the starkness of its discipline. Love had to re-enter the nationalist narrative.

Over the last decade of the century a new organizational principle, a new centre of gravity, was sought beyond conjugality. The axis was eventually located in the loving relationship between mother and son. This time, however, this was no flesh-and-blood woman, all too easily visible within an all-too-accountable household, but the new and supreme deity within the Hindu pantheon—the Motherland, the reified woman.[67] With the reoriented figure of the woman came a crucial shift in the very placing of the patriotic project. It was taken out of the problematic home space and into the wider, more public arena of the Hindu community—which is an abstraction. The defence of Hindu domesticity, the preservation of the Hindu home, fell away from the nationalist agenda. Vivekananda, who had found the whole age of consent agitation profoundly uncomfortable, proposed to add muscle and sinew to the decadent Hindu through work-oriented asceticism and social service. [...] The experience of something approaching a mass upsurge over the age of consent issue generated enabling rhetoric and techniques for political mobilization and agitation that were, for the moment, found to be more efficacious than the politics of petitions or the annual Congress forums. The very success of the struggle over domestic issues, paradoxically, carved out a political sphere that could now be separated from the domestic arena.

Questions of internal power arrangements were not to be completely resolved. They constituted—as I suspect or hope they still do now—implacable pitfalls, the internal limits within the discourse. Bankim, in the last pages of his last novel, had mocked the grandeur of his own apocalyptic vision through the casual gossip of common people who dismissed the Hindu–Muslim war as supremely irrelevant for themselves. Vivekananda was asked by an American woman missionary in 1898 if he foresaw any hope of eliminating child marriage and cruelty to widows. Sadly, he said, no. The missionary went on with her account: 'Even at the height of his popularity, with the Hindu world at his feet, the Swami shows a strange foreboding of ultimate failure. I cannot give you an adequate impression of the effect, but sitting there at twilight, in the large, half-lighted hall, it seemed like listening to a cry.'[68]

NOTES

1. Edward Said's *Orientalism* (London, 1978) has acquired enormous canonical value for recent perspectives on the colonial period. For an equally influential application of Saidian dicta, see Partha Chatterjee, *Nationalist Thought and the Colonial World: A Derivative Discourse?* (New Delhi, 1986).

2. See Asok Sen, *Iswar Chandra Vidyasagar and His Elusive Milestones* (Calcutta, 1977). In fact, the presumed naive faith and hope of the early reformers can be looked at very differently. For a more pessimistic reading of that phase, see Sumit Sarkar, 'The Complexities of Young Bengal', in *A Critique of Colonial India* (Calcutta, 1985).

3. All experimentation with courses and pedagogic methods gradually dried up after the Despatch of 1854 which introduced a drab uniformity through a systematic examination system. See Romesh Chandra Mitra, 'Education: 1833-1905', in N.K. Sinha (ed.), *The History of Bengal, 1757-1905* (Calcutta, 1967). See also Kissory Chand Mitra, *On the Progress of Education in Bengal* (July 1887), reprinted in *Nineteenth Century Studies* (January 1975).

4. See Swarajit Chakraborti, The *Bengali Press, 1818-1868—A Study in the Growth of Public Opinion* (Calcutta, 1976). According to Reverend Long's evidence before the Indigo Commission, in 1860, the controversy on widow remarriage alone gave birth to twenty-five new publications in the vernacular press and the issues of early marriage and female education were similarly widely discussed. Benoy Ghose, 'The Press in Bengal', in N.K. Sinha (ed.), *The History of Bengal*, p. 227.

5. Ibid.

6. William G. Archer, *Bazar Paintings of Calcutta* (London, 1953). Regarding the circulation of reading matter, visual and art objects, and cultural performances within a popular circuit, see Jyotindra Jain, *Kalighat Paintings: Images from a Changing World* (Ahmedabad, 1999).

7. See Brajendranath Bandyopadhyay, *Bangiya Natyashalar Itihas, 1795-1876* (Calcutta, 1943), p. 151.

8. For the reorientation of this traditional myth under colonial conditions, see Sumit Sarkar, 'The Kalki Avatar of Bikrampur: A Village Scandal in Early Twentieth-Century Bengal', in Ranajit Guha (ed.), *Subaltern Studies VI: Writings on South Asian History and Society* (Delhi, 1989).

9. *Bangadoot*, 1829. Cited in R.C. Majumdar, *History of Modern Bengal, Part I, 1765-1905* (Calcutta, 1975), p. 253.

10. Hitesranjan Sanyal, *Social Mobility in Bengal* (Calcutta, 1981), pp. 36-44.

11. See P.J. Marshall, *Bengal: The British Period in Eastern India 1740-1828* (Cambridge, 1987), pp. 25-9, 139.

12. See a discussion on Shakta poetry in Shashibhushan Dasgupta, *Bharater Shakti Sadhana O Shakta Sahitya* (Calcutta, 1960).

13. Frank Perlin, 'Proto Industrialisation and Pre-Colonial South Asia', *Past and Present*, 1983, p. 56. Although he ascribes the major structural changes to a period well before the establishment of colonial rule, there is no doubt that colonial innovation and interferences sharpened the processes in the nineteenth century.

14. Marshall, *Bengal*, p. 4. It is interesting that findings about the formation of the moribund delta became widely known by 1833.

15. Ibid.

16. Chowdhury, 'Agrarian Economy and Agrarian Relations in Bengal 1858-1885', in N.K. Sinha (ed.), *The History of Bengal*, pp. 241-3. Also Marshall, *Bengal*, pp. 5, 18-19.

17. Marshall, *Bengal*, p. 4.

18. See, for instance, Rajnarayan Basu, *Sekal O Ekal* (reprinted Calcutta, 1988), pp. 31-6.

19. *Garhasthya* (monthly journal: Calcutta, 1884).

20. Marshall, *Bengal*, pp. 160-1.

21. Ghose, 'The Press in Bengal'. See also Chakraborti, *The Bengali Press*.
22. See Nilmoni Mukherji, 'Foreign and Inland Trade' in Sinha (ed.), pp. 339-62. Also Sabyaschi Bhattacharya, 'Traders and Trade in Old Calcutta', in Sukanta Chaudhuri (ed.), *Calcutta: The Living City*, vol. I (Calcutta, 1990), pp. 204-8. Also Marshall, *Bengal*, pp. 166-7.
23. Debendranath Tagore, *Atmacharit* (Calcutta, 1898), reprinted in *Atmakatha* (Calcutta, 1981).
24. Marshall, *Bengal*, p. 13.
25. Bhattacharya, 'Traders and Trade in Old Calcutta'.
26. *Sambad Prabhakar*, 11 August 1892 in Ghosh, (ed.), *Samayik Patre Banglar Samajchitra* (Calcutta, 1978), p. 127.
27. Sumit Sarkar, 'Kaliyug, Chakri and Bhakti: Ramakrishna and His Times', *Economic and Political Weekly*, 18 July 1992. See also, Chatterjee.
28. See Tanika Sarkar, 'Nationalist Iconography: The Image of Women in Nineteenth-Century Bengali Literature', *Economic and Political Weekly*, 21 November 1987.
29. Chowdhury, *Agrarian Economy*, pp. 295-9.
30. A mechanical application of a simple divide between the home and the world is derived from an untenable extension of a mid-nineteenth-century Victorian situation into a very different socio-political context. Partha Chatterjee argues along the lines of a series of binaries since he sees the nineteenth-century 'nationalist' agenda as being a mimetic gesture. See Partha Chatterjee, 'The Nationalist Resolution of the Women Question', in Sangari and Vaid (eds), *Recasting Women*. The concept of the Victorian home and its separation from the public sphere, again, is an undifferentiated social construct, taking an active entrepreneurial segment as representative of the middle class. For a very different positioning of the domestic sphere within a less activist, non-entrepreneurial world of the clergy, see Howard M. Wach, 'A "still, small voice" from the Pulpit: Religion and the Creation of Social Morality in Manchester, 1820-1850', *The Journal of Modern History*, September 1991.
31. Narayan Ray, *Bangamahila* (Calcutta, n.d.), p. 51.
32. *Garhasthya* (monthly journal: Calcutta, 1884), p. 1.
33. Monomohan Basu, *Hindur Achar Vyavahar* (Calcutta, c. 1872), p. 99.
34. Chandrakanta Basu, *Sangjam Shiksha* (Calcutta, c. 1904), p. 81.
35. See Tanika Sarkar, 'Conjugality and Hindu Nationalism'.
36. Ibid.
37. Basu, *Hindur Achar Vyavahar*, p. 31.
38. Pratapchandra Majumdar, *Stri Charitra* (Calcutta, n.d.). Interestingly, the model for the chaste Hindu widow is Queen Victoria. Also Kamakhyacharan Bandyopadhyay, *Stri Shiksha* (Dacca, c. 1901). Interestingly, even Rev. Lal Behari Dey, who had converted to Christianity, became rather lyrical in his praise of chaste Hindu widows. The most unqualified admiration was evoked by Sister Nivedita. See *The Web of Indian Life*, first published Calcutta, 1904 (reprinted Calcutta, 1955).
39. Ibid., p. 57.
40. Sati was routinely evoked as the climax, the highest proof and the essence of the Hindu wife's chastity. 'The woman's chastity is the bright jewel

of an Aryan family. The chaste wife is sitting at the heart of flames, with the feet of her husband clasped on her breasts. She is chanting Hari's name with a face radiant with love and joy. Whenever we think of that, we are filled with pride.' See Girijaprasanna Raychaudhury, *Grihalakshmi* (Calcutta, c. 1887), p. 67.

41. Bankimchandra Chattopadhyay, 'Kamalakanter Daptar', *Bankim Rachanabali*, vol. II (Calcutta, 1954).

42. Sumit Sarkar, *The Swadeshi Movement in Bengal, 1903–1908* (Delhi, 1972), pp. 47–63.

43. See Tanika Sarkar, 'Conjugality and Hindu Nationalism'.

44. Bhabataran Datta, *Bangladesher Chhara* (Calcutta, n.d).

45. On this, see Ghulam Murshid, *Reluctant Debutante: Responses of Bengali Women to Modernisation* (Rajshahi, 1983).

46. See Tanika Sarkar, 'Conjugality and Hindu Nationalism'.

47. On the importance of this twelfth-century text, see S.K. De, *Early History of the Vaishnava Faith and Movement in Bengal* (Calcutta, 1961), pp. 9–11.

48. Rasikchandra Ray, 'Nabamir Gan', in Prabhat Goswami (ed.), *Hajar Bacharer Bangla Gan* (Calcutta, 1969).

49. Datta, *Bangladesher Chhara*.

50. Nandalal Sil, *Vratakatha* (Calcutta, 1930).

51. Prasad Das Goswami, *Amader Samaj* (Serampore, 1896), p. 14.

52. Bhattacharya, *Banga Vivaha* (Calcutta, c. 1881), p. 76.

53. Ibid., p. 194.

54. See for instance, Saudamini Gupta, *Kanyar Prati Upadesh* (Dacca, third edition, c. 1918). Even though it teaches the daughter how best and most graciously she can submit to patriarchal discipline and demands in her married life, the text simultaneously undermines the patriarchal hegemonic claim by asserting, again and again, that this was going to be a life of sorrow and problems, 'All women must live out their lives without their relatives or close ones near them (p. 3) [...] My child, I cannot advise you on when or how much to eat, for whatever you do, you must know that, you will most probably be criticised.' (p. 41)

55. Kailashbashini Debi, *Hindu Mahilaganer Heenabastha* (Calcutta, n.d.), p. 62.

56. Ibid., p. 45. Also *Narishiksha*, part I (Calcutta, 1884: first edition c. 1868), p. 6.

57. Rashsundari Debi, *Amar Jiban*, 1876, reprinted in *Atmakatha* (Calcutta 1981). See also Sarada Debi, *Atmakatha* (Calcutta, 1979), for a similar longing for the written word. In her case, however, it remained unfulfilled.

58. Charles Heimsath, *Indian Nationalism and Hindu Social Reform* (Princeton, 1964), pp. 91–4.

59. Tanika Sarkar, 'Conjugality and Hindu Nationalism'.

60. On folk poems about the Rukmabai episode sung on Calcutta streets, see Asit Kumar Bandyopadhyay, *Bangla Sahityer Itihas*, vol. V.

61. See Tanika Sarkar, 'Conjugality and Hindu Nationalism'.

62. Chandranath Basu, *Hindutva (Hindur Prakrita Itihas)* (Calcutta, 1892).

63. *Bangabashi*, 25 December 1890, *Report on Native Papers* (hereafter *RNP*), Bengal, 1890.

64. *Dainik O Samachar Chandrika*, 14 January 1891, *RNP*, Bengal 1891.
65. Cited by Nagendranath Bandyopadhyay, *Balyavivaha* (Calcutta, 1888), p. 31.
66. Cited in *Hindoo Patriot*, 19 September 1887.
67. On the composition and control of a dominant cultural symbol and its relationship to a real physical support in society, see Luisa Accati, *The Larceny of Desire: The Madonna in Seventeenth-Century Catholic Europe*, in Obelkevich, Roper, and Samuel (eds), *Disciplines of Faith: Studies in Religion, Politics and Patriarchy* (London, 1987).
68. Lucy E. Guiness, *Across India at the Dawn of the Twentieth Century* (London 1898), p. 147.

Limits of the Bourgeois Model?*

DIPESH CHAKRABARTY

In nationalist representations, the colonial experience of becoming modern is haunted by the fear of looking unoriginal. This is understandable, for some of the founding myths of European imperialisms of the last two hundred years were provided by narratives which, as Meaghan Morris has recently reminded us, always portrayed the modern as something that had already happened somewhere else.[1] Nationalist writings therefore subsume the question of difference within a search of essences, origins, authenticities, which, however, have to be amenable to global-European constructions of modernity so that the quintessentially nationalist claim of being, 'different but modern' can be validated.[2] While nationalist thought thus mobilizes for its own ends the cultural field of difference, its resolutions, whether of the 'woman question' or that of the 'nation' itself, are inherently unstable and require, for their continued survival, much more than just the force of persuasive rhetoric. Differences are too heterodox for the nationalist project of modernity to contain them.

The issue of domesticity helps me to chart the movement of some of these questions in colonial Bengal. That English education often brought in its trail a sense of crisis in Bengali families—a certain degree of waywardness in young men which led to their neglecting their duties towards their families and the elders—was a most commonly voiced

---

* Originally published as 'The Difference-Deferral of a Colonial Modernity: Public Debates on Domesticity in British Bengal', in David Arnold and David Hardiman (eds), *Subaltern Studies VIII* (New Delhi: Oxford University Press, 1994) pp. 50–88. For the complete text see the original. In the present version, some portions of the essay have been removed and notes rearranged accordingly.

complaint against the Young Bengal of the early nineteenth century. The British in India pushed the question further by promoting the idea that husbands and wives should be friends/companions in marriage. 'Friendship', of course, had a very particular range of meaning in these nineteenth-century discussions on domestic life. It reflected the well-known Victorian patriarchal ideals of 'companionate marriage' which the British introduced into India in the nineteenth century and which many Bengali male and female reformers embraced with great zeal.[3]

It is the debates around this question—in particular, those around the ideals of the Bengali housewife—that act as my starting point. What interests me, however, is a particular problem. Hidden in these debates were statements about how the personal/domestic are to be distinguished from the communal/public, the distinction itself reflecting some of the compulsions that modern colonial rule brought with itself. This essay is an effort to understand the many contradictory and heterodox moves through which the Bengali modern has negotiated this distinction in (re)constituting itself within a world-system fashioned by imperialism. My aim is to attend carefully to nineteenth-century Bengali contestations over received bourgeois models for relating the personal to the public world of civil and political life.

The British instituted some kind of a civil society in colonial Bengal. The modern civil society carries with itself the distinction of the 'public' and the 'private'. This distinction, in turn, raises the question of the state. As Philippe Ariés says, the modern public/private split fundamentally relates to the positioning of the individual with regard to the (modern) state, that is, the casting of the individual into the role of the citizen.[4] Since the colonial relationship was one that denied the colonized the status of the citizen, Bengali engagements with 'modernizing' the domestic cannot be discussed in separation from nationalism, the ideology that promised citizenship and the nation-state, and thus the ideal civil-political society that the domestic order would have the duty of servicing. What I discuss, however, are the ways the project of creating citizen-subjects for Bengal/India was/is continually disrupted by other imaginations of family, personhood, and the domestic.

The debates about domesticity that I examine here took place within what I would call '*public* narratives of the nature of social life in the family'. I emphasize of the word '*public*' because the documents on which I base this essay are both products as well as constituents of a modern print-culture or the public sphere—in the European, or even Habermasian, sense—that arose in Bengal (and elsewhere in India) as a result of our encounter with a post-Enlightenment European imperial nation. [...] What these documents capture are fragments of Bengali self-fashioning in the context of the formation of a modern public life, for these writings were definitely subject to a growing body of conventions about desirable forms and topics of speech in public.[5] This entailed, as it has elsewhere, the development of rules for representing, within this so-called public, aspects of life seen as constituting its opposite—the private, the personal, the domestic. Bengali modernity has thus produced its own share of artefacts that narrate 'the private' in 'public', for example, novels, autobiographies, diaries, letters, and other forms.

This history, then, tells us very little about what went on it the everyday lives of actual, empirical, *bhadralok* families. Something of those lives can indeed be traced in my documents—and there is evidence to suggest the existence of relatively autonomous domains for women which the coming of a print-culture may have significantly eroded.[6] But what I focus on is primarily a conflict of attitudes that marked what was said *in print,* within the emergent conventions of bookish writings, about, the ideals of the housewife and about desirable forms of marriage and domestic life.

I should also explain as part of these preliminaries that it is a small group of people whose history is discussed in this essay. I write about the so-called Hindu bhadralok, the respectable people of the middle classes. It is partly my lived, intimate knowledge of this group that informs the questions I discuss here.

I

In many ways, the expression 'domestic life' as it is used here was a European category of thought. The assumption that cultures were not properly understood until the 'domestic' had been opened up to scholarly (or governmental) scrutiny, itself belonged to an intellectual tradition that objectified the idea of 'culture' and that seems to have marked much European writing and thinking on India in the eighteenth and early nineteenth centuries. James Mill in *The History of British India* (1817) quotes Bentinck, then the Governor of Fort St George, Madras, as expressing the opinion that the Europeans knew 'little or nothing of the customs and manners of the Hindus...their manner of thinking; their domestic habits and ceremonies, in which circumstances a knowledge of the people consists. [...]'[7]

Mill, as is widely known, was to erect upon this concern with the domestic and 'women's question' an entire edifice, his voluminous *History*, that condemned India as an inferior civilization. The concern with 'domesticity' was very much a part of this civilizational critique of India. The idea of 'civilization', a product, as Lucien Febvre has shown, of European thought in the 1760s, saw the world as both united as well as hierarchical. The hierarchy was defined by a scale of civilization that constructed the world as one—why else would a single scale be universally valid?—while dividing it up into more and less civilized countries.[8]

The universalist indictment of this civilizing discourse aroused in Bengali (male) social reformers of the nineteenth century a strong desire to participate in what was now seen as a world-community of countries, peoples or nations (these words being used in this period some-what interchangeably). [...]

As this civilizing-cum-nationalist body of thought proliferated in the second half of the nineteenth century to incorporate influences coming out of Victorian England, the personal and the domestic came to be tied ever more closely to the idea of the nation. Bengali books on education of the young now argued, following the likes of Samuel Smiles, that 'the individual was a physical embodiment of the nation' and the latter improved 'only if the individual had undergone all-round improvement'.[9] The Victorian fetishes of 'discipline', 'routine', and 'order' became some of the most privileged elements in Bengali writings on domestic and personal arrangements, constituting in themselves objects of desire and beauty.

The internal 'discipline' of 'the European home' was now seen as a key to European prosperity and political power. Bengali books on 'domestic science' extolled the 'attractive' qualities of 'the house of any civilized European' which was now compared to 'the abode of gods'. It was a place where *srinkhala* (discipline) reigned, things were clean, attractive, and placed in order. The Bengali/Indian home—itself a colonial construct, as we shall see—suffered badly in comparison. It was said to be like hell—dirty, smelly, disorderly, unclean, and unhealthy.[10] [...]

Order was thus linked to notions of cleanliness, hygiene, health, and a certain regimentation of time expressed in the 'virtue' of punctuality. The question of health, in turn, reflected the relations of power under colonial rule, the idiom of gender (the imperial theme of the emasculation of the colonized) in which it was often manifested, and the extent to which the male body itself had become a signifier for these relationships.[11] [...]

[...] Nationalism was [...] also at work in redefining childhood. Anukulchandra Datta, one of the early writers on 'domestic science', wrote: 'well-trained children are the pride of the country. With bad training and corrupt morals, they only bring grace to the family and [become] the scum of the nation.'[12] A regimen of routine regulating children's eating habits, games, work, and manners, was what the housewife was now being called upon to administer.[13] [...]

The civilizing discourse that propelled both imperialist and nationalist thought thus produced the figure of the 'uneducated housewife/mother' as one of the central problems that the project of making Bengalis into citizen-subjects had to negotiate. The lack of books in Bengali on the subject of 'domestic science' was now deplored by authors who came forward, with a sense of patriotic duty, to fill in this perceived void. [...]

It was thus that the idea of the 'new woman' came to be written into the techniques of the self that nationalism evolved, which looked on the domestic as an inseparable part of the national. The public sphere could not be erected without reconstructing the private.

II

My attempt to understand how the question of difference was played out in this (re)construction of the domestic realm in bhadralok life will take as its point of departure a generally accepted observation often made about this history: that in nineteenth and early-twentieth-century Bengali tracts supporting women's education and even the idea of 'friendship' between husbands and wives, the ideal of the 'modern', educated housewife was almost always tied to another ideal, 'the older patriarchal imagination of the mythical divine figure of the goddess Lakshmi.[14]

Lakshmi, regarded as Vishnu's wife by *c.* AD 400, has for long been upheld in puranic Hinduism as the model Hindu wife, united in complete harmony with her husband in a spirit that combined submission with loyalty, devotion, and fidelity. [...]

Lakshmi, however, has a reverse side, Alakshmi (Not-Lakshmi), her dark and malevolent Other. The innately heterogeneous puranic literature ascribes the origins of this malicious mythical woman to diverse sources. [...]

However she originated, Alakshmi came to embody a gendered conception of inauspiciousness and the opposite of all that the Hindu lawgivers upheld as the *dharma* (proper moral conduct) of the householder. When she entered a household, she brought jealousy and malice in her trail, brothers fell out with one another, families and their (patri)lineages (*kula*) faced ruin and destruction, the highest misfortune that Hindu patriarchal minds could ever imagine. [...]

Lakshmi and Alakshmi were mutually exclusive categories. A house where the spirit of Alakshmi prevailed was said to be unbearable for Lakshmi, who always left such a household and bestowed her favour on others who, and in particular whose women, did not flout the rules and rituals that made them auspicious. The Lakshmi–Alakshmi cycle has often been used in pre-British and folk literature to explain family (mis)fortunes and social mobility.[15]

What kind of women would be termed Alakshmi's in our nineteenth-century tracts on new domesticity? Two kinds, of which the first were women without any formal education for it was they who were bringing the nation into disrepute. [...] One important argument often advanced in favour of educating women was that education of the right kind would help to get rid of the poison of jealousy that ignorance produced and would thus help to restore in women their true Lakshmi-like nature.

Clearly then the invocation of Lakshmi was not an instance of a 'tradition' fighting 'modernity'. The 'modern' Lakshmi, to be produced through education, was an indispensable part of a nationalist, and self-consciously articulated, search for domestic 'happiness'. [...] Converting women into *grihalakshmi*s (Lakshmi of the household) through the novel means of formal education was the self-appointed task of a civilizing nationalism. [...]

But a 'lack of education' was not the only factor that made some women behave in an Alakshmi-like spirit. Education itself could also be dangerous. It could produce its own variety of Alakshmis, women who were allegedly arrogant, lazy, immodest, defiant of authority, and neglectful of domestic duties. As one author of a textbook on 'domestic science' put it: 'In today's women, education produces an [inordinate] fondness for luxury and comfort. They do not have much sympathy for others in the family, nor much modesty, and unlike [women] in the past, do not look on their husbands as divine beings....The proper aim of women's education is to correct these faults'.[16]

Several negative terms were used to describe such women or their behaviour: *bibi* (the feminine form for *babu*, a dandy), *memsahib* (European women), *boubabu* (a housewife who behaves like a babu), *beshya* (slut), and such others. [...] These imaginary 'ultra-modern' women were portrayed in fiction and non-fiction as selfish and self-indulgent people who had overturned the domestic order by their disrespectful attitude towards the *grihini* of the household, the mother-in-law. [...] The alleged neglect of *grihakarma* (domestic work or duties) by '(over) educated' women was the subject of complaint and banter in Manmohan Bosu's book on Hindu rituals. Speaking of 'the effort to destroy' the Hindu home now apparently at work in the *antahpur* (the inner apartments or women's quarters), he said.

On all sides we hear the cry: Be civilized, learn manners, don't touch cow-dung [traditional purifier/cleanser] or dirty cooking pots, don't handle the broomstick, and don't even go near the hearth! After all, you are the ladies of the household, does it suit you to do the work of the maidservant? If you spend the whole day in the kitchen, when will you apply yourselves to the cultivation of the mind? [...][17]

Bosu's reference to the maidservant is a reminder that what was at issue was not the question or even the quantum of actual physical exertion by middle-class women. The physically harder part of domestic labour, one could reasonably assume, would have been performed by hired servants (or retainers) in many bhadralok families—subaltern groups whose histories we have not even begun to imagine. The invocation of 'household duties' or grihakarma/*grihakarya* worked rather as a cryptic cultural code for the qualities of personhood that made a woman both 'modern' and desirable. Education was essential to the production of this desirability, for 'an uneducated woman', as a book on *naridharma* (women's dharma) put it: 'cannot be skilled in grihakarya [domestic work]. At the same time, a woman who neglects grihakarya for the sake of learning, will find her learning to be useless. The most successful wife is she who combines education with skills in household tasks.'[18] Grihakarya or household work was a culturally shared way of referring to the qualities of grace/modesty and obedience which were described in this literature as the two signs of Lakshmi-like auspiciousness in a woman. The attainment of both required modern education. [...]

Students of the social history of the bhadralok will know that it was not only the male writers of the period who wrote in this vein. Very similar points of view, in different forms, were often expressed by women (which is not to deny the dissimilarities that could distinguish women's writings from men's). I will also take for granted the by-now familiar point that the literature discussed originated as part of the historical process through which a modern patriarchal discourse was fashioned by the Hindu Bengali bhadralok under the twin pressure of colonial rule and emerging nationalist sentiments.[19] The very interchangeable use made in these writings of words such as *beshya* (whore) and memsahib (European woman) suggest a nationalist insistence on cultural stereotypes in a gesture of creating and maintaining boundaries that were patently false. Nor is there much intellectual mileage to be had from regarding the use of the Lakshmi-figure as an instance of the so-called 'modernity of tradition', for that only leaves all modernities looking the same.

For the purpose of this analysis, I will also take for granted another obvious point: that Alakshmi, beshya, boubabu, memsahib, and other such words were terms that stood for individual assertiveness on the part of women and its undesirability. They were the figures of imagination that helped demonize the 'free' and 'private' (female) individual whom the European writers on conjugality idealized. 'Friendship' between husbands and wives, grown in the privacy and freedom of bourgeois patriarchy, appear here to have run into opposition from the patriarchal structures that already existed. 'Freedom' in the West, several authors argued, meant *jathechhachar*, to do as one pleased, to be self-indulgent and selfish. In India, it was said, 'freedom' meant freedom from the self, the free person being one who could serve and obey voluntarily.

[...]

To read this conflict over the ideals of the Bengali housewife (the *sugrihini*)—grihalakshmi versus the memsahib—as a debate about the 'freedom' of the autonomous bourgeois self on the one hand, and the idea of subordinating the individual to the will of the clan or the extended family on the other, is not so much to misread it as to stay completely within the very terms of these colonial texts themselves.[20] After all, as is known, for nationalist and imperial historians alike, the 'woman question' has often acted as a measure of 'freedom' and quality of civilization.[21]

'Freedom', undoubtedly, was a key idea that shaped the Bengali modern. The emergent and new (bourgeois) individuality in Bengal in the nineteenth and twentieth centuries was deeply embroiled in the question of defining personal 'freedom' in the context of the norms of the extended family. Debates over 'free will' versus 'determination' or 'necessity' (sometimes read as 'fate' or 'destiny'), for example, provided some of the central motifs in quite a few of Bankimchandra's novels, an early edition of *Kapalkundala*, in fact, carrying a whole essay on the subject of 'freedom versus destiny'.[22] [...]

It is not my purpose here to sit in judgement over the nineteenth-century question of whether or not Bengali lives were 'free'. I do not want to essentialize or fetishize the idea. Investigations into 'unfreedoms' are obviously a matter of investigating concrete contexts that cannot be contained by the merely textual. Here, however, as I have already said, I am concerned with the textual alone. I want to read these texts—in particular, the debate over the ideals of the grihalakshmi—as illustrations of the different possible, and often non-commensurable, worlds we created for ourselves as we embraced our (colonial-nationalist) modernity. What I read in the terms in which the Bengali debates over new forms of domesticity were conducted are two radically different, though not unconnected, constructions of the social life of the family as narrated in public. They are both constitutive of our 'modernity', yet each of them posits a relationship between domesticity and civil-political life that is contradicted by the other. They can come together only by bringing each other into crisis. I do not claim that my reading of these texts exhausts the possibilities created in our modernity. But it may enable us to question the narratological closures that give this 'modernity', or its 'history', a semblance of homogeneous unity.

III

At the heart of the grihalakshmi/memsahib debate, then, were at least two contradictory articulations of the public/private distinction, both called into being by the exigencies of our colonial modernity. I have explained the way this relationship was conceived within the view that took as its task the 'civilizing' of Bengal/India. I will now demonstrate the structure of the second articulation by moving to an earlier period in the history of British colonialism in Bengal and begin by considering two documents from the year 1823. I choose these documents simply because they help me to lay bare the structure

Limits of the Bourgeois Model? 187

of a practice which, over time, got routinized and hence all too codified.

Both of these documents involved the prominent resident, journalist, and social commentator of early colonial Calcutta, Bhabanicharan Bandyopadhyay. One [...] is a well-known tract that he authored in 1823: *Kalikata Kamalalaya* (literally, *Calcutta: The Abode of Kamala* [*Lakshmi*]). The other one, a relatively obscure pamphlet published in the same year from Calcutta and now held in the British Library, is entitled: *Gauradeshiya samaj sangsthapanartha pratham sabhar bibaran* (literally: Minutes of the first meeting held in connection with the establishment/foundation of Gauradeshiya samaj [society/ association]). Bhabanicharan was one of the founders of this association. The other organizers were such contemporary Bengali stalwarts as Dwarkanath Tagore, Radhakanta Deb, Ramkamal Sen, Tarachand Chakrabarti, Ramdulal De, and Kashinath Mullick.

Gauradeshiya Samaj, one should remember, was itself part of a fledging civil society already visible in the schools, offices, workshops, press, voluntary associations in Calcutta of the 1820s. As the editor of the magazine *Samachar Chandrika*, Bhabanicharan was a luminary of the 'public sphere' that was emerging in Calcutta in this period. The published minutes of the Samaj themselves constitute interesting historical evidence of this [...]. More importantly, what makes this text a witness to the emergence of a 'public life' for the Bengali middle classes in Calcutta is the main subject that was discussed at the meeting. It was nothing other than 'the state of the country' and the possibilities of 'improvement'.

The country [...] is described in this document as being in a state of misery brought about by a combination of factors including the following: (a) lack of unity among 'us' [Hindus], and (b) declining status of scriptures and Brahmins, all compounded by ignorance on the part of the rulers (the British) of the dharma (moral order, proper action) of the land.[23] The appeal that this document makes to a dharmic code in discussing a political and social order will not surprise students of Bengali history. Books written early in the first decade of the nineteenth century by Bengali intellectuals patronized by the British interpreted the coming of the Raj by invoking this code. Mrityunjay Vidyalankar, 'for many years the Chief Pundit in the college of Fort William', saw the restoration of dharma, that is, the practice of *rajdharma* (the dharma of the king) as the divine purpose behind British rule.[24] [...]

There is no doubt a significant trace of this language in the way the minutes of Gauradeshiya Samaj use dharma as a shorthand for both land/country as well as for order/rule, that is, for a moral community. However, while in [...] Mrityunjay's prose dharma does not speak to any idea of 'nation' or 'civilization', the minutes of the Samaj are interestingly different. In the language of the minutes, dharma is made to work in tandem with the hierarchical and competitive European discourse of 'civilization'. One aim of the Samaj's resolve to 'protect Hindu dharma' was to prevent 'the humiliation of...the country, scriptures, and dharma' by especially the European missionaries. The theme of the decline of the country, though expressed in terms of dharma, differed from Mrityunjaya's [...] treatment of the subject in that it now included explicit comparison with European countries and their histories. [...] 'In the very distant past', the minutes continue:

the people of India [Bharat] were superior to the inhabitants of other islands. [...] They have become dependent and have been humiliated [and are now] immersed in abject misery. The unspeakable degree of our degradation can be comprehended if we compare our current state with the way intelligence and knowledge have influenced [other people]. But a combination of vanity and [our] current customs...prevents us from either acknowledging our sad circumstances or from making any effort to overcome them.[25]

The premise of this whole discussion was the idea of 'improvement' that we have already recognized as central to the idea of 'civilization'. The first requirement, Ramkamal Sen argued at this meeting, was unity and this was to be achieved by forming voluntary associations[...]. It was resolved at this meeting that the new 'Gauradeshiya Sabha of the bhadralok' would strive to eradicate the evil customs of the country by publishing Bengali translations of informative books from other countries, by promoting discussions among the scholars and pundits, by starting a school, and by acquiring European machinery to help the cause of knowledge, for, as it was observed in the minutes, 'a country lacking in printing presses and printed material...[to help disseminate] advice on conduct and rituals, will find the spread of harmful behaviour impossible to check, far less stop'.[26]

These minutes thus anticipate many of the features of that which came to characterize nationalist thought as the century wore on: the desire for a 'national' (still unclear in its outlines) unity, the desire for improvement in the state of the country, and the desire, finally, for a vigorous 'public sphere'—voluntary associations, presses and printed material promoting discussion on matters of public interest, formal meetings with all the rituals of 'public' life—elections, votes, resolutions, the recording of minutes, and other related practices—built into them. There is not yet an explicit desire for the modern nation-state here, but words like 'humiliation' and 'dependence' do refer back to a proto-national spirit that runs through this document and that distinguishes it from the texts of [...] Mrityunjay Vidyalankar who wrote in the early 1800s.

It is instructive, in this context, to consider Bhabanicharan Bandyopadhyay's tract *Kalikata kamalalaya* (hereafter *KK*) published in the same year as the minutes of the Samaj, 1823, as a guide to 'good conduct' in the urban life of Calcutta. Bhabanicharan, readers will recall, was one of the architects of Gauradeshiya Samaj and was an important editor in the emergent world of Bengali journalism. He had also worked in various capacities for a number of European business firms in the city. In other words, his participation in what we would now categorize as Bengali 'public life' was by no means negligible. Yet, as his book *KK* shows, public/private, home/world, or domestic/official were not the distinctions that he would have applied to his own life. *KK* is an interesting instance of the dharmic code being used to produce and organize an articulation of the relationship between domestic and civil-political life which was quite antithetical to that produced under the sign of 'civilization'.

KK is written in the form of a dialogue between an 'urban dweller', a Brahmin who lives and works in Calcutta, and a 'stranger', a newcomer from the country, who handles the city with a certain degree of anxiety and trepidation and who is therefore eager to find out about its ways. It is a book written very much in the colonial context and shares some of the sentiments expressed by [...] Mrityunjay Vidyalankar on the one hand, and Gauradeshiya samaj on the other. [...]

Unlike the texts of the Fort William College pundits, however, *KK* displays an inherent anxiety over the changes brought about by social mobility in Calcutta, in particular the role that 'new' money could play in undermining the 'proper' model of social order and the place of the Brahmins within it.[27] The word *kamalalaya* describing Calcutta as the abode of the goddess of wealth, Kamala (or Lakshmi), betrays this concern. This dissolution of kinship bonds in the city is mourned by the 'urban dweller' in *KK*, for it allowed people to engage in 'shameful acts'. Even religious ceremonies, he says, were not being observed in the proper spirit, ostentatious displays of money and wealth often being more important than any sacred intent. The celebration of

Durga Puja (worshipping of Goddess Durga) in Calcutta, said Bhabanicharan, had already acquired a bad name among many who called it, mockingly, 'chandelier puja', 'festival of *baijis* [dancing girls]', 'occasion for the worship of one's wife's jewellery and sarees', etc.[28] One sees why Bhabanicharan participated in the efforts of Gauradeshiya Samaj: constructing proper rules of proper conduct for the residents of colonial Calcutta is a concern shared by *KK* and the minutes of the Samaj.

'I hear that in Calcutta a large number of people have given up the right codes of conduct', the stranger says in *KK*. [...]

[...] [Among the] charges brought against the Calcutta bhadralok are [...]: salaried (or paid) work demanding long and fixed hours ('the whole day'), impurity of language, food and clothes; neglect of daily, sacred observances.

The 'urban dweller' in *KK* begins by conceding the validity of these charges. 'What you have heard is true,' he says, and adds, '...but a Hindu who behaves like that is a Hindu only in appearance [*Hindubeshdhari*: one dressed as a Hindu].' In spite of the new structuring of the day that the colonial civil-political society required, the true Hindu strove to maintain a critical symbolic boundary between the three spheres of action (karma) that defined life: *daivakarma* (action to do with the realm of gods), *pitrikarma* (actions pertaining to the realm of one's ancestors), and *vishaykarma* (action to do with the realm of worldly interests, that is, undertaken in pursuit of wealth, livelihood, fame, power, and other such intersts). The most commendable of the *vishayi* bhadralok (that is, bhadralok with worldly interests) were always able to separate the self-in-world from a transcendental, higher self:

People with important occupations such as *diwani* or *mutasuddiship* wake up early and meet with and talk to different kinds of people [visitors] [only] after completing their morning ablutions. ...Later on they rub their bodies with oil...Before eating, they engage in [different] puja [worship] ceremonies [including] *homa* sacrifice, *valivashya*, etc. [...] Middle-class people who are not wealthy...follow the same pattern, with the difference that they work harder, have less to give away in charity and can afford to entertain only a smaller number of [importunate] visitors. The more indigent bhadralok also live by the same ideas. But they have to work even harder and have even less to eat or give away.[29]

Of particular interest to us is how Bhabanicharan handled the question of the polluting effects of using foreign languages. [...] But 'what should we do,' he asked, 'when dealing with words that do not translate into Bengali or Sanskrit?' Bhabanicharan actually produces a list of such unavoidable words of which the following are in English. The list speaks for itself: 'non-suit, summons, common law, company, court, attachment, double, decree, dismiss, due, premium, collector, captain, judge, subpoena, warrant, agent, treasury, bills, surgeon [sergeant?], discount'.[30]

It is clear that these words belonged to the sordid domain of vishaykarma, the realm of worldly interests, which is where (British) rule was and Bhabanicharan's ideal was to prevent words from polluting the purer domains of daivakarma and pitrikarma. Using clothes, Ganga water, and other such items to mark the boundaries between the domains seems to have been a common practice among the upper castes in Calcutta in the early part of the nineteenth century. [...]

KK thus does not share the (later) nationalist urge to translate into Indian languages English words that had to do with modern statecraft or modern technology. An unmistakable expression of the nationalist and civic desire to appropriate the instruments of 'modern' rule is absent from this text. KK instead marginalizes the state (and by implication, the nation) by separating it from the purer aspects of personhood, by looking on it as a contingency and an external constraint, one of the many one has to negotiate in the domain of vishaykarma. [...] The serious business of 'nationalism—or indeed the all-consuming conception of the nation itself that one day, by dint of its sacredness, would demand the sacrifice of life at its alter—could not be born of such a spirit. [...]

This separation of the purer part of the self from the more polluting proceedings of public life and of the civil society had implications for Bhabanicharan's understanding of domesticity. He does not even mention women or children, their existence is contained within the definition of the life of the male, upper-caste, patriarchal householder. Nor does griha or home play any part in his thought as a spatial entity. There is no conception here of the 'home' being the man's castle, his personal refuge in love from the competitive world of the public sphere. The grihini, the housewife is not a separate subject of discussion here, presumably because it was assumed that she was only a derived aspect of the male grihi. [...]

There is in addition, nothing in Bhabanicharan's text that suggested any attraction to the idea that the time of the household should keep pace with the time of the civil-political society. The themes of discipline, routine, punctuality, all those particular constructions of human sociality that the themes of 'progress' and 'civilization' made both desirable and necessary and that so characterize what later nationalists wrote on domestic life, do not resonate through *KK*. If anything, there was an emphasis to the contrary. In the world that *KK* depicts, the ideal householder never spent more time at work than was minimally needed and concentrated on the higher levels of pitri and daiva karma. The self, in its highest from, was visualized as a part of the kula, the self-conception of the patriarchal, patrilineal, and patrilocal extended family, a self-conception that was more tied to a mytho-religious idea of time than to the temporality of secular history. The civil society here was a matter of compulsion, of unfreedom, a forced interruption of more important/purer acts.

IV

Let me then highlight the nature of the opposition between the two articulations of the domestic and the civil-political that Bengali modernity entailed, an opposition that I read into the neologism grihalakshmi, the two horizons as it were to which this compound word (griha=house+Lakshmi) points us. One is the horizon of the nineteenth-century European imagination of progress which was predicated on a split structure of consciousness, a consciousness that always perceived the present as 'unhappy' and therefore defined its worldly engagement as a struggle for 'happiness' (treated as synonymous with 'freedom') which was to be achieved within a historicized future. [...]

Discipline in public and personal life called for a dislodgment of the self from the mytho-religious time of the kula and its insertion into the historical narrative of 'freedom/happiness'. The Bengali modern, to the extent that's/he was the subject of this fable, was the embodiment of this unhappy consciousness struggling to transform itself. 'We become very sad,' wrote Krishnabhabini Das in the 1880s in her account of her travels in England, 'when we realize how unhappy the couples of our country are...Very few persons in our country know how the ideal husband-wife relationship should be. This is the reason why...Indian [couples] prove to be extremely unhappy.'[31] [...]

Yet Bengali public narratives of the social life of the family were replete at the same time with the opposite theme, that of 'degeneration', a view of the nineteenth century as 'the dark ages' or *kaliyuga*, a feature to which Sumit Sarkar has recently drawn our attention.[32] This was a theme that articulated the personal/domestic with the national in such a way that the civil-political society itself came to be seen as the site, if not the source, of unhappiness. To a degree, this was the flip-side of the narrative of improvement. It followed the civilizing discourse in picturing the present as unhappy and therefore in need of reform anyway. We also see the same use of 'woman' as a signifier of the quality of the times with the difference, however, that the value of the sign was changed from positive to negative. [...]

What was heard in the compound word grihalakshmi in the nineteenth century, then, were at least these two contrary ways of bringing together the domestic and the national in public narratives of the social life of the family. One way was to subordinate domesticity and personhood to the project of the citizen-subject and the goals of the civil-political sphere which, in turn, were seen as the site of work for the acquisition of improvement and happiness. The other was to imagine a connection between the domestic and a mytho-religious social—often equated in conscious nationalist writing with 'community' or the 'nation'—whereby the civil society itself became a problem, a constraint whose coercive nature was to be tolerated but never enjoyed.

V

What all this amounts to saying, it seems to me, is that the Bengali modern, implicated as it is in the structures and relationships of power that produce the social-justice narratives of the public sphere, is constituted by tensions that relate to each other asymptomatically. There cannot therefore be any one unitary history of its becoming. This 'history', that is ceaselessly gathered up as one by the exigencies of the historian's profession and by the needs of the state and governmentality, is always already not-one. Questions of this history/modernity have to be situated within a recognition of its 'not-oneness'.

This produces a fundamental problem for the construction of historical narratives, for if this subject is, at one and the same time, both historicist and hot, how can the historicist imagination of the historian speak for it (except by subordinating the whole to what is in effect only a part of it)? This is where I cannot agree with Sumit Sarkar's reduction, for instance, of the bhadralok critique of *chakri* (waged/salaried work) and civil society to a problem of historical time without in any way problematizing that very conception of time itself. 'The precise nature and implications of this [bhadralok] aversion to

chakri...needs some analysis,' comments Sarkar in his valuable essay on Ramakrishna, and then adds the following:
What made chakri intolerable was—its connotation of impersonal cash nexus and authority, embodied above all in the new rigorous discipline of work regulated by clock-time. Disciplinary time was a particularly abrupt and imposed innovation in colonial India. Europe had gone through a much slower, and phased, transition spanning some five hundred years...Colonial rule telescoped the entire process for India within one or two generations... Chakri thus became a 'chronotype' [sic] of alienated time and space.[33] [...]

It is unfortunate that Sarkar buries the question/histories of personhood in a phrasing that he does not himself contemplate: 'What made chakri intolerable was...its connotation of *impersonal* [emphasis added] cash nexus and authority.' The sociologese of this sentence, its use of 'impersonal', 'cash nexus', and 'authority', bespeaks a familiar narrative of transition to capitalist-modernity which renders all 'pre-capitalist' relations the same—'personal', 'face-to-face', embedded in kinship, and so-and-so forth. The modern or capitalist, then, is precisely its other—and therefore the same again the world over—and the transition is best understood by essentializing, hence sociologizing, the difference between the two!

Yet, this 'difference' is what has been at issue in my reading of Bengali public narratives of the social life of the family. The Bengali modern is not an 'incomplete' modern or even a 'bad' colonial one compared to some 'good' metropolitan model. The grihalakshmi is not a Rousseauvian solution of the question of 'womanhood' in phallocratic bourgeois modernity—the model of Sophy, educated and companionable but modest and obedient at the same time.[34] True, colonial rule introduced this model into bhadralok lives and the expression grihalakshmi partakes of it. But the concept of grihalakshmi, being tied to the mytho-religious time of the kula, also escapes and exceeds bourgeois time in all the three different senses that Lyotard has read into the word 'exceed' in a different context: to pass beyond, to fall outside of, to excise.[35] The expression 'grihalakshmi' shares in ideas of personhood that do not owe their existence to the bourgeois projects that European imperialism brought to India. Nor are these ideas mere historical residues, remnants of a past, left there only because the colonial-Bengali transition to modernity did not afford us the allegedly leisurely pace of the transformation in Europe. To say this is not to deny the cruelties of the patriarchal orders that this neologism of Bengali modernity, grihalakshmi, entails; it is, however, to claim that no adequate critique of this modernity can be mounted or practised from within secular-historicist narratives alone, which, by their very nature, are incapable of re-presencing what is not secular-historicist, except in an anthropologizing mode.

Let me elaborate a little further on this by discussing an obscure but by no means untypical text from the nineteenth century: a booklet called *Patibrata dharma* (with the English title: *A Treatise on Female Chastity*) written around 1870 by a Bengali woman called Dayamayi Dasi. The stamp of the bourgeois project of European modernity, of educating women to be both companies to their husbands as well as being devoted to them, is unmistakably present here. The very title of the book speaks of its concern with such feelings of devotion and its given English title places it firmly within the tradition of Bengali Victoriana. Encouraged by her husband to learn to read and write, Dayamayi Dasi wrote this tract on *kulakaminir kartabya* (duties of the woman of the Kula) which her husband published after her death. [...] In that sense, kula here was a term that tied the domestic to the national. As Dayamayi Dasi said, quoting from *the Brahmavaivartapurana*, to express her sense of nationalism: 'The land blessed with women of such nature [that is, devoted to their husbands] is comparable to heaven, and the people of that country should treat their women as goddesses'.[36] Besides, the very act of writing such books was part of becoming the new women that the ideal of citizen-subject demanded. Not only that. Women whose writings circulated in the public sphere were often those who had indeed experienced some measure of 'companionship' with their husbands, a 'friendship' that permitted this diffusion of knowledge between the sexes. Literacy itself was part of their experience of a new-found individuality and, in the context of the families structured by the patriarchal principle of kula, this was never achieved without struggle and pain.[37]

Yet the ideology of the patriarchy of the kula drips out of every word of what Dayamayi wrote in praise of this friendship and intimacy.

A woman has no better friend than her husband. It is because he helps cover [woman's shame] that he is called *bharta*. He is *pati* because he nurtures. He is *swami* because it is to him that the body belongs, he is the lord of the body. He fulfills [woman's] desires, that is why he is [called] *kanta*. He is a *bandhu* as he shares happiness, *parampriya* as he gives affection, and *raman* because he gives pleasure. It is he who, through his own semen, returns as the son, and that is why the son is valued. But for a *kulastree*, the husband is dearer than even a hundred sons.[38]

How would we understand this speech if we were not to classify it as some specimen of a 'low' or 'false' consciousness waiting to be 'raised' by the political subject? What kind of a modern was Dayamayi Dasi? To be sure, the project of bourgeois individuality was a strong factor in her modernity, the idea of the autonomous individual existing for her own ends was something that animated this modern. But kula, grihalakshmi, and other, for all their undeniable phallocentrism, were also ways of talking about formations of pleasure, emotions, and ideas of good life that associated themselves with models of non-autonomous, non-bourgeois, and non-secular personhood. [...] This is a recurrent theme in modern Indian public life—worked out here in public narratives of the social life of the family—that the highest form of personhood was one constituted by the idea of self-sacrifice, the idea of living for others, not in the secular spirit of civic virtue that Rousseau would have applauded but in a spirit of subordination to the non-secular and parochial principle of dharma. The idea, as I have argued elsewhere, was not at all innocent of power, domination, and even cruelty and violence but, whatever else it may have been, it was never merely a ruse for staging the secular-historicist project of the citizen-subject.[39]

The kula, then, was an integral part of the categories with which the patriarchal Bengali modern consolidated its ideology of new domesticity in the context of a growing public sphere that colonialism had instituted. I want to make two points relating to Dayamayi Dasi's and others' affectionate description of the patriarchy of the kula.

My first point is that an irreducible category of 'beauty', a non-secular and non-universalistic sense of aesthetics circulates in these writings, pointing us to a certain subject of pleasure/emotion that speaks through these documents. These texts on modern Bengali domesticity harp on the association between 'womanhood' and 'pleasantness'. Alakshmi was not only inauspicious, she was unpleasant as well, or, correspondingly, what was unpleasant in a woman was also inauspicious. [...]

That is why, our author explained, all the Sanskrit terms for 'wife' were meant to sound pleasant, all significantly ending with a long vowel—*jaya, bharya, grihalakshmi, ankalakshmi, grihini, sahadharmini, ardhangarupini*:

Even a five-year old child will be able to tell these names that the Hindu woman is not a slave even if she is skilled in domestic work. She is not a maidservant. Serving her husband does not make her a kept woman ... The Hindu woman is an object of great affection, care and pride.[40]

My second point follows from this. The connection between these pleasures and the ideology of the auspicious grihalakshmi, which is intimately tied to the concern for the well-being of the kula, always exceeds a straightforward bourgeois project of domesticating women in order to allow them into the modern and male public sphere. For the conception of mangal associated with the idea of 'auspiciousness', on which the survival of the line of the kula depends, can be only very inadequately translated as 'material prosperity' or simply 'well-being'. It is not a concept embedded in the secular time of the historicist imagination. An idea celebrated in the so-called 'medieval' Bengali texts, the *Mangalkavyas* (Mangal poems), where the human realm is never separated from the realms of gods and spirits, the word 'mangal' is a matter of everyday performance, clichéd no doubt but rooted deep in (chronologically pre-British) narratives/practices of kinship and family where Christian or historicist distinctions between the divine and the human do not apply. [...]

Needless to say, this imagination was at work in the nationalist aesthetics that marked the texts on domesticity that I have discussed here. Grihalakshmi signified a conception of the nationalist sublime which made the country ('not an object of the senses', as Kant would remind us[41]) 'comparable to heaven' (to return to the language of Dayamayi Dasi). And it was nationalism which used the term Alakshmi interchangeably with memsahib, European woman, a negative word charged with the impossible task of policing a false boundary between cultures.

But even this does not wrap up the Bengali modern. Dayamayi Dasi's own text provides us with a critical example of how even in these public narratives of domesticity and personhood, caught between the asymptomatic perspectives of the citizen-subject and of the grihalakshmi, there remained possibilities of other manoeuvres creating speaking positions that looked far beyond the patriarchy of the Bengali modern. Her book, which is a paean to the patriarchy of the kula, breaks completely out of its own framework at one point in the preface where she records the exhilarating sense of liberation that literacy brought to her: 'I had never entertained the thought that I would learn to recognise the alphabet or to read books ... But, in the end, I developed such a thirst for prose and poetry that I began to neglect my duties towards *samsar* (the world, the household, the family) and my husband'.[42]

This statement, which survives the patriarchy of the Bengali modern that speaks through the rest of Dayamayi's book, reminds us of the other struggles that modernity helped unleash.[43] But it is also a statement that, in its uncompromising resistance to duty (whether modern or ancient, civic, or familial) is not assimilable to the emancipatory visions that Eurocentric imaginations of civil-political life have bequeathed to us.

This conclusion cannot offer a closure, far less an explanation for a modernity that, as I have said, is itself not one. The modern, no doubt, is a myth in that it naturalizes history. The 'true' bourgeois does not exist except in representations of power and domination. Colonizing relationships, however, are not created through the complex attention to 'truth' that is often in evidence in academic debates. European imperialists would not have been able either to legitimize their colonial domination by using the idea of 'progress' or to sell this idea to the colonized, if their own representations of 'progress' were explicitly riddled with self-doubt. The certitudes that constitute the colonial theatre have not vanished with the demise of formal imperialism. The compulsion (and the temptation, as Heidegger once said) to think and translate the world through the categories of the European imperial-modern, is real and deeply rooted in institutional practices, both within and outside the university.[44] One cannot simply opt out of this problem, nor suffer, by a sheer act of will, the 'epistemic violence' that has been a necessary part of nation-and empire-making drives of the last two-and-a-half centuries.[45] History therefore cannot be a 'talking cure' from 'modernity'; the analyst is not the addressee of this story of colonial Bengal. I think of it, as Barthes once said with reference to Shaharazad of the *Arabian Nights*, more as a merchandize, a narrative traded 'for one more day of life'.[46] To attempt to write difference into the history of our modernity in a mode that resists the assimilation of this history to the political imaginary of the European-derived institutions—the very idea of the civil—political, for instance—which dominate our lives, is to learn from Shaharazad's technique of survival. It is to say, to every perpetrator or epistemic violence and in the voice of the woman-subject Shaharazad: 'Don't fuck me yet, for I still have (an) other story to tell'.

NOTES

1. This is an idea forcefully and illuminatingly argued in Meaghan Morris, 'Metamorphoses at Sydney Tower', *New Formations,* Summer, 1990, p. 10.

2. One of the best discussions of this argument is Partha Chatterjee's book *Nationalist Thought and the Colonial World: A Derivative Discourse?* (London, 1986).

3. The story is told in Meredith Borthwick, *The Changing Role of Women in Bengal 1849–1905* (Princeton, 1984), and Ghulam Murshid, *Reluctant Debutante: Response of Bengali Women to Modernization* (Rajshahi, 1983).

4. Philippe Ariès, 'Introduction' in Roger Chartier (ed.), *A History of Private Life: Passion of the Renaissance* (Cambridge, Mass., 1989), p. 9.

5. For examples of the way (male) reviewers controlled and regulated literary output of women, see Yogendranath Gupta, *Bange mahila kabi* (Calcutta, 1953), pp. 33–4, 58–9, 65–71, 125–8, 139, 220–1.

6. See Sukumar Sen, *Women's Dialect in Bengali* (1928) (Calcutta, 1979). Sen shows the prevalence in women's speech (of the 1920s) of older words that had gone out of use in male speech and writing.

7. James Mill, *The History of British India* (5th edition, (ed.) H.H. Wilson) (London, 1858), vol. 1, p. xxix.

8. Lucien Febvre, 'Civilisation: Evolution of a Word and a Group of Ideas', in Peter Burke (ed.), *A New Kind of History: From the Writings of Febvre* (London, 1973), pp. 219–57.

9. Somnath Mukhopadhyay, *Sikshapaddhati* (Dhaka, 1870), pp. 4, 33. This was one of the many books that self-consciously borrowed from Samuel Smiles.

10. Nagendrabala Saraswati, *Garhasthyadharma ba naridharmer parishista* [in Bengali] (Jamalpur, Burdwan, 1904), pp. 1, 29.

11. Ashis Nandy, *The Intimate Enemy: Loss and Recovery of Self Under Colonialism* (Delhi, 1987), has a stimulating discussion of this problem.

12. Atulchandra Datta, *Grihasiksha* [in Bengali] (Calcutta, 1906), p. 13.

13. Ibid., pp. 3–4, 34–9, 78, 80.

14. Both Borthwick and Murshid document this.

15. See Baikunthanath Majhi, *Baromaser Srisri lakshmidevir bratakatha o panchali* [in Bengali], revised by Madhusudan Bhattacharya (Calcutta, n.d.); Pasupati Chattopadhyay, *Baromese srisri lakshmidevir panchali o bratakatha* (Calcutta, n.d.).

16. Gupta, *Grihastha-Jiban*, p. 14.

17. Manmohan Bosu, *Hindu achar byabahar* [in Bangali] (Calcutta, 1873), p. 57.

18. Anon., *Naridharma* [in Bengali] (Calcutta, 1877), p. 27, puts this gloss on a *sloka* from the Mahabharata which says: '[Only] she is [the true] wife who is skilled in domestic work, who bears children and who lives for and is devoted to her husband'.

19. Partha Chatterjee, 'The Nationalist Resolution of the Women's Question', in Kumkum Sangari and Sudesh Vaid (eds), *Recasting Women: Essays in Indian History* (New Brunswick, 1990), pp. 233–53; Tanika Sarkar, 'Nationalist Iconography: Images of Women in Nineteenth Century Bengali Literature', *Economic and Political Weekly* (hereafter *EPW*), 21 November 1987, pp. 2011–15; Malavika Karlekar, 'Kadambini and the Bhadralok: Early Debates over Women's Education in Bengal', *EPW*, 21:17, 26 April 1986, pp. WS–WS31;

Jasodhara Bagchi, 'Representing Nationalism: Ideology of Motherhood in Colonial Bengal', *EPW*, 20-7 October 1990, pp. WS105-WS71.

20. Srabashi Ghosh's extensively researched article 'Birds in a Cage', *EPW*, 21:43, October 1986, pp. 88-96, demonstrates the continuing relevance of nineteenth-century questions.

21. Thus Altekar's nationalist study of Hindu women begins with a statement that could have come from Mill: 'One of the best ways to understand the spirit of a civilization and to appreciate its excellences and realize its limitations is to study the history of the position and status of women in it.' A.S. Altekar, *The Position of Women in Hindu Civilization: From Prehistoric Times to the Present Day* (Banaras, 1956), p. 1. For a statement typically seeing the extended family as an institution inimical to the growth of individuality, see Margaret M. Urquhart, *Women of Bengal: A Study of the Hindu Pardanashins of Calcutta* (Calcutta, 1926), pp. 33, 43-4.

22. See Amitrasudan Bhattacharya, *Bankimchandrajibani* [in Bengali] (Calcutta, 1991), pp. 90-1, and Sabyasachi Bhattacharya, 'Bankimchandra and the Subjection of Women: Kapalkundala's Destiny'. I am grateful to Professor Bhattacharya for allowing me access to this manuscript.

23. *Gauradeshiya samaj sangsthapanartha pratham sabhar bibaran* [in Bengali] (Calcutta, 1823), pp. 9-10, 12-14, 16-17, 21-2.

24. Mrityunjay Sharmanah [Vidyalankar], *Rajabali* [in Bengali] (Serampore, 1808), pp. 294-5, and the posthumously published *Prabodh chandrika* [in Bengali] (Serampore, 1846), p. 6.

25. *Bibaran,* pp. 6-9.

26. Ibid., pp. 4, 19-20, 27-8.

27. S.M. Mukherjee, 'Class, Caste and Politics in Calcutta, 1815-38', in Edmund Leach and S.N. Mukherjee (eds), *Elites in South Asia* (Cambridge, 1970), pp. 33-78.

28. Bhabanicharan Bandyopadhyay, *Kalikata Kamalalaya* (1823), Brajendranath Bandyopadhyay (Calcutta, 1952), pp. 5-6.

29. Ibid., pp. 8-9.

30. Ibid., p. 22. [...]

31. Krishnabhabini Das quoted in Murshid, p. 148.

32. Sumit Sarkar, 'The Kalki-Avatar of Bikrampur: A Village Scandal in Early Twentieth Century Bengal', in Ranajit Guha (ed.), *Subaltern Studies* VI (Delhi, 1989), pp. 1-53.

33. Sumit Sarkar, '"Kaliyuga", "Chakri", and "Bhakti": Ramakrishna and His Times', *EPW*, 27:29, pp. 1549-50.

34. See Jean-Jacques Rousseau, *Emile*, trans. Barbara Foxley (New York, 1977), Book V, and the discussion in Sarah Kofman, 'Rousseau's Phallocratic Ends' in Nancy Fraser and Sandra Lee Bartky (eds), *Revaluing French Feminism: Critical Essays on Difference, Agency and Culture* (Bloomington, 1992), pp. 46-59.

35. Jean-Francois Lyotard, *Heidegger and 'The Jews'*, trans. Andreas Michel and Mark Roberts (Minneapolis, 1990), p. 17.

36. Dayamayi Dasi, *Patibrata dharma* [in Bengali], (Calcutta, 1870) pp. 1-2.

37. Bharati Ray, 'Bengali Women and Politics of Joint Family', *EPW*, 28:32, 28 December 1991, pp. 3021-51.
38. Dayamayi Dasi, *Patibrata dharma* [in Bengali], pp. 1-2.
39. See my *Rethinking Working-Class History: Bengal 1890-1940* (Princeton, 1989).
40. Bosu, *Hindu achar*, pp. 58-60.
41. Immanuel Kant, *The Critique of Judgement*, trans. J.C. Meredith (Oxford, 1973). p. 97.
42. Dasi, *Patibrata*, preface.
43. See the discussion in my 'Postcoloniality and the Artifice of History: Who Speaks for "Indian" Pasts?', *Representation*, 37, 1992.
44. See Martin Heidegger, *On the Way to Language*, trans. Peter D. Hertz (New York, 1982), p. 15. The problem receives attention in my 'Postcoloniality and the Artifice of History' and 'Labour History and the Politics of Theory: An Indian Angle on the Middle East', in Zachary Lockman (ed.), *Workers, Struggles and Histories in the Middle East* (New York, forthcoming).
45. I have borrowed the idea of 'epistemic violence' from the work of Gayatri Spivak.
46. Roland Barthes, *The Grain of the Voice: Interviews 1962-1980*, trans. Linda Coverdale (New York, 1985), p. 89.

Re-Publicizing Religiosity*
Modernity, Religion, and the Middle Class

SANJAY JOSHI

The writings of Talal Asad, among others, have recently demonstrated how modernity restricted the meaning of religion to matters of private belief, its domain to the other worldly and the esoteric, and its legitimate place the world of rituals rather than realms of the public and the political.[1] Broadly defined, modernity in this sense refers to new models of organizing social, political, and economic relations, which, we are told, draw their inspiration from the ideas of the Enlightenment and material circumstances following from the triumph of industrial capitalism. While there is no doubt that modernity does in many ways define the world we live in, one wonders if we must assume such a one-way traffic between religion and modernity? Must we, in our representations of the world, empower modernity with such a totalizing force? Can we not, and given the evidence to the contrary that we see around us, should we not perhaps, consider the possibility of a more dialogic process—where religiosity is undoubtedly transformed by modernity, but also in some way, helps to shape and define the contours of the modern world? It is to explore such a possibility that this paper examines the emergence of what I term 'republicized' Hindu religiosity in colonial north India. Focusing

---

* Originally published in Derek Peterson and Darren Walhof (eds), *The Invention of Religion: Rethinking Belief and Politics in History* (Rutgers: Rutgers University Press, 2002), pp. 79-99. For the complete text see the original. In the present version, some portions of the essay have been removed and notes rearranged accordingly.

on the city of Lucknow, I demonstrate how a modernity shaped by Indian middle-class activists sought to transform multiple strands of beliefs and practices into a more or less monolithic 'Hinduism', and purge it of its divisive and hierarchical aspects so as to suit their own public sphere projects.

A close examination of these efforts also reveals, however, that this recasting of religion created powerful discursive templates which were then deployed in many different ways, for a variety of different political agenda. Not only did a transformed Hindu religiosity allow for the imagination of 'Hindu pride', often better known in its modern incarnation of *Hindutva* or Hindu nationalism, but such templates also served the project of a more liberal 'secular' nationalism. Exploring in some detail the nature of the modern political world fashioned by middle-class activists in India, therefore, raises some interesting possibilities of reinterpreting the relationship of religion and modernity. Not only does the modernity fashioned by this middle class bring religion back into the realms of the political, but this re-publicized religiosity becomes a central and constitutive feature of a political modernity. Such a modernity, this scenario suggests, allows for and perhaps makes necessary, the simultaneous avowal of secular and the religious, thereby smudging the boundaries between two terms so often read as binary opposites.

Why did religion become so important for middle-class nationalists in colonial India? Partha Chatterjee has offered us one of the best-known recent explanations. Chatterjee argues that the middle class intelligentsia of colonial India from the late nineteenth century onwards constructed an 'inner domain of cultural identity', from which to ready the nation for contestation with colonialism. He locates the concern with religion in the failure of middle-class projects in the 'outer' domain of politics. Middle-class intellectuals sought to claim complete sovereignty over their 'inner domain' which they defined primarily in 'spiritual' terms.[2] In other words, the concern with religion is born out of a failure, a lack. It is failures in the realm of 'true' public sphere politics, which in colonial India was governed by the 'rule of colonial difference', that animate middle-class concerns with religion.[3] Although Chatterjee is very aware of how middle-class activists then deploy religion to attempt their own counter-hegemonic project, religion in this work, as in many others, necessarily functions as an alternative to the realm of modernity, rather than a part of it. In the larger picture, Chatterjee's focus on middle-class religiosity helps explain why 'our modernity', the modernity of the colonized, had to be different from western modernity.[4]

Yet, there is a serious danger here of reifying 'religion' as possessing a timeless and unchanging essence. In accepting Chatterjee's thesis *in toto*, we open up the possibility of simply reinforcing the notion that the domain of the religious, by definition it seems, excludes negotiations over political power conducted in the public sphere. This is also one of the dangers posed by some recent postcolonial readings of Indian history, where 'religion' figures as a resource for academic critiques of modernity. Scholars, such as Chatterjee himself, have found in the presence of religion in politics a 'position' from which to critique the universalist claims of western modernity.[5] This is a valuable critique, both to show the limits of modern history, and to push all historians towards understandings of the past that do not simply universalize a particular ideal-typical modernity, so often attributed to the history of Europe.[6] However, one wonders if the best way to demonstrate the limits, or indeed the partiality, of a Eurocentric modernity's self-image is to reaffirm 'religion' as something outside of, and an alternative to, the modern? At a time when religious chauvinism is on the rise, there is for one, a danger of unwittingly valorizing this very different (and extremely modern) vision of religiosity.[7] Moreover, deploying religion in this fashion also appears to reaffirm the notion of religion as the essence of the non-modern, bringing us surprisingly close to colonial readings of the non-West. Religion, after all, was the basis on which Orientalist scholarship 'othered' India, to establish both the incapacity of Indians to rule themselves, and to reaffirm the rationality and the capacity of the West to rule over others.[8] This paper seeks to offer an alternative, by first examining the ways in which the concern with religion of the middle class brought religion firmly into the realms of public sphere politics, and then analysing the larger implications of this 'republicized religiosity'.

RE-PUBLICIZING RELIGIOSITY

A study of Lucknow's middle class does bear out Chatterjee's thesis to some extent. The tropes of what Sudhir Chandra termed an 'oppressive present', appear as important components of the middle-class imagination of the late nineteenth century.[9] Images of desolation and powerlessness abound in many of the writings of westernized middle-class men of nineteenth-century Lucknow. [...] [P.C.] Mookherji was concerned with the lack of achievement, the inability of the educated

Indians, to actually *do* anything to assert their presence in the city. As Mookherji said: 'With all that vast bookish knowledge, the so called educated native is helpless to the last degree. [...] They talk and speechify well—but cannot show any matter'.[10] The realization of the limits of their own participation in liberal politics initiated by colonial rule was, as Chatterjee suggests, evidently one factor prompting the despairing vision of the colonial middle class.

Though full of despair, and evidently dissatisfied with the amount of influence they were able to exercise over society, the auto-critique of the late nineteenth-century middle-class activists was hardly nihilistic. Contemporaries from differing ideological persuasions agreed that 'religion' in some way constituted an answer to their problems. The England-educated barrister, social reformer, and future President of the Indian National Congress, Bishan Narain Dar, attributed the absence of 'genius' in modern India to the lack of moral fibre in young men of his time, which in turn he attributed to their lack of religion. 'Morality,' he said, 'has been so closely connected with religion, since history began, that whenever religious sanction has grown weak, serious moral injuries have occurred to mankind.'[11] A present thought of as oppressive, corrupt, and alienating was blamed on the fact that society had gone astray from its religious ideals. Not only that, but the lack of religion was seen as one of the causes for their lack of freedom and strength. Partha Chatterjee's thesis it seems, stands vindicated with this evidence. The religiosity of the nineteenth-century middle class in Lucknow, as in the Bengali case Chatterjee studies, appears to closely reflect a concern with overcoming their perceptions of inadequacy and disempowerment, which, in turn, were seen by them as a direct product of the colonial experience.

Yet there are significantly different possibilities of reading this history. The controversy surrounding cow protection in the 1890s provides one context in where the concern of middle-class activists with religion was very evident. [...] Gyanendra Pandey, in his study of this movement, has pointed to the multiple meanings which participants brought to their actions. Especially, he points to the cohesion as well as the contradictions present in the invocation of a 'Hindu' identity in the mobilization efforts of the leaders and participants in the movement.[12]

Bishan Narain Dar, in his capacity as a lawyer, was called upon to defend some Hindus convicted of rioting in Azamgarh. He visited the area and independently published a report which blamed the 'meddlesomeness' of colonial authorities for the trouble between Hindus and Muslims.[13] His agenda was fairly explicit:

I have no particular liking for the [*Gaurakshini*] *Sabha* myself as I think that such institutions whether they be Hindu or Mohammedan, do more harm than good in the long run, yet I do not see the wisdom and even the justice in interfering with other people's religious persuasion.[14]

While turning a blind eye to the 'interference' which Hindu *Sabha*s had practised, Dar highlighted the actions of British officials in Azamgarh as evidence of interference of Government in the religious practices of Hindus. The prosecution of Hindu rioters was, by him, represented as 'religious persecution, pure and simple'.[15] Expressing grief at the partisan attitude of the colonial Government towards Hindus, Dar depicted the whole affair as one in a series of happenings where: 'Hindu religion is insulted and Hindu practices are treated with unconcealed scorn.'[16]

One could, with Chatterjee, argue that the roots of this imagination lay in the middle-class perception of their oppression at the hands of the colonial state, especially if we add to Chatterjee's thesis the gendered dimension of a perceived emasculation though the workings of a 'colonial masculinity'.[17] It was to overcome this perception of oppression, to seek new sources of self-respect, that middle-class activists like Dar sought to selectively celebrate aspects of what they perceived as evidence of 'Hindu manliness' in Azamgarh. In his report, for instance, Dar complained that Hindus, 'have for years and years been treated like the proverbial dog whom any stick is good enough to beat with'.[18] What he celebrated through this report, was the possibility that Hindu peasants' actions had opened up for the imagining of a strong and virile community in contrast to a disempowered and oppressed one. It was the desire to celebrate a strong, virile, 'native' self, which led Dar to adopt a position valorizing the collective violence against Muslims enacted in Azamgarh. Despite distancing himself from the actions of the rioters, Dar demonstrated pride in the actions of the Hindu sabha activists of Azamgarh, simply because their actions proved to him, 'that the Hindus are not quite such a meek, unmanly, and contemptible race as they have been imagined'.[19]

[...] [T]his was hardly a 'retreat' into any domain, uncolonized or otherwise. On the contrary, Dar used the report to criticize colonial official actions and bring the question of religion very much into the domain of public contestation with the state and its administration.[20] Of equal significance is how [...] Dar explicitly made his criticism as a self-appointed representative of the 'Hindu community'. His report, however, completely appropriated the complex web of events and ideas which had contributed to the disturbances in Azamgarh to the agenda of middle-class politics. The multiple meanings of 'Hinduness' present in Azamgarh were submerged in Dar's report. The report also made it evident that Dar's concerns were not really with Azamgarh or even the cow-protection movement. Despite acting as their lawyer, Dar described the cow-protection movement as, 'humane, though somewhat impractical'.[21] Moreover, in his report he was quite willing to acknowledge what he termed the 'good deal of latent barbarism' of the participants. The interventions of men such as Dar produced a new, and specifically middle-class discourse of Hindu religiosity. No doubt serving to overcome perceptions of middle-class inadequacy, the striking point about this modern Hindu religiosity was that, on the one hand, it distanced itself from the 'latent barbarism' of the religious practices of illiterate peasants of Azamgarh, yet on the other hand, used the opportunity to celebrate 'Hindu valour' and defend 'Hindu rights' in the domain of public sphere politics.

There is little doubt that middle-class men did indeed find in religion a resource for overcoming their perceptions of disempowerment. [...] But seeing 'religion'—at least the religiosity of the middle class in their political projects—as only constituting an 'inner' or 'uncolonized' domain seriously limits our understanding both of the nature of middle-class agenda and of the category of religion. For one, treating 'religion' as a synchronic entity ignores the ways in which religiosity itself was recast in very new terms through middle-class interventions in colonial India. Second, exclusively looking at religion as a way of contesting colonial hegemony glosses over the ways in which religion, like other middle-class interventions, was actively concerned with the empowerment of this social group over others. Together, these two lacunae obscure important historical connections between religion and power as they were being created anew through the politics of nationalism in India.

A number of studies of pre-colonial South Asia testify to the fact that religious institutions were very much a part of processes through which power and authority was constituted. The centrality of religion in political processes also made it a powerful locus for the creation of collective identities well before the advent of colonialism.[22] This was certainly the case in Lucknow, where Shia Islam played a significant role in the way politics and power were configured in the Nawabi courts.[23]

Colonial rule entailed the severing of many of these connections, and contributed in important ways to transformation of religious identities in India. Whether through Orientalist reinterpretations of texts,[24] or new administrative and legal categories and practices,[25] colonialism created the circumstances for very different perceptions and possibilities of imagining 'religious communities'. However, central to this process is also the often-overlooked role of middle-class activists who resisted the attempts of the state to push religion into the realms of the personal, by successfully 're-publicizing' religion through harnessing it to their interventions in the colonial public sphere. Such interventions not only created new understandings of religion, but also decisively shaped the nature of modern politics in India.

THE POSSIBILITIES AND LIMITS OF A PUBLICIZED RELIGIOSITY

References to Hindu religious practices or beliefs in Dar's report were either condescending or derogatory, even though he was representing the Hindus of his province and offered a spirited defence of their rights. Dar lived at a time when debates between Hindu reformers and revivalists were particularly keen. In fact, Dar was himself at the centre of a controversy about religious practices, when his decision to go to England to study law led to [...] his own temporary ostracism from the community.[26] Despite that, however, and the fact that he left behind copious amounts of writing, much of it stressing the importance of 'religion', we are left with no clue as to Dar's own position on matters of devotional practice; whether for instance, he advocated a 'return' to *varnashram dharma* (in which the fourfold caste hierarchy would be central), or some reformed variant of Hinduism. In fact, Dar, like many of his middle-class contemporaries, was articulating a new sort of religiosity, forged out of concerns of middle-class activists as they sought to create a larger place for their own endeavors in the public sphere.

Traditional conceptions of religion, prevailing religious practices, and beliefs could not easily serve projects which were part of the agenda of the emerging middle class. Existing 'Hindu' religiosity—with multiple traditions, metaphysical speculations, and most obviously, social practices governed by hierarchical principles—was particularly unsuitable as the basis of an ideology to mobilize a public, and create a 'community' which could be represented by the middle class. Middle-class constructions of Hindu religiosity therefore stressed its active, this-worldly orientation, as well as its non-divisive aspects. Through such reinterpretations, activists sought to create a religiosity which could most effectively be deployed in the public sphere. This republicized Hindu religiosity emphasized community rather than hierarchy, unity rather than divisions and difference, activism rather than 'mere' contemplation, and the exercise of reason over 'blind faith'. Much like other aspects of their public sphere politics in colonial India, however, this vision of a singular Hindu community too, was riven with contradictions. Attempts to mobilize this community often made these contradictions very visible, especially as the vision of an undivided Hindu community came into conflict with hierarchical beliefs and practices equally important for the middle class to maintain their social hegemony.

Involved in efforts at redefining religion, were not only lay public sphere activists, but also religious specialists, or those who had taken ascetic vows. Swami Vivekanand was probably the most famous of such 'patriotic *sanyasis*'.[27] In Lucknow it was Swami Rama Tirtha, and later his disciple Narain Swami, who caught the imagination of the middle class. After an MA in mathematics, Rama Tirtha was a professor of Mathematics at the Mission College in Lahore by 1896.[28] [...] Swami Rama Tirtha's religiosity was quite the opposite of any sort of 'otherworldly' speculation. 'Vedanta locked in cupboards will just not do, he wrote, thus breaking from the path of Upanishadic philosophical abstraction, and firmly establishing his Hindu religiosity in the public sphere.[29] Rama Tirtha's Vedanta had no place for rituals either. Rather than traditional animal sacrifices (*yagna*), he urged disciples to use the ingredients normally used in such sacrifices to feed the poor.[30] In the contemporary world, Rama Tirtha argued, 'sacrifice (*yagna*) requires, not innocent animals, but rather to consign to the flames of love, all our feelings of groupism, that is, caste and religious differences (*jati-bhed*) and envy, which alone can bring us heaven on earth.'[31] Real religion—politicians and poets, activists and ascetics alike seemed to agree—did not lie in philosophical abstractions, or blind devotion, or ritual practices. Rather, real religion was intimately tied up with the world, with the concerns and problems of people. [...] Such an anthropocentric view of religion, tied to ideas of humanity and national uplift, was a defining quality of the middle-class religiosity of the late nineteenth and early twentieth century.

These newly-created standards of a 'real' Hinduism were also deployed by middle-class activists to try and control or change existing traditions and practices. The *sadhu*s (wandering ascetics) of India were a favourite target, particularly for their 'indolence'. Undoubtedly, the fractious and fiercely independent nature of many ascetic sects, added to the desire to 'reform' the sadhus.[32] Rama Tirtha, despite his own ascetic vows, was highly critical of Indian sadhus, comparing them to 'unhealthy scum' on a lake. [...][33] His disciple, Narain Swami, attempted to discipline these wandering ascetics and set up a 'Sadhu Mahavidyalaya' (University for Sadhus) at Hardwar so that 'illiterate sadhus' could be given what was considered an appropriate Sanskrit education.[34][...] Equally important was the disciplining and reformulation of everyday religious practices, and here women were a particular target of reforming zeal, as they were not only perceived as inherently more religious, but also for their ability to produce and shape future, appropriately religious, subjects.[35] Sannulal Gupta's didactic manual aimed at middle-class women, *Strisubodhini*, sought to educate and improve women in this crucial aspect of their behaviour, in addition to offering other advice. Gupta warns women against 'superstition', and against 'charlatans' who adopt a religious guise. Most religious specialists, but particularly wandering ascetics claiming powers of divine possession or sorcery (though also venal Brahmin priests) are shown up to be frauds in Gupta's manual.[...][36] Ultimately, a woman's true religion, Gupta suggests, consists in following *stridharma* (literally a woman's religion/duties, effectively a religion of domesticity) and for that she has no need of either religious specialists or indeed to participate in fairs, festivals, or other public rituals.

Like contemporaneous movements among the Sikhs, and those led by middle-class Muslims, many of the innovations coming from middle-class Hindus at this time consisted of drawing boundaries between religions. At the level of religious practice, for instance, it was common for Hindus, and particularly women, to seek boons and blessings at the shrines of Muslim *pir*s or renown holy men. This form of popular worship which often cut across caste, class, sectarian, and religious boundaries, was unacceptable to middle-class reformers, who, undoubtedly influenced by a modern colonial epistemology, found such practices 'irreligious'. Reformers like Gupta took it upon themselves to wipe out syncretic religious practices among Hindus. *Strisubodhini*, accordingly, contains a major diatribe against worshipping at Muslim pirs' tombs, where the book seeks to invoke fear (such worship may make women barren), as well as castigating such worship for demonstrating a disrespect for one's 'own religion' because the shrines of Muslim pirs glorified individuals who were responsible for killing many Hindu men.[37] Although many of the changes initiated by reformers in the late nineteenth and early twentieth centuries were couched in terms of 'rediscoveries' of eternal truths about Hindu *dharma*, there is little doubt that such innovations were recasting if not reinventing religious traditions.[38] This new Hindu religiosity not only allowed greater facility in constructing bounded religious communities to represent, but also the opportunity of greater social control through the power or authority to define what did or did not constitute appropriate religious practice. This period also saw the emergence of new middle-class notions of religiosity, where 'religion' was separated from 'superstition', became more 'rational', and more amenable to the sensibilities of the middle-class educated men, and of course to their public sphere projects as well. [...] The attempt to fashion, address, and mobilize a singular 'imagined Hindu community' in the nineteenth century was a unique attempt, and one which reflected the concerns of the middle class, and also the new possibilities that were open to them in the colonial public sphere.[39]

However, as much as the writings of middle-class men reveal the tremendous confidence they undoubtedly had in their ability to transform social practices and beliefs at will, their projects remained necessarily partial and incomplete. At one level they were resisted by conservatives among their own ranks. A man like Shivanath Sharma, a prominent Hindi journalist and humourist of Lucknow, used his journal *Anand* to savagely lampoon the dress, eating habits, and even newer ways of relieving oneself, the Anglicized 'babu' unthinkingly copied from his masters.[40] At another, more quotidian level, middle-class efforts at transforming religious practices were resisted simply by being ignored! Arya Samaj sources inform us that the Lucknow branch of the Samaj was particularly strict in its enforcement of rules of conduct. [...][41] Yet, at the level of actual practice, these rules were evidently ignored. A report from the Lucknow newspaper, the *Advocate* of 1904 reveals that 'for some years' the president of the Lucknow Arya Samaj had been a gentleman by the name of Umrao Bahadur, who was born of a Hindu father and Muslim mother, and who had himself married a Muslim woman.[42] When even the president of a branch of the Arya Samaj, which prided itself on orthodoxy, so evidently transgressed boundaries the organization was seeking to reinforce, then we can only conclude that there was considerable gap between ideas and practice. Efforts of men seeking to create a monolithic, singular Hindu community were bound to remain unconsummated.

But a more serious limitation of the project of a public Hinduism, perhaps even more so than resistance at the level of praxis, was the fact that contradictions constitutive of the new modernity sought to be forged by middle-class activists worked to undermine their own efforts to construct this new entity. Nothing shows up these contradictions better than the vexed issue of caste. Caste was the foremost among the vast variety of social, cultural, and devotional practices that needed to be tamed and disciplined to produce the new Hindu religiosity. With the principle of hierarchy at its centre,[43] caste ideology as well as practices such as untouchability, interdictions on commensality, and restrictions on interaction between different castes were the biggest obstacles to the realization of the sort of unity desired by public sphere activists in colonial Lucknow. Rama Tirtha made the criticism of caste one of the central motifs of his writing.[44] [...] A true Hindu he said, 'must not observe any discrimination against anybody. For him there is no differentiation between the rich and the poor, high and low, and a Brahmin and Shudra."[45] [...] The modernity of Rama Tirtha's interpretation is most evident in his critique of the *Manu Smriti*. This fourth century canonical text, which most explicitly and unabashedly sets out caste and gender hierarchies and prescribes draconian punishments for transgressions, was taken to task by him because, 'instead of serving the people', the *Manu Smriti* acted as 'a despotic tyrant'.[46]

Despite theoretical rejection of caste by reformers, for many middle-class men upper-caste status was an important marker of their social respectability and their distance from lower classes and castes. Sannulal Gupta's book shows him to be a great supporter of the Arya Samaj, whose formal ideology also rejected notions of hereditary caste privilege or disability.[47] Yet [...] [t]he most convincing reason he can offer to dissuade women from worshipping 'un-Hindu' pirs is to point to the low caste origins of these saints. 'Isn't it a matter of shame,' Gupta asks, 'that even though we are high-born (*uchha kul*), we worship a base-born person?'[48] Worshipping these saints, Gupta points out, is to worship *chamar*s (an 'untouchable' caste) and even worse, *bhangi*s (scavengers, even lower on the caste scale). 'Ram! Ram' writes this Arya Samaj supporter, 'have we Aryas become so *irreligious and backward* that we should fold our hands to and worship Bhangis,

Chamars, Koilis, Chandalas, etc.'⁴⁹ Clearly, neither the 'religion' nor the 'progress' that Gupta or his kind were seeking to construct in colonial India, included any association with the lower castes. Rama Tirtha's fond hopes were evidently at odds with the sentiments and practices of many of the people he addressed. The new religiosity of the middle-class imagination revealed contradictions almost at the moment of its creation.

By the 1920s, caste issues were very much at the forefront of political debate in nationalist circles. This was also the time when an assertive Hindu nationalism, building on the templates of a new religiosity, was seeking to play a larger role in political affairs by championing the rights of a Hindu political community.⁵⁰ To successfully represent the 'rights' of Hindus and create a stronger, more assertive, Hindu self in colonial north India, it was crucial to the project of Hindu publicists in the 1920s to reiterate, at least rhetorically, the notion of a single 'Hindu community'. For instance, there were many highly charged, emotional, articles in support of allowing 'untouchables' entry to Hindu temples in the prominent Hindi journal of Lucknow, *Madhuri*. One of them compared the untouchables' situation with children prevented from embracing their father.⁵¹ Yet, [...] [t]his became one arena where the limits of the modern Hindu religiosity stood revealed most clearly. Immediately after an impassioned plea on behalf of allowing untouchables temple entry, *Madhuri* [...] warned against taking such reformism too far. While it was important to recognize certain 'Hindu birthrights', *Madhuri* argued, showing untouchables 'more compassion than was necessary' would only divide Hindu [...] ⁵² On an earlier occasion, *Madhuri*'s upper-caste editors had also criticized the attempts to force Hindu Sabha members to eat a meal cooked by untouchables. Their objections were expressed through a rhetorical question, asking if 'the natural and bodily impurity which made such *jatis* [castes] untouchable in the first place, [had] disappeared all of a sudden?' [...]⁵³ However much the editors may have liked to believe otherwise, fault-lines based on caste and class not only limited the Hindu Sabha members, but the very imagination of a modern publicized Hindu religiosity.

It is important not to dismiss such contradictions in middle-class Hindu nationalism as evidence of a simple political duplicity, or to suggest that this avowal of a single Hindu community was 'using' religion as a guise for more 'real' material or political interests. That would be tantamount to arguing that Bishan Narain Dar went to Azamgarh with the real agenda of undermining the religious sensibilities of the peasants there, even while claiming to represent the Hindu community; or that the editors of *Madhuri* were simply upper-caste bigots who put on a facade of liberality while writing some articles in the journal, but allowed their 'true' feelings to surface in some pieces. There is really no historical justification for such conspiracy theories. In fact, such dismissals have lurking at their root, the notion that 'real' religion needs to be concerned with the otherworldly, with individual worship, rather than political power. What middle-class interventions actually did was simply re-politicize religion in the contexts of the colonial public sphere. Of course, like all religiosities perhaps, the product of their efforts too reflected their own interests and the power configurations emerging in the late nineteenth and early twentieth centuries in colonial north India. This context included tensions and contradictions which were constitutive of the middle class. The coexistence of the old and the new, the hierarchical and the emancipatory, and the religious and the secular, are therefore better seen as examples of inevitably fractured modernities characteristic of middle-class politics. A closer look at other deployments of this republicized Hindu religiosity might make this more evident.

DEPLOYING RELIGIOSITY

[...] Tamed Hindu religiosity, liberated from specific contexts and practices, could and was deployed in different ways, as part of many political projects, and in many sorts of discourses. The varieties of explicitly nationalist projects were the most obvious of these. Having consigned caste and other inconvenient features of lived Hinduism to the realms of false religion, and emphasized the pristine purity of Advaita Vedanticism, Rama Tirtha and the more famous Vivekanand deployed the new religiosity to impress upon foreign and native audiences the glories of 'Hinduism'. It was equally necessary for caste and other parochial aspects to be defined as historical accretions upon a true Hindu essence, before India's first President and philosopher, S. Radhakrishnan, could claim that, 'Vedanta is not a religion, but religion itself in its most universal and deepest significance.'[54] A range of hierarchical precepts reinforcing caste and gender distinctions, and a significant history of sectarian conflicts within and between groups of rival Hindu religious specialists and ascetics needed to be marginalized, suppressed, or subsumed by this new notion of Hindu religiosity before Gandhi could define 'non-violence' as one of the essential virtues of Hinduism.[55] On the other hand, political activists like Bishan Narain Dar were not so concerned with the history and philosophy of Hinduism. But even for him to be able to appropriate subaltern religiosity in the name of representing the rights of a 'Hindu community' against the 'meddling' of the colonial state, it was necessary to have the idea of a Hindu community free of divisions, whose rights were to be defended by the middle-class activists like himself.

Abiding faith in liberal values, and commitment to the politics of nation-building may have led Dar to emphasize, even in his celebration of Hindu might, shared aspects of the history and culture of Hindus and Muslims.[56] In other contexts, however, the cultural politics of Hindu assertiveness could, and was, used to construct a much less plural vision of the nation, underscoring Hindu superiority while compelling Muslims to recognize their status as the vanquished.[57] This aggressive Hindu nationalism also drew upon the templates of middle-class modernized Hinduism, celebrating a 'real' Hinduism, not divided by caste, class, language, or region, as the ideological basis for a Hindu community it sought to represent. A rhetoric of community and solidarity, rather than hierarchy, as the characteristic of a modern Hinduism is equally necessary in order for the middle-class proponents of *Hindutva* today when they tear down mosques or carry out systematic pogroms of Muslims or Christians in the name of 'restoring Hindu pride'.

But this is, by now, well known. What is more surprising however, is that the discursive templates that allowed for the discourse of Hindu nationalism to emerge, also underpin large parts of the most liberal and 'secular' discourse of Indian nationalism. Jawaharlal Nehru is almost universally regarded as a quintessential modernist. His rationalism, belief in the progressive impact of western science and technology, and heavy industry, has often led unfavourable comparisons with Mahatma Gandhi, the 'indigenous' critic of modern industrial society. [...]. Nehru's own disdain for 'superstitious practices and dogmatic beliefs' and his outward rejection of religion because its 'method of approach to life's problems...was...not that of science', do, on the surface, appear to reinforce the image of Nehru the modern secularist.[58] What is quite surprising therefore, is to note the extent to which Nehru's narrative also draws heavily upon a republicized Hindu religiosity as he recounts his *Discovery of India*.

One reason that Nehru could not unequivocally celebrate the Indian past was because that past contained much that was evidently unsuitable for a progressive, modern, nation-state. Yet, that past needed to be appropriated, made available for the history of the modern nation. How then were hierarchical and non-modern institutions and ideas so much a part of that history to be accounted for? How was Nehru to square his dislike for non-scientific superstition and dogma of religion with the necessity of celebrating, taking pride in a past which so evidently consisted of much that was religious? Nehru's resolution was very much in the discursive pattern established by men like Rama Tirtha or Vivekanand. Expressing his admiration for the vitality of the Vedas, the spirit of enquiry and philosophical insights of the Upanishads,[59] Nehru celebrated the 'rational spirit of enquiry, so evident in ancient times, which,' he added, 'might well have led to the further growth of science' but then notes a historical and intellectual decline when such a spirit of enquiry is replaced by orthodox, orthoprax religion, and 'irrationalism and a blind idolatry of the past'. It is then that Indian life, In Nehru's view, becomes 'a sluggish stream, living in the past.'[60] It is this degeneration of an authentic tradition that leads to the sort of superstition and dogma Nehru associates with religion, which 'petrifies' a system of reasonable division of labour and a mechanism of group solidarity into the oppressive caste system.[61]

In common with much of nationalist writing, Nehru exhibited what has variously been described as the 'aporia' or the 'Janus-faced' character of nationalism, asserting simultaneously the 'objective modernity' and the 'subjective antiquity' of the Indian nation.[62] The tension between the two is never quite resolved. [...] The only way that Nehru could appropriate history to the Indian nation was to fall back on notions almost identical to those of a 'real Hinduism' which were deployed by the middle-class activists of the nineteenth century. What India needed, therefore, was not to reject the 'vital and life-giving' past, but break with '[...]the dust and dirt of the ages that have covered her up and hidden her inner beauty and significance, the excrescences and abortions that have petrified her spirit, set it in rigid frames, and stunted her growth'.[63] [...] A tamed, disciplined, religious heritage, unencumbered by the 'dust and dirt of the ages,' was the essence of Nehru's 'wisdom of the ancients.' Such a heritage, liberated from lived practices as well as a host of hierarchical and non-modern notions, could be polished, selectively appropriated, to serve as a glorious and untarnished resource available to the emerging

Indian nation. Ironically, therefore, it is the discursive template of republicized religiosity that allows Nehru the arch-secularist to detach religious ideas from their contexts, from religion itself as he understands the term. It is only a new way of thinking about religiosity which allows Nehru to celebrate the 'wisdom of the ancients,' and their spirit of enquiry, while condemning the rest as the 'dust and dirt,' as 'excrescences and abortions.' It is this religiosity that allows the secularist to first construct and then condemn only one part of a tradition as 'religion'.

CONCLUSION

Nationalist modernity in India evidently did not relegate religion to the realms of the private or personal belief. On the contrary, actions of middle-class men in colonial India brought the discourse of religiosity firmly into the domain of public politics: far from a being a 'consciousness other than a consciousness of reality', a republicized religion became constitutive of the realities of nationalist politics in India. Liberated from specific devotional beliefs, social and cultural practices, and detached from the world-views from which they emerged, republicized religiosity was easily deployed for a variety of modern projects in which the middle class played a central role. Of course, such interventions also transformed religion. The republicized Hindu religiosity of the middle class was considerably different from the myriad customs, beliefs, and practices which had previously characterized 'Hinduism'. Undoubtedly a modern phenomenon, this middle-class vision of Hindu religiosity however, cannot be dismissed either as non-religion or reduced to a duplicitous drive to acquire political power. Looking at this phenomenon in the context of a longer history, in fact, we could well see this as yet another instance where transformations in religious ideas both reflected as well as contributed to struggles over political power. Moreover, the very visible presence of religion in the modern arena of nationalist politics also allows us to question the ideal-typical model of modernity itself. [...]

[...] Rather than understand the Lucknow middle class' religiosity as a lack or failure, where they strive for and ultimately fail to achieve the secular-modern ideal, we can look at them as active producers and the products of a sacralized modernity which in turn produced a modernized religiosity in colonial India. This was a modernity shaped by their own concerns and contexts, and their rhetoric and politics were in turn shaped by it. Religion, or rather self-definitions based on religious categories, became a critical part of the modern self created by the colonial middle class. The modernity which middle classes constructed in colonial India, therefore, used the new and the old, looked ahead as well as back. The modern in this case was built on the traditional and coexisted with it, belying neat dichotomies between the modern and the traditional, the religious and the secular. It is this fractured modernity,[64] built upon but never erasing existing traditions, which allows for the simultaneous articulation of the traditional and the modern, the religious and the secular which are so characteristic of modern politics, not only in India but across much of the colonial and post-colonial world.

NOTES

1. Talal Asad, *Genealogies of Religion: Discipline and Reasons of Power in Christianity and Islam* (Baltimore, 1993).
2. Partha Chatterjee, *The Nation and its Fragments: Colonial and Postcolonial Histories* (Princeton, 1993), pp. 6–7.
3. Chatterjee, *The Nation*, pp. 16–18.
4. Partha Chatterjee, *Our Modernity* (Rotterdam/Dakar, 1997).
5. Dipesh Chakrabarty, 'Postcoloniality and the Artifice of History: Who Speaks for 'Indian' Pasts?' *Representations* 37, (Winter, 1992), pp. 1–26; Chatterjee, *Modernity*; Ashis Nandy, 'The Politics of Secularism and the Recovery of Religious Tolerance', in Veena Das (ed.), *Mirrors of Violence: Communities, Riots, and Survivors in South Asia* (New Delhi, 1990), pp. 69–93.
6. Chakrabarty, 'Artifice of History'
7. Sumit Sarkar, *Writing Social History* (New Delhi, 1997).
8. Ronald Inden, *Imagining India* (Cambridge, Massachusetts, 1990); Gyanendra Pandey, *The Construction of Communalism in Colonial North India* (New Delhi, 1990).
9. Sudhir Chandra, *The Oppressive Present: Literature and Social Consciousness in Colonial India* (New Delhi, 1992).
10. P.C. Mookherji, 'The Pictorial Lucknow'. Unpublished Galley Proofs dated 1883. Oriental and India Office Collection (London), pp. 145–6.
11. Bishan Narain Dar, *Collected Speeches and Writings of Pt Bishan Narain Dar*, vol. I, edited by H.L. Chatterjee (Lucknow, 1921), p. 89.
12. Pandey, *Construction of Communalism*.
13. Bishan Narain Dar, *An Appeal to the English Public on behalf of the Hindus of Northwestern Province and Oudh* (Lucknow, 1893).
14. Dar, 'An Appeal', *Collected Speeches and Writings*, Appendix, 6.
15. Ibid., Appendix, 9.
16. Ibid., Appendix, 10.
17. Mrinalini Sinha, *Colonial Masculinity: The 'Effeminate' Bengali and the 'Manly' Englishman in Nineteenth Century Bengal* (Manchester, 1995); John Rosselli, 'The Self-Image of Effeteness: Physical Education and Nationalism in Nineteenth-Century Bengal', *Past and Present*, 86 (February 1980), pp. 121–48.

18. Dar, 'An Appeal', *Collected Speeches and Writings*, p. 30.
19. Ibid., p. 28.
20. This is also how it was primarily read by the administration. Dar's report was widely cited and criticized within the administration for its anti-government tone. For one such interpretation, see the official report on Dar written at the time he was elected President of the 1911 session of the Indian National Congress. Government of India. Home Political, January 1912, B 121-3 (National Archives of India).
21. Dar, 'An Appeal', *Collected Speeches and Writings*, p. 8.
22. Peter van der Veer, *Religious Nationalism: Hindus and Muslims in India* (Berkeley,1994); Susan Bayly, *Saints, Goddesses, and Kings: Muslims and Christians in South Indian Society, 1700–1900* (Cambridge, 1989); Arjun Appadurai, *Worship and Conflict under Colonial Rule* (Cambridge, 1981).
23. J.R.I. Cole, *Roots of North Indian Shi'ism in Iran and Iraq: Religion and State in Awadh, 1722–1859* (New Delhi, 1989).
24. Peter van der Veer, 'The Foreign Hand: Orientalist Discourse in Sociology and Communalism', in Carol Breckenridge and Peter van der Veer (eds), *Orientalism and the Postcolonial Predicament* (Philadelphia, 1993), pp. 23–44; Inden, *Imagining India*, 1990; Romila Thapar, 'Imagined Religious Communities? Ancient History and the Search for a Hindu Identity', *Modern Asian Studies*, 23 (1989).
25. Bernard Cohn, *An Anthropologist among the Historians and Other Essays* (New Delhi, 1987); Appadurai, *Worship and Conflict*; Robert E. Frykenberg, 'The Emergence of Hinduism as a Concept and as an Institution: A Reappraisal with Special Reference to South India', in Gunther-Dietz Sontheimer and Hermann Kulke (eds), *Hinduism Reconsidered* (Delhi, 1997), pp. 1–29; J.D.M. Derrett, 'The Administration of Hindu Law by the British', *Comparative Studies in Society and History* IV, 1 (1961), pp. 10–52; Gregory C. Koslowski, *Muslim Endowments and Society in British India* (Cambridge, 1985); Lata Mani, *Contentious Traditions: The Debate on Sati in Colonial India* (Berkeley, 1998).
26. Henny Sender, *The Kashmiri Pandits: A Study of Cultural Choice in North India* (New Delhi, 1985).
27. Tapan Raychaudhri, *Europe Reconsidered: Perceptions of the West in Nineteenth Century Bengal* (New Delhi, 1988); Sumit Sarkar, '"Kaliyuga", "Chakri" and "Bhakti": Ramakrishna and his Times', *Economic and Political Weekly* (18 July 1992) pp. 1543–66.
28. Pt Brijnath Sharga, *Life of Swami Ram Tirtha* (Lucknow, 2nd edition, 1968); Puran Singh, *The Story of Swami Rama: The Poet Monk of India* (Lucknow, revised edition, 1974); S.R. Sharma, *Swami Rama Tirtha* (Bombay, 1961).
29. Swami Rama Tirtha, *Bharat Mata: Bharatiya Ekta aur Unnati ke Mool Mantra* (Lucknow, 1982), Aphorism # 83, 15.
30. Rama Tirtha, *Bharat Mata*, Aphorism # 16, 3.
31. Rama Tirtha, *Bharat Mata*, Aphorism # 60, 11.
32. See William R. Pinch, 'Soldier Monks and Militant Sadhus', in David Ludden (ed.) *Contesting the Nation: Religion, Community, and the Politics of Democracy in India* (Philadelphia, 1996), pp. 140–62.
33. Sharga, *Swami Ram Tirtha*, p.155.
34. Ibid., p. 25.

35. Sanjay Joshi, *Fractured Modernity: The Making of a Middle Class in Colonial North India* (New Delhi, 2001), pp. 59-95; Anshu Malhotra, 'Pativratas and Kupattis: Gender, Caste, and Identity in Punjab, 1870s-1920s'. (PhD dissertation, School of Oriental and African Studies, University of London, 1998); Gail Minault, *Secluded Scholars: Women's Education and Muslim Social Reform in Colonial India* (New Delhi, 1998).

36. Sannulal Gupta, *Strisubodhini*, Pandit Rupnarayan Pandey (ed.) (Lucknow, 1954), pp. 635-76.

37. Gupta, *Strisubodhini*, pp. 643-5.

38. See Harjot Oberoi, *Construction of Religious Boundaries: Culture, Identity and Diversity in the Sikh Tradition* (New Delhi, 1994); Kenneth W. Jones, *Arya Dharma* (Delhi, 1989); van der Veer, *Religious Nationalism*.

39. After the death of Rama Tirtha for instance, his disciple, Narain Swami, decided that the most fitting memorial for his spiritual mentor was the establishing of the 'Rama Tirtha Publication League', which later became the 'Swami Rama Tirtha Pratishthan', and undertook the task of publishing and disseminating the message of his Guru to the largest possible audience. Swami Rama Tirtha Pratishthan, *Swami Narayana: Some Reminiscences with a Brief Life Sketch* (Lucknow: Rama Tirtha Pratishthan,1975), p. 26.

40. Shivanath Sharma, *Mister Vyas Ki Katha* (Lucknow, Vikram Samvat 1984, ca. 1927).

41. Satyaketu Vidyalankar and Haridutt Vedalankar, *Arya Samaj ka Itihas* vols I-II (Delhi, 1984), I: 589-90 and II: 288.

42. *Advocate*, 27 October 1904, cited in the report of 'City Arya Samaj, Lucknow' *Report of the Nineteenth Indian National Social Conference* (Benaras, 1905), xlv-xlvi.

43. Louis Dumont, *Homo Hierarchicus: An Essay on the Caste System*, Mark Sainsbury (trans.) (Chicago, 1970).

44. Singh, *Swami Rama*, p. 221; Rama Tirtha, p. 42.

45. Rama Tirtha, *Sanatan Dharma* (Lucknow, n.d.).

46. Sharga, *Swami Ram Tirtha*, p.146.

47. Jones, *Arya Dharma*, p. 33.

48. Gupta, *Strisubodhini*, p. 645.

49. Ibid., p. 647, emphasis added.

50. van der Veer, *Religious Nationalism*; Pandey, *Construction of Communalism*; Joshi, *Fractured Modernity*.

51. *Madhuri*, 30 April 1925, 564-6.

52. *Madhuri*, 30 April 1925, 564-6, emphases added.

53. *Madhuri*, September 1924, 275.

54. van der Veer, *Religious Nationalism*, p. 68.

55. M.K. Gandhi, *Hindu Dharma* (Delhi, 1995), p. 8.

56. Dar, *Collected Speeches*, p. 23.

57. van der Veer, *Religious Nationalism*; Pandey, 1990.

58. Jawaharlal Nehru, *The Discovery of India* (Calcutta, 1946; reprint, New Delhi, 1982), pp. 13-14.

59. Nehru, *The Discovery of India*, pp. 78-95.

60. Ibid., p. 47.

61. Ibid., pp. 284-95.

62. Tom Nairn, 'The Modern Janus', *New Left Review* 94, (November–December, 1975), pp. 3-29; Benedict Anderson, *Imagined Communities: Reflections on the Origin and Spread of Nationalism* (London, 1983); Prasenjit Duara, *Rescuing History from the Nation. Questioning Narratives of Modern China* (Chicago, 1995).

63. Nehru, *The Discovery of India*, p. 620.

64. For an elaboration of this argument, please see Joshi, *Fractured Modernity*.

Middle Class and Secularization*

MARGRIT PERNAU

[...] In this paper I will attempt to shed some light on the interrelation between the middle classes and secularization in the Islamic context, by focusing on Delhi. In the first part I will concentrate on the question of whether a Muslim middle class existed at all, how it was composed, and from which sources it drew its cultural identity. The second part will centre on religious changes and the moving forces behind them. What were the relations between the reformist Islam and the rising middle class? In which ways and for what reasons were both the theology and the forms of piety provided by this movement taken up by the middle class? What was the position of the *ulama* within the middle class? In the last part I will discuss [... the] concept of secularization. [...] The question will be, whether there has been an evolution towards this kind of secularization in the nineteenth century, and what were its relations to reformist Islam and its striving for an enhancement of piety.

WAS THERE A MUSLIM MIDDLE CLASS IN DELHI?

The images drawn of the Muslims in the nineteenth century still tend to depict them as either decadent *nawab*s or illiterate, fanatical masses. But is it true that the middle class consisted only of Hindus and Jains? Was there really no Muslim middle class in north India?[1]

---

* Originally published as 'Middle Class and Secularization: The Muslims of Delhi in the Nineteenth Century', in Imtiaz Ahmad and Helmut Reifeld (eds), *Middle Class Values in India and Western Europe* (Delhi: Social Science Press, 2001) pp. 21–41. For the complete text see the original. In the present version, some portions of the essay have been removed and notes rearranged accordingly.

The *ashraf*: The nobles and the well-born

Unlike in the European context, for nineteenth century north India it is difficult to draw a definite line between the nobles and the middle classes. Who was regarded as noble? What constituted the nobility of a nobleman? On the one hand nobility could be defined primarily with reference to the royal court. In this case, the nobles were those who served the monarch in an exalted position and received rewards in the shape of land grants and titles. However, this constituted only one aspect of the Mughal nobility, the one which pointed out the dependence of the nobility: a noble was noble because the emperor honoured him of his free will. On the other hand, nobility could be linked with noble descent: here a noble was noble because he descended from a noble lineage. In this case, the honour the emperor bestowed upon him was not constitutive, but a recognition of what was due to the scion of an illustrious family.

This pride in descent from a family of noble immigrants from outside India (*ashraf*), as opposed to the descendants from converts (*ajlaf*), however, was not limited to the titled and landed nobility. Thus, according to context, ashraf can be translated either as well-born or as noble. Although in theory this status could only be inherited—hence to a certain extent it contradicted the free choice of the monarch—this group would also include all those, whose social status denoted so much respectability that they could successfully claim foreign descent. Thus, within limits, it was lineage that followed status, and not the other way round.[2]

The decisive conceptual dividing line hence separated not three groups, but two: the respectable and well-born, and the rest. The notion of ashraf linked the nobility and those whom we would qualify as middle class in the European context, defined in terms of economic position, profession and cultural habitus. This is not to deny that within this group there existed multiple and intertwining differentiations. During the first half of the nineteenth century however, they did not lead to the formation of a 'middle class', perceiving itself as basically different from the nobility, nor to the evolution of the nobility into a closed estate, the entry into which was legally codified.[3] It would be a matter for separate investigation, in how far this development was linked to the different position the towns occupied in European and in Indian history.[4] Notably, it would be interesting to see how the enhancement of self-administration by the leaders of the trades, neighbourhoods and communities, which seems to have followed the decline of the Mughal authority in Delhi, can be seen as a 'pre-history' of the middle-class formation.[5]

Professions for the ashraf

Traditionally, the quickest way to ashraf status lay in military career, permitting access to both land and titles, often within a single generation. To a slightly lesser extent, administration, too, provided appropriate employment for those who already laid claim to ashraf status and to newcomers. Administrative jobs ranged from the prestigious tasks in the immediate surroundings of the emperor to revenue collectors, police, and judicial officers. The grant of land revenue and pensions secured the acquired status for future generations and delinked it from the actual exercise of a profession.

Though the advent of the British rule reduced the possibilities of a rapid rise through warfare, and though in Delhi the administration of civil and criminal justice shifted to the court of the Residency, leaving the Mughal with nominal power of control, the structure of the administration was left intact and remained largely in the hands of the same families as before.[6] As far as grants and pensions were concerned, except in the case of the Mughal emperor himself, the British interfered only to a limited extent but slowly tightened their control from the 1830s.[7]

Not all the ashraf, however, were in the service of the Mughal or colonial state or lived on their revenue income and pensions. Parallel to the political decline, since the second half of the eighteenth century, Delhi had witnessed a remarkable renewal of intellectual activity. In the decade before the revolt, the city counted as many as six madrasahs, which drew a large number of students from all over north India and beyond.[8] In addition to this, the 1850 map of Shahjahanabad shows another four non-identified madrasahs, and it can be supposed that many of the over 100 mosques of the city also included provisions for teaching.[9] Delhi had nine newspapers in Urdu and Persian, not including the five journals published from the Delhi College, and a number of printing presses, which catered to increasingly diversified needs.[10] We know of the biographical data of more than 130 Unani doctors for the nineteenth century—the actual number of medical practitioners, however, must have been many times that number.[11] What was new in this period was, of course, not the existence of a Muslim intellectual strata, but the fact—although this still has to be investigated in detail—that this group turned their knowledge into a liberal profession, which both guaranteed their livelihood and rendered them independent from the patronage of a single noble.

It is one of the classic topoi of Urdu poetry to lament the decay of the city and its culture and to point out how the noble Muslims were reduced to poverty and had to bow before the rich Hindu traders. Is it true that the nascent Muslim middle class scorned the trade? As yet, we have no detailed information on the Muslim traders and entrepreneurs in the first half of the century. Although the merchant community of the Quam-e-Punjabian had already migrated to Delhi in the seventeenth century, their economic rise seems to date from the period after 1857. Two indications, however, document the possible existence of rich Muslim merchants even before this period: first, the papers which were recovered by the British from the royal palace after the fall of Delhi contain a petition by a large number of Muslim merchants, pleading their inability to further finance the revolt, as the military events had disrupted their trade routes to Calcutta, Benares, Kanpur, Ambala, and Lahore;[12] second, the figures for the Delhi Municipality from 1863 to 1931, collected by Narayani Gupta,[13] show that even at this late stage, 19 out of 36 merchants were Muslim. Their presence in the Municipality indicates not necessarily their status as ashraf, but nevertheless a certain respectability. This is an area which certainly needs further investigation, both as to the composition of this group and their social status.

Middle-class Identity? Sharif versus Nawabi in the Second Half of the Century

Though the titled nobility and the simply well-born could be distinguished at the beginning of the nineteenth century, the line which divided them was not demarcated sharply as they shared a common cultural horizon in the notion of *sharif*. However, this very notion of sharif began changing its meaning in the second half of the century, and came to imply a bourgeois habitus, which no longer encompassed the nobility but stood in stark contrast to what was perceived as a *nawabi* comportment.

This new meaning of sharif laid less emphasis on birth, noble lineage, and inherited qualities and more on behaviour and achievement. While this in itself could be taken as an indicator for a new middle-class consciousness, the required behaviour, too, underwent a significant change. In contrast to the values of the nobility, which emphasized abundance of money as well as time, and despised petty calculating, here the husbanding of resources received primary importance. Demonstrative consumption and spontaneity were no longer important; instead hard work, the capacity to plan and to stick to planning, and punctuality became the new key words. The very venues which formerly marked a person as sharif, the poetical gathering until late in the night, the revelries in the houses of the courtesans, the ability to extemporize in Persian, now became suspect—Nasuh's burning of his son's library in Nazir Ahmad's *Taubat un Nasuh* being the most drastic poetical image of the opposition between the old and the new values. The same comportment, which at the beginning of the nineteenth century still had indicated cultural capital, producing and securing social status, became the symbol of nawabi decadence, from which the new middle class wanted to distinguish itself: the twofold division between the ashraf and the rest had given way to a three-layered structure. The middle class fought hard—but with different arguments—to strengthen its boundaries from the old elite as well as from the menial classes.[14]

The genealogy of this development needs further research. The decisive event seems to have been the failure of the revolt of 1857, which deprived the traditional culture of its centre and patronage, and discredited the leadership of the nobility. If the Muslims were to rebuild their houses after this catastrophe, they felt it had to be on a new basis.[15] At the same time, this critique also drew from the no less traditional topics of reproving the nobility for their lifestyle, which was described as luxurious and sensual, lacking in seriousness and in commitment to values, which had time and again been brought forth by *sufi*s and scholars, to the extent of refusing gifts from nobles.[16] In this context, Delhi claimed for itself to embody the more sober, one might almost say, bourgeois characteristics, while depicting Lucknow as the centre of the decadent feudal culture.[17]

Piety and Ashrafization

Thus, what is new for the second half of the nineteenth century in Delhi (unlike for instance in the Presidency towns and more especially in Calcutta) is not so much the emergence of a new curriculum, leading to new professions, but a reshifting of alliances within the traditional framework, endowing the middle group with an identity of its own, clearly demarcated both from the nobility and the lower classes. If one wants to avoid the term of class for this group, which is linked with a common economic position, and if estate on the other hand usually denotes a position safeguarded by law, they could in Weberian terminology meaningfully be called an 'estate-like associative social relationship' (*ständische Vergesellschaftung*). The link for this group, the basis of their identity, could thus be seen in a common lifestyle and a claim for social prestige based on this lifestyle.[18] This new lifestyle, on its part, was heavily intertwined with the teachings of reformist Islam.

Without having to decide here whether the reformist ideas brought about the rise of the middle class or whether the social changes induced corresponding changes in the religious ideology, for the purpose of this paper, it is enough to claim an elective affinity between theology and the forms of piety brought forth by reformist Islam since the last quarter of the eighteenth century and the rise of the 'new ashraf' to a position of social leadership in the nineteenth century.

While we are fairly well informed about the forms of piety advocated by the later-day reformists, notables of Deobandi provenance, research on reformist Islam in the second half of the eighteenth and the first half of the nineteenth centuries has so far concentrated more on theological aspects than on the piety propagated for the lay followers.[19] Two trends, however, emerge. First, the emphasis shifted towards this-worldly activity as a means to salvation. This holds true even for the religious specialist, who is now supposed to experience the final stages of his way towards God only once he has returned to the world and has assumed the leadership of the community.[20] Second, the concentration on the revealed texts, the Quran and the Hadith, reduced not only the possibility, but also the necessity of mediational activity of the religious experts. This contributed both to the possibility of a rationalization of the relations of cause and effect on an everyday basis, and to a religious recognition of the values of personal achievement.

The behaviour thus induced became the central hallmark by which the ashraf were to be identified. It gave an internal coherence to the group and demarcated them both from the nobility and from the lower classes, both of which continued their reliance on traditional Sufi practices.[21] As these new forms of piety were, at least in principle, accessible to everyone, they constituted an ideal vehicle for *ashrafization*, providing rising groups with the possibility to convert their economic status into social respectability by conforming to high religious standards. The connection between reformist movements and trading groups, while still to be proven in detail, seems a highly probable hypothesis.[22]

At the same time, this development dovetailed with British expectations as to the religious organization of Indian society and also the shared assumption that religion was all the more authentic, the more it was based on scriptures as opposed to practice and custom. However, one should be careful not to jump to the conclusion that reformist Islam owed itself only or to a large extent to the encounter with the colonial power, or even to see it as the result of colonial constructions. As for other areas, here too the element of dialogue and the mutuality of the encounter has to be further investigated, the interests that some sections of society shared with the colonial power, and also the limits of the commonality of interests. As long as they did not on their part head for a conflict with the colonial power, the representatives of reformist and scriptural Islam stood in good chance of being recognized as the speakers for the community.

REFORMIST ISLAM
Was there an Islamic Enlightenment?

Commonly, historiography assumes a close relationship between the rise of the middle classes in Europe, enlightenment, and secularization. At the same time, the period and the philosophy of enlightenment have been seen as the great dividing line between European and Oriental history,[23] as the point where the common world history ended with Europe taking the route towards modernity, rationality, and progress, and the Orient towards stagnation, from which it could only be redeemed by western influence. For Islam, this assumption of the missing enlightenment has recently been challenged by Reinhard Schulze, who pointed out that this idea was based on a very restricted notion of the European enlightenment, reducing it to those stands, which criticized both the churches and the revealed texts, and posited human reason as the only means for arriving at the truth.[24] Rather than bringing out the 'missing enlightenment' in the Indian tradition, while leaving intact European self-perceptions, the task of a comparative study would be to deconstruct the very dichotomy between the rationalistic West and the religious East. Pointing out both the continuous importance of religious traditions in Europe, even in the very centre-stage of modernity, the creation of the public sphere,[25] and the importance of the rationalistic debates in Indian

Islam, permits the depiction of a problem common to both cultures: the reconciliation of human reason and faith, of individual autonomy and scriptural authority. [...]

Traditional Islamic learning, prevalent in India since the advent of Muslim rule, systematized in the *dars-e nizami* in the beginning of the eighteenth century has been associated with the Firangi Mahal in Lucknow. It was based on the one hand on the revealed text of the Quran and the Hadith of the Prophet, and on the other, this theology was strongly influenced by Greek, notably Aristotelian philosophy, emphasizing the central place of human reason and hence attempting to evolve a basis of communication across the borders of the Sunni-Shia and the Hindu-Muslim divide. This *ma'qulat* tradition (from *'aql*, the human faculty of reasoning) thus laid the greatest emphasis not only on the study of logic, philosophy and epistemology, but also included mathematics, astronomy, law and sometimes medicine, providing a comprehensive training for future administrators.[26]

Since the middle of the eighteenth century, this tradition came under attack from two schools, both based in Delhi: the reformed Naqshbandi order of Mirza Jan-e Janan (1700-81) and the madrasah of Shah Wali Ullah (1702-62), who was later acclaimed as forefather by almost all the different groups of Islamic reformers. They were united in their effort to discard what they perceived to be innovations and deviations from the pure revealed Islam, notably the excessive veneration of saints[27] and the syncretistic elements of popular Islam.[28] Distrusting the ability of '*aql* to arrive at the divine truth, they emphasized the study of *naql*, the revealed traditions (hence the name of *manqulat* for this curriculum), translated the Quran, thus facilitating the direct access to the revelation, prepared critical editions of the Hadith of the Prophet, systematized the exegesis and called for punctilious obedience of the Shari'at.[29]

[...] While the *man'qulat* tradition deprecated individual human reasoning on a theoretical level, its turn against the outstanding position of the mystic guide in favour of the possibility of a direct access to the sources of faith in fact enhanced human agency—if not for everyone, at least for the educated, who could arrive at the revealed truth through their own mental efforts.[30] To this new individual responsibility corresponded the increase in debate, both at the level of the *munazaras*, public religious debates,[31] and the pamphlet wars: religion thus became the vehicle through which the middle classes constituted the public sphere.[32]

The ulama and their networks

What was the exact relation between the reformist Islam and the middle classes? Who were the scholars, who aimed at the diffusion of these ideas? What was their social position and by whom were they supported? The main sources of information on the ulama in the eighteenth and nineteenth centuries are the so-called tazkirahs, collective biographies regrouping either the scholars of a certain area or a certain tradition. [...]

Scholars usually received their initial training in their hometown, either from their father or some learned relative, or from a local teacher. At a fairly young age, they then proceeded to a centre of learning, the choice being sometimes a personal one, but more often followed either the family tradition, or the tradition of the township. Though each school had its own network, these networks were not exclusive. Thus it was quite common for a young man who had arrived in Delhi to study at the Madrasa Rahimiya to take lessons from the scholars of the Khanqah of Mirza Jan-e Janan, while studying Arabic with a professor from the Delhi College, and eventually becoming a disciple at the shrine of Khwaja Mir Dard. After finishing his studies, the young man would either return to his hometown, or search for employment in the service of the British or a princely state.

To gather information from the tazikirahs as to the social status of these scholars is more difficult . [...] Usually the scholars would, in a double way, have belonged to the same group of established or aspiring ashraf, who provided the main support for the reformist movement.[33] On the one hand, the majority of these scholars originated from this strata and remained linked to it throughout their life. In the first half of the nineteenth century, the cultural habitus of an *alim* differed only very gradually from the other members of his family and social group, with whom he shared both the canon and the *adab*. On the other hand, families who regularly brought forth ulama, usually after some time were successful in claiming ashraf status. In exceptional cases, this ascent could even take place within a single generation, as in the case of the founder of the Deoband seminary.[34]

It is even more difficult to come to a conclusion as to the financial position of these scholars. It has often been claimed that the loss of professional perspectives and thus of livelihood has been one of the reasons why educated Muslims joined the revolt of 1857. However, until the middle of the century, this type of education still qualified a person for all but the very highest administrative and judicial posts in north India, and it might well be that the expansion of the area covered by state intervention in the wake of the British conquest extended rather than diminished the number of jobs available. Nor was there—with the single exception of the Khanqah of Mirza Jan-e Janan—a marked reluctance to learn English and to take up employment with the British on the part of the north Indian Muslims.[35] The scholarly family of the Khairabadis, a stronghold of the ma'qulat tradition in Delhi is a good case in point. Fazl-e Imam Khairabadi held the office of Sadr us Sudur, the supreme judge at the Delhi court, in the first few decades of the nineteenth century. His brother worked as a newswriter in the service of the British at Rajasthani courts, his three sons held judicial offices in the service of the East India Company and different princely states, while two nephews worked as personal secretaries to General Ochterlony.[36] Nevertheless, while his official position had still permitted Fazl-e Imam to occupy a position of outstanding respectability in Delhi, his son Fazl-e Haq felt that his talents no longer received the recognition they deserved and left British employment for a career in princely states.[37]

Beneath the surface, the social position of the ulama and their function in society had started changing. These changes were brought to a culmination in and after the revolt of 1857, but they cannot be reduced to the influence of a single event. It is to them that we now turn.

[...]

The changing position of the ulama

An alim is a person who possesses *ilm*, which can be quite translated as knowledge, both worldly and religious. At the beginning of the nineteenth century, the plural of alim, ulama, still carried the same meaning.[38] Ulama were the people who possessed knowledge, the scholars, independently of the character of the knowledge implied. If the connotation of religious scholars was intended, as for instance in the case of the teachers at the Khanqah of Mirza Jan-e Janan, the term used was *ulama-e din*.[39] However, it seems that even in this instance it was rather the pious lifestyle which was implied, than a differentiation between worldly and religious scholarship.

While ilm and, to some extent, also alim have retained their original meaning until today, the term ulama since the middle of the century began to acquire the significance of a group of scholars, who dealt only with the traditional religious sciences [...] The scholarship of these 'new' ulama was restricted to knowledge relating to redemption and salvation [...] and now excluded knowledge relating to rule and administration [...] as well as the knowledge relating to culture [...]. [40] Thus, the ulama trained at the great theological colleges of the second half of the nineteenth century, at Deoband, the Nadwa or one of their dependencies, already by their professional formation were excluded from taking up employment in any field other than the religious subsystem. The British construction of the 'Mutiny' as a revolt in which Muslims for religious reasons took a leading part, and their consequent distrust of the ulama certainly was one of the central reasons for this development. However, even in a princely state like Hyderabad, which by its treaties was protected from direct British intervention in the field of education, and to some extent also of administration, a similar transformation took place. In the middle of the century, Salar Jang's foundation of the *Dar ul Ulum*, based on a traditional curriculum, had still aimed at providing the state with competent administrators to carry through a thorough reform of the state government. Soon, however, it became clear that the alumni of this institution would not fulfil the hopes set on them and increasingly the state relied on students coming from the 'modern' universities, from Aligarh or from the Nizam College.

For the ulama, this development implied a loss of income and possibly also of social status. While the theological movement of return to the original sources of the faith together with the translation and propagation of the central texts tended to enhance the possibility of every learned person forming his own judgements on appropriate religious behaviour, thus undermining the exclusivity of the ulama's position, the social movement tended to point in the opposite direction. The differentiation of religion into a subsystem with its own set of specialists, who even developed a 'professional consciousness' of sorts, who tried to find institutionalized ways of conflict resolution and to co-ordinate their action [41] led to a situation opposing the laity with an increasingly organized set of religious specialists. The sacralization of religion, the autonomy of a 'secular' worldly sphere are closely linked and enhance each other. However, more research on the transformation of the piety of the ashraf, and notably on their relation to the ulama, is needed, before it will be possible to tell how this differentiation was translated into everyday practice.

Tajdid or transformation of religion?

[...] The leaders of reformist Islam did not see their endeavours as something new, but on the contrary, as one of the periodically necessary movements of return to the pristine purity of the religion. For them, the new religion was the old one.[42]

However, in the *fatawa* of Shah Abdul Aziz, written in the first decades after the British seizure of Delhi, it is possible to discern a theological response to social differentiation. This differentiation was certainly exacerbated by the fact that the different sub-systems were submitted to the colonial power in a very different degree, and that assigning a sphere to 'religion' as opposed to 'politics' might render it less permeable to British intervention. As in Europe, the endeavour of the religious specialists to ward off interventions of the state, here too, it may have constituted an important factor for not only their coming to terms with the division between the sacred and the secular, but also for their active propagation of this separation. Although the contemporary British perceptions of private and public may have provided an opening for this argumentation, only the detailed examination of the way established arguments have been used and transformed can show the reciprocal weight of tradition and British influence.

Though Shah Abdul Aziz ruled that India had become a *dar ul harb* by reason of the British holding the supreme political power—collecting revenue, exercising civil and criminal jurisdiction—it still did not come under that category of *dar ul harb* which necessitated either *jihad* or emigration, as the British did not prohibit the calling of the prayer, the observation of the fast, and the preaching of Islam.[43] This may be interpreted as the— certainly very qualified—recognition of an autonomy of the political sphere. In the same way, he did not prohibit the acquisition of an English education, as long as it did not interfere with Muslim religious obligations (cultural autonomy), nor the taking up of service under the British government (economical autonomy).[44]

This tendency to constitute the private as the true sphere of religious identity, to hope for a regeneration of the community of believers through a renewal of personal faith of the individuals—and above all of their wives and daughters—continued with increasing intensity in the second half of the nineteenth century. However, as Sanjay Joshi had pointed out for the Hindu community,[45] for the Muslims, too, this emphasis on individual and private piety by no means implied renouncing the public sphere—on the contrary, the debates, first on education, then on the need for a world-wide Islamic solidarity, effectively combined personal religious feelings and political action.[46] How did the transformation of religion we have just described impinge upon its place in the public sphere? How did the relation between religion and politics change under the conditions of a beginning secularization? It is to these questions that we turn in the concluding paragraph, drawing our examples from the Khilafat agitation after the First World War.

Secularization : An irreversible process?

If [...] we consider secularization as a reaction to the increase of social complexity, this process is irreversible as long as this complexity continues to exist. How then is a movement like the Khilafat agitation to be interpreted, which is commonly seen as the result both of religion entering politics and of the alliance between the ulama and the politicians?[47] Isn't the very success this movement enjoyed, at least until the abolition of the Khilafat by the Turkish National Assembly an indication of the fragility of whatever secularization had taken place in the nineteenth century? How do we interpret the multiple statements, both by religious leaders and by Muslim politicians that a separation of politics and religion is not possible in Islam?

Two levels of argumentation have to be carefully distinguished. The first involves the structure of the society and, derived from it, the place of religion. It is at this level that it has to be decided whether secularization takes place or not, whether politics and religion constitute distinguishable sub-systems or an integrated whole. The Khilafat movement was led by an alliance between the politicians whom Francis Robinson has called the 'Young Party in Muslim Politics',[48] and parts of the ulama. In no respect did this alliance lead to a merger between these categories. Even when Muhammad Ali started using religious arguments to back up his political position after his conversion in prison, this did not transform him into a member of the ulama. In the eyes of the Muslim politician, the latter remained religious specialists—in no way did their knowledge, related to redemption and salvation, endow them with a special competence in politics.[49] And while the Khalif was certainly a powerful symbol of Islam and to a certain extent claimed as a spiritual ruler, there was no attempt to endow him with worldly power over the Indian Muslims. Thus, the conceptual and structural division of the spiritual and the secular not only remained intact even at the height of a religio-political movement, but even became reinforced.

The second level of argument concerns the normative interpretation of this social reality: here it is not secularization which is at stake, but secularism. It is to this level that the statements about the impossibility of the division of politics and religion belong. They refer not to the actual transformation of social structure, but to the legitimacy of a policy furthering or even acknowledging these developments. The absence of an ideology of secularism, however, is no indication whether or not secularization did take place.

This clear-cut distinction between secularization and secularism, between social structure and ideology enables us to perceive and thus further investigate the 'fractured modernity' [50] of the middle class, which provided the driving force for both secularization as well as reformist re-Islamization.

NOTES

1. Even Sanjay Joshi (2001) in his otherwise excellent work starts his discussion on the emergence of the middle class in religiously neutral terms, but in the course of the book focuses more and more on how the public sphere, gender relations and religion were discussed among the Hindu middle class.
2. Ahmad (1996), pp. 268–78. See also the nineteenth century saying: 'Last year I was a Julaha, a weaver, this year I am a Shaikh and next year, if prices rise, I shall be a Syed'. Quoted in Muhammad Waseem (1997), p. 19.
3. For the European context, see Serna (1998), pp. 42–98.
4. Rothermund (1992), pp. 273–84.
5. See the negotiations between the court and these leaders during the Siege of Delhi in 1857, Imperial Record Department.
6. Panigrahi (1968), pp. 121–58.
7. Spear (1951).
8. These were the Delhi College, the Madrasa Rahimiya, the school Azurda had reopened near Jama Masjid, the Khairabadi Madrasa, the Husain Bakhsh Madrasa, and the school of the shrine of Mirza Jan-e Jahan.
9. Malik (1993), pp. 43–65.
10. Khan (2000), pp. 260–78.
11. Zill ur Rahman Hakim Saiyyid (1995).
12. Yadav, (1980), pp. 106.
13. Gupta (1981), pp. 235–8.
14. For a comparison with the rising middle class, see Joshi (2001).
15. For the field of literature, this development has been depicted by Pritchett (1994).
16. Only a careful reading of the extensive *malfuzat* literature can show whether this refusal indicates a condemnation of the riches and such or only of certain ways of acquiring and spending them.

17. Petievich (1992)
18. Lepsius (1992), pp. 8–18.
19. Fusfeld (1981); Rizvi (1982); Gaborieau (1999b) pp. 295–307, and (2001); Troll (1978).
20. Fusfeld (1981).
21. See the continuing patronage of the Mughal Court for the shrines of Nizam-ud-Din and Qutb-ud-Din Bakhtiyar Kaki, as well as the veneration of the royal family of the descendants of Shah Kalimullah and notably, in the years immediately preceding the revolt, for Kale Mian (Nizami, 1985), pp. 517–19.
22. While for Delhi at least, the relationship at the end of the nineteenth century between the Punjab merchants and the Ahl-e Hadith, seem to have been fairly tight, the link between the Shah Wali Ullahi school and the merchant communities remains to be proven. However, the fact that mercantile interests seem to have provided an important rationale for declaring India *dar ul harb*, indicate a strong probability. See also Malik (2000) and Masud (2000), pp. 298–315.
23. Schilling (1998), pp. 41–52.
24. Schulze (1990), pp. 140–59 and Schulze (1996), pp. 276–325.
25. van der Veer (1995), pp. 15–43.
26. Malik (1997).
27. Gaborieau (1999a).
28. Gaborieau (1996).
29. This necessarily sketchy picture of the two traditions only aims at drawing attention to different trends. In reality, of course, the revealed texts and obedience to the *Sharia* were important to the Firangi Mahalis too, and on the other hand, even the Madrasa Rahimiya relied on the *dars-e mizamia* for the daily teachings.
30. The one person, who is always quoted in connection with Islamic enlightenment in Indian, Sir Sayyid Ahmad Khan, initially came from this tradition. However, he is not dealt with at length in this article, as his central writing already belonged to a later stage and was so stongly influenced by western philosophy, that its impact on his contemporaries remained limited.
31. Powell (1993).
32. Joshi (2001), pp. 96–132.
33. Metcalf (1982), pp. 235–64.
34. Ibid., pp. 246–7.
35. See the discussion between Shah Abdul Aziz and Shah Ghulam Ali in Qadiri (1992), pp. 14–15.
36. Ibid., pp. 17–19.
37. Ibid., pp. 23–6. See also, Russell and Islam (1994), pp. 61–2.
38. See for instance *Burhan-e Ghiaz ul Lughat*; Karim ul Lughat [1861]; *Lughat ul Kishore* [1891]; *Encyclopedia of Islam*, 1960 ff.
39. See for instance Khan (2000 reprint), who differentiates between *masheikh* (pp. 461–96) and *ulama-e din*, which he reserves for law scholars and teachers of the Madrasa Rahimiya (pp. 517–84).
40. Scheler quoted in Lepsius (1992), p. 13.

41. For the motivation behind the foundation of the Nadwat ul Ulama see Malik (1997); for the foundation of the Jamiat-ul Ulama and the discussions on its scope of action see Rozina (1980).
42. Metcalf (1982), pp. 3–15.
43. Rizvi (1982), pp. 225–37.
44. Ibid., pp. 237–44.
45. Joshi (2001), pp. 106–13.
46. For further references, see Pernau (2002).
47. Minault (1982).
48. Robinson (1997).
49. See the speech at the first session of the Jamiat ul Ulama-e Hind by Sayyid Jalib, editor of the *Hamdard* in which he claims that while politicians were willing to accept the religious lead of the ulama, the political representation of the community did not lie with them but with the Muslim League. [Rozina (1980), pp. 34].
50. Joshi (2001).

REFERENCES

Ahmad, Imtiaz. 1996. 'The Ashraf-Ajlaf Dichotomy in Muslim Social Structure in India', *Indian Economic and Social History Review*, pp. 268–78.

Conrad, Dieter. 1986. 'Max Weber's Interpretation des Dharma und sein Begriff der Eigengesetzlichkeit', in Irma Piovano (ed.), *Max Weber el'India. La Tesi Weberiana della razionalizzazione in rapporto all induismo e ill buddhismo*, Torino.

Fusfeld, Warren Edward. 1981. *The Shaping of Sufi Leadership in Delhi: The Naqshbandiyya Mujilddidiyya, 1750–1920*, Pennsylvania.

Gaborieau, Marc. 1996. 'Les Débats sur L'Acculturation Chez Les Musulmans Indiens au Début du XIXe Siècle', *Purusartha, 19, Altérité et identité, Islam et Christianisme en Inde*.

———. 1999a. 'Criticizing the Sufis: The debate in early eighteenth century India', in Frederick de Jong, Bernd Radtke (eds), *Islamic Mysticism Contested. Thirteen Centuries of Concwversies and Polemics*, Leiden.

———. 1999b. '"Forgotten Obligation": A Reinterpretation of Sayyid Ahmed Barelwis's Jihad in the North West Frontier, 1826–1831', in Jackie Assayag (ed.), *The Resources of History. Tradition, Narration Nation in South Asia*, Paris.

———. 2001. 'Le Mahdi oublié de l'Inde britannique: Sayyid Ahmed Barelwi (1786–1831), Ses Disciples, Ses Adversaires', in Mercedes Garcia-Arenal (ed.), *Mahdisme et Millenarisme dans le Monde Musulman, Revue des Mondes Musulmans et de la Medilerannie*, Aix-en-Provence.

Gupta, Narayani. 1981. *Delhi Between Two Empires*, Delhi.

Hahn, Alois. 1997. 'Religion, Sakularisierung und Kultur', in Hartmut Lehmann (ed.), *Säkularisierung Dechristianisierung, Rechristianisierung im neuzeitlichen Europa*, Gottingen.

Imperial Record Department. 1921. *Press List of Mutiny Papers 1857: Being a Collection of the Correspondence of the Mutineers at Delhi; Reports of the Spies to English Officials and Other Miscellaneous Papers*, Calcutta.

Joshi, Sanjay. 2001. *Fractured Modernity: Making of a Middle Class in Colonial India*, Delhi.
Khan, Nadir Ali. 1991. *A History of Urdu Journalism*, Delhi.
Khan, Sayyid Ahmed. 2000. *Asar us Sanadid*, Delhi.
Lepsius, M. Rainer. 1992. 'Das Bildungsburgertum als Standische Vergesellschaftung', in M. Rainer Lepsius (ed.). *Bildungsbürgertum im 19. Jahrhundert. 3, Lebensführung Und Ständische Vergesellschaftung*, Stuttgart.
Madan, T.N. 1997. *Modern Myths, Locked Minds. Secularism and Fundamentalism in India*, Delhi.
Malik, Jamal. 1993. 'Islamic Institutions and Infrastructure in Shahjahanabad', in Eckhard Ehlers, Thomas Kraift (eds), *Shahjahanabad/Old Delhi. Tradition and Colonial Change*, Stuttgart.
——. 1997. *Islamische Gelehrtenkultur in Nordindien: Entwichlungsgeschichte und Tendenzen am Beispiel von Lucknow*, Leiden.
——. 2000. 'Encounter and Appropriation in the Context of Modern South Asian History', in Jamal Malik (ed.), *Perspectives of Mutual Encounters in South Asian History, 1760–1860*, Leiden.
Masud, Muhammad Khalid. 2000. 'TheWorld of Shah Abd al-Aziz (1746–1824)', in Jamal Malik (ed.), *Perspective of Mutual Encounters in South Asian History, 1760–1860*, Leiden.
Metcalf, Barbara Daly. 1982. *Islamic Revival in British India: Deoband 1860–1900*, Princeton.
Minault, Gail. 1982. *The Khilafat Movement: Religious Symbolism and Political Mobilisation in India*, Delhi.
——. 2000. 'Qiran al Sa'adain: The Dialogue between Eastern and Western Learning at the Delhi College', in Jamal Malik (ed.), *Perspectives of Mutual Encounters in South Asian History 1760–1860*, Leiden.
Nizami, K.A. 1985. *Tarikh-e Mashaikh-e Chisht*, Delhi.
Panigrahi, Devendra. 1968. *Charles Metcalfe in India: Ideas and Administration, 1860–1835*, Delhi.
Pernau, Margrit. 2002. 'From a "Private" Public to a "Public" Private Sphere: Old Delhi and the North Indian Muslims in a Comparative Perspective', in Gurpreet Mahajan, Helmut Reifeld (eds), *The Public and the Private: Democratic Citizenship in Comparative Perspective*, Delhi.
Petievich, Carla. 1992. *Assembly of Rivals. Delhi, Lucknow and the Urdu Ghazal*, Delhi.
Powell, Avril. 1993. *Muslims and Missionaries in Pre-Mutiny India*, London.
Pritchett, Frances. 1994. *Nets of Awareness: Urdu Poetry and its Critics*, Berkeley.
Qadiri, Muhammad Ayub. 1992. 'Maulana Fazl-e Haq Khairabadi: Daur-e Mulazamat', in Fazl-e-Haq Qarshi (ed.), *Maulana Fazl-e Haq Khairabadi: Ek Tahaqiqi Mutala*, Lahore.
Rizvi, Saiyid Athar Abbas. 1982. *Shah Abd al-Aziz: Puritanism, Sectarian Polemics and Jihad*, Canberra.
Robinson, Francis. 1997. *Separatism among Indian Muslims: The Politics of the United Provinces Muslims 1860–1923*, Delhi.
Rothermund, Dietmar. 1992. 'Town and Country in India', in Jens Christian Johansen (ed.), *Clashes of Cultures: Essays in Honour of Niels Steensgaard*, Odense.

Rozina, Parwez. 1980. *Jamiyat ul Ulama-e Hind: Dastaviz Markazi Ijlas, 1919–45*, Islamabad.

Russell, Ralph and Khurshid ul Islam. 1994. *Ghalib 1797–1869: Life and Letters*, Delhi.

Scheler, Max. 1960. *Die Wissensformen und die Gesellschaft*, Bern.

Schilling, Heinz. 1998. 'Der religionssoziologische Typus Europa als Bezugspunkt inner-und interzivilisatorischer Gersellschaftsvergleiche', in Hartmut Kaelble, Jurgen Schriewer (eds), *Gesellschaften in Vergleich. Forschungen aus Sozial-und Geschichtswissenschaften*, Berlin.

Schulze, Reinhard. 1990. 'Das Islamische Achtzehnte Jahrhundert, Versuch einer historiographischen Kritik', *Welt des Islam*.

———. 1996. 'Was ist Islamische Aufklarung', *Welt des Islam*.

Serna, Pierre. 1998. 'Der Adlige', in Michel Vovelle (ed.), *Der Mensch der Aufklärung*, Frankfurt.

Spear, Percival. 1951. *Twilight of the Mughuls: Studies in Late Mughul Delhi*, Delhi.

Troll, Christian W. 1978. *Sayyid Ahmad Khan: A Reinterpretation of Muslim Theology*, Karachi.

Veer, Peter van der. 1995. The Moral State: Religion, Nation and Empire in Victorian Britain and British India', in Peter van der Veer, Hartmut Lehmann (eds), *Nation and Religion, Perspectives on Europe and Asia*, Princeton.

Waseem, Muhammad. 1997. 'Introduction' in Garcin de Tassy, *Muslim Festivals in India and Other Essays*, Delhi.

Yadav, K.G. 1980. *Delhi in 1857. Vol. I: The Trial of Bahadur Shah*.

Zill ur Rahman Hakim Saiyyid. 1995. *Dilli aur Tibb-e Unani*, Delhi.

One Step Outside Modernity*
Caste in the Middle-class Imaginary

M.S.S. PANDIAN

'...although I try to forget my caste, it is impossible to forget.'

—Kumud Pawde, 'The Story of my Sanskrit'.

The autobiography of R.K. Narayan, the well-known Indian writer in English, is perhaps a useful place to begin one's explorations into the complex interrelationship between caste, identity politics, and public sphere. When I read it recently, one of the things that struck me the most was how Narayan, whose fictional world dealt substantially with the life of rural and small town south India, was almost completely silent about his caste identity. In an autobiographical text running into 186 pages, he mentions his caste only in two places. First, when he recollects his schooling in colonial Madras during the 1910s. He was the only Brahmin boy in his class in the missionary-run school. The context was the scripture classes in the school where Hinduism and Brahmins were deliberately chosen for systematic lampooning. The second instance was from his adult life as a journalist working from Mysore. Here, he wonders how he, a Brahmin, was employed as a stringer for the official newspaper of the South Indian Liberal Federation (or the Justice Party), *The Justice*, which vigorously enunciated anti-Brahminism in colonial south India. Interestingly, both are occasions when others bring his caste into being—the rabid

---

* Originally published as, *One Step Outside Modernity: Caste, Identity Politics and Public Sphere* (Amsterdam/Dakar: SEPHIS-CODESRIA, 2001). For the complete text see the original. In the present version, some portions of the essay have been removed and notes rearranged accordingly.

fundamentalist Christians in one instance; and the exclusivist non-Brahmins in the other. But for their incitement, caste perhaps would not have made even those two appearances in the rich and textured story of Narayan's life.[1]

For a man born in 1906 and witnessed the most acute battles around caste—whether it be M.K. Gandhi's threat to suicide which robbed by means of the Poona Pact the 'untouchable' communities of separate electorate, or the nationwide movement for temple entry by the untouchables, or the rise of the non-Brahmin politics in the Madras Presidency during the early decades of the twentieth century—Narayan's forgetfulness about caste comes through as a bit surprising. But this feeling of surprise fades away when one does a closer reading of his autobiography. All through the autobiography, caste masquerades as something else and makes its muted modern appearance. For instance, writing about his difficulties in getting a proper house to rent in Mysore, he writes, '[...]our requirements were rather complicated—separate room for three brothers, their families, and a mother; also for Sheba, our huge Great Dane, who had to have a place outside the house to have her meat cooked, without the fumes from the meat pot polluting our strictly vegetarian atmosphere; a place for our old servant too, who was the only one who could go out and get the mutton and cook it.'[2] It does not need much of an effort to understand what 'strictly vegetarian atmosphere' or meat, which is specified as mutton (that is, it is not beef) encodes. It is caste by other means.[3]

The subtle act of transcoding caste and caste relations into something else—as though to talk about caste as caste would incarcerate one into a pre-modern realm—is a regular feature one finds in most upper-caste autobiographies. Caste always belongs to someone else; it is somewhere else; it is of another time. The act of transcoding is an act of acknowledging and disavowing caste at once.

In marked contrast to the upper-caste autobiographies, the self-definition of one's identity, as found in the autobiographies of the lower castes, is located explicitly in caste as a relational identity. The autobiographical renditions of Bhama or Viramma, two Dalit women from the Tamil-speaking region, the poignant autobiographical fragments of Dalits from Maharashtra, put together by Arjun Dangle in his edited volume *Corpse in the Well*, and Vasant Moon's *Growing up Untouchable in India* are all suffused with the language of caste—at times mutinous, at times moving.[4] Most often the very act of writing an autobiography for a person belonging to a lower caste is to talk about and engage with the issue of caste.⁵

In other words, we have here two competing sets of languages dealing with the issue of caste. One talks of caste by other means; and the other talks of caste on its 'own terms'. My attempt in the rest of the paper is to understand the implication of these two sets of languages for the play of identities in the public sphere under the long shadow of modernity.

A COLONIAL STORY

First, let us have a look at the historical conditions that facilitated and made possible these two competing modes of talking about castes. This straightaway takes us to the domain of culture as articulated by dominant Indian nationalism, in its battle against colonialism. In an influential formulation, Partha Chatterjee has argued that anti-colonial nationalism marks out the domain of culture or spirituality as 'its own domain of sovereignty within colonial society well before it begins its political battle with the imperial power.'⁶ As Chatterjee shows, in the discourse of nationalism, 'The greater one's success in imitating Western skills in the material domain, the greater the need to preserve the distinctness of one's spiritual culture.'⁷

In arguing so, Chatterjee departs from Benedict Anderson who treats anti-colonial nationalism as already imagined in the West, and recovers a space of autonomous national imagination for the colonized. Clearly, Chatterjee's argument, in displacing the centrality of the West, relocates political agency in the colonized.

While I agree with the new possibilities opened up by Chatterjee's argument about nationalism in the colonial context, if we pluralize 'national community' and 'national culture', the obvious triumph of dominant nationalism over colonialism would at once emerge as a story of domination over varied sections of the subaltern social groups within the nation. In other words, if we foreground dominant nationalism in an oppositional dialogue with the subaltern social groups within the nation—instead of colonialism—the divide between the spiritual and material, inner and outer, would tell us other stories—stories of domination and exclusion under the sign of culture and spirituality *within* the so-called national community itself. That is, the very domain of sovereignty that nationalism carves out in the face of colonial domination, is simultaneously a domain of enforcing domination over the subaltern social groups such as lower castes, women, marginal linguistic regions, by the national elite. For example, Partha Chatterjee, in discussing Tarinicharan Chattopadhayay's *The History of India*, notes, 'If the nineteenth-century Englishman could claim ancient Greece as his classical heritage, why should not the English-educated Bengali feel proud of the achievement of the so-called Vedic civilization?'[8] If we keep aside the obvious sense of irony in this statement, what we find is a valorized opposition between colonialism and nationalism. The nationalist invocation of Vedic civilization indeed challenges the claims to supremacy by the colonizers. However, it also carries an unstated hierarchization of different social groups that go to make the nation. The normativity of a Vedic civilization, reinvented by dominant nationalism, would accommodate vast sections of the Indians only as inferiors within the nation.[9] It is not so much the triumph of non-modular nationalism over colonialism, but its inability to exercise hegemony over the life of the nation, is where we can locate the source of two competing modes of speaking caste.

I shall illustrate this by journeying through the biography of a prominent public figure in colonial Madras, P.S. Sivaswami Aiyer (1864-1946). Among other things, Sivaswami Aiyer was Assistant Professor at Madras Law College (1893-9), Joint Editor of *Madras Law Journal* (1893-1907), Member of the Madras Legislative Council, and Vice-chancellor of Madras University (1916-18).[10] In keeping with his pre-eminent location in this modernized colonial public, his life in the material domain was governed by what one may term as canons or protocols western modernity. The telling instance of this was the way Sivasami Aiyer organized his time: '...daily walks, hours set apart for reading newspapers or magazines, fixed time for bath and food, appointment for interview of visitors, intervals devoted to correspondence and private accounts and family affairs—these made up Sivaswami Aiyer's well-arranged routine.'[11] As one of his life-long friends, C.R. Narayana Rao, recounted, 'his habits [were] regulated by clocks and watches.'[12]

However, this modern selfhood of Sivaswami Aiyer in the material domain accounts for only part of his life. The rest was one of 'tradition':

In his personal habits he never changed much from the Indian tradition even after his long tours in foreign lands. As a matter of fact, the reason why he spent extra money on a personal attendant throughout his long tours was his anxiety not to depend on food and victuals supplied at foreign hotels... In his life he had hardly any occasion to have food outside except at intimate friends' places on invitation. His bath at stated time, performance of Sandhyavandanam in the morning, afternoon and evening, annual observances of Sraddhas for his parents—all connoted the immutability of time-honoured regulations that he respected. All religious festivals and special fasts were observed by him... Religious expositions from Srimad Bhagavata or Devi Bhagavata used to be conducted by some learned pundits and listened to with faith by his wife and himself. Brahmins were fed in his house in the ancient manner with all the paraphernalia of a Hindu ritual.[13]

Here we have a description of what the author claims as 'Indian tradition'. It includes, among other things, notions of pollution, Sandhyavandanam, Sraddhas, Srimad Bhagavata, Devi Bhagavata, and feeding of Brahmins. In short, what gets encoded here as Indian culture is what culture to the Brahmins/upper castes. The logic of exclusion from and the inferiorization of lower-caste 'traditions' within the so-called national tradition are too obvious for elaboration. Let me also mention here that the book which carries this description of 'Indian tradition' has been published in the 'Builders of Modern India' series by the Government of India.

T.K. Venkatrama Sastri, one of his early juniors, captured the hybridity that Sivaswami Aiyar was, in the following words: 'In the very first week came my test. One night he put into my hands Ruskin's "Sesame and Lilies" and asked me to read the title of the book. When I read "Sesame" as a word of three syllables, I passed the first test. He was very punctilious about pronunciation... Another night he bade me to read the Bhagavata Purana, a favourite study of his. After I had read it for some time, he took it back and read it with feeling...'[14]

The seemingly effortless co-existence of Ruskin and Bhagavata Purana in the everyday world of Sivaswamy Aiyer in colonial Tamil Nadu can of course be written as a straightforward story of resistance to colonialism. This is indeed the way the elite Indian nationalism scripted the story by working through the binaries of spiritual/material, inner/outer, and valorizing the inner or spiritual as the uncolonized site of national selfhood. But it had a less triumphal implication for the subaltern classes.

First of all, courting the West in the material domain by means of accessing English education, falling in line with certain time discipline, participating in the language of law and so on, provided the Indian elite with the means to take part in the colonial structures of authority (though indisputably as subordinates to the colonizers).

Often such authority, working itself through the language of English and disciplinary institutions like the court of law, meant a compelling moment of exclusion and disempowerment for the subordinate social groups within the 'national community'. For instance, *Pradabha Mudaliar Charitram*, the first novel in Tamil language published in 1879, talks of the effect of conducting court proceedings in English for the ordinary people, as follows: 'They returned home without any gain like a blind man who went to watch theatre and like a deaf man who went to listen to Music.'[15]

Simultaneously, the so-called sovereign domain of culture uncolonized by the West remained a domain to affirm elite upper-caste culture/spirituality as *the* culture of the nation. We have already seen this through the instance of Sivaswamy Iyer's spirituality. This act of mobilizing a part of the national to stand for the whole, not only inferiorized vast sections of lower castes as inadequate citizens-in-the-making;[16] but also significantly *delegitimized the language of caste in the domain of politics by annexing it as part of the cultural*. It is only by unsettling the boundaries between the spiritual and material, inner and outer, the lower castes (and women) could contest the logic of exclusion inherent in the so-called national culture and talk caste in the colonial public sphere.

The intersection between the act of unsettling the boundary between spiritual and material, and the efforts of dominant nationalism to enforce this very boundary is the point at which we can trace the arrival of the two modes of talking about caste which I have mentioned earlier. In fact, much of the politics of Periyar E.V. Ramasamy or Babasaheb Ambedkar can be read as an effort to unsettle the boundary between the spiritual and the material, and recover a space for the language of caste in the colonial public sphere. However, it is a far more interesting story how the mainstream nationalists, in confronting this language of caste in the domain of politics, responded to it.

In 1933, the Municipality of Pollachi, a small town in Western Tamilnadu, introduced a regulation to do away with the separate dining spaces marked out for the Brahmins and the non-Brahmins in hotels. Sivaswami Aiyer opposed the move by claiming that it was interference in personal matters.[17]

Here is an obvious story of pushing back caste into the inner domain of culture. But most often, caste, once brought into the public domain, refused to heed such nationalist advice. It stayed on speaking its own language, though from marginal and stigmatized spaces.

In the face of such stubbornness, caste often gets written out as a part of colonial strategy of 'divide and rule' and, thus, its invocation in the domain of politics stigmatized. The story of how the nationalisms of E.V. Ramasamy and Ambedkar are suspect even today; and how they, in the dominant nationalist thinking, remain as 'collaborators' with the British, would illustrate this.[18] At another level, caste gets transcoded as a modern institution in an effort to shut out the language of caste from the public sphere. Let me take the case of untouchability. There was an avalanche of publications in the first half of the twentieth century, which explained away untouchability by resorting to a discourse of hygiene. P.V. Jagadisa Aiyyer, whose monograph *South Indian Customs* published originally in 1925 but in print even today, has the following to say,

The Indian custom of observing distance pollution, etc., has hygienic and sanitary considerations in view. In general the so-called pious and religious people are generally most scrupulously clean and hence contact with people of uncleanly habits is nauseating to them...people living on unwholesome food such as rotten fish, flesh, garlic, etc., as well as the people of filthy and unclean habits throw out of their bodies coarse and unhealthy magnetism. This affects the religious people of pure habits and diet injuriously. So they keep themselves at a safe distance which has been fixed by the sages of old after sufficient experience and experiment.[19]

This quote is interesting on several counts. There is not a moment when it acknowledges caste. The upper castes, on the one hand, get encoded here as 'so-called pious and religious people' or as 'religious people of pure habits'. The lower castes, on the other, are encoded as 'people living on rotten fish, flesh, garlic, etc.' Fish, flesh, and garlic—all are tabooed in the world of the Brahmin and certain other upper castes. Interestingly, Jagadisa Aiyyer does not invoke merely experience, but experimentation as well. The authority of experimentation summons science to validate caste pollution.[20]

In other contexts, caste, in the hands of the upper castes and dominant nationalists, reincarnates as division of labour. Though one can easily provide several instances to illustrate this, let me just confine to one. In an editorial, appropriately titled as 'How Caste Helps?', *New India*, the journal of Theosophical Society edited by Annie Beasant, noted, 'However much we may declaim against the thraldom of caste in details, the fundamental four divisions of men are so much part of the natural order of things that they will remain as long as servants and traders and soldiers and teachers perform their duties amongst us.' It further added, '...caste in itself is not peculiar to India, but is found everywhere. Servers, merchants, fighters and rulers, priests, every people has them, though the name is different according to the Nation.'[21] Here, Annie Besant, a vociferous defender of Brahminism who tried her best to wreck the non-Brahmin political mobilization in colonial Madras Presidency, naturalizes caste. In doing so, she assimilates caste as part of a universal structure of division of labour and denies it any socio-historical specificity. Both the acts of naturalizing caste and denying it any specificity, work in tandem to invalidate caste as a relevant category in public sphere and politics.

In tracing the historical moment of the arrival of two modes of talking about caste in Indian public sphere, as it unfolded in the womb of colonialism, let me emphasize two key points: first, the very nationalist resolution founded on the divide between spiritual and material, rendered the mode of talking caste on its own terms in the material/public sphere, an illegitimate project. Two, its response to those who still chose the language of caste in the domain of politics by crossing the divide between the spiritual and material, is one of mobilizing modernity (hygiene and division of labour as instances we have seen) and nation to inscribe the language of caste as once again illegitimate.

The intimacy between modernity and the desire to keep caste out of the public sphere had its own particular career in post-colonial India, to which now I turn.

POSTCOLONIAL ANGST

With the end of colonial rule, the ambivalence towards the modern exhibited by the Indian nationalist elite during the colonial period, withered. Now it is modernity on the terms of the 'nation' itself. The character of this new journey along the path of the modern by the Indian nation-state, has been captured by Partha Chatterjee in the following words: 'The modern state, embedded as it is within the universal narrative of capital, cannot recognize within its jurisdiction any form of community except the single, determinate, demographically enumerable form of the nation.'[22] However, it is important here to recognize that this very opposition between the state (and/or capital) and the community, would make community indispensable for the articulation of the nation. After all, only by recognizing the presence of communities, the nation-state can deny their legitimacy and affirm the nation. This simultaneous inseparability and antagonism between the modern state and community is of critical importance to understand the politics of two modes of talking caste in postcolonial India.[23]

In exploring this connection between modernity and caste in postcolonial India, the writings of M.N. Srinivas, who was committed at once to the developmental state and sociology,[24] are the most helpful. Let us have a look at his much-hyped theory of Sanskritization and Westernization. Stripped down to its basics, the theory, within a comparative framework, claims that the lower castes sanskritize and the upper castes westernize.[25]

Taking a cue from Johannes Fabian's argument about how the West constructs its Other by 'the denial of coevalness',[26] we can immediately locate a teleological scheme within Srinivas' comparative analysis. The teleology moves from lower caste practices to sanskritization to westernization. This very teleology sets caste as the Other of the modern.

But we need to remember here that what looks here like the unmarked modern is stealthily upper caste in its orientation. What M.N. Srinivas offers us as the history of westernization in India is eminently instructive here. He writes,

Only a tiny fraction of the Indian population came into direct, face-to-face contact with the British or other Europeans, and those who came into such contact did not always become a force for change. Indian servants of the British, for instance, probably wielded some influence among their kin groups and local caste groups but not among others. They generally came from the low castes, their Westernization was of a superficial kind, and the upper castes made fun of their Pidgin English, their absurd admiration for their employers, and the airs they gave themselves. Similarly, converts to Christianity from Hinduism did not exercise much influence as a whole because first, these also came from the low castes, and second, the act of conversion often only changed the faith but not the customs, the general culture, or the standing of the converts in society.[27]

Very clearly, for M.N. Srinivas, the source of the Indian modern cannot be the lower castes. Their attempts could only remain superficial trapped in pidgin English and absurd admiration for their employers. Interestingly, this is one of those several paragraphs in Srinivas' book, which refuses the distinction between his own view and that of others whom he is talking about.

Let me stay with this theme a bit more. M.N. Srinivas, in the course of his book, gives us a list of 'Westernized intelligentsia' who were, in his words, 'the torchbearers of a new and modern India.' The list runs as follows: Tagore, Vivekananda, Ranade, Gokhale, Tilak, Gandhi,

Jawaharlal Nehru, and Radhakrishnan.[28] Let us for the moment not get caught in the question of how complex figures like Gandhi find a place in this list of westernized intelligentsia. What is of interest here is the glaring absence of the names of those who courted the modern for the mobilization of lower caste. Babasaheb Ambedkar and Periyar E.V. Ramasamy are obvious instances here. It is evident that the Indian modern, despite its claim to be universal—and of course, because of it—not only constitutes lower caste as its Other, but also inscribes itself silently as upper caste. Thus, caste, as the Other of the modern, always belongs to the lower castes.[29]

Given this particular character of the Indian modern, it proscribes and stigmatizes the language of caste in the public sphere. It does so even while it talks caste by other means. In understanding the politics of this authorized language of the public sphere, M.N. Srinivas is once again helpful. It was thanks to Edmund Leach that Srinivas, who spoke all the time about caste in general but never about his own, spoke of his caste identity. In a review of Srinivas' *Caste in Modern India*, Leach called his Sanskritization model 'Brahminocentric' and taunted him whether his interpretation would have been different if he were a Sudra.[30] If the incitement of the rabid Christians and the non-Brahmins occasioned R.K. Narayan's acknowledgement of his upper-caste identity, the incitement of Edmund Leach prompted Srinivas to concede his own caste identity. He claimed,

...my stressing of the importance of the Backward Classes Movement, and of the role of caste in politics and administration, are very probably the result of my being a South Indian, and a Brahmin at that. The principle of caste quotas for appointments to posts in the administration, and for admissions to scientific and technological courses, produced much bitterness among Mysore Brahmins. Some of these were my friends and relatives, and I could not help being sensitive to their distress.[31]

This is familiar enough. Distress of the Brahmin is the theme song of the post-Mandal modern public sphere of India. M.N. Srinivas, to his credit, talks of it even earlier. But what is quite illuminating here is that as soon as he confesses his caste identity (with the caveat of 'very probably'), he hastens to enfeeble it. In the place of his sensitivity to the distress of the Mysore Brahmins, now he presents a range of things that has nothing to do with caste as such, as the reason for his opposition to caste quotas. He could not help being sensitive 'to the steady deterioration in efficiency and the fouling of interpersonal relations in academic circles and the administration—both results of a policy of caste quotas. As one with a strong attachment to Mysore, I could not but be affected by the manner in which conflicts between castes prevented concentration on the all-important task of developing the economic resources of the State for the benefit of all sections of its population.'[32]

M.N. Srinivas, at one level, emerges here as one of '...those "experts" on caste who consider it their duty to protect caste from the pollution of politics.'[33] Here is a torrent of words—'decline of efficiency', 'fouling of interpersonal relations', 'the benefit of all sections of the population'—all conspire to keep caste out of public articulation. In the heart of all of it what we find is the well-known principle of 'common good' as a civic ideal. As the feminist and other minoritarian critiques of civic republican ideal of 'common good' has shown us, the deployment of 'common good' as the so-called democratic ideal elbows out the politics of difference based on inferiorized identities and sports the interest of powerful as that of the society as a whole. As Chantal Mouffe has argued 'all form of Consensus are by necessity based on acts of exclusion.'[34]

However, this is not merely a story of interests, but of democracy and its articulation in the public sphere. The deracinated language of 'common good' comes in the way of the formation of an inclusive public sphere. The pressure exerted by the modern most often forces the subordinated castes into silence and self-hate. D.R. Nagaraj, a fellow traveller and a scholar of the Dalit movement in Karnataka, notes, 'The birth of the modern individual in the humiliated communities is not only accompanied by a painful severing of ties with the community, but also a conscious effort to alter one's past is an integral part of it.'[35] The moving story of Nansaheb Wankhede, as recounted by Vasant Moon, then a deputy county commissioner in Nagpur, is instructive here: 'We went to the house of Nansaheb Wankhede, the retired deputy county commissioner...Nanasaheb was an extremely warm person, but he lived completely apart from the community. He didn't care to mix with me even as a deputy commissioner.' He told Moon, a fellow Mahar, that displaying books on Ambedkar and Buddhism would land him in trouble. But when the news of Ambedkar's death was brought to Wankhede, 'he broke into tears.'[36] It is not words of dialogue in the public, but moments of despair in the private, that the Indian modern offers the lower castes. It demands and enforces that caste can live only secret lives outside the public sphere.

The response of the Indian modern, when the insurrection of the prohibited language of caste occurs in the public sphere, would illuminate the contradictory relationship between modernity and mass politics in India. The year 1990 when V.P. Singh as the Prime Minister of India decided to implement a part of the Mandal Commission Report, was such a moment. As an illustration, let me take the response of Ashok Mitra, well-known Marxist and a believer in 'People's Democracy'. His modern selfhood is not in doubt at all. In a rather revealing statement, he claimed, 'The government's decision... represents the ultimate triumph of the message of Babasaheb Ambedkar over the preachings of secularists.'[37] Sullied by the language of caste, Ambedkar cannot be part of the secular-modern. He goes on, as a Marxist, to enumerate national ills—which are, for him, more real—such as misdistribution of arable land, near-universal illiteracy, and general lack of health. Caste is, however, refused a place in his secular-modern reckoning.[38]

Then comes his ruminations about mass politics:
For the nation's majority, the oppressive arrangements the system has spawned are little different from what obtained under medieval feudalism. With just one exception, medieval tyrants did not have to worry about votes. Modern leaders have to. They cannot therefore ignore pressure groups, who claim to speak on behalf of neglected classes or sections. These groups have to be taken at their face value for they supposedly represent solid vote banks. Revolutions are not next door, but the threat of votes withheld, or being hawked around to other bidders, works.[39]

The simultaneous disenchantment of the Indian modern (even in its Marxist incarnation) with the language of caste as well as that of mass politics is all too transparent here. The perceptive comment about the doctrinaire modernist made three decades back by Rajini Kothari, still holds true:
Those who in India who complain of 'casteism in politics' are really looking for a sort of politics which has no basis in society. They also probably lack any clear conception of either the nature of politics or the nature of the caste system (many of them would want to throw out both politics and caste system).[40]

CONCLUSION

In concluding this paper, let me dwell a bit on how the Indian modern's revolt against democracy has shaped the lower-caste responses. In their response, the modern is both mobilized and critiqued, for the promises of modernity and what it delivers in practice are often in contradiction. A fragment from the real-life story of how Kumud Pawde, a Mahar woman, became proficient in Sanskrit, is a good instance to explore the distinguishing features of these responses.

It is a story of intense struggle, discouragement, and ridicule. However, with determination, Kumud Pawde pursues Sanskrit, gets a post-graduate degree, and teaches it in a college. Gokhale Guruji, an orthodox Brahmin, was exemplary as a teacher. Her caste did not matter to him. But when she began her MA course in Sanskrit, her own professor—someone other than Guruji—disliked her learning Sanskrit. As Kumud Pawde narrates the events:

The Head of the department was a scholar of all-India repute. He didn't like my learning Sanskrit, and would make it clear that he didn't. And he took a malicious delight in doing so... I would unconsciously compare him with Gokhale Guruji. I couldn't understand why this great man with a doctorate, so renowned all over India, this man in his modern dress, who did not wear the traditional cap, who could so eloquently delineate the philosophy of the Universal Being, and with such ease explain difficult concepts in simple terms, could not practice in real life the philosophy in the books he taught. This man had been exposed to modernity; Gokale Guruji was orthodox. Yet one had been shrivelled by tradition, the other enriched by it...[41]

Here is an anguished statement of wonder from a Dalit woman of great accomplishment about how to delineate the meaning of the modern and the non-modern in the context of caste. Modern experience and modern expectation are obviously at loggerheads.[42] However, it would be a mistake to read this as the lower-caste rejection of modernity. It is at once a critique of the modern for its failure as well as an invitation to it to deliver its promises. In other words, the lower-castes' relation to modernity can best be described as 'antagonistic indebtedness'—a felicitous term used by Paul Gilroy in the context of Black politics.[43]

It is by critiquing/rejecting the civilizational claims of modernity that the lower castes, at one level, could claim a space for their politics. The vast corpus of literature produced by the Dalit intellectuals during the past decade in Tamil Nadu is illustrative here. For instance, Raj Gowthaman, one of the leading Tamil intellectuals and a Dalit literary critique, rejects the civilizational claims and the teleology of modernity, and instead recuperates the past of lowly hill cultivators, hunters, fisher people, pastoralists, and the like as the high point of human achievement. He characterizes their social life as communal, with people pooling together and sharing food with a sense of equality, without much internal differentiation. Flow of history ceases to be civilizing and Raj Gowthaman incites the Dalits to step outside it.

One Step Outside Modernity

In carrying forward his agenda of carving out a space for those who are outside the pale of civilization in Indian modern's reckoning, he argues that one needs to resignify as positive those cultural practices which are deemed by the upper castes as lowly. Beef-eating, drinking, speaking in Dalit dialect are necessarily part of this cultural politics.[44] The need to reclaim what has been stigmatized is essential because that alone would end the self-hate that Indian modern has produced in the lower castes. Like D.R. Nagaraj, Raj Gowthaman is aware that the lure of Indian modern is capable of silencing them:
We could see the elements of these protest cultures disappearing among those Dalits who have migrated to urban areas seeking education and jobs... We could see the Dalits avoiding and covering up these counter-cultural elements because of the consciousness that they are uncivilized.[45]

It is evident that this new political project is addressed to the lower castes. And it gives raise to a sphere of politics outside the modern civil society/public sphere. The very appellation 'Dalit' attached to everything that takes place in this sphere signals it.[46] The refusal to concede the demands of Indian upper-caste modernity to hide and at once practise caste, has alone ensured this subaltern counter-public.[47] And this is a public where the language of caste instead of the language of speaking caste by other means, is validated, encouraged and practised. However, it should not be forgotten that this is a public which is simultaneously in constant dialogue with the modern civil society which, in its invocation of modernity, has and continues to resist the articulation of lower-caste politics. We do know that most often this dialogue about the new sphere of politics, takes place in the sheer despair and condemnations that is expressed in the modern civil society. The response which the arrival of Dalit literature and Dalit literary criticism in Tamil Nadu brought has forth from the *avant garde* little magazines is a case in point. For instance, responding to the claim that Dalit writings constitute a separate literary genre, Tamil Selvan, an activist of the cultural front of the Communist Party of India (Marxist) and a Thevar by caste, noted in anger, '...stop your pointless howling. Some professors are organising here and there conferences [on Dalit literature]. They rebuke others. They try to impose on others' heads what is in their heads. These are unnecessary conflicts.' In a move—perhaps inspired by Marxism—towards conflict-resolution, he suggested to the Dalit writers, 'Give up your pointless howling. [Instead] produce serious writing.'[48] In other words, the subaltern counter-public, in extracting the response of the modern authorized public sphere with its upper-caste protocols, is engaged in an antagonistic dialogue with the Indian modern. Equally important is the fact that this sphere of politics, outside the modern civil society, is in constant dialogue, collaboration, and discard with the other strand of lower-caste politics which mobilizes modernity and speaks a language of universal freedom.

This contradictory engagement with modernity by the lower castes has an important message for all of us: That is, being one step outside modernity alone can guarantee us a public where the politics of difference can articulate itself, and caste can emerge as a legitimate category of democratic politics. Being one step outside modernity is indeed being one step ahead of modernity.

NOTES

1. R.K. Narayan, *My Days: A Memoir* (Mysore, 2000 [1974]).
2. Ibid., p. 161.
3. There are uncritical admirers of R.K Narayan who would object to this mode of reading his writings. For instance, N. Ram, a co-biographer of Narayan, writes, 'The criticism is occasionally heard, from literary scholars and others, that Narayan's Malgudi is a literary cocoon, where real-life conflicts, turbulence, and socio-economic misery are not encountered. Naipal, for one, seems to have given some credence to this complaint. But when Narayan is in flow, such criticism seems misdirected, almost banal. Who is to say with what theme or problem or slice of life or imaginative experience a novelist must deal?' (*Frontline*, 8 June 2001, p. 12). Such generosity towards the flow of creativity locates creativity outside the social and declines to interrogate critically what an author chooses *not to engage with* is as important as what he chooses to.
4. Bhama, *Karukku* (Madurai, 1994); Viramma *et al., Viramma: Life of an Untouchable* (London, 1997); Arjun Dangle (ed.), *A Corpse in the Well: Translations from Modern Marathi Dalit Autobiographies* (Hyderabad, 1994 [1992]); and Vasant Moon, *Growing Up Untouchable in India: A Dalit Autobiograph,*. tr. Gail Omvedt (Lanham, 2001).
5. Though the paper talks about caste in general, it draws its instances from the Brahmins and Dalits. It is so because, given their location in the caste hierarchy, their instances can be of help in delineating sharply the argument of the paper.
6. Partha Chatterjee, *The Nation and Its Fragments: Colonial and Postcolonial Histories* (New Delhi, 1995 [1993]), p. 7.
7. Ibid.
8. Ibid., p. 98.
9. Partha Chatterjee is not unaware of this problem. However, even while acknowledging this problem, the primary focus of the book is on the opposition between nationalism and colonialism. It is my plea that if we shift the emphasis from the contradiction between nationalism and colonialism

One Step Outside Modernity   255

to the contradictions within nationalism, the outcomes would be rather different.
   10. K. Chandrasekharan, *P.S. Sivaswamy Aiyer* (New Delhi, 1969), pp. 152–3.
   11. Ibid., p. 119.
   12. Ibid., p. 113.
   13. Ibid., p. 114. This story of Sivaswami Aiyer is not an exceptional story. One can produce innumerable similar accounts about the Tamil Brahmin elite.[...]
   14. K. Chandrasekharan, *P.S. Sivaswamy Aiyer*, p. 23.
   15. Mayuram Vedanayagam Pillai, *Prathaba Mudaliar Charitram* (Chennai, 1984 [1879]), p. 302.
   16. It is rather instructive here to take note of what Stuart Hall and David Held have to say about citizenship: 'The issue around membership—who does and who does not belong—is where the *politics* of citizenship begins. It is impossible to chart the history of the concept very far without coming sharply up against successive attempts to restrict citizenship to certain groups and to exclude others. In different historical periods, different groups have led, and profited from, this "politics of closure": property-owners, men white people, the educated, those in particular occupations or with particular skills, adults.' Stuart Hall and David Held, 'Citizens and Citizenship', in Stuart Hall and Martin Jacques (eds), *New Times: The Changing Face of Politics in the 1990s* (London, 1989), p. 175.
   17. *Gandhi*, 6 November 1933.
   18. For a recent attempt to characterize Ambedkar as a British collaborator, see Arun Shourie, *Worshipping False Gods: Ambedkar and the Facts which Have Been Erased* (New Delhi, 1997). Characteristically, one of the chapters in the book is titled 'The British Stratagem and Its Indian Advocate'.
   19. P.V. Jagadisa Aiyyar, *South Indian Customs* (New Delhi, 1985 [1925]), p. ix.
   20. Here is yet another instance of bringing forth Western authority to defend caste pollution: *Arya Bala Bodini*, a children's magazine brought out by the Theosophical Society, wrote in 1897, 'The Brahmins, particularly the Vaisnavites, insist that they be not seen by others while at dinner. The custom is denounced and declared silly. Efforts are made now and then to bring a miscellaneous crowd to eat together and any success that might attend such gatherings is advertised as grand. People, who ought to know better, exult in such *small triumphs*, as they would put it, over blind orthodoxy. Let us, however, see what a distinguished Westerner has to say on this subject. Says Professor Max Muller in the *Cosmopolis* thus: "The Hindus seem to me to show their good taste by retiring while they feed, and re-appear only after they have washed their hands and face. Why should we be so anxious to perform this no doubt necessary function before the eyes of our friends? Could not at least the grosser part of feeding be performed in private, and the social gathering begins at the dessert, or, with men, at the wine..."' (*Arya Bala Bodinin*, III (5), May 1897, p. 114).
   21. *New India*, 58 (77), 1 April 1916.
   22. Partha Chatterjee, *The Nation and Its Fragments*, p. 238.

23. For a recent and highly sophisticated account of the simultaneous inseparability and antagonism between state and community, see Sankaran Krishna, *Postcolonial Insecurities: India, Sri Lanka and the Question of Nationhood* (Minneapolis and London, 1999). Let me also note here that the relationship between the narrative of capital and that of community need not always be one of opposition. They can come together in denying a universal Western narrative of capital. For example, see Aihwa Ong, *Flexible Citizenship: The Cultural Logic of Transnationality* (Durham and London, 1999).

24. Emphasizing these two roles of a sociologist, M.N. Srinivas wrote, 'The Government of India has an understandable tendency to stress the need for sociological research that is directly related to planning and development. And it is the duty of the sociologists as citizens that they should take part in such research. But there is a grave risk that "pure" or "fundamental" might be sacrificed altogether.' M.N. Srinivas, (ed.), *India's Villages* (Bombay et al., 1963 [1955]), p. 5.

25. M.N. Srinivas, *Social Change in Modern India* (New Delhi, 1972).

26. Johannes Fabian, Time and the Other: How Anthropology Makes Its Object (New York, 1983). Walter Mignola characterizes the 'denial of coevalness' as 'the replacement of the "other" in space by the "other" in time... and the articulation of cultural differences in chronological hierarchies.' Walter D. Mignola, *The Darker Side of Renaissance: Literacy, Territoriality & Colonization* (Ann Arbor, 1995), p. xi.

27. M.N. Srinivas, *Social Change in Modern India*, p. 60.

28. Ibid., p. 77.

29. This is very similar to the manner in which race figures in the Western discourse. As Paul Gilroy notes, '...the history of slavery is somehow assigned to blacks. It becomes our special property rather than a part of the ethical and intellectual heritage of the West as a whole.' Paul Gilroy, *The Black Atlantic: Modernity and Double Consciousness* (Cambridge, 1996 [1993]), p. 49.

30. M.N. Srinivas, *Social Change in Modern India*, p. 148.

31. Ibid., p. 152.

32. Ibid., pp. 152-3.

33. Rajni Kothari (ed.), *Caste in Indian Politics* (New Delhi, 1986 [1970]), p. 6.

34. Chantal Mouffe, 'Feminism, Citizenship and Radical Democratic Politics', in Judith Butler and Joan W. Scott (eds), *Feminists Theorise the Political* (London, 1992), p. 379.

35. D.R. Nagaraj, *The Flaming Feet: A Study of the Dalit Movement* (Bangalore, 1993), pp. 7-8.

36. Vasant Moon, *Growing Up Untouchable in India*, p. 159.

37. Asghar Ali Engineer (ed.), *Mandal Commission Controversy* (Delhi, 1991), p. 190.

38. In fact, Ashok Mitra's view on the implementation of Mandal Commission is not different from that of M.N. Srinivas. M.N. Srinivas too lists, in the context of his opposition to the Mandal Commission recommendations, a similar set of problems as the real ones: 'Social and educational backwardness are best tackled by anti-poverty programmes. Backwardness is due in large measure to poverty and the many ills that go with it. Malnutrition affects

productivity; illiteracy is inseparable from ignorance and superstition. The lack of access to shelter, clothing, and hygiene and sanitation makes people backward. There is such a thing as a "culture of poverty"' (ibid., p. 133). The obvious similarity between Ashok Mitra and M.N. Srinivas points to the elite consensus on the question of caste despite their differing ideological locations.

39. Ibid., pp. 190–1.
40. Rajni Kothari (ed.), *Caste in Indian Politics*, p. 4. For a similar argument, see D.L Sheth, 'Changing Terms of Elite Discourse: The Case of Reservation for "Other Backward Classes"', in T.V. Sathyamurthy (ed.) *Region, Religion, Caste, Gender and Culture in Contemporary India* (New Delhi, 1996).
41. Arjun Dangle (ed.), *A Corpse in the Well*, p. 32.
42. See Paul Gilroy, *The Black Atlantic*, p. 49.
43. Ibid., p. 191.
44. A more systematic statement of the same can be found in Kancha Illiah's notion of 'Dalitisation'. See Kancha Illiah, *Why I am Not a Hindu: A Sudra Critique of Hindutva Philosophy, Culture and Political Economy* (Calcutta, 1996), chap. VII.
45. I have analysed Raj Gowthaman's Writings in detail elsewhere. The material used here are drawn from 'Stepping Outside History; New Dalit Writings from Tamilnadu', in Partha Chatterjee (ed.), *Wages of Freedom: 50 Years of the Indian Nation-State* (New Delhi, 1998).
46. Upper caste politics which refuses to speak caste as caste is what gets written as *politics* without any qualification. Politics that invokes caste is always Dalit politics or the politics of the 'backwards'.
47. On the notion of subaltern counter-public, see Nancy Fraser, 'Rethinking the Public Sphere: A Contribution to the Critique of Actually Existing Democracy', in Craig Calhoun (ed.), *Habermas and the Public Sphere* (Cambridge, Mass., and London, 1996 [1992]).
48. Quoted in V. Arasu, 'Tamil Sirupathirigai Choolalum Dalit Karuthdalum', in Ravi Kumar (ed.), *Dalit Kali-Illakiyam-Arasiyal* (Neyveli, 1996), p. 217.

Four

Whither Middle Class Studies? The Middle Class and the Everyday World

'In Those Days There Was No Coffee'*
Consumption, Popular Culture, and Middle-class Formation in Madras

A.R. VENKATACHALAPATHY

The sociological imagination necessitates, above all, being able to 'think ourselves away' from the familiar routines of our daily lives in order to look at them anew. Consider the simple act of drinking a cup of coffee. What could we find say, from a sociological point of view, about such an apparently uninteresting piece of behaviour? The answer is—an enormous amount.
—Anthony Giddens, *Sociology*, Cambridge, 1989, p. 20

One can write a whole *puranam* on coffee.
—A.K. Chettiar, *Kudagu*, Madras, 1967, p. 126

To go without my morning cup of coffee is like the world in an acute economic crisis.
—Pudumaippithan, 'Chinna Vishayam', *Manikkodi*, 7 October 1934

'In those days there was no coffee,' observed Va. Ramaswamy Iyengar (Va.Ra.) in his essay 'Aimpathu Varushangalukku Mun' (Fifty Years Ago) written in 1943.[1] U.V. Swaminatha Iyer, in his classic autobiography, remarks that 'The morning cup of coffee was unknown to people of those days'.[2] N. Subramanian, the historian and author of *Sangam Polity* and *The Brahmin in the Tamil Country*, makes a similar observation in his autobiography that 'The habit of coffee-drinking, I

---

* Originally published as, '"In Those Days There Was No Coffee": Coffee-drinking and Middle-class Culture in Colonial Tamilnadu', *The Indian Economic and Social History Review*, vol. 39, nos 2 and 3 (2002), pp. 301-16. For the complete text see the original. In the present version, some portions of the essay have been removed and notes re-arranged accordingly.

believe, entered our household only a few years before my birth [1915] [...] Probably, it was only after 1918 that coffee drinking became a tradition with my father.'[3] Such observations recur frequently in the reminiscences and memoirs of the late nineteenth and early twentieth centuries.[4] Drinking coffee, it appears, was no simple quotidian affair. Much like history, the nation-state or even the novel,[5] coffee too was a sign of the modern. This chapter explores how coffee became entrenched in late colonial Tamil society. I will try to map the cultural practices surrounding coffee and the employment of coffee as a metaphor for a range of signifying practices.

DRINKING COFFEE

Standard accounts of the history of coffee hark back to its origins in Ethiopia. By the seventeenth century, coffee, along with tea, is said to have reached the shores of India.[6] Enthusiasts of coffee take great delight in describing, first its discovery and then its triumphant spread to the entire world.[7] Such antiquarian enthusiasms will not detain us here. For not until the end of the nineteenth century did coffee and its cultural 'other', tea, become a phenomenon in India. Being plantation crops, the cultivation of tea and coffee was closely tied to colonialism. As Anthony Giddens observes, 'Although coffee originated in the Middle East, its mass consumption dates from the period of Western colonial expansion about a century and a half ago. Virtually all the coffee we drink in the Western countries comes from areas ... that were colonized by the Europeans.'[8]

The economics of such cultivation and its exploitative nature have received considerable attention from historians and sociologists. The Tamil diaspora has spread over a good part of the world, working as labour, especially in tea and coffee plantations: hence the Tamil language's dubious distinction of giving the word 'coolie' to the world. This chapter, however, will have little to say about the production of coffee. Rather, what it meant to consume coffee in late colonial Tamil society is its concern.

Though coffee was possibly being raised in the Mysore region even by the eighteenth century, it was largely a beverage for Europeans. Most of the produce found its way to the market in London, while a small part of it was consumed by Europeans here.[9] Even at the turn of the twentieth century, Ayothidas Pandithar, the radical Dalit intellectual, refers to coffee as being the drink of Europeans.[10] By the early twentieth century, references to the use of coffee crop up often.

For instance, F.R. Hemingway, in the *Tanjore Gazetteer*, writes, 'Among the higher classes coffee in the morning ... is taken ... Of recent years however a tendency has become noticeable among *Shudra*s, even of the poorer classes, towards the use of coffee in the early morning in preference to cold rice.'[11] In a similar vein, H.R. Pate wrote of the Tirunelveli district:
The old practice of taking *kanji*, or cold rice-water, in the early morning is rapidly giving way to coffee drinking, a degenerate innovation at which the older generation shake their heads. Even Pallans [a Dalit caste] in some parts insist on having their cup of coffee before they go out to work; with the younger members of the richer classes the custom of drinking coffee is almost general.[12]

'New beverages like coffee and tea have become the order of the day. Without such drinks no work gets done,'[13] commented a contemporary Tamil scholar and critic.

Coffee began to gradually displace *neeragaram*, especially in the countryside. Made by fermenting water drained after cooking rice, and adding water and salt to taste, neeragaram's demise was lamented by many intellectuals—a sign of their cultural anxiety. We have already mentioned Pate's observation in this regard. 'In those days people lived a hundred long years' as they drank neeragaram ... 'Now times have changed. Even the women who work the fields demand coffee. There is not a single household without a coffee drinker.'[14] Apart from its unique taste which varied according to the food grain used, neeragaram, it was claimed by its advocates, apart from being cheap and nutritious, was wholesome, good for one's health and nourished the body exhausted by work.[15] In a 1914 chapbook titled *Englandu Kappikkum Indian Palayathukkum Nerntha Chandai Chindu*, 'Cold Rice' accused 'Coffee' of marginalizing curd and buttermilk; even coolies had ceased to take neeragaram, demanding coffee in its stead.[16]

However, coffee was not a mere substitute for some traditional drink, whatever be its nutritive value and cultural position. Coffee was a drink in its own right. Displacing neeragaram, *conjee* or gruel was the least of its exploits, as we shall see as the saga of coffee unfolds. The incursion of coffee into Tamil society was marked by a cultural anxiety which was matched only by the enthusiasm with which it was consumed. The ambivalence and tension, between the threat that coffee was supposed to pose to both Tamils' physical and cultural health on the one hand, and the fascination with coffee as a beverage with all its attendant cultural associations on the other, is something that the Tamils have yet to get over. 'The pleasure that a man derives from drinking coffee is magnificent. It is doubtful if even heavenly bliss that people speak of could be compared to the cheer obtained from a cup of coffee. ... If you ask me, coffee is a wonder.'[17] 'Coffee is the elixir that drives away weariness. Coffee gives vigour and energy',[18] claimed an advertisement for those times.

But this enthusiasm for coffee had to contend with a volley of criticism, before coffee could manage to become a cultural marker for the Tamil middle class. 'Coffee-drinking is not required in our nation. Our ancestors never ever consumed it' was the primary criticism of conservatives.[19] Some arguments against coffee were couched in the language of modern medicine, health, and hygiene.[20] Every conceivable, and inconceivable, malady was blamed on coffee. For instance, one D. Ramaswamy Iyengar (of course, a BA, BL) compared coffee and tea unfavourably with even liquor: while alcohol, he argued, was actually a depressant despite the seeming excitement it caused to the drinker, both coffee and tea were stimulants which finally turned the users into addicts. They meddled with one's sleep pattern and spoilt the appetite, a complaint that has not ceased to this day.[21] 'With the increase in coffee-drinking in our country, infant mortality, diabetes, constipation and other lowly diseases have begun to afflict our brothers and sisters.'[22] While Ramaswamy Iyengar warned non-users, who he rightly suspected were not many, to keep off these beverages, he advised moderation to those already habituated to them,[23] one 'Anjanenjan', whose avowed aim was to reform the rapidly rising Nattukkottai Chettiars, was more categorical when he proclaimed, 'Filter coffee is more addictive than even beer and arrack!'[24] In fact, fundamentalist Gandhians had even christened it *'kutti kal'* ('the junior alcohol').[25]

These days the enemies called tea and coffee have entered all homes, wreaking havoc. They are not food. They seem to stimulate cheer for a little while after drinking, but gradually subvert the vitality of the digestive organs, and when the body is weak, they create all sorts of unknown diseases

argued *Stri-Dharma*, the organ of the Women's Indian Association.[26] Maraimalai Adigal, the father of the Pure Tamil movement and known for his puritanical views on culture, made arguably the most forceful plea against coffee and other beverages:

In the last few years some obnoxious stuff has emerged as eatables: coffee, tea, cocoa and liquor. Many people have begun to consume the decoction of coffee, tea or cocoa four times a day, in the morning, at noon, in the evening and at night. Even the country folk who never knew this drink have learnt to drink these beverages and now proclaim that they cannot live without them!²⁷

The West transgressing into the sovereign realm of culture, especially the supposedly unblemished, pristine, and untainted countryside and its folk is a fear that seems to have constantly stalked the colonial middle class. We found such fear being expressed in the way coffee is supposed to have displaced neeragaram. The chapbook that we referred to earlier, it may be noted, poses a contrast between *English* coffee and *Indian* soaked rice (*palayathu*: leftover rice soaked in water overnight and consumed in the morning). In the debate between the two, Cold Rice personifies Coffee as an immoral woman, who has led people astray and disturbed the (fasting) austerities connected with *amavasai, karthigai,* and *ekadesi*.²⁸

Not surprisingly, similar fears were expressed about coffee's transgression into another avowed sovereign realm: women. A correspondent wrote to Gandhi:

The greatest obstacle in the way of success to our [non-cooperation] movement in Madras are our women. Some of them are very reactionary, and a very large number of the high class Brahman ladies have become addicted to many of the Western vices. They drink coffee not less than three times a day, and consider it very fashionable to drink more.²⁹

Stri Dharma was more forthright in its views on the supposed ill effects of coffee on (presumably Indian) women:

Alas! This damned thing has got hold of women! Two cups of coffee have become the order of the day. The number of women who are proud of feeding their kids with cups of coffee is on the rise! This habit has taken over even aged women. These old women who were once adept in home remedies now rush to the doctor, making a beeline for the hospital for the slightest headache.³⁰

If old women lost touch with home remedies, 'emaciated by coffee-drinking, young women are unable to suckle their children with the god-given, ambrosia-like breast milk and instead feed them with bottled milk bought with money.'³¹ Moreover, after the spread of coffee-drinking, avaricious milkmen milked the cows dry, depriving the calves of milk and thus impoverishing the nation of cattle-wealth.³²

Thus the incursion of coffee was not just a threat to the health of a nation and its people, but affected its very vitals: the pristine, sylvan countryside, with its unassuming and credulous folk was exposed to the dangers of the West and its modernity. Conjee, cold rice, and neeragaram were relegated to oblivion. Women, the bearers not only of posterity, but also of culture and tradition, were getting addicted to coffee. Even old women, the repositories of old world wisdom, were losing touch with their roots. Despite these perceived, if not actually manifest, dangers, coffee could not be wished away; it had simply come to stay. As Maraimalai Adigal rued, 'People who claim accomplishment in education, wealth and culture have begun to see the consumption of beverages through the day as both indispensable and a matter of pride.'[33] Therein lay the secret of the success: coffee and tea were becoming cultural markers which distinguished the 'high' and the 'low'—a phenomenon that figured in Tamil society through the cultural practices surrounding these stimulating beverages.

The emerging Tamil middle class could not, therefore, dismiss an artefact with such wide cultural import. It had to perforce contend with it and ultimately appropriate it in conformity with its preferred goals. Educated in modern schools and occupied with jobs created by colonialism and increasingly tending to cluster in Madras city and other towns of the presidency, this middle class was trying to articulate a consciousness of its own. Its struggles were not limited to the political arena, but stretched into civil society. Cinema, the novel, music, or drama—even an apparent trifle like the use of harmonium in Carnatic music renderings—nothing was left out of its purview. In this complex realm, coffee too was actively negotiated.

Drinking coffee came to be tied to a whole range of cultural practices. In fact, coffee for many, became the touchstone of hospitality. Every guest to a Tamil middle-class home was offered a cup of coffee.[34] R.K. Narayan goes so far as to say that a (middle-class) South Indian 'cannot feel that he has acquitted himself in his worldly existence properly unless he is able to ... ask any visitor who may drop in "Will you have coffee?"'[35] Advertisements for coffee through this period revolved around the theme of coffee as a fitting drink for guests. One advertisement showed a woman reclining on the chair with pride writ large on her face: 'She has served Narasu's Coffee to her guests. She's sure they loved it', ran the advertising copy.[36]

In the fictional writings of the 1930s and 1940s, we find any number of instances of coffee being offered to guests.[37] It should be remembered here that most of the writers of this period were brahmins with just a sprinkling of non-brahmin upper castes, especially the vellalars. In the writings of Pudumaippithan (1906–48), arguably the greatest of Tamil short story writers, coffee is often served to visitors. Murugadas, the failed writer in his 'Oru Nal Kalinthathu' offers coffee to his friends

Sundaram Pillai and Subramania Pillai as soon as they enter his home.[38] Similar incidents may be cited in his other short stories like 'Velippuchu' and 'Nisamum Ninaippum'.[39] In his classic 'Kadavulum Kandasami Pillaiyum', when Lord Sivan visits the earth and meets Kandasami Pillai at the intersection of Esplanade and Broadway in Madras, the latter instinctively leads Him to a nearby coffee hotel.[40]

To just say, 'Let's have some coffee', was a way of welcoming a guest and the ultimate insult to a person was to say that he would not even offer a cup of coffee to visitors.[41] The 'darkest condemnation of a family would be the warning uttered at their back, "Their coffee is awful."'[42] The widespread use of metal tumblers with rims, unlike the rimless North Indian ones, is a Tamil (brahmin) invention: enabling the drinking of coffee without sipping the tumbler, it facilitated the balancing of hospitality and avoiding ritual pollution.[43] It has been observed that taking coffee or tea was considered legitimate even where caste restrictions came in the way of eating food.

However, it was not just any coffee that the middle class could either drink or offer to its guests—it was a coffee defined in a certain manner that had nothing to do with how it was savoured, for instance, in the West. The best coffee was made of freshly roasted and ground beans for every occasion. R.K. Narayan provides the most elaborate description of these processes.

[His mother] selects the right quality of seeds almost subjecting every bean to a severe scrutiny, roasts them slowly over a charcoal fire, and knows by the texture and fragrance of the golden smoke emanating from the chinks in the roaster whether the seeds within have turned the right shade and then grinds them into perfect grains; everything has to be right in this business.

After the careful roasting and grinding of the beans, comes the actual task of making coffee.

... decoction drawn at the right density, on the addition of fresh warm milk turned from black to sepia, from which ultimately emerged a brown akin to the foaming edge of a river in flood, how the whole thing depended upon one's feeling for quality and eye for colour; and then the adding of sugar, just enough to mitigate the bitterness but without producing sweetness. Coffee making is a task of precision at every stage.[44] [...]

Referring to the early days of coffee, Va.Ra. observed, 'In those days nobody drank coffee. Only a few rich households consumed it. Even there, they did not know how to make *proper* coffee. It would be jet black like *kasandu* [dregs]. Drinking such coffee, they would smack their lips.'[45]

Bad coffee, as designated by the Brahmin middle class, was the butt of many jokes. A self-proclaimed expert on coffee had this to say about coffee served at one particular cafe: 'A liquid was brought ... . In a cup of hot water something like milk was added to something black with something like sugar sprinkled upon it.'[46]

Good coffee could be made only with cow's milk—with all the ritual importance associated with the cow in Brahmin discourse. R.K. Narayan emphatically declared that 'Only pure milk, untampered and taken straight from the cow could be a true coffee component.'[47] Making coffee with buffalo's milk was a sign of cultural and moral degeneration.[48] Coffee made with unadulterated cow's milk, quite popular to this day in Thanjavur and Kumbakonam, is still referred to as 'degree coffee'. Recently, the Tamil critic A. Marx has drawn attention to the ubiquitous signboard of 'Pasumpal Kapi Klub" (Cow's Milk Cafe) in Kumbakonam, the stronghold of Tamil Brahminism; whereas in North Arcot district, historically at the margins of Brahminism, this phenomenon is not only absent but also 'beef biriyani' is widely available and advertised.[49]

If the making of good coffee was defined in terms of cow's milk, and the first decoction of freshly roasted and ground coffee beans, the middle class also codified the right manner of drinking coffee. Scorn and ridicule were heaped on those who could not drink coffee 'properly'. For the middle class, unacceptable ways of drinking coffee was usually associated with the countryside. Ki. Rajanarayanan provides two instances in this regard. One Mr M. is said to have drunk coffee from his dinner plate after his meal, while Mr K. used to mix cold water with piping hot coffee from fear of scalding his tongue![50] Apart from such detestable practices, the uncultured also gulped coffee in huge tumblers instead of savouring it in small doses![51]

Thus, sipping 'good' coffee at frequent intervals, savouring its flavour and aroma was a mark of cultural attainment. Such coffee-drinking gradually became a habit. So indispensable did it ultimately become for the middle class that withdrawal of coffee was said to cause headaches. 'I need to drink a cup of coffee at about one in the afternoon ... .Without it my head begins to ache', commented a writer.[52] [...]

[...]

Coffee constituted an important part of the life of a middle-class family. The humorist S.V.V.'s delightful essay, 'Don't Meddle With Coffee', makes this point with typical sheepish humour. To balance the ever-deficit family budget, S.V.V. and his wife decide to forego coffee. They also rationalize this decision by invoking health reasons for arriving at this decision. After a few days, the withdrawal of coffee becomes unbearable with both husband and wife getting quarrelsome and edgy. Finally, wisdom dawns on the middle-class family: I cannot understand why every domestic cost-cutter starts with coffee. But that he does; ... this step develops in the human body canine tendencies of the most ferocious character. I tell you seriously, and after bitter experience; whatever you do, don't cut out coffee. You may cut out food, you may go out in rags, or walk three miles to your office, but don't meddle with coffee.[53]

COFFEE AS METAPHOR

Coffee was not only a fine beverage but also a good thing to think about. Tamil writings through the 1930s and 1940s increasingly employed coffee as a metaphor to put across various views. A range of issues was argued in and through coffee which attests to the cultural importance it had gained with the rise of the middle class. [...]

One of the most striking cases of thinking through coffee would be the debate on coining technical terms in Tamil. In late colonial Tamilnadu, there raged in the Tamil public sphere a debate on the principles that should underlie the coining of technical terms in Tamil. While one school contended that a uniform national vocabulary based on Sanskrit roots should be used, another group, closely linked to Tamil identity politics, argued for the uniqueness of Tamil and advocated the use of Tamil root words.[54] This was an acrimonious debate where no punches were pulled, and the pro-Sanskrit group seems to have taunted the Tamil group on the issue of coffee. Murugu Subramanian, a leading figure in the vanguard of Tamil cultural politics, wrote: 'There are so-called creative writers who denounce Pure Tamil as the demand of a handful of people. The so-called "journalists" ridicule [us]: "Is it at all possible, sir? What is Tamil for coffee?"'[55]

Thus coffee was no mean thing. The widespread use of coffee in its turn appears to have been a constant concern for the middle class. Arguments about Tamilness—what constituted Tamil identity, how the Tamil language was to keep pace with the demands of modernity, and the like were articulated through coffee.

C. Rajagopalachari [Rajaji], in an essay written to argue the case for accepting loan terms into Tamil, creates a fictitious conversation between a man and his wife; the wife brings coffee, and a conversation ensues about the coffee made by her. Rajaji uses this conversation about coffee to point out the numerous Arabic and Persian terms that have become part of the Tamil language.[56]

Unlike Murugu Subramanian, many other Tamil enthusiasts took such taunts in their stride. Refusing to take extreme positions, they argued for retaining *'kapi'*,[57] which is but the Tamilized form of the term 'coffee'. U.V. Swaminatha Iyer, the doyen of Tamil scholarship commented, 'When we adopt words from other languages we should change their form [i.e. Tamilise]. *Erangi* [hearing], *uyil* [will], *pathiri* [padre], *vangi* [bank], *kapi* [coffee], etc. are some words formed in this manner.'[58] Periyar E.V. Ramaswamy argued a similar case more elaborately.

When we need to accept in our language an idea that did not earlier exist in our language, we should work very carefully to coin a term. The term that we discover or coin should not only be able to express the idea clearly but also be easy to pronounce. For example, let us take the term *'kapi'* [coffee]. For most of us today, this beverage has become indispensable. There is no term for this in our language. Instead of coining a new term for this, we may accept this term, which is already in vogue. When we require terms for certain useful scientific ideas, if the English terms are in consonance with Tamil pronunciation, it is better to accept them as such.[59]

It is striking that two rather diverse personalities occupying two ends of the ideological spectrum should employ the same example.

'COFFEE HOTEL'

With the widespread use of coffee in Tamil society, a new institution, popularly referred to as 'coffee hotel' or 'coffee club' which served coffee (and not tea) along with what was called 'tiffin' emerged in the towns and cities of Tamil Nadu. This phenomenon was widely noticed and commented upon from the 1920s well until the 1950s. G.A. Natesan observed, 'It has been said that every third house is either a hair dressing saloon or a coffee hotel. Possibly there is some exaggeration in this ...'[60] These coffee hotels were so popular and such money-spinning enterprises that the satirist Kuttoosi Guruswamy, the ideologue of the Dravidian movement likened them 'to printing currency notes in one's own press'.[61]

The Tamil equivalent of the *Devil's Dictionary* was more blunt when it defined a coffee club as 'A public tavern instituted by Brahmins. A messenger from God to break Brahmin orthodoxy'.[62] A.K. Chettiar, a keen observer of contemporary culture, wrote in a lighter vein:

The coffee hotel is one of the most indispensable things for human society ... Some find it difficult to cajole their wives to entertain friends at home. Such persons seek refuge in coffee hotels. The coffee hotel is not just an eating joint. In villages it is a place of congregation. In towns it is the place where traders clinch deals. Wage earners, school-going students and sub-editors, who down 'half a cup' by the hour—all depend on the coffee hotel. There are people who, sick of homemade food, go to eat at these hotels with their family every week ... Moreover, what can one do when visitors turn up without notice?[63]

A.K. Chettiar's elaborate account of this phenomenon points to the institutionalization of coffee in Tamil society. What is missing in this account however, is the fact that the coffee hotel was generally run by brahmins, and in the popular mind, was associated with them. 'Iyer! Bring me a cup of coffee'[64] was a cry that was heard often in coffee hotels. In fact, some hotels were called 'Brahmanal Hotel'—a practice whose vestiges can still be found in out-of-the-way mofussil towns. When Bharatidasan, the fiery poet of the Dravidian movement, once wanted to criticize some brahmin adversaries, he derisively called them *'kapi kadai mundangal'* (coffee-shop wretches).[65]

Thus, not only coffee, but also the coffee hotel was closely identified with brahmins, even if they happened to be fallen ones. I would suggest that the attribute of the fall was only a way of articulating the ambivalence about the brahmin's negotiation with modernity. The complaint that coffee hotels were unclean was repeated ad nauseam by many contemporary middle-class observers: cups got reused without proper rinsing; the milk was adulterated; the waiters and cooks were dirty; the unclean ambience aided the spread of contagious diseases.[66] Such complaints only go to show their cultural anxiety at an institution which was negotiating in its own way the demands made by modern living in an urban context.

While such critics couched their cultural anxiety about loss of caste in the dubious language of health and sanitation, nationalists like G.A. Natesan were taking pride over 'how quietly yet, effectively [coffee hotels] have levelled up distinction! Could education or legislation have done that work with equal rapidity?'[67] However, this pride concealed the fact that separate space was reserved for brahmins in coffee hotels which was out of bounds for non-brahmins. This was a zealously guarded privilege. For instance, in 1933, when the municipality of Pollachi town introduced a regulation to do away with this reservation, P.S. Sivaswami Iyer opposed it on the grounds that it amounted to interference in personal matters.[68] It was left to Periyar

E.V. Ramaswamy to articulate the radical non-brahmin perspective on this institution: 'Even in the wretched coffee hotels there is no equality. There too hang the boards: "Brahmins" and "Shudras"; "Panchamas", lepers and dogs not to enter.'[69] In the historic Self Respect Conference held at Chengalpat in 1929 a resolution was passed condemning coffee hotels which reserved space for brahmins and urging local authorities to withdraw licences to such establishments.[70]

After such discrimination had formally been abolished, Periyar launched a campaign to remove the adjective 'brahmin' from the names of hotel establishments. His first successful attempt was at railway canteens where separate sections were designated for brahmins. Periyar called upon the government to cancel licences issued to establishments persisting with the use of 'brahmin' in their nomenclature. 'Caste oppression in its experiential form is largely determined through food. Therefore, why should the government permit the use of caste in the names of hotels?'[71] In a well-known agitation in the 1950s, Periyar tarred the word 'brahmin' on the nameplate of Murali's Cafe in Tiruvallikkeni, Madras.

TEA, THE OTHER

As coffee came to be increasingly the cultural marker of the Tamil, especially brahmin, middle class, tea was constructed as the other of coffee: tea and its consumers came to be identified with what coffee and its consumers were not.

Tea came to be related to the urban working class. Advertisements issued by the Tea Market Expansion Board, set up to promote the consumption of Indian tea, were pitched at the urban working class. 'Low Price. High Quality'. screamed the baseline of one such advertisement.[72] Price was an important argument in favour of its promotion as a working-class drink. Another ad claimed. 'By spending one paisa [one] can have five cups of this most excellent beverage'.[73]

For workers, there is no better beverage than Indian tea. It is very cheap. It costs one pice only ... .When you are tired, it is Indian tea that dispels your weariness and gives increased pleasure. It is India tea that gives pleasure and vigour to crores and crores of workers all over India.

Indian Tea—One Cup A Dime.[74]

Another advertisement released by the same Board portrayed a fireman enjoying a cup of (presumably strong) tea: 'The fire brigade is the fearless fighter of India ... Tea is their very life. It is tea that gives the firemen the strength and vigour to combat fire.'[75]

In contrast to the widespread consumption of tea in north India cutting across caste and class barriers, in Tamil Nadu it continues to be pre-eminently a working-class drink. By the 1940s tea even came to be institutionalized in its position. For instance, in the Buckingham & Carnatic Mills of Madras, the management had made arrangements in conjunction with the Indian Tea Marketing Board for a tea canteen which supplied a daily cup of tea to all workers at 4 annas per month.[76] By 1943, as the Factories Act: Administration Report recorded, scores of mills across Tamil Nadu, in Coimbatore, Madurai, Tuticorin, Tiruchi, and Madras, served only tea to its workers. Only the *Hindu*, the acknowledged seat of brahminhood, served coffee to its press workers.[77]

In this context, the middle class identified tea with the working class. Here is a revealing description of the rickshaw-puller, the Tamil middle-class's archetype and symbol of the urban lower class.
The Tamil world is vast. Its countryside is considerably large. Crores of people live there. Like the rickshaw-puller they do not have the faintest idea of literacy. But then there is a major distinguishing feature. Due to his urban living, the rickshaw-puller is familiar with urban culture. He always has some money on hand. He may not drink conjee; but he never fails to visit the toddy shop ... Nor does he fail to drink cups of tea at frequent intervals ... Smoking the beedi is his very breath of life.[78]

Apart from the unfavourable comparison with the pristine and simple country folk, drinking tea was a crucial marker of the degenerate urban working class. It is such workers who frequent roadside 'teashops' (as they are called to this day). Though such shops serve coffee also, it is primarily and predominantly meant (and seen) as teashops for lower class people. The middle class resorts to hotels (the adjective 'coffee' having been dropped in the last few decades) where tiffin, coffee, and usually not tea, is served. If, as we have seen earlier, the coffee hotel was seen as a brahmin institution, serving and consuming good coffee a brahmin habit, tea had another derisive association apart from its working-class patronage. To this day, it is generally accepted that the best tea can be had only at Muslim households and non-vegetarian restaurants, run often by Muslims (popularly called 'military hotels').

Pudumaippithan, whenever he wanted to call somebody crazy, would remark that 'You are a chap who drinks tea at a brahmin hotel.'

G. Alagiriswamy, his close associate, who has recorded this habit of Pudumaippithan, has glossed it with the comment, 'In his view, coffee at brahmin shops was best, while Muslim shops served excellent tea.'[79]

CONCLUSION

Coffee in India began its career as a beverage of Europeans. Despite its early advent, it did not take root until well into the late nineteenth century when Indians began to consume it in significant numbers. This phenomenon drew the attention of the middle-class intelligentsia who saw coffee as a threatening, alien substance—a symbol of the West/modernity—which weakened the very vitals of Indian/Tamil society. They declared that coffee transgressed into Indian culture especially by invading the domains of the countryside and that of women.

By the turn of the twentieth century, however, coffee had captured the imagination and the diet of the middle class, which ultimately appropriated it to suit its goals. From despising the beverage, the middle class now defined the cultural practice of coffee drinking: how it was to be made, how it was to be consumed, and how it was to be thought about. Through such an appropriation it defined 'tea' as the 'other' of coffee. While coffee became the cultural marker of the Tamil middle class, tea was seen as a working class/Muslim drink. Moreover, coffee also figured as a metaphor in a range of cultural debates of the time.

This conclusion far from exhausts the richness of coffee. Perhaps it is better to give the inveterate coffee-drinker, R.K. Narayan, the last word: 'I never tire of writing about coffee. It seems to me an inexhaustible, monumental theme. I sometimes feel that it is a subject which may well occupy the space of a whole saga, if we may define a saga as a worthy theme expanded to a worthy length.'[80]

NOTES

1. *Ananda Vikatan*, 24 October 1943.
2. U.V. Swaminatha Iyer, *En Charithiram*, Madras, 1990, p. 125 (This autobiography was serialized in the popular Tamil weekly *Ananda Vikatan* during 1940–2).
3. N. Subramanian, *En Valkai Varalaru*, Udumailaippettai, 1993, p. 17.
4. See Thi.Ka. Shanmugam, *Enathu Nadaga Valkai*, Madras, 1986, p.66. Also see Thi. Ja. Ra. (*Poluthupokku*, Madras, 1953, p. 190; essays written in the late 1930s) who observes, 'The public never desires anything. Twenty years ago, did anybody petition asking for soaps and coffee?'

5. For an exploration of the appropriation of the novel into Tamil society, see my 'Domesticating the Novel: Culture and Society in Inter-War Tamilnadu', *The Indian Economic and Social History Review*, 34(1), 1997.
6. George Watt, *The Commercial Products of India*, London, 1908, p.337; A.K. Chettiar, *Kudagu*, Madras, 1967, p.121; K.T. Achaya, *Indian Food: A Historical Companion*, Delhi, 1994, pp. 229–30; B.G.L. Swamy, *Bothaiyin Pathaiyil*, Madras, 1978, p.159. Also see Irfan Habib, *The Agrarian System of Mughal India*, Bombay, 1963, p. 46.
7. Claudia Roden, *Coffee*, Harmondsworth, 1981.
8. *Sociology*, Cambridge, 1989, p. 20.
9. S. Muthiah, *A Planting Century: The First Hundred Years of the United Planter's Association of Southern India, 1893–1993*, New Delhi, 1993.
10. Gnana. Aloysius, (ed.), *Ayothidasar Chinthanaigal*, Vol. I, Palayamkottai, 1999, p. 273 (originally published in *Tamilan*, 17 August 1910).
11. *Madras District Gazetteers: Tanjore*, Madras, 1906, p. 65.
12. *Tinnevelly District Gazetteer*, Madras, 1917, p. 105.
13. Mu. Arunachalam, *Nilalarumai Veyililae*, Madras, 1944, p. 28.
14. 'Anjanenjan' [So. Murugappa], *Namathu Palasarakku Kadai*, Karaikkudi, Thunmathi (Tamil calendar, 1921–2), p. 78.
15. Ki. Rajanarayanan, *Karisal Kattu Kadithasi*, Sivagangai, 1991, p. 73.
16. Written by Choolai Munuswamy Mudaliar and published from Choolai, a working-class locality of Madras. For Tamil popular publishing, see my 'Songsters of the Cross-roads: Popular Literature and Print in Colonial Tamilnadu', *South Indian Folklorist*, 3 (1), October 1999.
17. 'Rakki', 'Ore Oru Cup Kappi', *Sakti*, February 1947.
18. *Grama Ooliyan*, 16 March 1947. For similar advertisements issued by Narasu's Coffee see *Swadesamitran* (Weekly), 27 June 1943.
19. *Lokobakari*, 21 June 1928.
20. Coffee and tea do not figure in the indigenous medicinal texts and traditions. While native *materia medica* refer to even tobacco, coffee and tea do not find a place probably because they are rather late entrants. However, popular beliefs hold that coffee and tea are heat- and bile-producing substances.
21. *Tamilar Nesan*, 7(9), December 1923.
22. *Navasakti*, 15 June 1927.
23. *Tamilar Nesan*, 7(9), December 1923.
24. 'Anjanenjan', *Namathu Palasarakku Kadai*, p. 18.
25. Not that it stopped many Gandhians from drinking coffee. Of C. Rajagopalachari's love for coffee, it has been said (by no less than A.K. Chettiar, another Gandhian) that he would have been mighty pleased if the entire Kaveri were to run with coffee. See A.K. Chettiar *Kudagu*, p.119. Many Gandhians were taunted with the question whether the followers of Gandhi could drink coffee.
26. *Stri-Dharma*, June 1926.
27. Maraimalai Adigal, *Makkal Noorandu Valkai*, Madras, 1976, pp. 205–6 (first edition 1933).
28. *Englandu Kappikkum Indian Palayathukkum Nerntha Chandai Chindu*, Madras, 1914.

29. 'Of Tamil Women', *Young India*, 25 August 1921.
30. *Stri-Dharma*, June 1926.
31. *Lokobakari*, 21 June 1928. Also see *Ooliyan*, 11 August 1925.
32. *Lokobakari*, 21 June 1928.
33. Maraimalai Adigal, *Makkal Noorandu Valkai*, p. 206.
34. A.K. Chettiar, *Kudagu*, p. 122; B.G.L. Swamy, *Bothaiyin Pathaiyil*, pp. 156-7; 'Anjanenjan', *Namathu Palasarakku Kadai*, p. 78.
35. R.K. Narayan, *A Writer's Nightmare: Selected Essays*, New Delhi, 1988, p. 56.
36. *Swadesamitran* (Weekly), 7 November 1943.
37. Ka. Naa. Subrahmanyam draws attention to Kalki's comment that, in the short stories of the day (the 1930s and 1940s) the wife should make an appearance with a cup of coffee in her hands! *Vimarsanakkalai*, Madras, 1984, p. 120.
38. A.R. Venkatachalapathy, ed., *Pudumaippithan Kathaigal*, Nagercoil, 2000, p. 381.
39. Ibid., pp. 254, 605.
40. Ibid., p. 552.
41. B.G.L. Swamy, *Bothaiyin Pathaiyil*, p. 156; Ki. Rajanarayanan, *Karisal Kattu Kadithasi*, p. 75.
42. R.K. Narayan, *My Dateless Diary*, Mysore, 1960, pp. 2-3.
43. A.K. Chettiar, *Kudagu*, p. 125. Also see Gnanakoothan's preface to Vathsala, *Suyam*, Madras, 2000, p. 7.
44. R.K. Narayan, *My Dateless Diary*, p. 3.
45. *Ananda Vikatan*, 24 October 1943, emphasis added.
46. *Sakti*, February 1947.
47. R.K. Narayan, *My Dateless Diary*, p. 3.
48. *Navasakti*, 2 November 1923.
49. A. Marx, *Udaipadum Punithangal*, Coimbatore, 1997, p. 112-16.
50. Ki. Rajanarayanan, *Karisal Kattu Kadithasi*, p. 74.
51. Ibid., p. 75.
52. Chitti, 'Oru Cup Kapi', *Manikkodi*, 29 September 1934. This essay, written in the fashion of A.G. Gardiner and Hilaire Belloc, was acclaimed as a classic (*Kalamohini* 15 Aadi, Chithrabanu - Tamil calendar, 1942). Also see, A. Ramgopal, 'Teilai', *Kalaimagal*, October 1948.
53. S.V.V., *Soap Bubbles and More Soap Bubbles*, Madras, 1988, p. 98 (first edition 1946).
54. For an extended discussion of these debates, see A.R. Venkatachalapathy, 'Coining Words: Language and Politics in Late Colonial Tamilnadu', *Comparative Studies of South Asia, Africa and the Middle East*, vol. 15, no. 2, 1995.
55. *Mullai*, No.4 [1946]. As late as 1967, A.K. Chettiar was commenting, 'We hear demands like "light coffee", "medium coffee", "strong coffee", "double strong coffee" at cafes. Tamil terms for these are yet to be coined,' *Kudagu*, p. 125.
56. *Rajaji Katturaigal*, Madras, n.d., pp. 12-13. See *Rajaji Kathaigal* for a short story about rivalry in the coffee trade between two dealers.
57. The Tatas have recently introduced a new brand specially meant for south India called 'Kaapi'.

58. U.V. Swaminatha Iyer, *Nallurai Kovai*, vol. 2, Madras, 1991, p. 53. Originally delivered as a presidential address of Tamilanbar Manadu, Madras, 1933.
59. Ve. Anaimuthu (ed.), *Periyar Ee.Ve.Ra. Chinthanaigal*, vol. 2, Tiruchy, 1974, p. 922. Originally written in 1948.
60. G.A. Natesan, 'Changing Times', *Indian Review*, August 1938.
61. Kuttoosi Guruswamy, *Ambe Sivam*, Madras, 2004, p. 115.
62. *Navasakti*, 29 October 1926.
63. A.K. Chettiar, *Ulagam Suttrum Tamilan*, Madras, 1957, pp.125–6.
64. 'Rakki', 'Oru Cup Kapi', *Sakti*, February 1947.
65. *Kuyil*, 15 August 1948.
66. 'Kapi Hotelgal: Janangalukku Erpadum Keduthalgal', *Navasakti*, 2 November 1923; 'Kapi Hotelgalin Seerkedana Nilamai', ibid, 15 June 1927; Su.Aa. Ramasamy Pulavar, *Ilagiri Porulgala? Emathoothargala?*, Madras, 1955, p. 26.
67. *Indian Review*, August 1938.
68. *Gandhi*, 6 November 1933.
69. Ve. Anaimuthu (ed.), *Ee.Ve.Ra. Chinthanaigal*, vol. 3, pp. 1783–4 (originally published as an editorial in *Kudi Arasu*, 3 July 1938).
70. *Kudi Arasu*, 24 February 1929
71. Ibid., vol. 3, p. 1849.
72. *Manikkodi*, 2 February 1936.
73. *Stri-Dharma*, August–September 1935.
74. *Manikkodi*, 2 February 1936.
75. *Swadesamitran* (Weekly), 23 May 1943. Another advertisement in this series portrayed a sailor (Ibid., 21 November 1943).
76. G.O. No. 1527, Public Works (Labour), 30 July 1943, Government of Madras (Administration Report—Factories Act—1942, Appendix III).
77. G.O. No. 2092, Public Works, 22 July 1944, Government of Madras.
78. Mu. Arunachalam, *Indraiya Tamil Vasananadai*, pp. 89–90.
79. G. Alagiriswamy, *Nan Kanda Eluthalargal*, Madras, 1988, p. 102.
80. R.K. Narayan, *Story-Teller's World*, New Delhi, 1989, p. 44.

A Case of Indian Exceptionalism
Bengali Middle-class Patronage of Sport in Colonial Bengal

BORIA MAJUMDAR

> Without doubt the middle classes have suffered a bad press in some academic quarters. Apologists for other classes have set about them or set them aside. It is now time for a revisionist reassessment in the interests of balance, accuracy and impartiality, and time to break free of an intellectual deadlock.
>
> —J.A. Mangan, 'Introduction' to *Victorian and Edwardian Middle Class England at Play*.[1]

Paraphrasing Mangan, it can be argued that as in the case of England, the contribution of the Bengali middle classes too remains 'inexcusably undervalued and underappreciated' in the evolution and spread of Indian sport. Also, 'there has been far too little interest in pressing the merits of investigation.' This paper is a corrective.

Cricket in Bengal, unlike in other parts of the country, owed much to the patronage of the educated Bengali middle classes. The *bhadralok*, as this class was referred to, collaborated with the Maharajas of Natore, Cooch Behar, Mymensingh, and other native states in their efforts to make the game representative of Bengali society from the close of the nineteenth century. Desire to attain recognition in British eyes together with the longing to defeat the British on their own turf were at the root of this middle-class initiative, and, to that extent, Bengali cricket was a nationalist enterprise. The bhadralok, products of the public school system the English had imported into India, though openly advocating the 'games ethic', often employed sport as a tool of subversion. It was a well thought out strategy. On the surface it demonstrated to the colonial masters the success of the 'games ethic' as an imperial tool. Accordingly, British administrators hardly ever thought of suspending sports promotion in academic institutions.

Rather, the colonial masters, on many occasions, took the lead in providing equipment, necessary infrastructure, and funding so that sporting activities could flourish. That the 'games ethic' was actually subverted in these institutions and in the province in general makes the story of Bengal cricket different from that in other parts of the country, particularly Bombay.

Cricket in Bombay was promoted by Parsi business classes and was rooted in an urge for social mobility within the colonial framework. Cricket, it was hoped, would aid the Parsi bourgeoisie's rise up the social ladder. In Bengal, on the other hand, middle-class patronage of the sport, it may be argued, was partly rooted in an urge to negate the charge of effeminacy labelled against the Bengali male.

It is commonly believed that in Bengal the popularity of cricket is relatively recent, comparable to soccer only from the 1980s. This assumption finds corroboration in most historical treatises on Indian cricket, which spare little thought for the origin and proliferation of the game in the province.[2]

While recorded history speaks of stray matches in Calcutta from 1792 onwards, the year that the Calcutta Cricket Club was founded,[3] a startling entry in Hickey's *Bengal Gazette* testifies to a flourishing cricket culture in Bengal at an earlier date. The report ran as follows: *News extraordinary from the Cricket Club*: The gentlemen of the Calcutta Cricket Club are themselves into wind and preparing to take the field for a very active campaign—Calcutta Cricket Club enjoys today the use of a splendid site as good as can be found anywhere.[4]

These are, however, scattered references to the game, and evidences testify that cricket was firmly established in Calcutta from the early nineteenth century.[5] At this point, the game was confined to the white population of the metropolis, and it was from the 1870s and 1880s that the Bengali middle class started playing the game on an organized basis.

Existing studies, in complete disregard of this rich tradition of cricket in Bengal, treat the early history of Indian cricket as one synonymous with the history of the sport in Bombay. The reason behind this early Parsi patronage was the desire of the newly emerging Parsi bourgeoisie to strengthen ties with the colonial state. Parsi intellectuals also welcomed prowess in the game as a sign of the renewal of physical vitality of a race sapped by centuries in tropical climes.[6]

The colonizers, aiming to use cricket as a tool of governance, encouraged the Parsi initiative as part of the imperial agenda of

civilizing the colonized. As has been shown by J.A. Mangan and others, sport, and especially cricket, was essential to British imperial dominance in the colonies.[7] Even as late as 1934-5, when cricket had been indigenized and 'subverted'[8] in most colonies, the MCC[9] issued a greeting card with the following text:
We breathe in the teeth of the north wind,
We bask'neath a Southern Sky,
And the bonds that our empire doth bind
Shall never was old nor die.[10]

The illustration on the card and the poem by the MCC Secretary, W. Findlay, outlines the close bond between cricket and the empire, a bond that often led the colonial state to ignore the sport's 'subversion'.

In fact, early cricket in India has largely been understood as an alien sport appropriated as part of an emulative enterprise. The close links, if any, between cricket and civism are generally regarded as a twentieth-century phenomenon. Their linking, historically, is still regarded an unfounded proposition, evident from the following comment by Richard Cashman:
Indian nationalism was less radical, in a cultural sense, than Irish where the nationalists attacked cricket and other English sports as objectionable elements of colonial culture and patronised Gaelic sports instead. The Indian nationalist leaders attacked the political and economic aspects of British imperialism but retained an affection for some aspects of English culture.[11]

Contrary to existing assumptions, a study of the middle-class initiative in Bengal demonstrates that Indians other than the Parsis started playing the game for reasons more complex than simply trying to emulate the British or achieve social mobility within the colonial framework.

THE TURN TO CRICKET IN BENGAL

All the factors that stimulated the Parsi initiative were noticeable among the Bengali bhadrolok of the early nineteenth century. They were a western educated, upwardly mobile community and had been compradors of the colonial state. Yet they did not take to cricket until the 1870s and 1880s. It, therefore, becomes obvious that the explanations advanced thus far fail to successfully account for the proliferation of cricket in parts of the country other than Bombay. Further, as vernacular sources[12] indicate, from the 1870s the Bengali bhadralok made serious attempts to spread the game beyond the confines of their own community, an effort hardly replicated by the Parsis.

In existing studies, cricket in Bengal has been confined to the initiatives of the royal families of Natore and Cooch Behar. The death of the Maharaja of Cooch Behar (1911), Edward Docker argues, sounded a death knell of the game in the province:

Before the first war the Maharaja Sir Nripendra Narayan of Cooch-Behar had maintained at his own expense no less than three cricket teams, two based mainly in Calcutta and a third in Darjeeling...Local Calcutta and Bengali cricket prospered tremendously as a result, but in 1911 the Maharaja died in England, and then the other of the two sons who succeeded him died within the following ten years, and a very fruitful period of contact between European and Indian cricket temporarily came to an end. Calcutta, by the early 1920s had simply ceased to be an important centre of Indian cricket, football being all the rage instead.[13]

While acknowledging that the royal families of Natore and Cooch Behar played key roles in promoting cricket in Bengal, it needs to be asserted that such initiatives were part of a broader interest in the game among the educated Bengali middle class.[14] Princely patronage was a later development, which made an appreciable difference from the early twentieth century.

HISTORY OF SPORTS IN COLONIAL BENGAL

Sports in Bengal in the early years of the nineteenth century present a peculiar incongruity. While games like cricket and football were looked upon as exclusive European preserves, indigenous sports like wrestling were confined to the lower classes. The educated middle class remained aloof from all kinds of sporting activity. The following passage in a European travelogue (1843), is telling of the English monopoly over cricket:

In such a climate as that of India those who have never entered through the *ghaut*s of Calcutta might conclude that no such laborious sport as cricket would be pursued there. Yet if the voyager arrived during the comparatively cold season and land in the evening at the Chandpal Ghat, he will at once ascend to the first view of the City of Palaces, looking upon it across a plain forming the most magnificent Cricket Ground in the World, and where the Calcutta Club play regularly. On the Cricket Ground stand two spacious tents, not like the paltry affairs bearing that name in England, but lined with fancy chintz, furnished with looking glasses, sofas, chairs and each player's wants are supplied by his turbaned attendants whether it be a light for his cigar, iced soda water or champagne. The natives do not at all enter into the pleasures of this manly game, neither do the servants of the players, if desired to stop a stray ball, think it at all meritorious to risk stinging their fingers by stopping it while in motion, they amble by its side until it has ceased rolling and then pick it up.[15]

The significance of cricket in Bengal's social life is borne out by the advanced nature of sports writing in the province in the first half of the nineteenth century. Records indicate that most reports on sport in Bengal in the early nineteenth century were in English. These, in most cases, were concerned with cricket, a favourite of the British soldiers and sailors. The earliest sports journals in Bengal, the *Bengal Quarterly Sporting Magazine* and the *India Sporting Review*[16] date back to the 1820s and 1830s. Sports coverage was of a fairly accomplished level and detailed rules of cricket and horse racing were published.

The early sports magazines also printed scorecards and statistics of cricket matches played in and around Calcutta during a season. Detailed year-end statistics on the performances of players was a typical item in such publications.[17] It was cricket's visible presence in Bengal's public life that played a decisive role in attracting educated Indians to the game by the 1870s.

Between 1800 and the 1860s, the bhadralok patronized indigenous sports like wrestling, though they did not themselves participate in such activity. They organized competitions in which their servants fought against each other amidst great excitement and enthusiasm, as attested by the following report from the *Samachar Chandrika*:

A wrestling competition was organised in the garden house of one Raja Baidyanath Roy. There were thirty wrestlers in the fray. The Europeans used to be regular spectators in such events. Palmer *sahib* had a servant built like a giant. He fought against a young servant of Nanda Kumar Tagore. Baidyanath (Nanda Kumar's servant) was the victor and was cheered lustily by the audience present. A delighted Nanda Kumar rewarded the winner with his own gown. All the fighters who entered this competition were duly rewarded from a fund amassed for this purpose.[18]

These reports often extolled the feats of leading Bengali *byambirs*,[19] possibly as an effort to counter the charge of effeminacy labelled against the Bengali male.

This picture underwent a transformation from the second half of the nineteenth century, a transition that may be dated from the 1870s and 1880s. From this period onwards, the educated Bengali middle classes strove to integrate sporting activity, rooted in physical culture, into their everyday lives. This transition may be located in the changed political conditions of Bengal in the aftermath of the Mutiny of 1857.

In the post-mutiny period, the educated Bengali middle class found it imperative to devise an effective strategy to counter the colonial charge of inferiority. Barred from staging violent demonstrations or other acts, which would be symbolic of 'physically challenging' British superiority, educated Indians looked upon 'leisure' pursuits with new eyes. Colonialism and the realities of being a subject population were the conditions that informed Bengali middle-class investment in sport. Drawing upon real life encounters between colonizer and colonized, leisure settings helped provide an exciting imaginary, minus the attendant risks that would otherwise characterize such situations.

That a new breed of Bengali intellectuals extolled the virtues of physical prowess is evident from the following account of an interaction at a gathering in the Sovabazar Palace involving Nagendraprasad Sarbadhikary, leading Bengali sports patron of the time:

... young family member ridiculed Nagendraprasad's powerful stature and stamina saying that a man needed only that much strength that would enable him to drink a glass of water by himself! Surrounded by armed retainers the babus present broke into laughter at the comment. Not amused in the least, Nagendraprasad stunned everyone present by lifting the young man off the ground and asking 'now that I shall fling you down, what do you imagine you will require to escape that fate?' It was only after the man apologised that Nagendraprasad set him down. He declared in disgust, 'those who speak like this—they are the ones who are afraid to step out on the streets with their wives and daughters; and when they do (they) are unable to safeguard their honour. Muslim drivers intimidate them before their wife and daughter, extract double the money due to them, and walk away with a swagger while the *babu* humours himself saying I can't stoop to being a *chotolok* with the *chotoloks*. Such behaviour is not becoming of a *bhadralok* but of a eunuch! The rate of female abductions from the homes of Bengali Hindus is unparalleled in any other community. Bengalis are effete, let them gain in physical strength,— with the return of masculine splendour, will come respect from others ... .'[20]

This investment in physical culture reached a climax with the organization of the World Wrestling Championship under the patronage of the Maharaja of Cooch Behar in 1892.[21]

MOVE TOWARDS EUROPEAN SPORT

It was as part of the new vision outlined above that the bhadralok began their tryst with European sports like cricket, one, which intensified in the 1880s. Noting that the charge of effeminacy continued to be labelled against them, evident during the Ilbert Bill controversy, the bhadralok realized that an investment in physical culture was not enough. Even Swami Vivekananda, the famous Bengali religious and social reformer, imbibed this view. He argued that, 'you will be nearer to god through football than through the Bhagwad Gita.' Children also imbibed the feeling of satisfaction that came from victories in competitions against the British. A passage from the contemporary journal *Sakha* is redolent with these sentiments. The editor recalls a conversation he had one evening with a 'young friend' who reported with glee that he had successfully beaten the sahib in a game of 'bat-ball'. 'I wondered,' he writes,

> ...what is so great about defeating the sahibs? Boys of all nations indulge in play. So what is it that has marked out English boys as superior to their young counterparts especially the Bengalis? The answer lies in the fact that while the *sahib*s play these manly games almost regularly Bengalis are averse to any form of physical exhaustion. Since the sahibs practice athletics, cricket etc. their bodies are strong and they acquire skills, which cannot be matched by the natives. Manly sports are therefore an exclusive English preserve.[22]

It was the act of defeating the colonizer on his own turf that filled his young friend with such glee. This interaction indicates that the 'significance' of defeating the sahibs at their own game had already filtered down to young Bengali boys by the middle of the 1880s.[23]

It might appear from the above account that the proliferation of cricket in Bengal was a linear trajectory, spurred by a desire to simply defeat the sahibs at their own game. The situation, however, was far more complex, and to fully capture its nuances one would need to study the nature of sports organization in Bengal in the period. The principles governing the functioning of the Mohun Bagan Club is a case in point:

> The ideals that the founders had set before themselves were high. At the inception, except for a limited few at the top it was the convention to accept only students as members. Each applicant for membership had to produce his guardian's permission for joining the Club. There was a probationary period of six months. The executives of the Club saw to it that each member combined the development of the body with the development of the mind. They prescribed a high moral code for the members. Some of the old members recall how J.N. Basu would suddenly line up younger members of the Club and test their educational progress in their schools and colleges. A young member was expelled from the club because he was found smoking.[24]

The above description indicates that the object was not simply that of defeating the English at their own game. Rather, initiative was geared toward the fashioning of a new identity and individuality for the Bengali male, and saw a growing bhadralok involvement in the game. In 1884, a Sri Lankan team visited Bengal giving Indians their first taste of international cricket.[25] This was followed by the organization of an international cricket match, played at the Eden Gardens between the Presidency Club and the Australians.[26]

The Prince of Wales, Dadabhai Naoroji, Surendranath Banerjee, and other Congressmen present in Calcutta to attend the second session of the Indian National Congress witnessed this match played at the Eden Gardens.[27] The performance of the Bengali cricketers in this match was commendable enough for them to be invited to a party hosted by His Excellency, the Rear Admiral Freemantle of the battleship HMS Boadecia.[28]

The initiation of organized native cricket by the middle classes in Bengal stimulated the formation of numerous cricket clubs in the 1880s. The Boys Club was the first regular club formed in 1880 by Nagendra Prasad Sarbadhikary. The Howrah Cricket Club, later renamed the Howrah Sporting Club was formed the next year. It was the strongest Indian club in those days and produced renowned cricketers like Bama Charan Coondoo and Bhutnath Chunder. The Town Club, established by Professor Saradaranjan Ray followed. Saradaranjan and his brothers Muktidaranjan and Kuladaranjan collaborated with Zamindar B.K. Ray Chaudhuri in setting up the club. The Town Club became the foremost Indian cricket club in the province, and played an annual fixture against the Calcutta Cricket Club—the premier European team, at the Eden Gardens since 1895. To Saradaranjan also goes the credit for introducing cricket in Aligarh, as Professor of Mathematics at the Aligarh College in 1888-9.[29]

The records of the Mohun Bagan Club indicate that towards the close of the nineteenth century the club had regular fixtures against teams like Town, Aryans, Kumartuli, B.E. College Shibpur, and the Calcutta Medical College. Prominent players of the time were Moni Lal Sen, Dr A.N. Das, Dr Girish Ghosh, Sailen Bose, Ganen Mitter and D.N. Guin.[30] These men hailed from renowned bhadralok families of Calcutta, a reflection of the Bengali middle-class' interest in cricket, one that continued to grow in the early years of the twentieth century.

The premier educational institutions of the city, attended by middle-class students, also bestowed significant patronage on the game. Though the earliest mention of cricket in St Xavier's College goes back to 1860, cricket in this institution gained popularity in the late nineteenth century. There soon developed a culture of matches played against visiting sides. These were elaborate and well-organized events, evident from the following circular sent to the Old Boys of the institution in 1906:

A cricket pavilion has been a long felt want in St. Xavier's College. The school teams have a large number of fixtures during the year on the college ground and it has been suggested that we should have some better means of entertaining our visitors...We appeal to the Old Boys and to the kind friends of St. Xavier's for funds to enable us to erect the pavilion, which will be a permanent memorial of the kindly interest they still take in the institution...[31]

The circular met with a prompt and generous response, with the pavilion fund rising to Rs 400 within a few days.[32] Letters received in support of the initiative point to the growing popularity of cricket in Bengal in the early years of the twentieth century.[33] The tradition of cricket at St Xavier's College was not exceptional and the college cricket club had antecedents in similar initiatives at the Metropolitan College (currently Vidyasagar College) under Professor Saradaranjan Ray[34] and at Presidency College under Professor Bipin Behari Gupta in 1891.

At Presidency College, the earliest mention of cricket dates back to 1879. It received institutional foundation under the superintendence of Professor Bipin Behari Gupta, when students set up a regular cricket and football club in 1891, and a suitable plot of ground on the *maidan* was solicited and acquired for the club's use. The grant was the outcome of an application made to the Commissioner of Police, Calcutta.[35]

School cricket too was firmly established by this time, and the first inter-school cricket tournament in the country, the Harrison Shield, was started in Calcutta in 1887. School cricket was not confined to the metropolis of Calcutta. Leading members of the Presidency College Cricket Club were students from East Bengal, often belonging to families of modest means.[36] Teams from East Bengal colleges and clubs regularly toured West Bengal from the mid-1880s.[37]

The growing importance of cricket in late nineteenth-century Bengal can be discerned from the advertisements of sporting gear published in leading dailies of the 1880s and 1890s.[38] Marketing and promotional strategies were made full use of, pointing to the element of competitiveness among the various concerns.[39] In fact, Indian enterprise in the field had been launched in Bengal in 1895 with Saradaranjan Ray setting up 'S. Ray & Co'. He also wrote the first cricket-coaching manual in Bengali in 1899.[40] To popularize cricket among the masses, Saradaranjan, in this manual, compares cricket with the popular indigenous game of *danda gulli*:

Bengali boys who have not seen or played *danda gulli* are very rare. Cricket can be justifiably described as a variant of *danda gulli*. However, like the great difference in the Bengali and Sahib way of eating fish, there is an even greater difference between the Bengali and Sahib version of *danda gulli*. While the playing of *danda gulli* is a very trivial pursuit for the Bengali, for the Sahib, cricket is a national treasure. The respect accorded to a good cricket player by the *Sahibs* finds no parallel.[41]

The popularity of cricket in Bengal at the close of the nineteenth century is borne out by the glorious reception given to Ranji in Calcutta in January 1899. Contemporary reports indicate that more than 10,000 spectators attended the matches to see Ranji play. On the day of his arrival, players and officials of the city welcomed him at the Howrah station with bouquets and garlands. The Town Club organized a felicitation at the Town Hall incurring an expense of rupees 3,000, a huge sum by contemporary standards.[42]

The growing popularity of cricket, it may be noted, had much to do with a series of changes affecting the social life of the province since the 1860s. In Dhaka, as Sharifuddin Ahmad demonstrates, the twenty years between 1864-84 witnessed considerable progress in civic matters under the tutelage of British civil servants. These men, accustomed to sanitized conditions of living in England, did much for the improvement of civic amenities in Dhaka. Welfare activities undertaken contributed to an improved standard of living in the city. Dhaka, suffering from economic decline since the 1840s, received a great boost from the construction of new roads, improved conservancy, filtered water supply, and health care services. The Municipality undertook the task of filling up tanks and establishing parks and playgrounds, giving a fillip to sport in East Bengal.[43]

In Calcutta, as Amiya Bagchi demonstrates, the Municipal Act of 1888 increased the area under the jurisdiction of the municipality by over 72 per cent. In contrast, population in the city had increased by only 45 per cent.[44] This change, resulting in a lower density of population in the city, it may be surmised, allowed increased space for leisure activities. From 1888, the Municipal area came to include the locales of Chitpur, Maniktala, Kashipur, and Ultadanga. An examination of the location of the city's sporting clubs in the late nineteenth century shows that most of these were located in the newly appended areas.[45] However, sporting facilities were still lacking and it was only in the early years of the twentieth century that the Calcutta Improvement Trust set up a number of parks in the city. Such efforts were significant, because Bengal, as Pradip Sinha shows, was the least urbanized region of India at the end of the nineteenth century. In 1891, the proportion of urban to total population in the province was only 4.8 per cent. In contrast, the Madras urban population bordered around 10 per cent, in Uttar Pradesh around 12 per cent and in Bombay near 20 per cent.[46] Initiatives such as those of the Calcutta Improvement Trust generated an ambience for heightened sporting activity in Bengal from the beginning of the twentieth century.

From the early twentieth century, Presidency, St Xavier's, and Vidyasagar Colleges had regular fixtures with local club sides and hosted teams from other parts of the country.[47] Bombay's Elphinstone College had undertaken a series of cricket tours to various parts of the country between 1903–13, playing a series of matches in Calcutta.[48] The college magazines of this period are full of reports that speak of a thriving cricket culture in these institutions. The Vidyasagar College magazine of September 1926 mentions that in 1916–17, students of the college played cricket, football, hockey, and tennis. They played 28 cricket matches, registering victories in 25 of these encounters. They won the Hardinge Shield, the Lansdowne Shield, and the Senior Harrison Shield tournaments. Saradaranjan Ray, the principal of the college was himself a great cricketer and played a pivotal role in promoting cricket among the students of the institution. In September 1911, the College Council, to commemorate the visit of the Governor General, proposed the institution of prizes for the encouragement of cricket among the students of the college, and the boys of the school attached to it. The proposal was conveyed to the Private Secretary of the Governor General on 28 February 1911 and was gracefully accepted by the dignitary. On 4 March 1911 the Secretary communicated that the Governor General had no objection to the institution of prizes, as he too had been captain of his own college team.[49] On receipt of this letter, six prizes designated 'Hardinge Prizes', two in each department of the game; batting, bowling, and fielding were instituted. The annual value of the prizes was fixed at Rs 160, no mean sum by contemporary standards.[50] The advanced nature of the game in the educational institutions is evident from the number of trophies competed for by the schools and colleges. There were three annual tournaments.[51] While the Junior Harrison Shield was a competition for boys under 18 years of age, the Senior Harrison Shield was a college students' affair. The Lansdowne Shield, presented by Lord Lansdowne when he was

Viceroy, was to be played for annually by Indian students' clubs of the various Calcutta Colleges.⁵²

What is unique about the game's promotion in the educational institutions in Bengal is the deep-rooted urge to use cricket as a means to challenge British rule. This is best exemplified by the history of sport at Presidency College, Calcutta, the foremost symbol of middle-class ascendancy in colonial Bengal. At Presidency, a gymnastics class for the college students was started in 1856 but was abandoned a year later. The class was resumed in 1879, a year after the passing of the oppressive Vernacular Press Act.⁵³

In the 1880s, when nationalist resistance in Bengal was gathering momentum, the sporting field contributed in a large measure to challenging British supremacy. From the early years of the nineteenth century, the British had attempted to portray the Bengali male as effete, a portrayal that acquired a specific connotation by the late nineteenth century. By this time, it was directed almost exclusively at the educated Bengali middle classes. It is hardly surprising, therefore, that the gymnastics class was made compulsory for all students of the college in 1891, soon after the Age of Consent controversy.⁵⁴ Rigorous physical exercise, it was thought, was a way to counter to the British stereotype of the effeminate Bengali. The move to playing cricket and football is not a coincidence either. The realization that cultivation of masculine strength by participating in indigenous sports like wrestling and bodybuilding were not enough prompted the shift to cricket and football. The futility of the physical culture movement, as evidenced during the Age of Consent controversy, determined the shift to 'manly' colonial sports like cricket, football, and tennis.

Not surprisingly therefore, the first decade and a half of the twentieth century was the golden age of sport in the leading educational institutions of Bengal,⁵⁵ a period of heightened nationalist resistance. The Swadeshi movement, a concerted campaign against the partition of Bengal, which eventually led to the annulment of partition in 1911, and a phase of revolutionary terrorism marked the political life of Bengal in the period.⁵⁶ In the first decade of the twentieth century, when nationalist resistance was at its peak, the Presidency College won the Elliot Shield, the premier intercollege soccer tournament for five years in succession between 1904–8.⁵⁷ In 1912, all major intercollege football competitions were won by the college. The importance given to sport is evident from the detailed reports published in the college magazine soon after it was started in 1914.

The first cricket match described in detail in the college magazine is one against the European Calcutta Cricket Club played at the Eden Gardens. 'In 1907 in an exciting match, Sri P.C. Ray tells us, the College defeated the formidable Calcutta Cricket Club at the Eden Gardens by one wicket. Debendra Lahiri scored 90 not out, a remarkable performance for those days.'[58] This was a historic triumph and was reported in vernacular journals of the period. The college secured the double in 1912-13 winning the Lansdowne and Harrisson Shields. In 1914-15 and 1916-17 they drew against the Calcutta Cricket Club.[59] However, in 1914, when the college lost to the all European La Martiniere side, the players were severely criticized.[60] This draws our attention to the importance attached to winning, more so against European institutions:

But the big defeat of the college team by La Martiniere College cannot be forgiven. The conduct of some of the players on that day was anything but sportsmanlike. The game was supposed to commence at 11 o'clock punctually, but after the toss there were only four or five players present. The result, of course, was a foregone conclusion; a lost match and a loss of prestige for the college team.[61]

It is striking to note that almost every year the annual report on the cricket season in the college magazine included detailed comments on the match against the Calcutta Cricket Club. Even when the report is a relatively smaller one in comparison to other years, this match is never left unmentioned. The 1928 cricket report, a comparatively small one, went thus:

We have had very strong fixtures this season. Up to this date games have mostly been drawn ones, including the games with H E Governors XI and with the Calcutta CC. These games drew admiration from the local press for our team. Our performance was also highly praised by His Excellency the Governor and Hon. Lady Jackson as well as by other distinguished visitors. Ardhendu Das's brilliant 56 not out, attracted the notice of distant papers like the *Times of India* of Bombay. Ardhendu Das and Bishnu Sarkar (Captain) have been honoured by His Excellency's invitation to play for his team against the Anglo-Indians. H E the Governor told the Captain that he would ask Messrs Lagden, Hosie, Lee, and others of the Calcutta Cricket Club to coach our players from the next season.[62]

In the next year, though the cricket report was an even smaller one, the college's performance against the Calcutta Cricket Club and the Governor's XI was described in detail:

We had a very strong fixture this session. The games have mostly been drawn including the games with H E the Governors XI and with the Calcutta CC. Our captain, Mr B Sirkar and Mr Ardhendu Das deserve special mention; as they were included in His Excellency's cricket team, an honor which comes rarely to few players of Bengal.[63]

The match against the Calcutta Cricket Club, it may be surmised, was the central attraction of the college's cricket season and its temporary discontinuance in the early 1930s resulted in a decline in the college's cricket fixtures. By the 1920's therefore, Bengal cricket had acquired considerable prominence, and teams from Bengal could easily compete with the best teams of the country.

In East Bengal too, the period between 1900-20 witnessed a spurt in cricket enthusiasm. The partition of Bengal in 1905 had, as Ratan Lal Chakrabarty argues, re-established Dhaka's eminence as a capital of Bengal after a period of nearly two hundred years. As the capital of Eastern Bengal and Assam, Dhaka received a host of grants from the government that contributed to improving living standards in the city.

Though the annulment of the partition in 1911 once again reduced Dhaka to the status of a district town, the annulment was accompanied by some compensatory promises from the government. Among these was the promise to establish the University of Dhaka, an institution that later emerged as a hotbed of sporting activity. The establishment of the university contributed to enhanced economic, intellectual, and political activity in the city, with sport becoming an integral part of student life at the university. However, with the institution developing into a hub of nationalist activity, governmental investment declined from the late 1920s, leading to a gradual decline in sporting activity.[64]

DOWNTURN AND REVIVAL

By the 1940s, the well established tradition of cricket in Bengal waned, Bombay perpetuating its hegemony over Indian cricket in the 1930s and 1940s. In this phase, Bengal cricket gradually lost out to Bombay, failing to come to terms with a rapidly changing political and economic milieu. The history of Bengal cricket from the third decade of the twentieth century speaks of the fate of a sport that failed to come to terms with the forces of urbanization and commercialization. The atmosphere of political and economic uncertainty that had gripped the province during and after the Civil Disobedience movement gathered momentum in the 1940s, seriously affected the fortunes of the game. The period of political turmoil in the decades preceding partition, coupled with the atmosphere of economic uncertainty prevailing in the province eventually relegated cricket to a secondary status in Bengal's public imaginary.

The situation finally underwent a transformation following India's victory in the Prudential World Cup in 1983. This victory brought in its wake an unparalleled commercialization of the game, transforming cricket into the country's foremost national passion. The victory initiated a trend of huge investments in cricket all over the country, including Bengal, leading to a resurgence of cricket among the middle classes. Cricket was not elite leisure; in the 1980s and 1990s the game transcended this barrier. With corporate investment bolstering the game, it became once again a career option for the middle classes—in the 1990s the middle-class dreamboat. The growing interest in the sport saw the setting up of a series of cricket coaching clinics in Bengal, ones that soon competed with the noted educational institutions of the region as centres of excellence.

CONCLUSION

In conclusion it can be argued that the Bengalis did not play cricket simply to be like the British and to then defeat them on their own turf. Bengali cricket was not simply an act of mimicry,[65] but was conceived of as a tool for remedying deeper, more serious allegations that underplayed native abilities. The roots of Bengal cricket went deep—to help permeate ideas of self-respect, manliness, and self-worth among the natives. Educated men from middle-class backgrounds promoted cricket, trying to legitimize physical activity in Bengali society and win respect for the players. The sport emerged as the mirror wherein an Indian/Bengali identity started to reassess itself, and in that sense Bengal cricket was certainly part of a nationalist enterprise.

At the same time, the genesis of cricket in Bengal cannot be explained merely in terms of the urge to valorize native physical culture. The latter had been tried and marginalized as a project towards the end of the nineteenth century. *Akharas* and indigenous games had failed to gain the kind of social pervasiveness a European sport like cricket enjoyed, factors that go to explain the continued popularity of cricket in post-independence India.

Despite its political character, cricket was accompanied by no discernible radical intonation associated with other proto-nationalist ventures, which led to their suppression. Sport, therefore, emerged as a sphere of competition sans violence. It was this element that made cricket a safe haven where sentiments pertaining to the inculcation of self-worth and strength of character could be articulated without the tension and fury that would accompany them in the 'political' sphere.

What the Bengal story draws attention to is that one cannot claim to write a social history of 'Indian' cricket by simply looking at the history of the game in one province or region. By studying cricket as a middle-class investment in colonial Bengal, I have tried to dwell on the whole question of the relationship between leisure and middle-class identity, which continues to animate Indian history even after the demise of colonialism.

NOTES

1. J. A. Mangan (ed.) *A Sport-Loving Society: Victorian and Edwardian Middle-Class England at Play.* (London, 2005), pp. 1.

2. In most works on the history of Indian cricket there is little mention of any cricketing tradition in Bengal, except that the Calcutta Cricket Club had been founded in 1792. Even this is incorrect as has been demonstrated in this paper. For details see, Ramchandra Guha, *'Cricket and Politics in Colonial India', Past and Present,* 161, (November 1998), p. 158; Edward Docker, *History of Indian Cricket,* (Delhi, 1976); Richard Cashman, *Patrons, Players and the Crowd,* (Calcutta: Orient Longman, 1979); Arjun Appadurai, 'Playing with Modernity: Decolonization of Indian Cricket', in Carol Breckenridge (ed.), *Consuming Modernity: Public Culture in Contemporary India,* (New Delhi, 1996); Sandeep Bamzai, *Guts and Glory: The Bombay Cricket Story,* (Calcutta, 2002).

3. *The Madras Courier* of 22-3 December 1792 carries the report that on both these days the Calcutta Cricket Club played competitive cricket against the Gentlemen of Barrackpore and Dumdum. This entry in the Madras Courier has hitherto been identified as the date when the Calcutta Cricket Club was founded.

4. *Bengal Gazette,* 16 December 1780; Major H. Hobbes, V.D., *John Barley Corn Bahadur: Old Time Taverns In India,* (Calcutta, 1944), pp. 436-7.

5. Narendranath Ganguly, *Calcutta Cricket Club: Its Origin and Development,* (Calcutta: Calcutta Historical Society, 1936); Thomas Rebeiro (ed.), *Bengal Quarterly Sporting Magazine,* vol. 1: 4, (1844), p. 433; *The Calcutta Monthly Journal,* (1836), p. 71.

6. Cf. Mankasji Kawasji Patel, *A History of Parsi Cricket* (Bombay, 1892).

7. J.A. Mangan (ed.), *Pleasure Profit Proselytism: British culture and sport at home and abroad, 1700-1914* (London, 1988); J.A. Mangan (ed.), *The Cultural Bond: Sport Empire Society* (London, 1992).

8. For an analysis of how and why the game's ethic was subverted in the colonies see, Richard Cashman, 'Cricket and Colonialism: Colonial Hegemony and Indigenous Subversion', in Mangan (ed.), *Pleasure Profit Proselytism*, pp. 259-60.

9. Generally accepted as the world's oldest cricket club founded in 1787.

10. David Cooper, 'Canadians Declare, "It Isn't Cricket": A Century of Rejection of the Imperial Game: 1860-1960', in *Journal of Sport History*, Spring (1999), pp. 52-3.

11. Cashman, *Patrons, Players and the Crowd*, pp. 22-3.

12. Most of the vernacular journals published in Bengal carried detailed accounts on cricket. This trend may be traced back to the 1890s. Journals like *Mukul, Sakha, Pradip, Manasi, Manasi o Marmabani, Tarpan, and Sandesh*, edited and published by leading Bengali intellectuals, published accounts of cricket matches. *Tarpan* had dedicated a whole issue to Saradaranjan Ray, hailed as the father of Bengal cricket, after his demise in 1925.

13. Docker, *History of Indian Cricket*, pp. 8-9; For similar views, see Appadurai, 'Playing with Modernity'.

14. This fact hardly finds mention in existing works on Indian cricket, which equates the early phase of Indian cricket with a phase of princely patronage. It is erroneously appraised that 'cricket, as an elite sport, required the sort of time and money not available to the bourgeois elites of colonial India'. Appadurai, 'Playing with Modernity', p. 29; Nissim Mannathukaren, 'Subalterns, Cricket and the "Nation": The Silences of Lagaan', *Economic and Political Weekly*, 8 December (2001), pp. 4580-4.

15. George W. Johnson, *Three Years in Calcutta, Or Stranger in India*, (London, 1843), pp. 60-3.

16. *Bengal Quarterly Sporting Magazine*, vol. 1: 4, (1844); *India Sporting Review* (Calcutta: 1845).

17. *India Sporting Review*, (1845).

18. Anil Chandra Ghosh, *Byame Bangali* (Calcutta, 1928), p.100.

19. They were men renowned for their physical strength. The stories of these men taking on the might of their foes are part of Bengali folklore. For a large number of such stories celebrating the feats of leading Bengali byambirs, see Ghosh, *Byame Bangali*.

20. Saurindra Kumar Ghosh, *Krida Samrat Nagendra Prasad Sarbadhikary 1869-1940*, (Calcutta, 1964), pp.180-1.

21. Moti Nandy, 'Sports in Calcutta', in Sukanta Chaudhuri (ed.), *Calcutta—The Living City*, (Calcutta, 1990), p. 328.

22. *Sakha*, vol. 12, December (1883); Also see *Sakha*, February, (1891).

23. Bengalis took similar pride in the achievements of their Parsi counterparts. Commenting on the Parsi victory against the touring English side led by G.F. Vernon, the Bengali journal *Sakha* urged the Bengalis to take pride from the Parsi victory and motivate themselves to achieve similar feats on the sporting field. The notion, that defeating the English at their own game was no mean achievement was not unique to Bengal. Rather, as W.H. Mandle has argued sighting the case of Australia, 'The drawing of parallels from the example of manly sports, especially from cricket, was an Anglo-Saxon habit in the nineteenth century, and the assertion that ability at cricket indicated

national superiority was commonplace. Some examples of the English variety of chauvinism may serve to demonstrate the nature of the weight placed upon cricket as an indicator of national strength and moral cricket. The *Quarterly Review* of October 1857 favourably compared games playing English public school boy with the 'pale faced student of Germany, or the over taught pupil of the French polytechnique'. The Englishman had nothing to fear from them, games had given him pluck, blood, and bottom', Mandle, 'Cricket and Australian Nationalism in the Nineteenth Century'.

24. *Mohun Bagan Platinum Jubilee Souvenir*, (Calcutta, 1964), p. 4.
25. S.S. Perera, *The Janashakthi Book of Sri Lanka Cricket*, (Colombo, 1999), p. 50.
26. Ghosh, *Krida Samrat*, pp. 125-6.
27. Ibid., p.124.
28. Ibid., p.126.
29. Kiran Bala Ray and Kamala Bala Ray (eds), *Tarpan: Saradaranjan Sankhya*, (BS, 1332).
30. *Mohun Bagan Platinum Jubilee Souvenir*, p. 131.
31. *The Xaverian* (Calcutta, 1906), p. 10.
32. Ibid.
33. Ibid., p.11.
34. *Sakha*, February (1890), p. 25; *Sandesh*, November (1925), p. 293.
35. *Presidency College Register* (Calcutta, 1927), pp.28-9.
36. Ibid., p. 24.
37. Ibid., February (1891), p. 24; *Sandesh*, November (1925), p. 292.
38. *The Statesman, Amrita Bazar Patrika,* and *The Englishman* carry numerous advertisements of sports equipment and gear from the 1880s. These advertisements point to the prominence of sport in social life, a fact also attested by the proliferation of sports goods shops in Bengal in the late nineteenth and early twentieth century.
39. *The Statesman*, 22 January (1901). The text of the advertisement read: CRICKET BATS, Ours are the cheapest, because they are priced the lowest and last the longest and because with every bat above 10 we give a superfine quality extra stout rubber bat handle free. S.Ray & Co,, 62, Bowbazar Street, Calcutta, Patronized by the Calcutta Cricket Club.
40. Saradaranjan Ray, 'Cricket khela', in Siddhartha Ghosh and Prasadranjan Ray, *Cricket Majar Cricket*, (Calcutta, 1999), pp. 130-6.
41. Ibid.
42. Ibid., pp. 131-2.
43. Sarifuddin Ahmad, *Dhaka: Itihas O Nagar Jiban*, (Dhaka, 2001), pp. 196-256.
44. Amiya Kumar Bagchi, 'Wealth and Work in Calcutta: 1860-1921' in Sukanta Chaudhuri (ed.), *Calcutta—The Living City*, pp. 212-23.
45. Mohun Bagan, Sovabazar, Kumartuli, and other sporting clubs were all located in north Calcutta, in the areas newly added to the city's municipality.
46. Pradip Sinha, 'Calcutta and the Currents of History', in Sukanta Chaudhuri (ed.), *Calcutta—The Living City*, pp. 31-44.
47. Detailed reports of matches played by these colleges are to be found

in the publications brought out by these institutions. Each year's magazine contained reports of that year's sporting activities under separate headings, such as, Soccer, Cricket, Hockey, and other sports.

48. For a detailed report of these tours see J.D. Antia, *Elphinstone College Tours* (Bombay, 1913).
49. *Vidyasagar College Magazine* (1925–26).
50. Ibid.
51. *St Xavier's College Magazine* (1909–10).
52. Ibid.
53. The Vernacular Press Act, passed in 1878 by Lord Lytton, was one in a series of oppressive acts passed by the colonial state to curb nationalist tendencies among the Indians.
54. *Presidency College Register*, p. 27.
55. As a case study, see, *Presidency College Centenary Volume*, pp. 191–202; *Presidency College Register*, pp. 27–32.
56. For details on the political climate of Bengal in the first decade of the twentieth century see, Sumit Sarkar, *Swadeshi Movement in Bengal—1903–1908* (New Delhi, 1973).
57. *Presidency College Centenary Volume*, pp. 191–202.
58. Ibid., p. 197.
59. Ibid.
60. *Presidency College Magazine* (1914–15), p. 296.
61. Ibid.
62. Ibid. (1928), p.185.
63. Ibid. (1929), p.91.
64. Interview with Dr Sharifuddin Ahmad at the Bangladesh National Archives, Dhaka, 6 September (2001).
65. For an entirely different understanding of mimicry, see Homi Bhabha, *The Location of Culture* (London, 1994).

Middle-class Cinema*

M. MADHAVA PRASAD

[...] This chapter deals with the realist cinema of the subject, or what is commonly known as the middle-class cinema. In *Sara Akash* ('The Whole Sky', 1969) the urban middle-class world is treated with a solicitous detachment that was to disappear with the further development of the middle-class cinema. This mild trace of ethnographic objectification is a sign that [Basu] Chatterji had not as yet recognized the possibilities of a cinema of identification based on realist principles. The interventionist agenda of the FFC [Film Finance Corporation of India] project and the freedom from considerations of marketability no doubt contributed to this. The objectification effect in *Sara Akash* is achieved through an emphasis on the characters' immersion in a feudal culture, although the joint family home in which the story unfolds is located in an urban milieu. The potential for a cinema of identification was still concealed by the burden of ethnographic distancing which the FFC's realist programme placed on the film-maker. [...] [T]he story deals with the problem of modern individuals still caught up in a network of feudal customs and mental habits. A university student marries an educated woman but both are in the grip of family traditions which determine their lives. The marriage is arranged by the family. Unhappy with a relationship brought about in this manner, the hero rejects the woman, while his family burdens

---

*Originally published as 'Middle Class Cinema', in M. Madhava Prasad, *Ideology of the Hindi Film: A Historical Construction* (New Delhi: Oxford India Paperbacks, 2000), pp. 160–87. For the complete text see the original. In the present version, some portions of the essay have been removed and notes rearranged accordingly.

her with all the housework. When she goes away to her parental home, the hero finds himself missing her company. A reconciliation is brought about when, after her return the wife becomes more assertive and rejects him.

While employing the imagery of feudalism to effect an ethnographic distancing, the film does not undertake a critique of feudalism. Instead, it attributes the failure of the couple's union to their shyness and immaturity. The film tries to produce a nuclear couple within the confines of an extended family. Since both members are educated, there is a possibility of their overcoming the initial extraneous compulsion that brought them together and of establishing intimacy. In their ability to do so lies the value of the aesthetic: to wrest from the feudal space a couple who can be relocated in the space of modernity. In this task it is equally necessary to distance the feudal structure of the extended family as well as foreground the couple as the object of our sympathy. A visit to the cinema is an important moment in the film: the scene where the couple walk to the theatre, with the wife walking several steps behind the husband, heightens the pleasures of realism. On the one hand, the ethnographic interest is aroused by the recognition of the image: who has not seen such a phenomenon? (The answer of course is: those who walk like that, in single file; but the pleasure of recognition that realism offers us is not diluted by such reminders of realism's institutional/class determination.) On the other hand, the narrative proceeds to 'demonstrate' that the possibility of closing the gap between husband and wife depends on a process of psychic, rather than social, reform.

The middle-class cinema is predominantly characterized by an emphasis on the extended familial network as the proper site of production of nuclear couples. Even when, as in *Rajnigandha*, no such common ground of kinship is suggested, the idea of *endogamy* is strongly inscribed in the narrative delineation of the class. This is because middle-class narratives are confined to the world of the upper castes. These castes find themselves dispersed in an urban world, and define themselves as the middle class in the language of the modern state, while maintaining their endogamous identities. In deference to the semiotic prohibition which inaugurates the modern state, the caste identity of this urban society is generally concealed behind the term 'middle class'. It is thus that the paradoxical thematics of 'class endogamy' emerge as a narrative element in films like *Guddi* and *Rajnigandha*.

The middle class, however, also carries the burden of national identity on its shoulders. While one sector of the middle-class cinema represents a community hemmed in by the larger society and devoted to its own reproduction, there is another that presents the class' national profile, its reformist role in the drama of class and religious conflicts within the nation-state. Here the realist aesthetic draws upon the tradition of Gandhian melodrama, including Bimal Roy's *Sujata* and *Bandini*, and the films of his pupil Hrishikesh Mukherjee from before the FFC era, such as *Ashirwad* and *Satyakam*.

Thus, there are two broad sectors of the middle-class cinema, of which one is oriented towards asserting the role of the class while the other is committed to the construction of an exclusive space of class identity. While the first sector enjoyed a strong pre-FFC history, in the post-FFC era it was redefined around the political pressures of the moment. Three significant films of this type are *Anand*, *Namak Haram* (both by Hrishikesh Mukherjee), and *Mere Apne* (Gulzar). All three take up the question of national and class reconciliation in a period of political crisis.

The second-sector, concerned with the consolidation of middle-class (upper-caste) identity, can be further divided into three sub-types based on thematic differences. The first sub-type would include films like *Guddi* and *Rajnigandha*, both of which raise the question of the threat to class identity posed by the lures of the outside world, to which women in particular are susceptible. The second sub-type includes *Abhiman*, *Kora Kagaz,* and *Aandhi* where the post-marital tensions of the middle-class family arise from the ambitions and individualistic tendencies of one or both the partners. Films of the first sub-type differ from the second mainly in that they resolve the conflicts prior to marital union. The third sub-type includes films which take up the question of the space for middle-class existence, the dependence of middle-class life on the possibility of privacy. [...]

NARRATIVES OF NATIONAL RECONCILIATION

National reconciliation acquired urgency in the context of the disaggregation of the social already discussed. Martyrdom is the cleansing event which produces the possibilities of reconciliation in all the three films in this category. In *Mere Apne*, the martyr is an old peasant woman. In *Anand* and *Namak Haram*, he is a middle-class individual (played by Rajesh Khanna) who rises above the conflicts that surround him and reunites a divided world by dying.

In *Mere Apne* ('My Dear Ones', Gulzar, 1971), an old woman is brought to the city by her relative who needs household help, while he and his wife go out to work. The woman is thrown out when she questions the exploitative motive behind the altruistic gesture, and finds refuge in an old ruined building where two orphans live. A student gang leader, estranged from his family, also spends his nights there. In the midst of daily confrontations between two rival youth gangs, the woman's motherly affection and innocent and upright behaviour win the hearts of the gang members. At election time the two gangs are hired by rival candidates. In the explosion of campaign violence, the woman is killed by a police bullet as she tries to stop the street fighting between the gangs.

During a conversation with the gang members, the old widow recounts an event from her past which identifies her as a patriotic woman along the lines of the heroines of *Bandini*, *Mother India*, and the Tamil film *Anda Naal* (1954). Set in pre-independence India, the flashback recounts the events of a night when the woman and her husband hid a freedom fighter who was being pursued by the police in their bedroom. This scene serves as a reminder of the sacrifices made in the past to produce the community which is now breaking apart.

A conversation between some gang members at the beginning establishes the film's reading of the contemporary world. Socialism has become a mere collection of empty slogans which all parties, including communal ones, use indiscriminately. On the other hand, the blood ties which united people in the past have become an excuse for exploitation. The well-to-do extract free labour by using the rhetoric of kinship while the poor and the young find themselves helpless in a world in which parents and college principals do not understand their idealism or the frustrations of the unemployed. The woman functions as the agent of an infusion of binding affect into a world divided by class and generational conflict.

While the peasant woman is the textual agent of resolution, the affect deployed in the movement towards resolution is a complex one, combining values drawn from several sources. One such source is the village, which figures in the text as an 'elsewhere', untouched by the conflicts that are tearing the urban community apart. Another source is the past, the history of nationalist struggle, of which the woman serves as a reminder. Thirdly, there is the maternal element that the peasant woman brings to the urban scene. The hero's disaffection with the world is partly attributed to the fact that his mother died early. The only urban mother in the film is the wife of the peasant woman's relative. She is a working woman with a character that is completely negative. She colludes with the husband in exploiting relatives as unpaid servants and readily abandons her child to the servant's care in order to enjoy the pleasures of the city. Finally, part of the affect is also drawn from the star system. The legendary actress Meena Kumari is cast as the peasant woman while young trainees of the Film Institute play the roles of the gang members. The nostalgia evoked by the presence of Meena Kumari, combined with the emerging star identities of actors like Vinod Khanna and Shatrughan Sinha, enabled a textual compromise between old and new which reinforced the narrative drive towards a resolution of present conflicts through the restoration of links with the past and the far away.

In *Anand* and *Namak Haram*, the martyr figure is male and clearly identified as belonging to the urban middle class, Nevertheless, Anand, the eponymous hero of the first film, is closer to the woman in *Mere Apne* in being a figure of national reconciliation whereas *Namak Haram* directly takes up the question of class struggle. The story of *Anand* (Hrishikesh Mukherjee, 1970) is narrated by a doctor. The film opens in a literary gathering where Dr Banerji (Amitabh Bachchan), is being honoured for a novel based on his diary entries about a man who defied death by living life to the full and spreading happiness wherever he went. In his address to the assembly, the doctor recalls his own state of mind at the point of time when Anand (Rajesh Khanna) first came into his life. An idealist, Banerji had devoted himself to treating the poor who could not afford to pay for his treatment or buy the medicines they needed to recover from their illnesses. His helplessness against the social 'diseases' of poverty and unemployment had driven him to a state of utter despondency. At this point a fellow doctor and friend who runs a small hospital informs him of the imminent arrival from Delhi of a patient with a fatal illness. Anand arrives, a day early, and with his charming ways, endears himself to all. He becomes a living enigma for everyone around him. He knows that he does not have long to live but will not let that spoil his fun. Doctor Banerji feels angry with himself for being unable to cure him. Moving into Banerji's house, Anand hides his own private anguish and involves himself in good deeds. He reunites the doctor with his girlfriend (Sumita Sanyal), whom he had neglected in his idealist pursuits. He adopts doctor Prakash's wife as his sister, the matron in the hospital, Sister D'Souza (Lalita Pawar), as his mother, and a theatre owner,

Isabhai (Johnny Walker), as a friend. Hindu, Christian, and Muslim pray to their respective gods for the health of Anand. On his deathbed Anand asks for a tape of Banerji's poetry to be played and he dies as the poem ends. When Banerji, who was away, returns with some medicine, Anand and his laughter, taped inadvertently, bursts forth to break the spell of grief. The last words in the film, spoken by Banerji are 'Anand is not dead, anand (joy) does not die.'

In *Anand* as in *Mere Apne* the central character comes from elsewhere and brings purpose and meaning into the lives of those who were drifting apart and sinking into despondency. Anand functions as a focus for the scattered, free-floating affect of his acquaintances. Failing in their commitment to social causes, they take him up as a surrogate cause. He is an exemplary figure who teaches the despondent to value all that life offers. In contrast, Dr Banerji's clear and unambiguous perception of the evils of society makes him despair. As a doctor he rejects the path taken by his friend Prakash (Ramesh Deo) who thrives on the anxieties of his rich patients. On the other hand, he perceives that society is plagued by evils that are for the most part beyond the healing power of medicine. His clarity of vision makes him anxious. The arrival of Anand serves as a distraction from this anxiety. Anand is an enigma. In a world whose reality had seemed so transparent to Banerji a moment ago, there now appears a mystery. The paralysing effect of intellectual clarity is reduced as the enigma reactivates the emotions. The centripetal force of the enigma effects a displacement so that the spectator can participate in a surrogate resolution for the world's problems.

In *Namak Haram* ('Traitor', Hrishikesh Mukherjee 1973), the martyr is explicitly named as a member of the middle class. The film is roughly modelled on the Richard Burton and Peter O'Toole starrer *Beckett*. Somu (Rajesh Khanna), a middle-class youth, and Vijay (Amitabh Bachchan), a big industrialist's son, are close friends. When Vijay takes over the running of a factory, he refuses to concede a legitimate demand for compensation and abuses the trade union leader (A.K. Hangal). Faced with a strike, he is forced to apologize to the union leader. Swearing vengeance, he recounts the whole affair to Somu. The latter offers to help him. Joining the factory as a worker, Somu (now called Chander), with the help of Vijay, scores a couple of successes as a self-proclaimed workers' leader. His popularity grows as the workers find that his confrontationist ways pay quicker dividends than the old union leader's slow, rule-bound methods. He defeats the old leader in the union elections. Having had his revenge, Vijay wants Somu to leave the job and go back to his old life. But Somu, having lived in the workers' colony and become acquainted with their misery, has had a change of heart. Vijay's father (Om Shivpuri), who believes in the policy of divide-and-rule, realizes the threat posed by a middle-class man whose conscience has been awakened. He deliberately exposes Somu's real identity before the workers. When the workers turn against him, it is the old trade union leader, who has recognized Somu's change of heart, who defends him. Vijay goes to the slum to bring his friend back but Somu declares his intention of staying on with the workers. Rejected, Vijay prepares to fly to another part of the country where his father is setting up a factory. In his absence, the father hires some criminals to get rid of Somu. Vijay misses his flight, and on returning home, learns about the plot. He arrives too late to save his friend, who is run over by a lorry. Knowing that his father is too powerful to be convicted of a crime, Vijay takes the blame for the murder on himself and goes to prison. [...]

At the heart of the film is a long speech by the industrialist who tells his son about the unreliability of the middle class. They are usually pliable and can be useful, but every now and then, when their conscience is aroused, one of them decides to aspire for greatness. Somu, fulfilling this prophecy, becomes a martyr to the cause of working-class rights. But in the process he also unites the classes: Vijay rejects his father's divide-and-rule strategy as anti-national and pledges to continue Somu's struggle. In terms of the film this does not mean Vijay's transformation into a trade union leader but a process of reform whereby capitalists abandon their loyalty to British values and enter into a mutually beneficial pact with workers. The virtues of socialism are proclaimed in the film by Vijay's girlfriend, daughter of another industrialist. The camp of capitalists is thus shown to be internally divided and containing the seeds of a self-transformation. The middle-class martyr functions as a catalyst of reform, cleansing the capitalist class of its colonial habits.

In these narratives, political conflicts are resolved by aesthetic and affective infusions mediated by disinterested subjects whose power lies in their ability to serve as distractions. Gandhi is the prototype for this magnetic point, whose charismatic power draws the spectator into the fiction of a surrogate resolution and liberates her/him temporarily from the obligation of decisive action imposed by intellectual clarity. These narratives thus propose a non-political resolution of political conflicts as the middle-class' contribution to national cohesion. They assert the role of the middle class as a depoliticizing influence, as a repository of affect that absorbs and neutralizes class conflict.

The second type of middle-class narrative, on the other hand, attempts to represent the class as struggling to maintain its unity and identity in the face of disruptive intrusions and external pressures. Hrishikesh Mukherjee bridges these two segments. Firmly committed initially to Gandhian melodrama, which portrayed the middle class as the force of national reconciliation and reform, Mukherjee turned, with *Guddi*, to the new aesthetic of identity in which middle-class isolationism was the primary theme. The two forces that threaten middle-class identity in these films are sexuality and politics.

THE MIDDLE CLASS AS ENDOGAMOUS UNIT

In *Guddi* (Hrishikesh Mukherjee 1971), the sexual economy of a middle-class upper caste extended family is disrupted by the lure of the cinema. *Guddi* is the pet name of Kusum (Jaya Bhaduri), a charming school girl who is obsessed with the film star Dharmendra, who plays himself in the film. A chance meeting with the star turns this fan's admiration into a serious sublimated love for him which is modelled on the medieval saint Meera's love for the god Krishna, a love that is unrequitable but eternal. The change is registered by of a linguistic shift, with Kusum adopting the grandiose prose of popular film dialogue. This love threatens the endogamous network within which she has been marked out as the future wife of Navin (Samit Bhanja), her brother-in-law, an engineer from Bombay who is in search of a job. A visit to Bombay provides an opportunity for visiting the studios, where her uncle (Utpal Dutt), entering into a secret pact with the star, introduces Kusum to the 'reality' behind the images seen on the screen: the low-paid workers, the screen villains who are kind souls in real life, the stuntmen who substitute for the stars in fight sequences, and other 'real' characters. She also discovers her friend's brother (Asrani), who had run away to Bombay to be a film star, working as an extra and struggling to stay alive. These revelations apart, the star and the uncle, in a patriarchal plot to direct the girl's desire towards the legitimate object, provide opportunities for Navin's courage and masculinity to be revealed in a dramatic form. Kusum's education, a two-pronged process of demystification of the cinematic image and a remystification of the legitimate male's image and the patriarchal system, is complete when she expresses her love for Navin of her own will.

Hrishikesh Mukherjee, the maker of *Guddi*, was one of the people involved in the implementation of the new FFC policy. He also played an important role in transferring the realist aesthetic to the commercial sector. In this context, *Guddi* can be read as an ingenious allegorical representation of the construction of a constituency for the realist sub-sector of the commercial cinema. The subject who is liberated from the spell of commercial cinema in the film, is also the subject who is addressed by the film. As we watch Guddi maturing into responsible middle-class womanhood, we too go through a process of maturation at the end of which we, and Guddi with us, become rational, intelligent film-goers. Through our privileged access to the machinations of the well-intentioned men who undertake to educate Guddi, we become partners in an operation to reclaim the middle-class woman from her captivity to an irrational obsession. [...]

Guddi [...] offers a narrative suffused with iconic and situational authenticity, inviting spectator identification. At the same time it softens the critique of popular cinema through a 'disclosure' of the human world behind the illusion. The film industry emerges from the process unscathed, with the stars absolved of any blame for the fantasies the industry puts into circulation. One of the devices employed to produce a 'realist' effect in the film is that of 'not going to the cinema'. Guddi and Navin set out to go to the cinema but Navin changes plans and takes her to an archaeological site. This deflection or re-routing of the characters gives what follows a realist significance. Taking shelter from the rain in a cave at the site, Guddi offers to sing a film song but is persuaded to sing a 'classical' song instead, reinforcing the withdrawal from cinematic fantasy. At this stage in the film, *Guddi*'s obsession with films is contrasted with Navin's complete dislike for them. In the concluding segment, at a party to celebrate her birthday, Guddi sings a film song. But this time the song, '*Aa ja re pardesi*' has been wrested from the fantasy world of film and redeployed as an external aid to the resolution of a 'real' narrative. (Its difference is also guaranteed by the fact that it is from a film—*Madhumati*—made by Bimal Roy, one of the revered precursors of the middle-class cinema.) The song, whose meaning is appropriate to the context (while Guddi is singing, Navin is absent and thus becomes the addressee of the song), serves as an illustration of the ideal attitude to adopt towards cinema. This attitude consists of a detached indulgence, a knowing and provisional surrender to its pleasures. The subject must be able to draw affective material from the cinema for the narratives of real life without being sucked into its illusory world. The middle-class cinema thus provokes a dis-identification with the mainstream only to open up the possibility of a reidentification based on a compromise.

The carefully produced authenticity-effect is the source of the positive counter-popular valence that is assigned to this cinema. Its ideological function differs from that of the New Cinema in that its site of intervention is not only a 'real' in which new subject positions, allied to a shared political anxiety need to be produced; further, rather than a representation of an alternative reality in its distinction from the reality represented in the popular cinema, the middle-class cinema confronts the popular cinematic image and exposes its falsehood, its unworthiness as an object of emulation. At the same time, by means of the very cinematic devices which conceal the realities of the industry, it renders the 'real' world of the endogamous petty bourgeoisie desirable in itself. The new screen image is not a fantasy creation with no basis in reality, it is coded as the spectator's own image reflected back to him/herself. The mirror is adjusted to remove the look of surprise from its face.

In this world, endogamy—the signifier of class solidarity—has to be enforced in order to maintain that solidarity, which rests on the affirmation of patriarchal authority. Meera Bai, the *bhakti* poet and devotee of the god Krishna, whose example Kusum wishes to emulate, is an instance of the disruptive power of a love that transgresses the rules of endogamy: Meera was a princess who abandoned her royal family for a life of spiritual love and devotion. Woman is the displaced site of the struggle over the re-integration and re-identification of the class which hitherto shared the spectatorship of the popular cinema with the lower classes. If Kusum is not cured of her spiritual love, Navin would have to go to his new posting alone, increasing the potential for the breakdown of the network. The reconciliation between the cured Kusum and the engineer takes place in the nick of time, a few hours before his departure to his posting.

The film rescues the popular cinema from its own critique in another way too: Navin, the man who never goes to the movies, however finds a good friend in Dharmendra. The industry, as an economic enterprise, is thus represented as redeemable even as its product, the screen image, is rejected. The logic of this is not difficult to see. In the first place, the rejection is only partial: cinema as a source of discursive devices for use in the real world is approved. What is criticized is the absorption of real subjects into the screen image displacing, ungrounding of the spectator from his/her true being. Besides, by endorsing the industry and the entrepreneurial spirit behind it, the film is more firmly restricting its audience membership, for it does not dispute the suitability of the fantasy screen image for another kind of person, another class of people. It situates its audience on the other side of the camera as potential participants in the economy of film-making, which effectively renders the top strata of film personnel the class allies of the real world characters as well as the implied audience, thus distancing itself from those whose only access to the film world is through the image on the screen.

Basu Chatterji's *Rajnigandha* ('Tuberoses', 1974) also includes, at the very beginning, a scene of not going to the cinema. The scene begins with the heroine waiting in front of a theatre. Her boyfriend arrives, but has forgotten to bring the tickets. She is disappointed but agrees to go to a restaurant. This initial turn away from the cinema, which in *Guddi* occurred a little way into the narrative, is even more effective in establishing the authenticity of the rest of the narrative as a representation of the real world. The story centres round Deepa (Vidya Sinha), who is writing her PhD thesis and looking for a teaching position, and her boyfriend Sanjay (Amol Palekar), who is a clerk awaiting a promotion as officer. Sanjay's initial indifference to the movies is a character trait—when he does go, he eats constantly, disturbs his neighbours and goes out for a stroll whenever a song begins. His eyes are never fixed on the screen like the others in the theatre.

Sanjay's promotion faces two hurdles—one, a rival in the office who has the advantage of being from the same region as the boss, a strain of mild social satire which provides some gentle humour. The second hurdle is Deepa herself and her conflicting desires: the impending PhD which signifies her independent ambition, her job search, which threatens to take her away from Delhi (where they live), and Navin, a college boyfriend whom she has almost, but not quite, forgotten. The possible negative outcome of her transgressive desires is prefigured in a nightmare, with which the film opens. An interview call from a college in Bombay is the occasion for the surfacing of the anxieties over these potential threats to their stable life. Sanjay jokes about the imbalance that her PhD will cause and the equalizing potential of his promotion. He does not object to Deepa's desire to go to Bombay for a job, and even talks of taking a transfer in order to be with her. In response to her anxieties about getting around in Bombay, Sanjay jokingly drops the name of Navin, which Deepa has forbidden. Bombay itself (as in *Guddi*) is a possible threat, the city of disruptive fantasies.

Arriving in Bombay alone, Deepa is met by Navin (Dinesh Thakur), who has been sent by Ira, Deepa's host and former college friend who couldn't come herself. Navin is wearing sunglasses and khadi clothes—the sole mark of continuity between his college days, when he was a student radical, and his current life as an ad film-maker with high connections. In a flashback that followed Sanjay's mention of Navin we have already seen him and Deepa as students, at the moment when they break up because of a difference of opinion over a strike. Deepa insists on breaking the strike and going to classes, which leads to an argument and Navin's words of rejection. Deepa's apolitical subjectivity is shown on one more occasion when, trying to persuade Sanjay to leave his urgent office work and meet her, she suggests, 'Why don't you start a strike?' Her indifference to the strikes that preoccupy the young Navin and the promotion-hungry Sanjay is a repudiation of politics. But while Navin's radical politics is as threatening to middle-class integrity as his later ad-world lifestyle, Sanjay's trade-unionism, restricted to economic demands, is not subjected to any critique—it is presented with humour and equanimity as an unavoidable means to upward mobility.

Deepa's forgotten fascination for Navin resurfaces almost instantly. Ira tries to encourage her and Navin to rediscover their old passion. [...] The recurring image of Navin with sunglasses (Deepa too begins to wear them in the course of her outings with Navin), like the images of the cinema, is irresistible. Sometimes the image is interrupted by that of Sanjay, but reasserts itself. The transgression, thus, is located in the obsessive return of a cinematic image of Navin which, like Kusum's absorption in the screen image, is a form of possession, a capture by an alien force which portends a ruinous loss for the endogamous sexual economy. Navin is not blamed (any more than the film-makers are in *Guddi*) for causing this obsession. On the other hand, Navin's use of his connections to fix Deepa's interview is presented with no moral overlays. At once (economically) useful and (sexually) dangerous, the figure of Navin is invested with both the fears and desires of the class.

Returning to Delhi and awaiting news of her interview results, Deepa continues to be haunted by Navin's image. Sanjay, who has meanwhile been regularly bringing a bunch of tuberoses to replace the old ones in the vase, has had to go away on duty and is absent in this period of continued fascination with the screen image. When Navin's letter arrives, it proves to be quite formal, informing her of her success in the interview, Wishing her well, but with no hint of any other emotion. The image finally fades and at that very instant, as she is still holding the letter in her hand, Sanjay reappears at the door with a bunch of tuberoses, smiling—the image is repeated lingered over, till it suffuses her lately evacuated being. Sanjay has got his promotion, Deepa decides (on the spot) not to take the job in Bombay.

While in *Guddi* the endogamous group was still represented as a natural (blood-related) one, *Rajnigandha* takes the logical step forward by introducing a stranger into Deepa's life—a stranger who is familiar, instantly recognizable, trustworthy. They meet one rainy day when Sanjay invites her to share his umbrella on the way to college. He quickly becomes a member of the family and endears himself to all with his wit and charm. He talks non-stop about his job, the union, his rival for promotion, the coming strike, and cannot be persuaded to act romantically. The familiar grammar of romance which everybody has learnt from the movies is foreign to Sanjay but we are assured that a more genuine love lurks behind the clerical facade, signified by the constant supply of tuberoses that he brings to Deepa. The title song, which is heard as Deepa paces her home and arranges the flowers, speaks of her longing for the man's love to flourish in her heart as the flowers do in the vase. When the song exclaims, 'How enjoyable is this bondage', it speaks of the flowers uncomplainingly standing in the vase in a corner as well as the woman who stays at home. Another song, played against Deepa and Navin's wanderings in Bombay, tells of the mind's (natural) boundaries which it breaks on occasion and goes in search of 'unfamiliar desires'.

In moments of crisis, thus, the spotlight is turned on woman, locating all threats to class identity in the transgressive nature of female desire, a desire that takes its own undiscriminating route to fulfilment, threatening to establish undesirable contact with the lower classes (through the cinema) and disruptive political movements (through declassed individuals like the student radical turned ad film-maker). The polymorphous sexuality of the Bombay woman, Ira, who whispers in Deepa's ear on her departure, that she will 'miss her in bed' provides a glimpse into the future in store for Deepa if she were to abandon the security of Sanjay's love for the exhilaration of a renewed affair with Navin.

The third set of middle-class films deal with post-marital conflicts arising from a variety of factors. In *Abhiman* and *Kora Kagaz*, the couples are torn apart by envy and pride. Of these *Abhiman* ('Pride', Hrishikesh Mukherjee 1973) is the more significant film from our point of view because its narrative of domestic conflict is intermeshed with certain cultural questions important to the middle-class cinema's identity. Subir Kumar (Amitabh Bachchan), a popular singer, marries Uma (Jaya Bhaduri), daughter of a traditional brahmanical scholar and herself a singer in the classical style, although she only sings for her own pleasure. After marriage they decide to sing together (and only together) in public. Her popularity soars and recording companies ask her to sing solos. She resists but Subir persuades her to break their pledge and accept the offer. Subir is consumed by envy and the suspicion that she is a better singer. In an attempt to save the marriage Uma gives up her career, but as the relationship deteriorates, she goes back to her father's house. She has a miscarriage and enters into a state of deep shock. Subir, now repentant and trying to save his wife, agrees to a plan that is aimed at making her cry and break out of the state of shock. At a public gathering, Subir sings a song which he had written in happier days, expressing their longing for a child. Uma breaks down and sings with him.

The contrast between the ordinariness of popular music and the superior skills required for classical singing is deployed in *Abhiman* to provide the affective aura within which domestic conflict is staged. The 'light classical' song was reinvented for the middle-class cinema with Vani Jayaram's *'Bol re papihara'* in *Guddi*. *Abhiman* includes some songs of this type. Unlike the popular song that Subir sings at the beginning of the film, the 'classical' song is not presented as a spectacle, with the singer dancing on stage. Popular music is meant for others' pleasure, while Uma's singing is not addressed to any audience. Parallel to this theme of musical traditions in conflict, the film also touches upon the question of the conflict between narrative and spectacle. Domestic harmony is broken when, in his desire to display Uma's talent to the world, Subir urges her to sing with him in public. [...] The disruptive effect of her popularity is not her own fault because she did not want to sing in public.

Gulzar's *Aandhi* ('The Storm', 1975) however, does not 'protect' its heroine in this way. Political ambition is the factor that disturbs domestic harmony in *Aandhi*. Arati Devi (Suchitra Sen), a popular politician, goes to a town for campaigning and stays in the only hotel there. It is owned by her husband (Sanjeev Kumar), from whom she has been estranged for many years. The husband lives in the hotel with his trusted servant. After their encounter at the hotel, a series of flashbacks cover the previous history of their relationship. Arati's father (Rehman) is a man with great political ambitions for his daughter and is impatient with her for wasting time in romantic frolic instead of pursuing a political career. For a while Arati tries to balance the two lives but ultimately decides to sacrifice family life for her political career. In the narrative present, Arati Devi's election campaign is jeopardized by gossip about her relationship with the hotel owner. At a public meeting where her rival is exploiting the gossip for political gains, she makes a confession of her true relationship with the hotel owner. After winning the election, she decides to subordinate her political career to her renewed domestic life.

Indira Gandhi may have been a possible model for the character of Arati Devi. Mainly for this reason, *Aandhi* was banned and then allowed to be re-released with changes. There are references within the film to Nehru and Indira Gandhi which leave us in no doubt as to the parallels being suggested. However, it is not a 'biopic' that purports to be based on Indira Gandhi's life. The protagonist emulates Indira Gandhi and brings suffering upon herself as a result. Arati feels suffocated by the dullness of domestic life and longs to return to public life. The husband contributes to her rebellion against domesticity by his authoritarian ways. In the movement towards resolution, both have to acknowledge and atone for their sins.

Arati Devi's political career serves as a narrative device to symbolize a threat to the middle-class family. Arati is an idealist in politics, and is oblivious to the shady dealings of her own supporters. She is thus represented as a pawn in the hands of male politicians, who exploit her sincerity and honesty. The cinema, the world of glamour and advertising, politics: all have the same function, in the middle-class cinema, to signify a threat to the integrity of the family. With the change in enemies, however, there is also a change in the protected object itself. The family unit in these films is nuclear while its field of existence is the class. This is a significant step away from the narratives of pre-crisis popular cinema, in which the threat was directed at the *khandan*'s property and honour, and where the couple's sexual and affective energies remained harnessed to the furtherance of the khandan's splendour and enjoyment. In middle-class cinema the class continues to be identified with an enlarged and more diffuse traditional unit, the kinship network or the caste, but the couple emerges into relative autonomy. The sources of conflict shift from the economic and moral domains to the realm of the psychic, where envy, ambition, pride, and other disruptive emotions reside. With the middle-class cinema, women's subjectivity becomes a cultural issue. [...]

The middle-class film foregrounds the problem of bourgeois subjectivity through the exploration of the contradictions and conflicts of conjugality. Sometimes the continued hold of the parental family over the conjugal scene is the source of the conflict, as in *Kora Kagaz* where the wife's rich family tries to compensate for the husband's meagre salary by providing modern amenities. In all cases, however, the woman is at the centre of bourgeois narrative, the journey towards the recognition of woman's subjectivity stands as proof of the arrival of bourgeois conjugality.

For middle-class cinema as an institution, the thematics of female subjectivity and the problem of domestic space form the basis of a new aesthetic. Homologous to the problem of the domestic space and its unresolved conflicts, the middle-class segment of the industry, in its products, confronted the problem of its own cultural space. In the populist/socialist political climate, the middle class, whose class identity was intimately tied up with an upper-caste status, was more amenable to the exclusivist aesthetic enclosure produced by the narratives of domestic conflict than the national integrationist role delineated in the narratives of martyrdom.

Annotated Bibliography

As the Introduction to this volume states, trying to synthesize the historiography on the 'Middle Class in Colonial India' is a daunting task because of both the paucity and plentitude of sources. Few studies have focused exclusively on the middle class as a category; yet it is impossible to summarize, even in bibliographic form, the range of literature that deals with the activities of middle-class activists in colonial India. The following bibliography presents what is necessarily a short selection of important scholarly work dealing with the activities of the middle class in colonial India, along with references to some studies that centrally explore the making of a social/cultural category called the 'middle class' in India. There are a few overlaps between works cited in the references to the introduction and this bibliography, though, for most part I have attempted in this volume, to create two separate, yet complementary, sources of bibliographic data. Some references to additional readings can be found in the endnotes to the Introduction to this volume. For the making of middle classes in other parts of the world, see endnotes 11–16. For readings on gender and the Indian middle class, consult endnotes 47–54. For more on caste and the middle class, see endnotes 57–62, and for further readings on middle class and everyday (and classicized) culture, consult endnotes 70–81. I strongly urge readers to use *both* sources for a bibliographic study of the middle class in colonial India. None of the sources from which essays in this volume are derived have been repeated in this bibliography.

For lack of room as well as an indication of my own linguistic limitations, I have left out a crucial resource for understanding the middle class of colonial India—fiction. With the novel as the predominant form after the late nineteenth century, fiction, particularly in the social realist genre, is an excellent way to gain insight into the contradictions and cohesions of middle class identity. I found the work of novelists such as Amritlal Nagar to be immensely helpful in understanding the making of a middle-class in colonial Lucknow, and continue to draw on the insights of creative writers such as Manohar Shyam Joshi for my ongoing work on Kumaon. However, the sheer range of available material, and my ignorance of languages outside of the Hindi–Urdu region, meant I could not possibly do justice with a representative collection of novels, short stories, or other forms of fictional narratives.

AUTOBIOGRAPHIES AND BIOGRAPHICAL ACCOUNTS

Other than fiction, an excellent way to understand the making of middle-class identities in colonial India is to read the accounts of their everyday and public life contained in biographical works. I have chosen to focus on the lives of well-known public figures while making this list. Though political figures dominate, I have tried to include a few others as well. The essay by Sankaran Krishna was to be part of this volume, but considerations of length led to its elimination at the last minute. However, it is one of the best examples of using a biographical approach to understand middle-class formation. The collection by David Arnold and Stuart Blackburn, Javed Majeed's work on life histories, and the essay by Judith Brown help us better read these biographical works. In no way should this list be read as representative of middle-class autobiographical writings, but rather as a way to read the more theoretical material on the middle class through the context of the lives of individuals. The presence of some subaltern and one clearly upper-class individual in this list, is to suggest the extent to which middle-class standards were becoming normative over the period of study. The variety of regions and professions in the following list should indicate the diversity within the middle class.

Ambedkar, B. R. 2005. *Ambedkar: Autobiographical Notes*. Pondicherry: Navayana.

Anand, Mulk Raj. 1985. *Autobiography*. New Delhi: Arnold-Heinemann.

Arnold, David, and Stuart Blackburn. 2004. *Telling Lives in India: Biography, Autobiography, and Life History*. Bloomington: Indiana University Press.

Azad, Abulkalam. 1988. *India Wins Freedom: The Complete Version*. Hyderabad: Orient Longman.

Brecher, Michael. 1959. *Nehru, a Political Biography*. London: Oxford University Press.

Brown, Judith M. '"Life Histories" and the History of Modern South Asia'. *The American Historical Review* 114, no. 3 (1 June 2009): 587–95.

Chattopadhyaya, Kamaladevi. 1982. *Indian Women's Battle for Freedom*. Delhi: Abhinav.

Chaudhuri, Nirad C. 1968. *The Autobiography of an Unknown Indian*. Berkeley: University of California Press.

Debi, Rashsundari and Tanika Sarkar. 1999. *Words to Win: The Making of 'Amar Jiban': A Modern Autobiography*. Delhi: Kali for Women.

Devee, Sunity. 1921. *Autobiography of an Indian Princess: Memoirs of Maharani Sunity Devi of Cooch Behar*. London: J. Murray.

Gandhi, M. K. 1949. *Gandhi, an Autobiography: The Story of My Experiments with Truth*. London: Phoenix Press.

Gopal, Sarvepalli. 2004. *Jawaharlal Nehru: A Biography*. Abridged. New Delhi: Oxford University Press.

Hardiman, David. 2004. *Gandhi in his Times and Ours*. New York: Columbia University Press.

Kelkar, Vinayak Chintaman. 1980. *Autobiography of Gurudev R.D. Ranade: A Discovery*. Poona: I.P.Q. Publication, University of Poona.

Krishna, Sankaran. 'The Bomb, Biography and the Indian Middle Class.' *Economic and Political Weekly of India*, vol. XLI, no. 23 (10 June 2006).

Majeed, Javed. 2007. *Autobiography, Travel and Postnational Identity: Gandhi, Nehru and Iqbal*. Basingstoke: Palgrave Macmillan.

Majumdar, Janaki Agnes Penelope. 2003. *Family History* edited and with an introduction by Antoinette Burton. New Delhi: Oxford University Press.

Nanda, B. 1985. *Gandhi and His Critics*. New Delhi: Oxford University Press.

——. 1977. *Gokhale: The Indian Moderates and the British Raj*. Princeton: Princeton University Press.

——. 1962. *The Nehrus: Motilal and Jawaharlal*. London: Allen & Unwin.

Nanda, Reena. 2002. *Kamaladevi Chattopadhyaya: A Biography*. New York: Oxford University Press.

Nehru, Jawaharlal. 1936. *Jawaharlal Nehru, an Autobiography: With Musings on Recent Events in India*. London: John Jane.

Pal, Bipin Chandra. 1973. *Memories of My Life and Times*. 2nd ed. Calcutta: Bipinchandra Pal Institute.

Rai, Lajpat. 1965. *Lajpat Rai: Autobiographical Writings*. Jullundur: University Publishers.

Ray, Praphulla Chandra. 1958. *Autobiography of a Bengali Chemist*. Calcutta: Orient Book Co.

Tilak, Lakshmibai. 1950. *I Follow After: An Autobiography*. New Delhi: Oxford University Press.

Walsh, Judith E. 1983. *Growing up in British India: Indian Autobiographers on Childhood and Education Under the Raj*. New York: Holmes & Meier.

Zachariah, Benjamin. 2004. *Nehru*. New York: Routledge.

SCHOLARLY DEBATES AND DEFINITIONS OF THE MIDDLE CLASS
This is a short and somewhat eclectic selection of essays and books that deal quite centrally with the creation of a middle class in India. The divergence of perspectives on the study of the middle class is evident even in this short selection. While scholars such as Bruce McCully, B. B. Misra, Briton Martin, and to some extent, Christine Dobbin, see the middle class in colonial India only as a product of colonial policies, others such as Mukerjee paid more attention to the agency of Indians. Rajat Ray and others have followed with a more balanced understanding of the place of the middle class. Not all the works included in this section are by professional historians, as sociologists and students of politics, have, for obvious reasons, been equally interested in the middle class and the best of these, exemplified by the work of Andre Béteille, Satish Deshpande, or more recently, Leela Fernandes, have taken a historical perspective in their effort to understand the nature of the middle class in contemporary India. Obviously, these are to be read in addition to the works from which the essays in this volume have been taken.

Béteille, Andre. 2001. 'The Social Character of the Indian Middle Class', in Imtiaz Ahmad and Helmut Reifeld (eds) *Middle Class Values in India and Western Europe*. Delhi: Social Science Press.

Bhatia, B.M. 1994. *India's Middle Class: Role in Nation Building*. New Delhi: Konark Publishers.

Bhattacharya, Tithi. 2005. *The Sentinels of Culture: Class, Education, and the Colonial Intellectual in Bengal (1848-85)*. New Delhi; Oxford; New York: Oxford University Press.

Deshpande, Satish. 2003. *Contemporary India: A Sociological View*. New Delhi: Penguin Books India.

Dobbin, Christine. 1972. *Urban Leadership in Western India: Politics and Communities in Bombay City, 1840–85*. London: Oxford University Press.

Fernandes, Leela. 2006. *India's New Middle Class: Democratic Politics in an Era of Economic Reform*. Minneapolis: University of Minnesota Press.

Ganguli, B. N. 1977. 'Conceptualizing the Indian Middle Class' in K. S. Krishnaswamy and Ashok Mitra (eds) *Society and Change : Essays in Honour of Sachin Chaudhuri*. Bombay: Published for Sameeksha Trust by Oxford University Press.

Haynes, Douglas E. 1991. *Rhetoric and Ritual in Colonial India: The Shaping of a Public Culture in Surat City, 1852–1928*. Berkeley: University of California Press.

Joshi, Sanjay. 2001. *Fractured Modernity: The Making of a Middle Class in Colonial North India*. Delhi: Oxford University Press.

Martin, Briton. 1969. *New India, 1885; British Official Policy and the Emergence of the Indian National Congress*. Berkeley, University of California Press.

McCully, Bruce T. 1966. *English Education and the Origins of Indian Nationalism*. Gloucester [Mass.]: Peter Smith.

Mukerjee, Dhurjati Prasad. 1978. *Sociology of Indian Culture*. Originally published, 1948. Second edition; reprint. Jaipur: Rawat Publications.

Mukherjee, S. N. 1970. 'Class, Caste, and Politics in Calcutta' in Edmund Leach and S.N. Mukherjee (eds) *Elites in South Asia*. Cambridge: Cambridge University Press.

Ray, Rajat Kanta. 1980. 'Three Interpretations of Indian Nationalism' in B.R. Nanda, *Essays in Modern Indian History*. New Delhi: Oxford University Press.

Suntharalingam, R. 1974. *Politics and Nationalist Awakening in South India, 1852–91*. Tucson: University of Arizona Press.

SOCIO-CULTURAL–RELIGIOUS REFORM AND REVIVAL

Partha Chatterjee argues that attention to religion was an 'inward' turn by early middle-class nationalists in colonial India. Whether or not one agrees with this formulation (though even many of Chatterjee's critics do), there is overwhelming empirical evidence to suggest that social and cultural issues such as religion or language, as much as politics, framed the ways in which educated Indians came to define themselves as a middle class in colonial India. There is a plethora of work on the subject. It is difficult, indeed sometimes impossible, to separate this literature from that on religious revivalism or indeed religious nationalism—what is often termed 'communalism'—with middle-class activists seeking to redeploy new forms of religiosity in the politics of the colonial public sphere. For the sake of manageable reading lists, I have made some, fairly arbitrary, distinctions in classifying some works in this section of the bibliography, and others in the section under 'nationalism'. Needless to say, the list below is hardly exhaustive—rather it, represents a starting point for students and other scholars, indicating the different directions from which the scholarship on these subjects allows us to understand the making of a middle class in colonial India.

Appadurai, Arjun. 1981. *Worship and Conflict under Colonial Rule.* Cambridge: Cambridge University Press.

Brass, Paul. 1974. *Language, Religion, and Politics in North India.* Cambridge: Cambridge University Press.

Chandra, Sudhir. 1992. *The Oppressive Present: Literature and Social Consciousness in Colonial India.* New Delhi: Oxford University Press.

Dalmia, Vasudha. 1997. *The Nationalization of Hindu Traditions: Bharatendu Harischandra and Nineteenth Century Banaras.* Delhi: Oxford University Press.

Freitag, Sandria. 1989. *Collective Action and Community: Public Arenas and the Emergence of Communalism in North India.* Berkeley: University of California Press.

Hardy, Peter. 1972. *The Muslims of British India* . Cambridge: Cambridge University Press.

Heimsath, Charles H. 1964. *Indian Nationalism and Hindu Social Reform.* Princeton: Princeton University Press.

Inden, Ronald. 1990. *Imagining India.* Cambridge, Massachusetts: Basil Blackwell.

Jones, Kenneth W. 1990. *Socio-Religious Reform Movements in British India.* Cambridge: Cambridge University Press.

Joshi, V. C and Rajat Kanta Ray (ed.) 1975. *Rammohun Roy and the Process of Modernization in India.* Delhi: Vikas Publishing House.

King, Christopher Rolland. 1994. *One Language, Two Scripts: The Hindi Movement in the Nineteenth Century North India*. Bombay: Oxford University Press.

Kopf, David. 1979. *The Brahmo Samaj and the Shaping of the Modern Indian Mind*. Princeton: Princeton University Press.

Koslowski, Gregory C. 1985. *Muslim Endowments and Society in British India*. Cambridge: Cambridge University Press.

Lelyveld, David. 1978. *Aligarh's First Generation: Muslim Solidarity in British India*. Princeton: Princeton University Press.

Mani, Lata. 1998. *Contentious Traditions: The Debate on Sati in Colonial India*. Berkeley: University of California Press.

Metcalf, Barbara D. 1982. *Islamic Revival in British India: Deoband 1860–1900*. Princeton: Princeton University Press.

Minault, Gail. 1998. *Secluded Scholars: Women's Education and Muslim Social Reform in Colonial India*. New Delhi: Oxford University Press.

Oberoi, Harjot S. 1994. *Construction of Religious Boundaries: Culture, Identity and Diversity in the Sikh Tradition*. New Delhi: Oxford University Press.

Orsini, Francesca. 2002. *The Hindi Public Sphere 1920-1940: Language and Literature in the Age of Nationalism*. New Delhi: Oxford University Press.

Pandey, Gyanendra. 1990. *The Construction of Communalism in Colonial North India*. New Delhi: Oxford University Press.

Rai, Amrit. 1984. *A House Divided: The Origin and Development of Hindi/Hindavi*. Delhi; New York: Oxford University Press.

Ramaswamy, Sumathi. 1997. *Passions of the Tongue: Language Devotion in Tamil India, 1891–1970*. Berkeley: University of California Press.

Sarkar, Sumit and Tanika Sarkar. 2007. *Women and Social Reform in Modern India: A Reader*. 2 vols. Ranikhet: Permanent Black.

Sarkar, Tanika. 2009. *Rebels, Wives, Saints: Designing Selves and Nations in Colonial Times*. Ranikhet: Permanent Black.

Sen, Amiya (ed.) 1995. *Social and Religious Reform: The Hindus of British India*. New Delhi: Oxford University Press.

———. 1993. *Hindu Revivalism in Bengal 1872-1905: Some Essays in Interpretation*. New Delhi: Oxford University Press.

Troll, Christian W. 1978. *Sayyid Ahmad Khan: Reinterpretation of Muslim Theology*. Delhi: Vikas Publishing House.

Tucker, Richard P. 1972. *Ranade and the Roots of Indian Nationalism*. Chicago: University of Chicago Press.

van der Veer, Peter. 1999. 'The Moral State; Religion, Nation and Empire in Victorian Britain and British India.' In Peter van der Veer (ed.) *Nation and Religion: Perspectives on Europe and Asia*. Princeton: Princeton University Press.

——. 1994. *Religious Nationalism: Hindus and Muslims in India*. Berkeley: University of California Press.

NATIONALISM

While most fields in the historiography of colonial India have their share of contentious debates, Indian nationalism has perhaps had more than others, simply because it remains the master-narrative in historical accounts of colonial India. These debates, in turn, have also been directly or obliquely about the nature and constitution of the middle class. Hence, this is the only section of the bibliography which has two subsections, after a general list of works.

The first subsection is on the so-called 'Cambridge school'. The work of a group of like-minded researchers based in Cambridge University in the UK in the 1970s had a significant impact on the study of the middle class, as Michelgugliemo Torri suggests in his essay in this volume. Using recently available archival sources made available under amendments to the Public Records Act in 1967, these scholars began publishing detailed, regional studies of politics in colonial India, emphasizing the extent to which educated Indians' actions were a response to changing policies of the colonial administration. In doing so, they also debunked some of the more starry-eyed celebrations of the role of the Indian middle class nationalists and social reformers. The Cambridge scholars attracted their share of criticism, and the essays by Hardiman and Sarkar are representative of that critique. Partha Chatterjee also takes the Cambridge school to task in *The Nation and its Fragments: Colonial and Postcolonial Histories*, an extract from which appears in this volume.

The second subsection is on an even better-known historiographical intervention—of the scholars associated with the *Subaltern Studies* collective. The project began with a self-conscious focus on subordinated groups in Indian society. But, even at the start of the venture, essays such as those by Shahid Amin, or early monographs of David Hardiman and Gyan Pandey as well as Sumit Sarkar's short book, illuminate the making of middle class as well, if primarily through a somewhat stark distinction between subalterns and élites. As their concerns began to mesh more with the postcolonial critique, some of the major figures in the collective, such as Dipesh Chakrabarty, Partha Chatterjee, and Ranajit Guha, in particular, turned the attention of their work more directly to the Indian middle class. This, in turn has generated a degree of criticism from former colleagues such as Ramachandra Guha and Sumit Sarkar, or Tom Brass, also noted in the bibliography below.

Of course, classifications into 'schools' are often in the eyes of the beholder and not always the best way to understand scholarly development. A.R. Desai's analysis of Indian nationalism was clearly influenced by Marxist traditions, though it provides an understanding of the middle class quite distinct from Kapil Kumar or Dilip Simeon's critiques. Bipan Chandra combined a Marxist analytical framework with a sympathetic view of the nationalist endeavour. Then there are other scholars such as Ravinder Kumar, whose thoughtful analyses are more difficult to pigeonhole easily. Yet others, such as Christopher Bayly, have developed and transformed their analytical framework while remaining prolific scholars and hence feature in different sections of this bibliography.

Based on the existing historiography, it is virtually impossible to write a history of the middle class in colonial India without it also being in some way a history of Indian nationalism, and almost as difficult to write a history of nationalism that is not a history of the middle class. Thus there is a degree of arbitrariness in including some work in this category, as opposed as any of the others in this bibliography. My criteria for including some of the writing below is to illustrate the mutually constitutive relationship between the middle class and Indian nationalism.

Bayly, C. A. 1998. *Origins of Nationality in South Asia: Patriotism and Ethical Government in the Making of Modern India*. Delhi; New York: Oxford University Press.

Cashman, Richard I. 1975. *The Myth of the Lokamanya: Tilak and Mass Politics in Maharashtra*. Berkeley: University of California Press.

Chandra, Bipan. 1979. *Nationalism and Colonialism in Modern India*. Delhi: Orient Longman.

———. 1966. *The Rise and Growth of Economic Nationalism in India*. Delhi: People's Publishing House.

Desai, A. R. 1960 *The Social Background of Indian Nationalism*. Bombay: Popular Prakashan.

Gandhi, M. K. 1996. *Hind Swaraj or Indian Home Rule*. Ahmedabad: Navajivan Publishing House.

Gilmartin, David. 1989. *Empire and Islam: Punjab and the Making of Pakistan*. New Delhi: Oxford University Press.

Goswami, Manu. 2004. *Producing India: From Colonial Economy to National Space*. Chicago: University of Chicago Press.

Hasan, Mushirul. 1985. *Communal and Pan-Islamic Trends in Colonial India*. Delhi: Manohar.

Haynes, Douglas E. 1991. *Rhetoric and Ritual in Colonial India: The Shaping of a Public Culture in Surat City, 1852–1928*. Berkeley: University of California Press.

Jalal, Ayesha. 1985. *The Sole Spokesman: Jinnah, the Muslim League and the Demand for Pakistan*. Cambridge: Cambridge University Press.

Kumar, Kapil. 1988. *Congress and Classes: Nationalism, Workers, and Peasants*. New Delhi: Manohar Publications.

Kumar, Ravinder. 1989. *The Making of a Nation: Essays in Indian History and Politics*. Delhi: Manohar.

Masselos, Jim. 2005. *Towards Nationalism: Public Institutions and Urban Politics in the Nineteenth Century*. Delhi: New Dawn Press.

Markovits, Claude. 1985. *Indian Business and Nationalist Politics, 1931–1939: the Indigenous Capitalist Class and the Rise of the Congress Party*. New York: Cambridge University Press.

McLane, John. 1977. *Indian Nationalism and the Early Congress*. Princeton: Princeton University Press.

Mehrotra, S. R. 1971. *The Emergence of the Indian National Congress*. Delhi: Vikas Publications.

Raychaudhuri, Tapan. 1988. *Europe Reconsidered: Perception of the West in Nineteenth Century Bengal*. New Delhi: Oxford University Press.

Robinson, Francis. 1993. *Separatism Among Indian Muslims: The Politics of the United Provinces' Muslims, 1860–1923*. New Delhi: Oxford University Press.

Sarkar, Sumit. 1973. *The Swadeshi Movement in Bengal, 1903-1908*. Delhi: People's Publishing House.

Simeon, Dilip. 1995. *The Politics of Labour under Late Colonialism: Workers, Unions, and the State in Chota Nagpur, 1928–1939*. Delhi: Manohar.

Tagore, Rabindranath. 2005. 'Nationalism' in *Rabindranath Tagore Omnibus III*. Delhi: Rupa and Co., pp. 1-80.

Wolpert, Stanley. 1962. *Tilak and Gokhale: Revolution and Reform in the Making of Modern India*. Berkeley: University of California Press.

CAMBRIDGE SCHOOL AND THEIR CRITICS

Bayly, C. A. 1980. 'The Small Town and Islamic gentry' in Kenneth Ballhatchet and John Harrison eds. *The City in South Asia: Pre-Modern and Modern*. London: Curzon Press.

———. 1975. *The Local Roots of Indian Politics: Allahabad, 1880-1920*. Oxford: Clarendon Press.

Broomfield, J. H. 1968. *Elite Conflict in a Plural Society: Twentieth-century Bengal*. Berkeley: University of California Press.

Gallagher, John, Gordon Johnson, and Anil Seal (eds.) 1973. *Locality, Province and Nation: Essays on Indian Politics, 1870 to 1940*. Cambridge: Cambridge University Press.

Hardiman, David. 1982. 'The Indian 'Faction': A Political Theory Examined' in Ranajit Guha ed., *Subaltern Studies Vol. I*, New Delhi: Oxford University Press.

Johnson, Gordon. 1973. *Provincial Politics and Indian Nationalism: Bombay and the Indian National Congress, 1880–1915*. Cambridge: Cambridge University Press.

McGuire, John. 1983. *The Making of a Colonial Mind: A Quantitative Study of the Bhadralok in Calcutta, 1857–1885*. Canberra: Australian National University.

Sarkar, Sumit. 1983. 'Introduction'in *Modern India 1885–1947*. Delhi: Macmillan.

Seal, Anil. 1968. *The Emergence of Indian Nationalism: Competition and Collaboration in the Later Nineteenth Century*. London: Cambridge University Press.

Washbrook, David A. 1976. *The Emergence of Provincial Politics: The Madras Presidency, 1870-1920*. Cambridge: Cambridge University Press.

SUBALTERN SCHOOL AND THEIR CRITICS

Amin, Shahid. 1995. *Event, Metaphor, Memory: Chauri Chaura, 1922–1992*. Berkeley: University of California Press.

Amin, Shahid. 1984. 'Gandhi as Mahatma: Gorakhpur District, Eastern UP, 1921-22', in Ranajit Guha ed. *Subaltern Studies III: Writings on South Asian History and Society*. New Delhi: Oxford University Press, pp. 1–61.

Brass, Tom. 'Moral Economists, Subalterns, New Social Movements, and the (Re-) Emergence of a (Post-) Modernised (Middle) Peasant,' *Journal of Peasant Studies* 18, 2 (January 1991) pp. 173–205.

Chakrabarty, Dipesh. 2000. *Provincializing Europe: Postcolonial Thought and Historical Difference*. Princeton: Princeton University Press.

Chatterjee, Partha. 1986. *Nationalist Thought and the Colonial World: A Derivative Discourse?* Delhi: Oxford University Press.

Guha, Ramachandra. 'Subaltern and Bhadralok Studies', *Economic and Political Weekly* 30 (19 August 1995) pp. 2056-8.

Guha, Ranajit. 1993. 'Discipline and Mobilize,' in Partha Chatterjee and Gyanendra Pandey (eds) *Subaltern Studies VII: Writings on South Asian History and Society*. New Delhi: Oxford University Press, pp. 69-120.

Hardiman, David. 1981. *Peasant Nationalists of Gujarat : Kheda District, 1917-1934*. New Delhi: Oxford University Press.

Kaviraj, Sudipta. 1995. *The Unhappy Consciousness: Bankimchandra Chatto-padhyay and the Formation of Nationalist Discourse in India*. New Delhi: Oxford University Press.

Pandey, Gyanendra. 1978. *The Ascendancy of the Congress in Uttar Pradesh, 1926-1934: A Study in Imperfect Mobilization*. New York: .

Sarkar, Sumit. 1983. *Popular Movements and Middle Class Leadership in late Colonial India: Perspectives and Problems from a History from Below*. Calcutta: K.P. Bagchi and Sons.

——. 1997. 'The Decline of the Subaltern in *Subaltern Studies*', in *Writing Social History*. New Delhi: Oxford University Press, pp. 82-108.

Contributors

C.A. BAYLY is Vere Harmsworth Professor of Imperial and Naval History, St Catharine's College, Cambridge University. In 2007 he was knighted for his services to the discipline of History.

DIPESH CHAKRABARTY is Lawrence A. Kimpton Distinguished Service Professor of History, South Asian Languages and Civilizations and the College at the University of Chicago. He was a founding-member of the Subaltern Studies Collective.

PARTHA CHATTERJEE is Professor of Anthropology, Columbia University, New York and also teaches at the Calcutta and Jadavpur Universities in Kolkata. He was a founding-member of the Subaltern Studies Collective.

AUROBINDO GHOSH (1872–1950) was a nationalist member of the Indian National Congress who went on to become an important spiritual thinker after retiring to French-controlled Pondicherry.

FREDERICK TEMPLE HAMILTON-TEMPLE-BLACKWOOD (1826–1902), 1st Marquess of Dufferin and Ava, was Viceroy to India between 1884 and 1888.

SANJAY JOSHI is Associate Professor of History, Northern Arizona University.

PRASHANT KIDAMBI teaches Colonial Urban History at University of Leicester.

D.D. KOSAMBI (1907–66) made original contributions to a variety of intellectual disciplines ranging from mathematics to history. He is known for his original interpretations of Indian history.

BORIA MAJUMDAR is currently Senior Research Fellow, University of Central Lancashire.

CLAUDE MARKOVITS is Director of Research, Center of India and South Asia, National Center for Scientific Research (CNRS), Paris.

B.B. MISRA (Late) taught for many years at DAV College, Bihar University and held major appointments at the University of London and in the United States.

JAWAHARLAL NEHRU (1889–1964) was a leading nationalist activist and intellectual, who also served as the first Prime Minister of independent India.

M.S.S. PANDIAN is Professor of Contemporary History, Jawaharlal Nehru University.

MARGRIT PERNAU is currently Senior Research Scientist, Max Planck Institute for Human Development, Berlin.

M. MADHAVA PRASAD is Professor, Department of Cultural Studies, The English and Foreign Languages University, Hyderabad.

TANIKA SARKAR is Professor of History, Jawaharlal Nehru University.

MICHELGUGLIELMO TORRI is Professor of Modern and Contemporary History of Asia, University of Turin, Italy.

A.R. VENKATACHALAPATHY is Professor, Madras Institute of Development Studies, Chennai.